ANIME INTERVIEWS

The First Five Years of
ANIMERICA, ANIME & MANGA MONTHLY
(1992-97)

From the Editors of
ANIMERICA

Edited by
TRISH LEDOUX

Cadence Books
San Francisco, California

Publisher
Seiji Horibuchi

Editor in Chief
Satoru Fujii

Managing Editor
Hyoe Narita

Editor
Trish Ledoux

Senior Editor
Julie Davis

Contributing Editors
Takayuki Karahashi
Carl Gustav Horn
Junco Ito
Bruce Lewis
James Matsuzaki
Takashi Oshiguchi
Frederik L. Schodt
Toshifumi Yoshida

Editorial Assistants
Kit Fox
James Teal

Rights and Clearances
Kumi Kobayashi

Graphics and Design
Ted Szeto

Cadence Books
A Division of Viz Communications, Inc.
P.O. Box 77010
San Francisco, CA 94107 USA

ISBN 1-56931-220-6

First Printing, October 1997. Printed in Canada

contents

introduction

Like it says on the back cover, if you think "Japanimation," or "anime," is all about "big eyes, big boobs and big guns"...have we got some surprises for you.

This isn't a book about technique. It's not really concerned with the world of frames per second, camera pans, cel painting, computer graphics, or any other "how to" tips about which aspiring animators might be most eager to read. The technique of Japanese animation is a whole other book in itself, and not necessarily the one we wanted to write. What we *did* want to talk about in assembling this book wasn't about how Japanese animation is made, per se, or to compare its visual virtues to Western animation, but to examine the philosophy behind it, from the perspective of those who actually make it happen. To our way of thinking, Japanese animation's most arresting quality lies less in its technique and style—foreign as that style may be to those whose experience with animation goes no further than Disney features and Saturday morning cartoons—and more in the fact that, with its stories and themes, Japanese animation goes places and does things that Western animation rarely dares to do. *That*, we thought, was the part we wanted to talk about—the *why*, rather than the *how*.

Why do Japanese animators take on the tough subjects (wrenching drama, death, sex, and sorrow) and the tough settings (the high-tech, far-future sci-fi) that Hollywood seems comfortable addressing only in live-action? Why are Japanese comics so much more story- and character-oriented than their American counterparts? What *is* it about Japanese animation that draws fans from all cultures and nationalities—not just American—regardless of language?

How do these creators *do* it, this summoning up of the sometimes sketchily animated yet fully realized worlds which grasp our attention so firmly?

What makes these artists *tick*?

This book draws from interviews conducted over a period of five years, previously published in the magazine ANIMERICA, ANIME & MANGA MONTHLY. It's easy to analyze our philosophy as a magazine now, but back in the summer of '92 (which is when we were first talking about what kind of a magazine we wanted ANIMERICA to be), the biggest hurdle seemed to lie less in assembling a staff, but more in determining for whom, exactly, the magazine would be published.

As a magazine, we had several things going for us. First, there was the fact that the majority of the ANIMERICA editorial staff had come from an anime fan background. Veterans of an irregularly published yet consistently smart-alecky 'zine called ANIMAG, anticipating how anime and manga fans—our readers—were going to react to ANIMERICA was no problem, as the paths of fandom were well-trodden and known to us. Second, thanks to the connection of our publisher with its "parent" publisher in Japan, Shogakukan, the resources needed to publish a monthly magazine with the production values we wanted—and the fan sensibilities we were determined not to abandon—were assured.

But getting together a staff with a publisher was the easy part. The hard part was deciding which way we wanted to go: the safer, tried-and-true route of catering to established anime fandom (safer, but not necessarily in numbers—circulation could be limited, once maximum saturation of the existing fan base was established), or taking a risk and reaching out to what we hoped would someday be a larger and more diverse readership, one better in tune with our own experiences as anime fans, one which wouldn't necessarily need to have a background in fandom before enjoying the domestic import.

In 1992, which is when ANIMERICA started, Japanese animation and manga had yet to become fashionable or even widely known in most of the country, vague memories of *Speed Racer* notwithstanding. Attempting to canvass the full scope of Japanese animation was yet another hurdle, for just as the international cinema known as "Hollywood" has its distinct genres—romance, sci-fi, musical, etc.—so, too, does Japanese animation break down into unique genres of its own. From sports dramas to sci-fi, erotic fantasy to pure-hearted storybook adventures, Japanese animation is as well-rounded a creative realm as any film industry in the world; for proof, you need only page through this book, and study the wildly varied art styles of even the small portion of creators—many of them manga artists, the starting point for many animated projects—featured here.

As you're about to discover, there's something for every anime or manga fan here, from youngest child to most sophisticated adult. In effect, what we wanted to create with ANIMERICA was an anime version of PREMIERE or FILM THREAT, a magazine devoted to and written for fans of Japanese animation—*all* fans, and *all* Japanese animation—no matter what their age or gender might be. It's possible even within the videos released in English so far to find something for every imaginable taste...and the number of available videos continues to grow. Anime shows on American TV in recent years have created an amazingly widespread avenue of awareness for anime among the general public, much as the live-action "battle-team" or *sentai* show *Mighty Morphin Power Rangers* paved the way for the eventual broadcast of those same anime shows (do you think it's a coincidence *Sailor Moon* hit U.S. airwaves when it did?). The huge success of anime films such as *Akira* and *Ghost in the Shell*, always noted by aficionados, now draw mainstream attention to an artform which was once known only to a well-connected or Japanese-speaking few.

Now that Disney has acquired international distribution rights to several of the films of anime director Hayao Miyazaki, arguably Japan's most powerful filmmaker, it's possible that we'll be seeing "anime interviews" in other magazines, as well, and we for one welcome that possibility. Just as TV anime proved itself the catalyst needed for a relatively few number of pre-existing anime fans to swell into today's record audience (anime on MTV and the Sci-Fi Channel? who'd have thought it?), so, too, do we believe that more mainstream attention from the established American film industry will ultimately help to expand the library of the 1,300+ anime videos currently in release here in the U.S. on home video, be they subtitled or in English. For any artform in which the main purpose is popular entertainment—a category into which, *especially* in its native Japan, anime definitely falls—isn't increased access and availability what it's all about...?

What was most desperately needed, we realized, and something which we felt uniquely able to bring to the table, was a sense of perspective. To talk in any depth on the subject of Japanese animation required a little context on the continuing history of the anime industry in Japan, something by and large unknown to many Americans. Ever since the debut of creator Osamu Tezuka's *Tetsuwan Atom* in 1963 (NBC aired it across the U.S. as "Astro Boy" a year later), the Japanese anime industry has been producing TV series after TV series, and film after film. In more recent years, we've seen the birth of a new medium, the direct-to-home-video OAV or "original animation video," but the payoff has been the same: More great Japanese animation for us to love.

More than thirty years of TV animation, movies, and OAVs make for a very large body of work. To know *all* of Japanese animation—and not just the stuff that's been released here, which in itself is no mean feat—is like knowing all of thirty years of Hollywood, *plus* thirty years of television. (Although the first-ever Japanese-animated film goes back to 1917, the birth of the modern anime age is generally agreed to have begun in Japan with *Atom* in 1963.) Also, aside from animation, the overwhelming majority of Japanese comic or "manga" series—from which so many anime videos have been adapted—have yet to cross over to American shores, although manga-in-English publishers such as Antarctic, Dark Horse, Viz Comics, and others are making efforts to build that intercultural bridge.

Just like sci-fi, anime has its own myths and its own common lore. Unlike sci-fi fans, however, anime fans have more than novels and films and obscure British television programs with which to become familiar—they also have to contend with a completely different language! Once you make the decision to expand your horizons beyond the Japanese animation available on television and in English, you're looking at not only one but *three* new alphabets to learn…and that's *before* you're even reading at the level of an average Japanese elementary school student. Obviously, navigating your way through more than thirty years of animation in Japan is going to require more than the latest issue of the Japanese *TV Guide*.

This, we finally decided, is where ANIMERICA and *Anime Interviews* comes in. During the five years ANIMERICA has been in publication, we've had the privilege of speaking to many of the greatest talents in the Japanese industry, conducting exclusive, never-before-seen-in-English interviews not only with the big, established, "tiki heads" of anime Easter Island, but with some young and as-yet unproven talents, as well. To our knowledge, our two-part interview with *My Neighbor Totoro*'s Hayao Miyazaki remains to date the only full-length interview granted for an English-language publication; in it, he reveals the kind of thoughtful, challenging, speculative humanism you might expect to find more from a highly acclaimed, independent filmmaker at Cannes than from a director of what has been, to some extent in *both* Japan and the U.S., seen as "for kiddies only" animation.

As longtime fans of Japanese animation and manga ourselves, we were sometimes startled by the secrets that were so often casually revealed in these interviews, telling anecdotes that had never seen print in the *Japanese* anime press, much less the American. And, as we talked to more and more creators, certain patterns began to become clear—we began to see how each director, writer, character designer, mecha designer, or animator interlinked with the others to form one massive body of work, with influences and currents weaving through the entire thirty-year tapestry.

Many of these interviews have been expanded from their original appearance in ANIMERICA, with new material added that has never before seen print, with new introductions plus filmographies/bibliographies on each artist. In many cases, these "supplementary" materials are the only resource of which we know for non Japanese-speaking readers to research the backgrounds of these creators. In rare cases, a few of the more startling scoops of interest to anime fans had to be left within the pages of ANIMERICA, such as Leiji Matsumoto's revelation of the hidden connection between his *Ginga Tetsudô 999* characters "Maetel" and "Emeraldas" ("*They don't just know each other…they're sisters. I've never depicted them so, but they are sisters. Maetel and Emeraldas' common mother is Promethium*"), mostly due to simple space considerations, but also to help create a clearer, more sharply focused picture of each creator's work as a whole.

The creators represented here in this book are but a sampling of the talent working in Japan today. In most cases, the interviews which have appeared in ANIMERICA are the only English-language interviews on record. Some of our interview subjects are larger-than-life legends; some are relatively new on the scene; but all have created something that lives on its own, stories that have inspired and moved viewers and readers from Japan to America and beyond. If you're already familiar with Japanese animation and manga, here you will find fascinating insights about many titles you know and love, straight from the mouths and minds of the creators themselves. If you are new to anime and manga, it's our hope that the interviews in this book will give you an effortless entrée into a world that's provided all of us here at the ANIMERICA editorial staff so, so many hours of wonder and enjoyment.

—the editors of ANIMERICA
14 september, 1997

Yoshiyuki Tomino

Interviewed by James Matsuzaki and Frederik L. Schodt (1993)

Two years after the 1977 release of *Star Wars*, former film major and nouveau director Yoshiyuki Tomino debuted an animated mecha series that would forever redefine the "super-robot" genre. Titled *Kidô Senshi Gundam*, known from many a model kit box and poster as "Mobile Suit Gundam," the show received only a lukewarm reception during its original syndication run, but the subsequent theatrical release of three movie compilations of the story ignited a *Gundam* fever to accompany the runaway popularity of the *Space Cruiser Yamato* movies, which had themselves just given birth to anime fandom in Japan in general. The demand for *Gundam* toys and model kits caused near-riots in the aisles of Japanese toy stores, and variants on the *Gundam* model line have been produced regularly ever since.

But beyond merchandise sales, the *Gundam* series had a deeper effect. The giant robot genre that Tomino himself had helped to create in the '70s with heroic shows such as *Raideen*, *Daitarn 3* and *Zambot 3* received a subtle shift in attitude toward a kind of "robot realism" that fascinated audiences used to more formulaic fare. Though *Gundam* still featured all the conventions of the robot genre—from the transforming/combining prototype robot piloted by its creator's offspring, to the fight-of-the-week format against new and increasingly weird enemy robots and other contraptions—the spotlight had been moved from the usual sharp focus on the pilot-hero to a wider view, including the world in which he (and even she) lived.

Starting with an Earth shadowed by the L-5 space colonies postulated by Gerard O'Neill, Tomino made *Gundam*'s protagonists soldiers in a bitter civil war between the Earth and its orbiting colonies. Rather than heroic, intelligent robots, *Gundam*'s "mobile suits" are simply machines, and are piloted like fighter planes. The story as a whole explored themes such as war, man's relationship with technology, evolution, and manifest destiny in space. Tomino's *Gundam* series had introduced a new level of human drama and even existentialism to a genre where few had expected to find it.

And yet, what price success? In this interview, conducted at Anime Expo '92, Tomino in his grudging role as anime's Dr. Frankenstein gives the impression of a man who would gladly part with the title "Father of Gundam" if he could only disassociate himself from the mecha monster he's created.

Apocrypha regarding Tomino's love/hate affair abound. One oft-repeated story has him at a convention being plagued by fans about the next *Gundam* sequel. Tomino is rumored to have snatched up a nearby model, hurling it to his feet, whereupon he stomped it to pieces.

"*THERE'S* your *Gundam* sequel!" he's said to have cried. Another version has him stabbing it through the head with a pencil.

Part of this is understandable, especially when viewed from a career standpoint. Though easily the best known, *Gundam* is far from the *only* influential television series with which Tomino has been involved. He's had a hand in or a driver's-seat position for many of the mecha classics of the '70s including *Yûsha Raideen*—one of the handful of shows before *Gundam* in which he collaborated with character designer Yoshikazu Yasuhiko. Many of these, such *Raideen*, are viewed as classics in their own right. It was also during this era (and not from *Gundam*) that he earned the nickname "*Zen Kuroshi no Tomino*" ("Kill 'em all Tomino"), most notably with the TV series *Zambot 3*, which featured the hero's girlfriend being blasted to pieces as the result of a bomb implanted in her spine.

In the post-*Gundam* era, many of the '80s mecha TV shows were also Tomino's babies and are some of the best examples of his penchant for creating whole new worlds to explore: Ye olde medieval sword 'n' sorcery (with robots) in the faerie fantasy *Sei Senshi* ("Holy Warrior") *Dunbine*; far future sci-fi in the offbeat *Jûsenki* ("Heavy War-Machine") *L-Gaim*, cited by many to be the origin of Mamoru Nagano's *Five Star Stories*' universe, especially since Nagano himself worked on *L-Gaim* as a mecha designer; as well as the comedic Wild West robot adventure *Sentô* ("Battle") *Mecha Xabungle*, typically seen written in Japanese ads—in English—as "Blue Gale Xabungle." The inevitable *Gundam* sequels are there too, with *Z* ("Zeta") *Gundam*, *Gundam ZZ* ("Double Zeta"), as well as the theatrical feature *Kidô Senshi Gundam: Gyakushû no Char* ("Char's Counterattack"), which seemed to finally close the chapter on the characters from the original series. Another series of note in the post-*Gundam* era is the grim space saga *Densetsu Kyoshin Ideon* ("Legendary God-Giant Ideon"), often cited by director Hideaki Anno as an influence on his own series, *Neon Genesis Evangelion*.

An active writer and novelist aside from his animation work, Tomino has written novelizations of many of his works, many of them *Gundam*-related titles, such as "Gaia Gear" (originally serialized in NEWTYPE magazine and also adapted for a nationally broadcast radio version), which takes place 500 years after the original series' One-Year War. At the time of this interview, *Gundam* spinoffs produced by younger animators who had grown up watching the show were only just beginning to pick up speed; in 1992, the most recent one was *Gundam 0083: Stardust Memory*, a twelve-volume OAV series detailing an original story taking place between the original series' One-Year War and Tomino's sequel series *Zeta Gundam*. Tomino himself had only revisited the *Gundam* universe once in animation since 1989's *Char's Counterattack*, for a far-future movie titled *Gundam F-91*, which released theatrically at the same time as the first volume of *Stardust Memory*. In this interview, the director gives his thoughts on not only the origins of *Gundam* but also on some of his frustrations with the animation industry itself.

interview

ANIMERICA: How did you begin your career in anime?

TOMINO: You may be aware that in Japan, weekly half-hour television animation actually began one year before I graduated from college. The first series was *Tetsuwan Atom* [*lit., "Iron-Arm Atom," known in the U.S. as* Astro Boy—*Ed.*]. I majored in film, but when I graduated there was no chance of employment in the film industry. So I joined the *Tetsuwan Atom* production staff and went into

Mobile Suit Gundam: Char's Counterattack

the animation industry instead. I've probably directed more episodes of the TV series than anyone else.

ANIMERICA: What specific training did you receive?

TOMINO: In college, I was particularly interested in film direction. For the first two years in the program, we were required to write a lot of scenarios; I'd say it gave me a basic education in scriptwriting. I received no formal training in art, but because I knew that I wanted to become a director, I did study art and music to a certain extent.

ANIMERICA: What influenced your creation of the *Gundam* concept?

TOMINO: I don't think there are any animated works that have had a specific influence on the creation of the *Gundam* world. In regard to live-action, there have been quite a few that I have not only liked but been influenced by. I very much like Akira Kurosawa's films, especially the action films. I like the very quiet films of Yasujiro Ozu. And I particularly like the U.S. film *Destination Moon*. Its depiction of space did influence me; it's where I got my feeling for space conditions from. It's very outdated now, but it was revolutionary at the time.

ANIMERICA: How did the space-colony concept and the *Star Wars* movie influence *Gundam*?

TOMINO: The space-colony concept and *Star Wars* were very much an influence on me; in fact, you could say they're the basis for the whole *Gundam* drama. I already had the story outline done when the movie was released and, frankly, I felt extremely frustrated and bitter. In the United States a film like *Star Wars* could be made in live-action, whereas in Japan we were in a position—or *I* was in a position—where I had to make my story in robot animation...and I don't particularly *like* robot animation.

ANIMERICA: That brings up a point *Five Star Stories*' Mamoru Nagano brought up when he visited the United States in 1989. In many respects, he said, Japanese live-action films, especially in regard to sound effects and special effects, are by American standards outdated. Do you have any feelings on why this might be?

Mobile Suit Gundam

TOMINO: Yes. In Japan we have production staff and directors who are big, big admirers of special effects. But I think they regard the shooting of special effects as something too unique, too separate. That's one of the reasons that the films themselves are terrible. I think the biggest problem in the Japanese film industry is that people are not using special effects to tell a story; they're using special effects to use special effects. It's a big trend among many production companies. I would even go so far as to say that there are no live-action directors in Japan who can use special effects as an integral part of the story.

ANIMERICA: Going back to *Gundam*, how did you assemble the creative team that produced the first series?

TOMINO: There really is no creative "team" for *Gundam* as such. We just used whatever staff was currently available. For example, we were very lucky that on the first series we had Yoshikazu Yasuhiko (*Arion*, *Venus Wars*) as our character designer. In *Zeta* and *Gundam Double Zeta*, we had all kinds of creative staff involved. But because each series had a separate team, we weren't able to establish the overall continuity and uniformity that we should've had throughout the story, and that's unfortunate.

ANIMERICA: Is that why there were such big breaks in the storylines between the various series and *Char's Counterattack*?

TOMINO: Yes, that's the biggest reason. I think another reason why there were such big gaps was because, being both creator and director, I tried to do too much. Because both I and the producer felt that the element of human drama was the main reason for the success of the first series, I think I became too fixated. In *Zeta*, we emphasized this human-drama element too much and wound up with a bleak ending. We overcompensated in *Double Zeta* and ended up with a comical ending. I think many of the fans tend to see the whole *Gundam* story as one unified universe, but, frankly, I don't think of it that way. In my own mind, from *Zeta Gundam* on, every *Gundam* story stands on its own.

ANIMERICA: How involved were you with the two *Gundam* OAV series, *Mobile Suit Gundam 0080: A War in the Pocket* and the recently completed *Mobile Suit Gundam 0083: Stardust Memory*?

TOMINO: I had no involvement in either project. They're produced by Sunrise and under its direct control.

ANIMERICA: I understand that both *Char's Counterattack* and *F-91* were originally novel series.

From my standpoint as the original creator, the fact that I can't control the whole universe is sometimes very frustrating.

TOMINO: It's the other way around, actually. Whenever I write a novel, it's with the assumption that there'll also be a film. As for why, I don't know if I should say this, but...it's probably because my novels aren't strong enough to stand up on their own. I'd prefer to write the novels before the films, but the film production's got to come first. And since I'm involved in direction as well as production, the films always get priority and that's why the books come out later. I'd like to become a novelist, but I can't. I'm in a real dilemma.

ANIMERICA: In what way? Do you feel trapped by the *Gundam* concept?

TOMINO: It has absolutely nothing to do with *Gundam*. It's related to the fact that, for my generation, the print medium and novels in particular have a higher status than film. It's sort of everyone's dream, I guess, to be a novelist. But I am a TV animation director.

ANIMERICA: If you were a novelist, what sort of genres would you write in? Science fiction, perhaps?

TOMINO: No, I don't particularly care for science fiction.

ANIMERICA: In its time, *Gundam* was a revolutionary concept. In his book, *Inside the Robot Kingdom*, (author) Fred Schodt describes a '70s anime producer who told you how to write a proper robot story. Basically, have a young hero with a big robot smash the bad guy.

TOMINO: I was involved in a lot of films like that, actually. What I wanted to do was something very different. *Gundam*, of course, was a hit. Many times after that, I tried to create shows with a different feeling. Some of these I regard as failures.

ANIMERICA: What is your relationship with Sunrise?

TOMINO: In theory, I'm a freelance director. However, because of the success of *Gundam*, I am in reality directly linked to Sunrise. In many cases, Sunrise starts the project and then they pass it on to me. Because *Gundam* is so visible within the industry, people don't really see me as a freelance director. This has actually caused quite a personal problem. Until there are no more *Gundam* films made, I won't be getting any work. People won't give me any work.

ANIMERICA: What are your duties on a *Gundam* project? You've already mentioned that you're the overall director. Do you work on the screenplay as well?

TOMINO: I do everything that you mentioned. Whether it's a TV series or a theatrical feature, I'm involved in either drawing the storyboards or checking them. I discuss the drawings with the animators, I draw and check the cels—all of which takes 365 days a year. I really don't have time for other projects.

ANIMERICA: What would you like to be involved in if *Gundam* were terminated?

TOMINO: Nothing in particular. I'm a TV person—I've spent so much time in the industry, so many years being given the conditions under which I must create—I really

Garzey's Wing

don't think I could come up with anything on my own. I've been working under externally imposed conditions for thirty years. I've got all kinds of experience in being given certain conditions for planning and direction; I'm actually very confident working in an environment like that. But also, as I've said, because I've been working in this situation for thirty years, it's very difficult for me to put together my own ideas, to work from a "blank slate." In that sense, I am probably a very different creature from what you normally refer to as a creator.

For example, *Gundam* is part of the giant robot genre and, frankly, I don't really like the giant robot genre. But when I am put in the situation where I have to create within those parameters, I turn around and think, "Well, what can I do?" And then, if necessary, I try to introduce some new concepts. That's what happened with *Gundam*, and I think that's one of the reasons for its success. If I were left to my own devices, if I could do whatever I wanted, I probably wouldn't have the success of *Gundam*. It may not seem like a creative process, but I've recently begun to realize that as a creative method, it *is* legitimate.

ANIMERICA: Legitimate? How so?

TOMINO: When people think of a creative person in the industry, they probably think of someone who works from a blank slate. But actually, even the greatest geniuses tend to draw ideas from their environment. So I think what I described is a legitimate method of being creative.

ANIMERICA: Are there any future projects you're planning to work on?

TOMINO: In terms of the *Gundam* world, I would like to create one more story from the perspective of 10- to 15-year-old children. I'm also interested in doing something with the *Dunbine* world, maybe something in its future. It might be something, for example, where the inhabitants realize that only they can save the Earth from destruction.

ANIMERICA: How do you feel about the various print adaptations of the *Gundam* world? For instance, *MS Era* and *Gundam Sentinel*?

TOMINO: The fact that side-stories are popular is something I am pleased about. Sometimes the side-stories and the films made from them attract more fans than I'm able to generate. Because it does help to increase the *Gundam* market, I'm very happy for it. From my standpoint as the original creator, though, the fact that I can't control the whole universe is sometimes very frustrating. *Gundam*'s been around for over ten years. In terms of business strategy and development, the side-stories can be thought of as a vehicle to continue it for another ten. They're also another way to expand the market and continue it all over the world. In that sense, they're valuable.

ANIMERICA: Finally, if you had the chance to recreate *Gundam*, what would you change from the original story? Would it perhaps be more adult-oriented?

TOMINO: If it came to remaking the *Gundam* series...well, it would depend on the conditions. At this point I'm not even considering it. However, if I were given the opportunity and the conditions under which to do so, then I'd demonstrate to you how I'd go about it.

afterword

Since the time of this interview, things have begun to change for the *Gundam* juggernaut Tomino set in motion in 1979...and also for the creator himself.

In 1993-94, the new *Gundam* TV series referred to in this interview aired on Japanese TV under the title *Victory Gundam*. *V Gundam* (as it's usually abbreviated) was the first new *television* series to bear the *Gundam* name since *Gundam Double Zeta* in 1986. Featuring a 13-year-old hero, a surprisingly grim story, and a years-in-the-future setting in the world of the original *Gundam*, the show wasn't always the highest-rated of its timeslot (in comparison with evergreen hits such as *Dragon Ball* or the even younger-targeted *Crayon Shin-chan*, especially), but it did set in motion a new wave of popularity for the entire *Gundam* franchise.

These days, based on the popularity of such OAV series as *Stardust Memory*, the *Gundam* legacy keeps on rolling even without Tomino, with an ever-multiplying number of new series being created under the *Gundam* flag, most of which have no more to do with the original universe than a basic similarity in robot design, as each creative team picks out a different aspect of the series to emphasize. On TV, *V Gundam* was quickly followed by three back-to-back series—*G Gundam*, *Gundam Wing*, and *Gundam X*. An OAV series, *Mobile Suit Gundam: The 08th Mobile Suit Team*, is also currently in release, detailing an "alternate" story set in the original series' timeline.

Parody too, has been established—the *SD* ("Super-Deformed") *Gundam* series gives us strangely shrunken versions of familiar characters and is a seemingly endless font of slapstick pokes at the series, and in some ways (especially among small children) is even more popular than the original. Recently, Tomino has finally begun work on other series beside *Gundam* that inspire him, such as an OAV series, *Byston Well Monogatari: Garzey no Tsubasa* ("Tales of Byston Well: Garzey's Wing"). Set in the *Dunbine* world—yet lacking the robots that, it's long been rumored, were only added to the *Dunbine* story after pressure from the animation's then-sponsor—Tomino at last seems free to pursue his own vision quest.

Tomino's also tried his hand, of late, at writing for a manga series. Titled *Crossbone Gundam*, the series follows up on the story from the *Gundam F-91* movie, albeit with a Leiji Matsumoto-esque "tall ships and pirates" motif. One of Tomino's infamous name "homages" (he's admitted during a U.S. panel appearance that a good third of his characters' names, such as *Dunbine*'s "Shott Weapon," and *L-Gaim*'s "Full Flat," are gags) is the hero of *Crossbone Gundam*, "Tobias Arranax," whose name harkens to the hero of the classic Jules Verne novel *20,000 Leagues Under the Sea*.

Currently, it seems Tomino may be returning to his roots, as he's said to be working on a new, as-yet-untitled animation project for television.

Yoshiyuki Tomino
Select Filmography

ANIME アニメ

Known first and foremost as the "Father of *Gundam*," as you'll see below, Yoshiyuki Tomino has had quite a career in the anime industry, working as an animator on some of the biggest hits in the industry, as well as going on to create hits—not all of them *Gundam*, either—of his own. Involved recently in the writing of "Gaia Gear," a *Gundam*-inspired novella serialized in the pages of NEWTYPE magazine, Tomino has also published a series of *Gundam* novels through Del Rey here in the U.S., as translated by the redoubtable Fred Schodt. In terms of manga work, Tomino is currently involved in the writing of "Crossbone Gundam," an alternate *Gundam* series as published in SHÔNEN ACE. Finally, although one might reasonably argue that a byline is a byline, two things need to be noted: (1) not all Tomino's credits reflect actual work on the series, as his *Gundam 0080* and *0083* credits seem mostly honorary; and (2) we've elected not to list the numerous "SD" or "super-deformed" *Gundam* videos here, partly because Tomino's involvement in them is slight at best, and partly because there's just so darn many of 'em.

Tetsuwan Atom ("Iron-Arm Atom")
鉄腕アトム
Episode Director
193-episode TV series (1963-66); see entry for Sugii. *DOMESTIC RELEASE TITLE:* ***Astro Boy*** (The Right Stuf)

Ribon no Kishi ("Ribbon Knight")
リボンの騎士
Episode Director
52-episode TV series (1967-68); based on the Osamu Tezuka manga series of the same name which, incidentally, also happens to be Japan's first ever *shôjo* or "for girls only" manga title. *CURRENTLY IMPORT ONLY*

Moomin
ムーミン
Storyboards
65-episode TV series (1969-70); based on the children's stories by Finnish author Tove Jansson. Followed years later by several different sequel series. *CURRENTLY IMPORT ONLY*

Ashita no Joe ("Tomorrow's Joe")
あしたのジョー
Episode Director
79-episode TV series (1970-71); based on the popular, long-running manga of the same name by Tetsuya Chiba, as serialized in SHÔNEN MAGAZINE. *CURRENTLY IMPORT ONLY*

Sasurai no Taiyô ("Wandering Sun")
さすらいの太陽
Episode Director
26-episode TV series (1971); based on the *shôjo* manga series of the same name by Mayumi Suzuki, as published in weekly SHÔJO COMIC manga magazine. *CURRENTLY IMPORT ONLY*

Fushigi na Melmo ("Marvellous Melmo")
ふしぎなメルモ
Episode Director
26-episode TV series (1971-72); based on the Tezuka manga of the same name (Tezuka also acts as episode director). *CURRENTLY IMPORT ONLY*

Kokumatsu-sama no Otôri Dai ("Kokumatsu's 'Coming Through'")
国松さまのお通りだい
Episode Director
46-episode TV series (1971-72); based on the manga by *Ashita no Joe*'s Tetsuya Chiba. Updated remake of a series from Japanese television's "monochrome" or black and white age. *CURRENTLY IMPORT ONLY*

Umi no Triton ("Triton of the Sea")
海のトリトン
Director
27-episode TV series (1972); based on the Tezuka manga of the same name. In a rare departure from more "traditional" Tezuka anime, *Triton* focuses more on dramatic, morally charged conflicts between good and evil, reflecting, perhaps, what would eventually become Tomino's own preoccupation with same. *CURRENTLY IMPORT ONLY*

Yamanezumi Rockychuck ("Rockychuck the Woodchuck")
山ねずみロッキーチャック
Storyboards
52-episode TV series (1973); based on the children's book *Animal Tales* by Thornton W. Burgess. Adventures of a young woodchuck named "Rockychuck" and his woodchuck girlfriend, Polly. *CURRENTLY IMPORT ONLY*

Jinzô Ningen Casshan ("'New-Made Man' Casshan")
新造人間キャッシャーン
Episode Director
35-episode TV series (1973-74); representative work of Tatsunoko "Home of the Heroes" Productions. Although this original TV series has yet to be made available domestically, the *Casshan* story was recently updated as a new OAV series which is available in the U.S., through Streamline Pictures/Orion Home Video. *CURRENTLY IMPORT ONLY*

Samurai Giants
侍ジャイアンツ
Storyboards
46-episode TV series (1973-74); based on the manga by Ikki Kajiwara and Ko Inoue. At first glance your average baseball story, more thought actually went into *Samurai Giants* than you might think, mainly because its creators had set as a goal for themselves the creation of a story that *wouldn't* mirror the ubiquitous *Kyojin no Hoshi* ("Star of the Giants"). *CURRENTLY IMPORT ONLY*

Alps no Shôjo Heiji ("Heidi, a Young Girl of the Alps")
アルプスの少女ハイジ
Storyboards
52-episode TV series (1974); see entry for Miyazaki. *CURRENTLY IMPORT ONLY*

Hurricane Polymer
破裏拳ポリマー
Storyboards
26-episode TV series (1974-75); yet another entry in Tatsunoko Production's pantheon of heroes. Produced during a so-called "Bruce Lee boom" in Japan, perhaps it's true that the series does feature an unusual amount of kung fu style physical humor. On-air in Japan at roughly the same time as another Tatsunoko "hero" show, *Uchû Kishi* ("Space Knight") *Tekkaman*. *CURRENTLY IMPORT ONLY*

Uchû Senkan Yamato ("Space Battleship Yamato")
宇宙戦艦ヤマト
Storyboards
26-episode TV series (1974-75); see entry for Matsumoto. *DOMESTIC RELEASE TITLE:* ***Star Blazers*** (Voyager Entertainment)

Yûsha Raideen ("'Hero' or 'Brave' Raideen")
勇者ライディーン
Director / Episode Director / Storyboards
50-episode TV series (1975-76); based on the manga by Yoshitake Suzuki. The first "giant robot" anime show for Tohoku Shinsha, in the anime history books *Raideen* is said to be remembered for the slightly fantastic feel imparted to it by director Tomino. An updated, '90s remake was released in Japan recently, although it—like the show which inspired it—has yet to be made available domestically. *CURRENTLY IMPORT ONLY*

Haha o Tazunete Sanzen Ri
("Three Thousand Leagues in Search of Mother")
母をたずねて三千里
Storyboards
51-episode TV series (1976); see entry for Miyazaki. *CURRENTLY IMPORT ONLY*

Chô Denji Robo Combattler V
("'Super Magnetic Robo' Combattler V")
超電磁ロボコン・バトラーV
Episode Director / Storyboards
54-episode TV series (1976-77); based on the manga by Saburo Yatsude. Five robots combine into one, mightier robot warrior, thus the Roman numeral "V" in the series title. *CURRENTLY IMPORT ONLY*

Araiguma Rascal ("Rascal the Raccoon")
あらいぐまラスカル
Storyboards
52-episode TV series (1977); see entry for Miyazaki. *CURRENTLY IMPORT ONLY*

Chô Denji Machine Voltes V
("'Super Magnetic Machine' Voltes V")
超電磁マシーンボルテスV

Episode Director / Storyboards
40-episode TV series (1977-78); based on the manga by Saburo Yatsude. Second entry in the "Super Magnetic Robo" co-production founded by Toei and Sunrise. *CURRENTLY IMPORT ONLY*

Muteki Chôjin Zambot 3
("'Invincible Super Person' Zambot 3")
無敵超人ザンボット3

Executive Director / Original Story
23-episode TV series (1977-78); based on a story by Tomino and Yoshitake Suzuki. First animated series to be produced by Sunrise as an independent studio. The series' slant—that characters seldom knew why or for what they were fighting—is said to have been imbued directly by Tomino. *CURRENTLY IMPORT ONLY*

Mirai Shônen Conan ("Future Boy Conan")
未来少年コナン

Storyboards
26-episode TV series (1978); see entry for Miyazaki. *CURRENTLY IMPORT ONLY*

Peline Monogatari ("The Story of Peline")
ペリーヌ物語

Storyboards
53-episode TV series (1978); based on the novel *En Famille* by Hector Malot. Joining Tomino in the storyboard trenches for this series is Isao Takahata, frequent collaborator of Hayao Miyazaki. *CURRENTLY IMPORT ONLY*

Muteki Kôjin Daitarn 3 ("'Invincible Iron-Man' Daitarn 3")
無敵鋼人ダイターン3

Executive Director / Original Story / Episode Director
40-episode TV series (1978-79); based on an original story by Tomino, among others. Change of pace for director Tomino, incorporating a lighter tone than the usual *stürm und drang* for which he was already becoming famous. *CURRENTLY IMPORT ONLY*

Akage no Anne ("Red-Haired Anne")
赤毛のアン

Storyboards
50-episode TV series (1979); see entry for Miyazaki. *CURRENTLY IMPORT ONLY*

Kidô Senshi Gundam ("Mobile Suit Gundam")
機動戦士ガンダム

Executive Director / Original Story
43-episode TV series (1979-80); first entry in what would become the Franchise of Franchises for then-fledgling studio Sunrise. Before *Gundam*, giant robots in anime had been hulking, eccentric pets small boys could "sic" on others at will, or even, sometimes, ride; after *Gundam*, they became sleek, mass-produced weapons of war. The show that literally redefined the genre, the three *Gundam* movies available in Japan on home video are basically compilation or "digest" versions of the TV episodes, although the climactic final sequence in the third film was completely reanimated for dramatic effect. *CURRENTLY IMPORT ONLY*

Densetsu Kyoshin Ideon ("'Legendary God-Giant' Ideon")
伝説巨神イデオン

Executive Director / Original Story
39-episode TV series (1980-81); based on an original story by Tomino, among others. Follows up the iconoclastic reforging of the "giant robot" genre started by Tomino in *Gundam* by not only upping the size of the robots themselves, but also by escalating both existential musings as well as on-screen casualty counts. Followed by a two-part theatrical release in 1982. Also known as "Space Runaway Ideon," the studio-provided English subtitle. *CURRENTLY IMPORT ONLY*

Sentô Mecha Xabungle ("'War-Machine' Xabungle")
戦闘メカザブングル

Executive Director / Original Story
50-episode TV series (1982-83); based on an original story by Tomino, among others. Lovingly described by at least one diehard fan we know as *the* "Wild West Robot Show," the giant-robot (in this case, "walker-machine") action takes place in a world where Clint Eastwood might feel well at home. Also known as "Blue Gale Xabungle." *CURRENTLY IMPORT ONLY*

Ginga Hyôryû Vifam ("'Galactic Castaways' Vifam")
銀河漂流バイファム

Original Concept
46-episode TV series (1983-84). In this unique twist on Tomino's by-now familiar *oeuvre*, a passel o' younguns gets stranded in space and, with minimal adult supervision, must learn to pilot giant robots. Followed in 1984-85 by a four-volume OAV series, in which Tomino gets credit for "original concept" once again. Also known as "Round Vernian Vifam." *CURRENTLY IMPORT ONLY*

Sei-Senshi Dunbine ("'Holy-Warrior' Dunbine")
聖戦士ダンバイン

Executive Director / Original Story
49-episode TV series (1983-84); based on an original story by Tomino, among others. A mystic summons from an alternate world known as "Byston Well" summons ne'er-do-well Japanese youth Sho Zama (motorcycle and all) down the "Aura Road" to do battle in insectoid giant robots known as "aura battlers," aptly named after the metaphysical source of their power. Re-released in 1988 as a three-volume OAV compilation series, each of the three "rehash" volumes (VHS or LD) also include a brand-new, not-available-anywhere-else OAV episode. Also known as "Aura Battler Dunbine." *CURRENTLY IMPORT ONLY*

Jûsenki L-Gaim ("'Heavy War-Machine' L-Gaim")
重戦機エルガイム

Executive Director / Original Story
54-episode TV series (1984-85); features character and mecha design by a then-novice Mamoru Nagano (*Five Star Stories*). Re-released in 1986-87 as a three-volume OAV compilation. Also known as "Heavy Metal L-Gaim." *CURRENTLY IMPORT ONLY*

Kidô Senshi Z Gundam ("Mobile Suit 'Zeta' Gundam")
機動戦士Zガンダム

Executive Director / Original Story
50-episode TV series (1985-86); sequel to the popular 1979-80 series. With episode direction by Yasuhiro Imagawa (*Giant Robo*) and animation direction by Hiroyuki Kitazume (*Moldiver*), *Zeta Gundam* was an '80s focus point for the anime "name" industry of the '90s...especially as we know it here in the U.S. *CURRENTLY IMPORT ONLY*

Kidô Senshi Gundam ZZ
("Mobile Suit Gundam 'Double Zeta'")
機動戦士ガンダムZZ

Executive Director / Original Story
47-episode TV series (1986-87); in general, a more light-hearted sequel than *Zeta*, rising body counts in later episodes notwithstanding. Character design and animation direction by Kitazume. *CURRENTLY IMPORT ONLY*

Kidô Senshi Gundam: Gyakushû no Char
("Mobile Suit Gundam: Char's Counterattack")
機動戦士ガンダム：逆襲のシャア

Director / Screenplay / Original Story
120-minute theatrical feature (1988); resolves (more or less) the ambivalent rivalry of idealistic Gundam pilot Amuro Rei and charismatic leader Char Aznable as established in the 1979-80 television series. Character design and animation direction by Kitazume. *CURRENTLY IMPORT ONLY*

Kidô Senshi Gundam 0080: Pocket no Naka no Sensô
("Mobile Suit Gundam 0080: A War in the Pocket")
機動戦士ガンダム0080: ポケットの中の戦争

Original Story
Six-volume OAV series (1989). Tidy, complete-in-itself story, told through the eyes of a young boy and set chronologically about the same time Amuro and Char wage their final battle in the 1979-80 *Gundam* TV series (you don't need to have seen the TV series to enjoy the OAV series, however). Movingly bitter-sweet ending, with a screenplay by Hiroyuki Yamaga (*The Wings of Honneamise*). *CURRENTLY IMPORT ONLY*

Kidô Senshi Gundam F-91 ("Mobile Suit Gundam F-91")
機動戦士ガンダムF-91

Director / Original Story
115-minute theatrical feature (1991). The three caballeros of the original *Gundam*—creator Tomino, character designer Yoshikazu "Yaz" Yasuhiko of *Crusher Joe* fame, and mecha designer Kunio Okawara (*Votoms*)—reunite for this 1991 movie (thus, the perhaps not entirely coincidental "F-91" of the title). *CURRENTLY IMPORT ONLY*

Kidô Senshi Gundam 0083 ("Mobile Suit Gundam 0083")
機動戦士ガンダム0083: STARDUST MEMORY

Original Story
Twelve-volume OAV series (1991-92). "Mechanical stylings" by *Macross'* Shoji Kawamori are only a small part of the fantastic design work in this epic, sprawling *Gundam* "side-story." Although the OAV series itself has yet to be released domestically, as with the *Dirty Pair*, an "anime film comic" version is also available in the U.S. from Viz Comics which uses actual production cels from the series to illustrate the story. Followed in 1992 by *Kidô Senshi Gundam 0083: Zeon no Zankoku* ("Zeon's Fading Light"), a theatrically screened compilation version featuring a few minutes of new footage. *CURRENTLY IMPORT ONLY*

Mama wa Shôgaku Yon-Nen-Sei ("Mama's a Fourth-Grader")
ママは小学4年生

Opening Animation
51-episode TV series (1992) in which Tomino has no involvement other than in creating the opening animation sequence. (It's such a cute show—and, coming from the master of existential anime angst as it does, so unexpected—that we couldn't resist mentioning it.) *CURRENTLY IMPORT ONLY*

Kidô Senshi V Gundam ("Mobile Suit 'Victory' Gundam")
機動戦士Vガンダム

Executive Director / Original Story
51-episode TV series (1993-94). With a story designed to stand alone from the main *Gundam* continuity and a lead character aged purposefully younger in order to appeal to the model- and toy-buying kids who've helped make the series the phenomenon it's been over the years, the series nevertheless offers a strong attraction for older viewers as well, partially because of its story, and partially because of its unflinching approach to violence. *CURRENTLY IMPORT ONLY*

Kidô Butôden G Gundam
("Mobile 'Bushido Legend' G Gundam")
機動武闘伝Gガンダム

Original Concept
49-episode TV series (1994-95). When the series first aired, seasoned fans shook their heads gravely and applauded original creator Tomino for keeping his distance from what seemed a wholly gratuitous entry in the ongoing *Gundam* legend. However, as more recent critics have pointed out, the series is not without its appeal, especially if you're a fan of director Yasuhiro Imagawa (*Giant Robo*), whose aesthetic sense infuses the show from start to finish. *CURRENTLY IMPORT ONLY*

Shin Kidô Senki Gundam W
("The New 'Mobile Battle-Legend' Gundam Wing")
新機動戦記ガンダムW

Original Concept
49-episode TV series (1995-96). The Gundam franchise gets a whole new look, thanks to character designer Shuko Murase (*Ronin Warriors*/*Samurai Troopers*, *Night Warriors: Darkstalkers' Revenge*) and a cast of young, hunky Gundam prodigies. *CURRENTLY IMPORT ONLY*

Kidô Shin Seiki Gundam X
("The Mobile 'New Era' Gundam X")
機動新世紀ガンダムX

Original Concept
39-episode TV series (1996). Coming as it did on the heels of the popular *Gundam Wing*, expectations were high for this series, but even with the inclusion of oddities such as psychically enhanced "Newtype" dolphins and the like, *Gundam X* has seemingly suffered, at least in the hearts of finicky fans, what psychologists might describe as a "failure to thrive." *CURRENTLY IMPORT ONLY*

Kidô Senshi Gundam: Dai-08 MS Shôtai
("Mobile Suit Gundam: The Eighth Mobile Suit Team")
機動戦士ガンダム：第08MS小隊

Original Story
Six-volume OAV series (1996–); currently ongoing as of press time. In 1990, toy manufacturer Bandai released a collection of TIME-LIFE style "photos" (mock credits and contributor bios in all) to commemorate a fictional—yet crucial—event in the series' chronology. Titled *MS Era: The Documentary Photographs of the One-Year War*, the book uses original illustrations by top Japanese illustrators such as Masami Yuki (*Patlabor*), Yutaka Izubuchi (*Dunbine*), and Shoji Kawamori (*Macross*) to posit a documentary-style look at the conflict; the OAV series is an animated version of that same concept. Twelve OAV volumes planned for eventual release. *CURRENTLY IMPORT ONLY*

Byston Well Monogatari: Garzey no Tsubasa
("Tales From Byston Well: Garzey's Wing")
バイストン・ウェル物語（ガーゼイの翼）

Director/ Original Story / Screenplay
Three-volume OAV series (1996-97). Free at last of the sponsors who insisted his original *Dunbine* couldn't go on without the giant (albeit giant *insectoid*) robots, Tomino gets to do it his way in this updated (and robot-less) direct-to-home-video sequel to the 1983-84 TV series. *CURRENTLY IMPORT ONLY*

Key

- Japanese comics or "manga" series; may or may not be available in foreign-language (i.e., English) version
- TV series broadcast on-air in Japan. Note that, in the U.S., Japanese TV series are both broadcast on-air (*Ronin Warriors*) and released on home video (*Ranma 1/2*). Others (*Sailor Moon, Dragon Ball*) are available both in broadcast and home video versions
- Direct-to-home-video series; may also include compilations of TV episodes released to home video market
- Theatrical feature; may or may not receive equivalent theatrical release for U.S. version

Rumiko Takahashi

Interviewed by Seiji Horibuchi (1993)

"I think I'm in love."

They all say it, meeting her for the first time. Soft-spoken and full of laughter, petite even by Japanese standards, it's easy to see why Rumiko Takahashi is one of Japan's most beloved manga artists. What's not so easy is thinking of her as one of her country's wealthiest citizens. She's just so...*cute*.

Interviewer Seiji Horibuchi tells us he was "pleasantly surprised" when Takahashi personally opened the door. "I've spoken with her several times over the telephone," Seiji says, "but this was the first time for me to meet her in person. She's just so...*small*. Not only her size but her voice. Gentle, polite, modest—not at all what you'd expect from someone who makes more annually than Joe Montana.

"I fell in love immediately."

Takahashi was only twenty-one when she created *Urusei Yatsura*, the comic that would go on to sell over twenty-two million copies and establish her as one of Japan's premiere storytellers. The wacky boy-meets-alien romantic comedy enjoyed a seven-year serialization in WEEKLY SHÔNEN SUNDAY comic magazine and is currently available as thirty-four collected Japanese volumes, as well as in English under the title *Lum*Urusei Yatsura*.

"*Urusei Yatsura* is a title I had been dreaming about since I was very young," Takahashi says. "It really includes everything I ever wanted to do. I love science fiction because sci-fi has tremendous flexibility. I adopted the science fiction-style for the series because then I could write any way I wanted to."

Takahashi began her comics career under the tutelage of Kazuo Koike (*Lone Wolf and Cub*, *Crying Freeman*). She says she's a big fan of *Spider-Man*, adapted for a Japanese version by *Crying Freeman* and *Mai the Psychic Girl*'s Ryoichi Ikegami, who co-wrote it with Kazumasa Hirai.

Takahashi's unassuming red brick home is located in one of Tokyo's more quiet neighborhoods. The manga wunderkind was watching a rerun of a soap opera-like samurai drama when our interviewer arrived. "The first thing I noticed when I entered was the huge HDTV," he admits. "The high-definition television set was the only visible sign that this was the home of one of the world's most successful comic creators."

It was in 1977 that *Katte na Yatsura* ("Those Selfish Aliens"), the rough-yet-promising series which laid the early foundations for *Urusei Yatsura*, was nominated for Japanese mega-publisher Shogakukan's "Best New Comic

Artist" award. Her bestselling *Urusei* (the title is a pun on the Japanese *urusai*, as in "noisy/obnoxious," but written with the Chinese character for "planet") was published a year later at the encouragement of her Shogakukan editor. *Ranma 1/2*, described by Gerard Jones, the series' English rewriter, as "a bizarre martial arts sex comedy," was serialized in SHÔNEN SUNDAY for a total of thirty-eight *tankôbon*, or compiled manga volumes.

"I always wanted to become a professional comic creator," Takahashi says, "ever since I was a child. At first, my short stories were published in comic magazines, then I had the big chance to publish *Urusei Yatsura*. As you probably know, comics for girls are very popular in Japan. Most of girls' comics are created by women. Maybe that's why there are so many female comic artists here." According to some estimates, *shôjo* or girls' comics make up 30% of the entire Japanese manga industry—a significant figure, even though Takahashi herself works in a style more like that of *shônen*, or boys' comics.

"Although she's shy, she's also very, very determined," Seiji says. "Takahashi definitely knows what she's talking about. I think it's because she loves what she's doing. Do you realize that with the help of her assistants, she creates over one hundred original comic pages every *month*?

"With such a heavy work load, you'd think she'd be tired, but she was actually very refreshed...almost as if she were thriving under the pressure. She was very interested in hearing about her American fans, and is looking forward to meeting them." Although her schedule is among the most grueling in the manga industry, at the time of this interview Takahashi had been hoping she'd be able to visit the U.S. sometime in the future and see for herself what it is about her work that interests her English-speaking readers.

"Sure, there are cultural differences in my work," she says. "When I see an American comedy, even though the jokes are translated, there's always a moment when I feel puzzled and think, 'Ah, Americans would probably laugh at this more.'

"I suppose the same thing must happen with my books," she continues. "It's inevitable. And yet, that doesn't mean my books can't be enjoyed by English-speaking readers. I feel confident that there's enough substance to them that people from a variety of cultural backgrounds can have a lot of fun reading them."

No doubt about it, Takahashi is the darling of the manga and anime world, and not just in Japan. At the time of this interview, in the early spring of 1993, *Ranma 1/2* was still in serialization in SHÔNEN SUNDAY, only twenty-three of its final thirty-eight volumes had been released, and the idea of being a celebrity artist in America, as opposed to Japan, was still something of a novelty. Manga publishing in America was as yet only a few years old, and Takahashi was not its first star, that honor going instead to Ryoichi Ikegami, with the overwhelming success of the English translation of *Mai the Pyschic Girl* (ironically, as Takahashi herself admits, Ikegami's *Spider-Man* was one of her own influences as a young artist).

In the intervening years, however, the popularity of Takahashi's work not only caught up, but closed ranks with the bestselling manga artists in the country. Of all the manga and anime titles translated into English, Takahashi's work is easily among the most widely available—and widely popular—in the U.S. market, with nearly all of her manga in

Ranma 1/2

publication, including her more obscure short story work from various magazines, as well as the successful video series *Ranma 1/2*, *Maison Ikkoku* and *Urusei Yatsura* numbering among those most recognizable to American fans.

I think manga is all about feelings, of being scared or happy or sad. In that respect, I think we might all be the same.

In this early interview conducted with her U.S. publisher, Viz Comics, along with explaining the ideas behind *Ranma 1/2* and *Urusei Yatsura* (*Maison Ikkoku* had yet to achieve widespread familiarity among English-speaking readers), Takahashi expresses surprise at her own early popularity and discusses her feelings about success, international fame, the "universality" of her work, and the demands of being a manga artist.

interview

ANIMERICA: Since Viz Comics first released *Urusei Yatsura* about five years ago, several different companies have published English versions of Japanese manga titles. Some of them have sold extremely well. But did you know, among all of them, it's your works which enjoy the most continuing, stable popularity?

TAKAHASHI: Really? This is the first time I've heard about it.

ANIMERICA: Marvel Comics' English version of *Akira* is a consistent rival in sales, but you definitely have more fan support, readers who follow you regardless of title. Slowly but surely, you're becoming a household name among manga fans in America. How do you feel about that?

TAKAHASHI: It all just comes as a surprise.

ANIMERICA: You may have heard that in the U.S., comics aren't sold in regular bookstores. They're sold in comic specialty shops. With superhero titles such as *Superman* and *Batman* crowding the shelves, manga titles don't get quite the same exposure, so many fans go to comic conventions to get hard-to-find comics. Your works are among the most frequently requested.

TAKAHASHI: I've heard many animated versions of my manga titles are also available now.

ANIMERICA: Yes, English versions of the *Urusei Yatsura* TV series and films, as well as most of the *Rumic World* stories, are easily available. Any idea on why they're so popular?

TAKAHASHI: I don't have any idea. Maybe if I could understand what aspects the readers like about them....

ANIMERICA: In Japan, your works are big hits and enjoy great fan support. Those Japanese fans and American fans must have something in common.

TAKAHASHI: Because I consciously feature Japanese daily life such as festivals and the traditional New Year's holiday rather often in my manga, I sometimes wonder if American readers understand what they're reading. Maybe they just like the comics because they're exotic.

ANIMERICA: I'm sure there are at least some readers without any background in Japanese customs. On the other hand, readers who are interested in manga are usually interested in other aspects of Japanese culture. For example, there are probably many readers who wouldn't find anything strange about a dinner scene where everyone sits on the *tatami* of a traditional Japanese house. Do you think that mainstream readers, who aren't as familiar with the Japanese lifestyle, might be intimidated by too many cultural references?

TAKAHASHI: Once, when I was drawing *Maison Ikkoku*, I received a question about it from an American journalist. As you know, I created *Maison Ikkoku* to be a love story that could take place in the everyday world. I'm always curious about what attracts non-Japanese readers to my work, so I asked the reporter's opinion. The reply I got was that Americans could empathize with the emotions being depicted in the comics. For example, the feeling when you fall in love, and you want to express it, but you can't...the reporter said that emotions are all the same, no matter which country you're from. I thought about this for a little while and said to myself, "Come to think of it, that's true."

ANIMERICA: *Maison Ikkoku* is a story which takes place under unlikely circumstances, especially from an American point of view. It's possible it may have elements difficult for American readers to understand. However, it's also true that the original Japanese comic already has its own English-speaking fans. In the case of your works, I'd say it's the attractiveness of the characters, the story, the artwork...probably a combination of all of these.

TAKAHASHI: In terms of art style, the portion of *Urusei Yatsura* published in America is all early drawings, very distinct and completely different from how I draw now.

ANIMERICA: There have been fans who've made a point of mentioning the evolution of your art style. Because the later stories have better art, they say, they'd rather see the later stories printed than the earlier ones. But as publishers, we thought it was important to include the first story where Lum appears, so we started from the beginning.

The fans who worry about this sort of thing are more than likely to own the original Japanese comics anyway.

TAKAHASHI: But where do they get them from?

ANIMERICA: At the many Japanese cultural centers across the country, it's easy to purchase manga straight from their Japanese publishers. Many fans translate them on their own, sharing the books among themselves. There are *Urusei Yatsura* fan clubs, and some people even put out their own fan-published *dôjinshi* comics based on your characters. It's interesting that Lum seems to be as popular in America as she is in Japan. You've speculated in a previous interview that her appeal to American fans might be the exotic elements of a cute girl from the Orient. Has that opinion changed?

TAKAHASHI: Well, let's see. Is there a concept of *oni* in America?

ANIMERICA: I don't think so. The "devil" is a concept close to *oni*, but then that's a concept strongly associated with the occult. The *oni* is more of a mythological monster.

TAKAHASHI: With its many elements, it's difficult to describe *Urusei Yatsura* in one word. Maybe a school comedy/romance with some science fiction and what-not, based on a foundation of slapstick...? Add in the play on words such as the puns and the metaphors and the allusions...these aspects might be hard for the American reader to grasp. What does that leave us with as a reason for its popularity in America? The novelty of the characters?

ANIMERICA: Certainly, the comedy may have parts that are hard to understand, but owing to your artistic talent—that is, the wonderful visuals—some of it does come through. For example, right before the punchline, a character's mouth will be wide open, nostrils all dilated. The reader can sense something is coming up.

TAKAHASHI: The majority of Japanese *Urusei Yatsura* fans have been high school and college students, not children. In some ways that's been a problem. But you know, I can also say it was very easy for me back then because the readers were my own age. I was happy that people from my same generation could enjoy my manga. I was also happy that there were so many male readers. Come to think of it, though, that's not so surprising, since it was serialized in a boys' magazine. I *was* a little disappointed that it might have been too difficult for children. After all, I believe manga belongs fundamentally to children, and maybe *Urusei Yatsura* just didn't have what it took to entertain them.

ANIMERICA: Even in America, the age of the average reader is high...about 20, I'd say. Readers range even into their late 30s. For *Ranma 1/2*, also serialized in SHÔNEN SUNDAY after *Urusei Yatsura*, did you consciously try to draw something aimed more toward children?

TAKAHASHI: Yes, that was done on purpose. And also, I wanted it to be popular among women and children. *Ranma 1/2* is popular among girls now, but it seems as though it hasn't grabbed the boys yet.

ANIMERICA: I see. So it's more popular among girls?

TAKAHASHI: Yes. Let's see, it was around the time when the eighth graphic novel came out and the cumulative circulation had reached 10 million that I asked the editor if he could survey the readers. He placed a questionnaire postcard in the books. As it turned out, *Ranma 1/2*'s fans were similar to those of *Urusei Yatsura*. Both series had a peak readership of 15-year-olds, but in the case of *Urusei Yatsura*, the distribution spread toward the higher-aged males. Conversely, with *Ranma 1/2*, it spread toward younger females.

ANIMERICA: In America, the vast majority of comic book readers are male, but I think that with *Ranma 1/2* there's a definite increase in female readers. In fact, in America,

Ranma 1/2 is selling better than *Urusei Yatsura*. Issue One completely sold out by the time the fourth issue came out. It's evident that the number of readers is increasing.

TAKAHASHI: *Ranma 1/2* sells better in Japan, as well. There are some pretty hardcore *Urusei Yatsura* fans out there, but among all the serials I've done so far, *Ranma 1/2* is the number-one hit.

Japanese manga comes from a completely different form, where the artist does everything alone. It's not possible to excel in all tasks, but one can't succeed without a balanced combination of talents.

ANIMERICA: Is that so?

TAKAHASHI: Yes. Even when you look at the sales figures, there's a remarkable difference between the two. For me, though, I'll just be happy if someone remembers reading *Ranma 1/2* as a child, years after its serialization is over.

ANIMERICA: How long has it been since *Ranma 1/2*'s serialization started?

TAKAHASHI: Well, I don't remember exactly, but it's probably been five to six years.

ANIMERICA: Since there are so few female readers in this American market, it would certainly make us and the comics industry in general very happy if *Ranma 1/2* could increase the number of women reading comics. In my opinion, the concept of a man changing into a woman and a woman changing into man could be taken as an effort to enlighten a male-dominated society. After all, Ranma never knows what gender he'll be next. Did you intend this?

TAKAHASHI: It's just that I came up with something that might be a simple, fun idea. I'm not the type who thinks in terms of societal agendas. But being a woman and recalling what kind of manga I wanted to read as a child, I just thought humans turning into animals might also be fun and *märchenhaft*...you know, like a fairy tale.

ANIMERICA: So it's more that you never created the characters with a social agenda, but that they just happened to fit in with the *zeitgeist*?

TAKAHASHI: Yes, in that sense, that's exactly right.

ANIMERICA: I hear that, in Japan, the animated *Ranma 1/2* TV series has ended.

TAKAHASHI: That is so. I'm sad about it. It really was a fun show to watch.

ANIMERICA: Will there be new animation projects to follow?

TAKAHASHI: There seem to be many, but nothing I can talk about.

ANIMERICA: Incidentally, did you know that a rock singer named Matthew Sweet is a big fan of yours? He's even come to my office several times.

TAKAHASHI: Um, yes. Even getting a tattoo...I hope it's not permanent. [LAUGHS]

ANIMERICA: Did you know that he made a promotional video using nothing but *Urusei Yatsura* animation footage?

TAKAHASHI: I'm aware of it, yes.

ANIMERICA: Reportedly the song sold well and got a lot of airplay on MTV. It's probably one of the first times Japanese animation, although in a slightly modified form, was introduced to a major American TV medium.

TAKAHASHI: I hear he also did it with *Cobra*.

ANIMERICA: Yes. But his tattoo is of Lum.

TAKAHASHI: I heard a rumor that he started putting in Ran from *Urusei Yatsura* on his other arm, but will he go all the way? [LAUGHS]

ANIMERICA: In a previous interview you said that you often use Japanese folklore as a motif in your work. Do you ever receive inspiration from other media, such as contemporary movies or novels?

TAKAHASHI: Well, I've always liked Yasutaka Tsutsui's slapstick novels. I read them often. I've wished I could draw manga that were as absurd as that.

ANIMERICA: Could we say, then, that Yasutaka Tsutsui has had a great influence on your work?

TAKAHASHI: Yes, very much. I just happen to use folklore as a basis, but that's because it's easy to twist tales that everyone knows. As for movies, I only see them for entertainment.

ANIMERICA: Disney animation later influenced the story-oriented manga of the late Osamu Tezuka, which in turn became the basis of Japanese comics. Has animation ever influenced you?

TAKAHASHI: Not in particular. But then, Tezuka saw Disney animation and created the manga of today, and we as a generation grew up reading that, so I very much think I'm in that school.

ANIMERICA: This is an open-ended question, but I'd like to ask, just how busy *are* you...? I'll bet American artists probably can't imagine what it's like to be drawing over one hundred pages a month.

TAKAHASHI: Isn't American comic production done in a division of labor? So the artist is infinitely talented in drawing, and the writer is infinitely talented in making stories....

ANIMERICA: Yes. In America, there are very few artists who both draw and write stories.

TAKAHASHI: ...And so, Japanese manga comes from a completely different form, where the artist does everything alone. It's not possible to excel in all tasks, but one can't succeed without a balanced combination of talents. In that sense, it's difficult to strive for perfection, but the kind of perfection that *is* striven for by Japanese artists is different.

ANIMERICA: Are you ever dissatisfied with your stories?

TAKAHASHI: No, I'm always fully satisfied. [LAUGHS]

ANIMERICA: It would seem that it takes a vast amount of talent to succeed as a manga artist in Japan.

TAKAHASHI: I think so. If you can draw really well but can't write a story, you'd have to become an illustrator. Even with the help of a writer, if you can't come up with good layouts, you can't make it as a manga artist. You might become a wonderful illustrator, but not a manga artist.

ANIMERICA: In America, comics aren't too high in status, the industry is small, and sales figures are noticeably lower than in Japan. Even people who are in comics purely for the love of it tend to move on to other, more highly paid businesses just as soon as their talent is recognized. In Japan it's manga that's the big-money business, so people with talent flock to it. If you've got the talent, it's definitely more financially rewarding to become a manga artist or manga writer than a novelist.

TAKAHASHI: It's probably true everywhere, but people with talent go where the money is.

ANIMERICA: There must be a lot of people with great talent in America, too, and we'd like to give them a chance, within our limited means.

TAKAHASHI: But don't you think that manga is still looked down upon in Japan also?

ANIMERICA: There still probably are many people who hold biases against it.

TAKAHASHI: But if we wait just a little more, the day should come when the only generation left is the one which reads manga. [LAUGHS]

ANIMERICA: A day when compiled graphic novels taken from the pages of BIG COMIC magazine line the shelves of retirement homes....

TAKAHASHI: Yes. Manga is entertainment, after all. And because it's a form of entertainment rather than a separate culture, it's inevitable for cultural elements to creep in. It depicts the world we live in. That manga is read in America...well, I think it's truly wonderful if it can make people laugh across all sorts of borders. I think manga is all about feelings, of being scared or happy or sad. In that respect, I think we might all be the same.

ANIMERICA: I'm happy and encouraged that in America, *Ranma 1/2* has a different sort of readership than *Urusei Yatsura*.

TAKAHASHI: If that's true, then there's nothing that makes me happier.

ANIMERICA: What's your impression of America?

Urusei Yatsura

TAKAHASHI: I've only stayed for a single night in Los Angeles. I was scared then. I felt the L.A. airport was frighteningly mechanical.

ANIMERICA: Some people might say that town represents America itself.

TAKAHASHI: I tend to be short, so I was looking up at everything, and my eye-level seemed to be at the waists of the walking people. [LAUGHS]

ANIMERICA: Do you feel Europe suits you better?

TAKAHASHI: I like the Latin people. I was supposed to go to an Italian comic convention this year but, in the end, I was too busy. Spain and Italy are agreeable countries, don't you think? I wonder why, among all the countries of Europe, I feel so secure in those two places...?

ANIMERICA: There's a manga boom in Europe right now. It first caught on in Italy and then in Spain. We just signed a big contract there.

TAKAHASHI: It's interesting that Japanese manga is getting accepted in the Latin countries of Europe first.

One-Pound Gospel

ANIMERICA: We'd love to interview you again next year after your travels through Europe. In closing, do you have a message for your American fans?

TAKAHASHI: I'm grateful that you read my works, and it gives me encouragement to know that you enjoy them. My best regards to every one of you.

afterword

Four years later, Rumiko Takahashi had finished her serialization of *Ranma 1/2*, written and drawn several short stories—most notably a continuation of her *One-Pound Gospel* serial—and begun work on an all-new title, *Inu-Yasha*.

As a followup to her previous works, most of which were very much of a slapstick-comedy school, the more sober *Inu-Yasha* came as something of a surprise. A historical fantasy set in Japan's "Warring States" period, *Inu-Yasha* has not only a grimmer tone than nearly any of Takahashi's stories (save for her collection of "Mermaid" stories, in which the main characters, for all practical purposes, achieve immortality through the cannibalistic eating of mermaid flesh) but also a more purely *Japanese* story than nearly any of her previous works.

Although all of Takahashi's stories take advantage of their in-or-around Tokyo settings to parody daily life in modern-day Japan, the basic love stories of *Ranma 1/2*, *Urusei Yatsura* and *Maison Ikkoku* have a truly universal quality about them. *Inu-Yasha*'s historical time and place give an utterly different feel—Rumiko Takahashi crossed with an Akira Kurosawa samurai movie, perhaps.

In a 1997 interview conducted after *Inu-Yasha* had just begun, Takahashi simply expressed her hopes for the series as, "I wanted to draw a story-oriented manga. Also, I liked the idea of a historical piece. Something I could easily draw. That's the premise I started with." She also admitted right up front that *Inu-Yasha* was a story with fewer laughs than her previous *Ranma 1/2*, though she planned to try and work in more comedy as the series went on.

"I have a rough idea of how the personal relationships should work out, but that's all," she laughed when asked if she would share hints on where the story might be headed in the future. "I'm hoping the plot will follow. But I'm wondering about getting too tied up in relationships. So I'd really like to be able to improvise as I go."

Two years earlier, in 1995, Rumiko Takahashi had also become a member of a very exclusive club, as one of the few manga artists ever to sell over *one hundred million* copies of her compiled works—approximately one of her

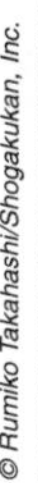

books for every person living in Japan. A gala celebration, staged by her Japanese publisher, Shogakukan, feted the artist with accolades from other manga artists, film clips of her works hosted by the animation voice-actors for her *Urusei Yatsura* characters "Ataru" and "Lum," and a star-studded exhibition wrestling match in her honor, kicked off by a bout between costumed characters "Genma-Panda" from *Ranma 1/2* and "Kotatsu-Neko" from *Urusei Yatsura*.

Her feelings on the subject of being a hundred-million-selling artist were expressed as something of a culmination of all her years of work—a life's goal, finally achieved, freeing her up to go on without having to reach so much for the stars.

"I didn't realize it myself when I started *Ranma 1/2*, but I must have been under pressure to match my previous two works, and I think I was rushing," Takahashi admitted. "I was thinking I *had* to create memorable scenes as soon as possible. In that sense, I think I feel like now I'm free to do what I *can* do." Even so, Takahashi was the last one to attribute her new sense of relaxation regarding her work with having "grown up."

"I'll always be a kid," she laughed.

Takahashi continues on, drawing *Inu-Yasha*. While a weekly serial is running, the artist has next to no opportunity for time off—during the nine-year run of *Ranma 1/2*, a 1994 trip to America to attend the nation's largest comic convention, San Diego Comic-Con, was about the only vacation she was able to take. After the end of *Ranma 1/2* and previous to *Inu-Yasha*'s serialization, a trip to the Yucatan Peninsula in Mexico constituted probably the only vacation Takahashi will have in quite a while. But still, she's as committed to being a manga artist as ever.

In a weekly serial, Takahashi's new ideas come from everywhere, from daily observations, from minute details in newspaper columns, to what's happening at her home, which also doubles as her workplace. For free time, Takahashi reads books, goes to the sumo wrestling bouts, and sees plays, even more than films. *Takarazuka* plays are a particular favorite—a Japanese artform that is the exact opposite of the traditional all-male casts of *Noh* and *Kabuki*, *Takarazuka* features female performers playing roles of both genders.

"I do feel pressure," she confessed on the subject of *Inu-Yasha*'s success, "but I'm starting to wonder if I'm at the age where I can keep on drawing *shônen* manga (boys' comics) forever. But I do...I do want to keep on drawing *shônen* manga until I die." Perhaps it's appropriate that, thanks largely to her efforts—and to those of fellow female manga artist Naoko Takeuchi, whose bestselling *Sailor Moon* has helped redefine English-speaking anime/manga fandom—not only youthful *shônen* boys but young *shôjo* girls are today enjoying her manga in equal measure.

Rumiko Takahashi
Select Bibliography & Filmography

MANGA 漫画

Somewhere along the way, during the rise of her popularity in the U.S., Rumiko Takahashi picked up the nickname "Queen of Romantic Comedy." We're not sure where it came from, exactly, but hey! it *fits*. Known not only in Japan but around the world for her uniquely charming, somehow reassuringly *on-target* tales of gentle war between the sexes (think Tracy and Hepburn, as compared to, say *War of the Roses*' Douglas and Turner), Takahashi seems to know just where the heart lives, as demonstrated by the titles (every one of them a bestseller) listed below. Note that Takahashi is both writer and artist on all titles.

Rumic World
るーみっくわーるど

Serialized in SHÔNEN SUNDAY and SHÔNEN SUNDAY EXTRA (1978-1984). Three compiled volumes total. Reprinted in 1984 by the same publisher. *DOMESTIC RELEASE TITLE:* ***Rumic World*** (serialized in MANGA VIZION)

Urusei Yatsura
うる星やつら

Serialized in SHÔNEN SUNDAY weekly magazine (1979-1986). 34 compiled volumes total. Reprinted in a "wide" edition in 1989. *DOMESTIC RELEASE TITLE:* ***Lum*Urusei Yatsura*** (Viz Comics)

Maison Ikkoku
めぞん一刻

Published in Shogakukan's "Big Comics" (1982-87); fifteen compiled volumes total. Reprinted in a "wide" edition in 1992. *DOMESTIC RELEASE TITLE:* ***Maison Ikkoku*** (Viz Comics)

Ranma Nibun no Ichi ("Ranma 1/2")
らんま１／２

Published in Shogakukan's "SHÔNEN SUNDAY Comics" (1988-96); 38 compiled volumes total. *DOMESTIC RELEASE TITLE:* ***Ranma 1/2*** (Viz Comics)

Ningyo ("Mermaid") Series
人魚シリーズ

Published by Shogakukan (1988-93); compiled short stories as originally serialized in SHÔNEN SUNDAY and SHÔNEN SUNDAY EXTRA. *DOMESTIC RELEASE TITLES:* ***Mermaid Forest, Mermaid's Promise, Mermaid's Scar, Mermaid's Dream, Mermaid's Gaze, Mermaid's Mask*** (Viz Comics)

Ichi-Pound no Fukuin ("One-Pound Gospel")
１のポンドの福音

Published in Shogakukan's "YOUNG SUNDAY Comics" (1989-96); originally serialized in YOUNG SUNDAY magazine. Three compiled volumes to date. *DOMESTIC RELEASE TITLE:* ***One-Pound Gospel*** (Viz Comics)

Takahashi Rumiko Kessakushû: "P" no Higeki
("Rumiko Takahashi Masterpiece Collection: The Tragedy of P")

高橋留美子傑作集：Ｐの悲劇

Published in Shogakukan's "Big Comic Special" (1994); originally serialized in BIG COMIC ORIGINAL. *DOMESTIC RELEASE TITLE:* ***Rumic Theater*** (serialized in MANGA VIZION)

Rumik World Takahashi Rumiko Tanpenshû: 1 or W
("Rumic World•Rumiko Takahashi Short Story Collection: One or Double")

るーみっくわーるど高橋留美子短編集：1or W（ワン・オア・ダブル）

Published by Shogakukan (1995); short story collection as serialized in various manga magazines in Japan. *DOMESTIC RELEASE TITLE:* ***Rumic Theater*** (serialized in MANGA VIZION)

Inu-Yasha
犬夜叉

Published in Shogakukan's "SHÔNEN SUNDAY Comics" (1997~); originally serialized in SHÔNEN SUNDAY weekly magazine. U.S. edition published almost concurrently with ongoing Japanese release. *DOMESTIC RELEASE TITLE:* ***Inu-Yasha: A Feudal Fairy Tale*** (Viz Comics)

ANIME アニメ

Given the popularity of her manga, it should come as no surprise that Takahashi anime series also weigh in as some of the most popular in the world. *Inu-Yasha*, her latest manga title, has yet to be animated, but it shouldn't be much longer before it's announced for upcoming release. Note that Takahashi gets "original story" credit for all titles.

Urusei Yatsura
うる星やつら

197-episode TV series (1981-86). *DOMESTIC RELEASE TITLE:* ***Urusei Yatsura/Those Obnoxious Aliens*** (AnimEigo)

Urusei Yatsura: Chance on Love
うる星やつら：チャンス・オン・ラブ

BGM & more one-shot music video compilation (1981-86). *CURRENTLY IMPORT ONLY*

Urusei Yatsura: Love Me More
うす星やつら：ラブ・ミー・モア

Opening & ending one-shot music video compilation (1981-86). *CURRENTLY IMPORT ONLY*

Urusei Yatsura: Mata Aeru'cha! Urusei Yatsura TV Yokoku Henshû
("We'll Meet Again! 'Next Time On...' TV Compilation")

うる星やつら：また逢えるっちゃ！うる星やつらTV予告編集

One-shot "next episode" trailer compilation, as seen on the original TV series (1981-86). *CURRENTLY IMPORT ONLY*

Urusei Yatsura: Symphony Kaisô
("Symphonic Reminiscence")

うる星やつら：シンフォニー回想

One-shot orchestral music video compilation (1981-86). *CURRENTLY IMPORT ONLY*

Urusei Yatsura: TV Titles
うる星やつら：テレビ・タイトルズ

Non-credit + stereo opening & ending one-shot music video compilation (1981-86). *CURRENTLY IMPORT ONLY*

Urusei Yatsura: Only You
うる星やつら：オンリー・ユー（ノーカット版）

110-minute (uncut) theatrical feature (1983). *DOMESTIC RELEASE TITLE:* ***UY Only You*** (AnimEigo)

Urusei Yatsura 2: Beautiful Dreamer
うる星やつら２：ビューティフル・ドリーマー

98-minute theatrical feature (1984). *DOMESTIC RELEASE TITLE:* ***UY Beautiful Dreamer*** (U.S. Manga Corps)

Urusei Yatsura 3: Remember My Love
うる星やつら３：リメンバー・マイ・ラヴ

102-minute theatrical feature (1985). *DOMESTIC RELEASE TITLE:* ***UY Remember My Love*** (AnimEigo)

Rumik World: Fire Tripper
るーみっくわーるど：炎（ファイヤー）トリッパー

One-shot OAV (1985). *DOMESTIC RELEASE TITLE:* ***Fire Tripper*** (U.S. Manga Corps)

Urusei Yatsura: The Original Animation Video Series
うる星やつら：OAVシリーズ

Eleven-volume OAV series (1985-90). *DOMESTIC RELEASE TITLES:* ***Inaba the Dreammaker, Raging Sherbet & I Howl at the Moon, Catch the Heart & Goat and Cheese, Date With a Spirit & Terror of Girly-Eyes Measles, Nagisa's Fiancé & Electric Household Guard, Ryoko's September Tea Party & Memorial Album*** (AnimEigo)

Urusei Yatsura 4: Lum the Forever
うる星やつら４：ラム・ザ・フォーエバー

94-minute theatrical feature (1986). *DOMESTIC RELEASE TITLE:* ***UY Lum the Forever*** (AnimEigo)

Rumik World: The Chôjo ("The Supergal")
るーみっくわーるど：ザ・超女（スーパーギャル）
One-shot OAV (1986). *DOMESTIC RELEASE TITLE:* ***Supergal**, later **Maris the Chôjo*** (U.S. Manga Corps)

Maison Ikkoku
めぞん一刻
96-episode TV series (1986-88). Heartwarming romance originally aimed at a college-age and older audience. *DOMESTIC RELEASE TITLE:* ***Maison Ikkoku*** (Viz Video)

Maison Ikkoku: Utsuri Yuku Kisetsu no Naka de
("Within the Changing Seasons")
めぞん一刻：移りゆく季節の中で
Single-volume, 90-minute TV series compilation released on home video (1986-88). *CURRENTLY IMPORT ONLY*

Rumik World: Warau Hyôteki ("Laughing Target")
るーみっくわーるど：笑う標的
One-shot OAV (1987). *DOMESTIC RELEASE TITLE:* ***Laughing Target*** (U.S. Manga Corps)

Ichi-Pound no Fukuin ("One-Pound Gospel")
1ポンドの福音
One-shot OAV (1988).The adventures of a gluttonous boxer and the (at least, on the surface) sweet nun who offers him spiritual solace. *DOMESTIC RELEASE TITLE:* ***One-Pound Gospel*** (Viz Video)

Urusei Yatsura: Kanketsu Hen ("Final Chapter")
うる星やつら：完結篇
93-minute theatrical feature (1988). *DOMESTIC RELEASE TITLE:* ***UY The Final Chapter*** (AnimEigo)

Maison Ikkoku: Kanketsu Hen ("Final Chapter")
めぞん一刻：完結篇
70-minute theatrical feature (1988). *UPCOMING DOMESTIC RELEASE*

Ranma Nibun no Ichi ("Ranma 1/2")
らんま１／２
18-episode TV series (1989). The first episodes from the enduringly popular martial arts comedy of the sexes. *DOMESTIC RELEASE TITLE:* ***Ranma 1/2*** (Viz Video)

Ranma 1/2: Nettôhen ("Ranma 1/2: Chapter of Hard Battle")
らんま１／２：熱闘編
143-episode TV series (1989-92). *DOMESTIC RELEASE TITLE:* ***Ranma 1/2: Anything-Goes Martial Arts*** *(22 eps.),* ***Ranma 1/2: Hard Battle*** *(24 eps.), plus more to come* (Viz Video)

Urusei Yatsura Saishinsaku vs. Maison Ikkoku Bangai Hen
("UY Latest Videos vs. MI Side-Story")
うる星やつら最新作 vs. めぞん一刻番外篇
One-shot OAV compilation: two ***Urusei Yatsura*** and one ***Maison Ikkoku*** (1990). *CURRENTLY IMPORT ONLY*

Ranma 1/2: Nettô Uta Gassen ("'Hot Song' Battle")
らんま１／２：熱闘歌合戦
Two-volume original animation music video (1990). *UPCOMING DOMESTIC RELEASE*

Maison Ikkoku Bangai Hen: Ikkoku Jima Nanpa Shimatsu Ki
("Maison Ikkoku Side-Story: Castaways of Ikkoku Island")
めぞん一刻番外編：一刻島ナンパ始末記
One-shot, 30-minute OAV (1990). *UPCOMING DOMESTIC RELEASE*

Urusei Yatsura: Itsudatte ("Always") **My Darling**
うる星やつら：いつだってマイダーリン
78-minute theatrical feature (1991). *DOMESTIC RELEASE TITLE:* ***UY Always My Darling*** (AnimEigo)

Ranma 1/2: Nekonron Dai-Kessen! Okite-Yaburi no Gekitô Hen!!
("Big Battle at Nekonron! The No-Rules, All-Out Battle")
らんま１／２：中国寝崑崙大決戦！掟やぶりの激闘篇！！
76-minute theatrical feature (1991). *DOMESTIC RELEASE TITLE:* ***Ranma 1/2: Big Trouble in Nekonron, China*** (Viz Video)

Rumik World: Ningyo no Mori ("Mermaid's Forest")
るーみっくわーるど：人魚の森
First of two OAVs animating Takahashi's "Mermaid" manga series (1991). *DOMESTIC RELEASE TITLE:* ***Mermaid Forest*** (U.S. Manga Corps)

Ranma 1/2: Kessen Tôgenkyô! Hanayome o Torimodose!
("Decisive Battle at Togenkyo! Get Back the Brides")
らんま１／２：決戦桃幻郷！花嫁を奪りもどせ！！
60-minute theatrical feature (1992). *DOMESTIC RELEASE TITLE:* ***Ranma 1/2: Nihao My Concubine*** (Viz Video)

Maison Ikkoku: Prelude
プレリュードめぞん一刻
One-shot, 25-minute TV series compilation (1992). *CURRENTLY IMPORT ONLY*

Rumik World: Ningyo no Kizu ("Mermaid's Scar")
るーみっくわーるど：人魚の傷
Second of two OAVs based on Takahashi's "Mermaid" series (1993). *DOMESTIC RELEASE TITLE:* ***Mermaid's Scar*** (Viz Video)

Ranma 1/2: TV Titles
らんま１／２：TVタイトルズ
Opening & ending music video compilation (1993). *DOMESTIC RELEASE TITLE:* ***The Ranma 1/2 Video Jukebox*** (Viz Video)

Ranma 1/2: Special
らんま１／２スペシャル
Six-volume OAV series (1993-94). *DOMESTIC RELEASE TITLES:* ***Ranma 1/2 Desperately Seeking Shampoo***, ***Ranma 1/2: Like Water For Ranma***, ***Ranma 1/2: Akane and Her Sisters*** (Viz Video)

Ranma 1/2: Super
らんま１／２スーパー
Five-volume OAV series (1995). *DOMESTIC RELEASE TITLES:* ***Ranma 1/2: An Akane to Remember***, ***Ranma 1/2: One Grew Over the Kuno's Nest*** *(one episode from* ***Ranma 1/2: Super***, *paired with 30-minute "movie" listed below),* ***Ranma 1/2: Faster, Kasumi! Kill! Kill!*** (Viz Video)

Chô Musabetsu Kessen: Ranma Team vs. Densetsu no Hô'ô ("Super Anything-Goes Battle: Team Ranma vs. the Legendary Phoenix")
超無差別決戦：乱馬チームvs.伝説の鳳凰
30-minute theatrical feature (1995). *DOMESTIC RELEASE TITLE:* ***Ranma 1/2: One Grew Over the Kuno's Nest*** *(paired with one episode from* ***Ranma 1/2: Super****)* (Viz Video)

Key

- Japanese comics or "manga" series; may or may not be available in foreign-language (i.e., English) version
- TV series broadcast on-air in Japan. Note that, in the U.S., Japanese TV series are both broadcast on-air (*Ronin Warriors*) and released on home video (*Ranma 1/2*). Others (*Sailor Moon, Dragon Ball*) are available both in broadcast and home video versions
- Direct-to-home-video series; may also include compilations of TV episodes released to home video market
- Theatrical feature; may or may not receive equivalent theatrical release for U.S. version

Hayao Miyazaki

Interviewed by Takashi Oshiguchi (1993)

"I don't want to spend the little time I've got left just for the benefit of young people who only like my lighter side," Miyazaki said in a 1989 interview with the manga magazine COMIC BOX. "I'd rather use my remaining energy as a filmmaker in a way which will be satisfying to me, and to the people around me.

"The most important thing that Japanese animation should *not* do is to categorize the fans as a certain kind of people and then make movies only for them," he continues. "How can we make films which will gain the acceptance of those people who've never seen animation before? We need to get nearer to that universal appeal of animation when making a movie, or all our efforts will have been for nothing."

Miyazaki is an icon in his native Japan, but outside of it he is little-known as yet—even the film that Japan submitted to the Oscars for the foreign film category, the animated film *Heisei Tanuki Gassen Pom Poko* ("Present-Day Tanuki War Goes 'Tum-Tum'"), which Miyazaki produced, never really "broke through" to the American mainstream audience. *My Neighbor Totoro*, praised by *At the Movies'* Roger Ebert, is the closest Miyazaki has yet gotten to recognition in America—but that may soon change. Distribution deals have been signed, and thanks to recent developments, the Japanese filmmaker who in his own country is more beloved than Walt Disney at his height may be able to spread his magic touch to a wider audience through none other than the Disney Corporation itself.

Born in 1941 in Tokyo, Miyazaki was graduated from Gakushuin University (the school that the members of the Japanese imperial family attend) and began his career as a filmmaker doing in-between work at Toei Animation in 1963. Never content to observe the status quo, one of the first things Miyazaki did after entering Toei was to march in front of the building in union demonstrations.

By as early as 1964, Miyazaki had been elected president of the studio's animation labor union and had begun wooing his future wife, whom he married in 1965. It wasn't long before Miyazaki was squaring off against the director of Toei's latest film project, *Gulliver's Space Travels* (1965), insisting that the ending was unsatisfactory and needed to be changed (Miyazaki won). Even as a mere in-betweener, Miyazaki was proving that he had the persistence of vision which would eventually make him one of the world's leading creators of animation.

Although his first production as a solo director didn't take place until *Future Boy Conan* (1978), Miyazaki had long been involved in the creative process, all the way back to the thousands of illustrations he drew for *The Adventures of Horus, Prince of the Sun* (1968). Other notable involvements from this early period include *Animal Treasure Island* (1971), a real "cartoon" adventure; *Lupin III* (1971), a 26-episode TV series not to be confused with the later 155-episode series; and *Panda, Panda Cub* (1973), a feature which strongly foreshadows the later *Totoro*.

In the early 1980s, Miyazaki began to move away from comedy to make animation which would appeal to a more mature audience such as *Lupin III: Castle of Cagliostro* (1979), as well as the six episodes he directed for *Sherlock Holmes* (1984-85). Ironically, it wouldn't be until ANIMAGE magazine's publication of his manga *Nausicaä of the Valley of Wind* in 1982 that Miyazaki would achieve a reputation as a serious filmmaker.

"I started drawing the manga only because I was unemployed as an animator, so I'll stop drawing it as soon as I find animation work," Miyazaki once said in an interview. The story of a spirited warrior-princess coming of age in a future world wracked by ecological disaster, *Nausicaä* is one of the few manga that Japanese cognoscenti will admit to reading. During its serialization, *Nausicaä's* popularity was such that the frequent hiatuses Miyazaki was obliged to take when he went back to the animation studio caused a minor furor amidst fans worldwide.

According to *The Art of Nausicaä* illustration book, ANIMAGE convinced Miyazaki to draw a manga for it with the specific promise that it wouldn't be used as the basis for some future animation project. It was also ANIMAGE that first broke the covenant when it approached Miyazaki about making a short, fifteen-minute *Nausicaä* film. Miyazaki declined the *Nausicaä* short but offered instead to work on a sixty-minute original animation video. When ANIMAGE's publisher Tokuma promptly came back with an offer to sponsor a full-length theatrical feature, the *Nausicaä* film was born and Miyazaki was firmly ensconced as a filmmaker to be reckoned with.

Since then, Miyazaki began to turn out a new movie nearly every other year—*Laputa, Castle in the Sky* in 1986; *My Neighbor Totoro* in 1988; *Kiki's Delivery Service* in 1989; *Porco Rosso* in 1992, various projects upon which

Laputa, Castle in the Sky

he served more as producer, such as Studio Ghibli's *Pom Poko*, and all the while, drawing his manga *Nausicaä*.

At the time of this interview, Miyazaki's latest work was *Porco Rosso*, the story of a 1930s biplane pilot (who also happens to be a pig), set against the political situation in Italy. More adult in tone than his previous works, *Porco Rosso* was nonetheless the top domestic-grossing film in Japan that year, breaking all previous records.

interview

ANIMERICA: First I'd like to ask you about *Porco Rosso*. It's received a lot of attention due to the fact that it's been the biggest money-maker of all your films. How do you feel about its box-office success?

MIYAZAKI: It was an unexpected hit. I was telling everyone, "This one's not going to go well, so don't get your hopes up." No one was more surprised than I when the film was a financial success.

ANIMERICA: Why is that?

MIYAZAKI: To my mind, animation is for children. *Porco Rosso* flies in the face of that assumption. Moreover, as a producer I still think *Porco Rosso* is too idiosyncratic a film for a toddlers-to-old-folks general audience. That it turned out to be a hit was an unexpected stroke of luck. It's actually kind of disturbing.

ANIMERICA: If you felt that way about it, why did you undertake the project in the first place?

MIYAZAKI: The biggest reason lies in Miyazaki's personality. [LAUGHS] The dangerous thing about him, particularly in terms of business, is that every once in a while he feels a sudden urge to stand everything he's ever done on its head.

I never trust the response of industry people.... If they knew what they were talking about, the movie business wouldn't be on the decline like it is.

I've very earnestly made a number of films for children, such as *My Neighbor Totoro* and *Kiki's Delivery Service* and, as a producer, *Omohide Poro Poro* (lit., "Falling Tears of Remembrance," also known as *Only Yesterday*). After that, frustration began to build. Somewhere in the back of my mind, this idea started to take root that animation should be more fun, more absurd, and I just couldn't control this feeling.

It was precisely at such a dangerous moment that, for a variety of reasons, we found ourselves committed to making a 45-minute film exclusively for screening on international flights. Actually, no one was more at a loss over this commitment than I. All the while I was saying to myself, "We're just doing this just for laughs," but as it turns out, everyone *else* was thinking of it as a new movie—so much so that I had to start taking their expectations seriously.

What's more, I began to realize that the staff—who I could have sworn were thoroughly sick of working on all these serious projects—weren't sick of them at all. I had totally misread the situation. I thought to myself, "This is no good. I've got to get my act together." So as I'm frantically trying to catch up, forty-five minutes turns into ninety minutes, we have trouble with the animation, and expenses begin to mount to the point where the only way we can hope to recover our investment is to make it a general theatrical release. Then one day our producer, Mr. Suzuki, announces his decision to make this into a full-fledged movie and I think to myself, "*YIKES!!* This is *bad*—there's no *way* this is going to be a hit!!" [LAUGHS] I was really worried.

ANIMERICA: As far back as a year ago, way before the film was released, I heard people talking about how the film had all the elements of success. It had a retro theme, it was animated, and Miyazaki was involved with it.

MIYAZAKI: Well, I never trust the response of industry people. [LAUGHS] They're too conservative. They've always been a step behind the times. If industry people knew what they were talking about, the movie business wouldn't be on the decline like it is. Moviegoers aren't fools. You might get lucky and score a hit with a film that has no substance, but you won't get away with it twice. Now, the decision to go ahead with *Porco Rosso* may have evolved in a half-assed way, but when it came to the actual production of the film, we gave it everything we had.

ANIMERICA: So it's not just anime but the Japanese film industry in general that's pretty rough?

MIYAZAKI: If this business were easy, it would be a sin. It doesn't bother me that it's rough. What's really rough, though, is that the damage from a single failure can be fatal. People become too timid and end up making boring stuff. It seems to me that things have gotten rough in the *American* film industry, as well. In the old days, all they had to do was make love-conquers-all type movies. I don't know how much the people in Hollywood actually believed in love personally...they were probably more concerned with getting a home in Beverly Hills. But at one time that illusion held sway throughout the world.

It doesn't anymore. It's become difficult to even pretend you believe in that anymore. Or rather, it might be more accurate to say that movies today are about the psychopathology surrounding love. And these days they seem obliged to overdo everything. The goal now is to throw a huge amount of money at a project, do a huge promotion, and mobilize a huge number of viewers. But don't you think most of the best movies are those which were the end result of small productions?

When you watch *Ben-Hur* these days, it's so ridiculous, it's embarrassing. But weren't *My Darling Clementine*, *The Third Man* and *Casablanca* small productions? And they're still excellent films. So it would be wrong to complain that it's particularly hard in Japan. Filmmakers throughout the world are dealing with difficult issues peculiar to their own societies. One thing that can be said with certainty about Japan is that people want to see quality films. The need is there. And the money is there. I think that in order to meet that demand, we need new talent.

ANIMERICA: The question everyone is asking is, "Why did you make the hero a pig?"

MIYAZAKI: It's because I wouldn't want to draw a character like that as a human being. [LAUGHS]

ANIMERICA: I've been reading MODEL GRAPHIX since the serial began. When *Porco Rosso* first showed up, I thought that it would make for some interesting animation....

MIYAZAKI: Pigs are creatures which might be loved, but they are never respected. They're synonymous with greed, obesity, debauchery. The word "pig" itself is used as an insult. I'm not an agnostic or anything, but I don't like a society that parades its righteousness. The righteousness of the U.S., the righteousness of Islam, the righteousness of China, the righteousness of this or that ethnic group, the righteousness of Greenpeace, the righteousness of the entrepreneur.... They all claim to be righteous, but they all try to coerce others into complying with their own standards. They restrain others through huge military power, economic power, political power or public opinions.

I myself have a number of things I believe are right. And some things make me angry. Actually, I'm a person who gets angry a lot more easily than most people, but I always try to start from the assumption that human beings are foolish. I'm disgusted by the notion that man is the ultimate being, chosen by God. But I believe there are things in this world that are beautiful, that are important, that are worth striving for. I made the hero a pig because that was what best suited these feelings of mine.

ANIMERICA: About mecha. Have you liked that sort of thing since you were a child?

The Princess Mononoke

MIYAZAKI: Hmm. It wasn't mecha so much as drawing tanks and warships that I liked. I was a shy boy who was not very good at expressing himself. I think such children find ways like that to express their yearning for power and strength. I suppose nowadays that takes the form of air guns, video games, remote-controlled craft and the like. Motorbikes, too, are often used that way. But as we grow to adulthood, the core of that interest shifts accordingly. At first, it's the capabilities and forms of the machines that fascinate us, but in my case, my interest shifted to the dramas of the people who build them and who are made to use them.

ANIMERICA: Did you ever want to become a pilot?

MIYAZAKI: No, I don't think so. Even now, if you were going to give me a plane ride, I'd like to fly through a sky with some interesting clouds. I would enjoy seeing what kind of view there is, but I'm not really interested in flying for the sake of flying. A lot of different flying sports have come into being, so I suppose I could do it if I wanted to, but in order to do that, I'd probably have to give up on something else. For example, I wouldn't want to have to cut back on time spent relaxing in a mountain cabin or pouring all my energy into creating a film. I'd like to have a seaplane, but there wouldn't be any point without a beautiful body of water to maneuver on and a place to hide out in. And most of all I would need a society where one could fly and land as one pleased. I'd be in trouble if I were forced into speaking with an air traffic controller in English. English is not my forte, after all. [LAUGHS]

ANIMERICA: A friend of mine whose pilot father had seen

your movies and read your manga wondered if you'd done a lot of research on technical matters.

MIYAZAKI: No, numbers aren't my forte either, so I don't read complicated books. Besides, I don't really like any airplanes that've been made since the Douglas DC-3. [LAUGHS] I'll fly in a jet airliner if I have to, but I'm the kind of person who wishes they made jets with *tatami* floors.

ANIMERICA: So it's really form that interests you?

MIYAZAKI: Yes, but there's more to it than that. I drive a certain German car and the wheel lugs are really hard to get off. They won't budge if you don't jump up and down on the wrench. When I'm doing something like that, I'll find myself thinking something along the lines of, "Man, I bet it must have been hard getting the lugs off the wheels of one of those heavy German tanks. It would be

My Neighbor Totoro

really awful if, to top it all off, there was sleet falling and you were knee-deep in mud and shells started exploding all around you." This sort of fantasy will be running through my head as I'm taking the tire off.

There was a triple-engine plane in Italy called the Savoia-Marchetti S.M. 79 for which I've just happened to get a good diagram. So, I'm trying to recreate in my mind what the interior space of that plane must have been like. If I went to Italy, I could see the actual airplane in a museum, but I'd much rather piece together the interior of the plane in my mind, than go and see the real thing.

It's something like philology.... It's strange, I know. But if I were to see the real thing, I'd lose my motivation. [LAUGHS] There was this diagram of a handle for which I didn't know the purpose, so I thought about it and thought about it until finally I figured out that it must have been used to pull a metal cover over the glass gondola in the belly of the S.M. 79 to protect it during landing. I was really thrilled with myself for figuring it out. [LAUGHS] I can just picture the Italian bombardier dragging the cover up.

ANIMERICA: There was a plane in *Lupin III* called the *Albatross*, wasn't there? I didn't realize at the time that a plane like that had actually existed once.

MIYAZAKI: There was something like that, yes. I believe it was the "Dornier Do X" or something like that.

ANIMERICA: When you see a plane like that in a black and white film, it looks even bigger, don't you think?

MIYAZAKI: They do look bigger. As if something that shouldn't be able to fly at all is flying magnificently. I prefer the planes from that period, from the '20s through the early '30s.

ANIMERICA: When illustrators in the early 1900s drew planes of the future, it wasn't jets they drew, but just a lot more propellers. I guess your own work is an extension of that.

MIYAZAKI: Those images really are interesting, even today. *20,000 Leagues Under the Sea* is still interesting when you read it today, don't you think? Later, when submarines were actually built, the bottom of the sea was portrayed countless times, but none of those images were particularly interesting. What makes *20,000 Leagues Under the Sea* so interesting even today is that the sea depicted there isn't just any sea—it's a sea of the mind. At one time, flight, too, was something that took place only in the world of imagination. It was portrayed with the sense that, "Wouldn't it be wonderful to be set free and fly through the sky?" Now it's strictly a matter of physics. I think it must have been different back then.

ANIMERICA: Even with all those propellers there's no way those things could have flown.

MIYAZAKI: No, they couldn't. But to children, those images make more sense. Children aren't interested in logic; to them, it's pure imagination.

ANIMERICA: *Porco Rosso* seems to be set in the 1930s....

MIYAZAKI: I'd wanted to do it somewhere around 1928, but the world depression hadn't begun at that time, and it still hadn't reached Italy by 1929, so it ended up taking place in 1930. We sort of fudged on the dates.

ANIMERICA: There were still biplanes at that time.

MIYAZAKI: Yes, there were a lot of biplanes in use. It's not that I have a particular love of biplanes, but that I have a love of technology which no longer exists. We can't go back and witness it, and there's something stirring about that impossibility, don't you think? That's what it is. That's what makes the past so stirring...the fact that you can never return to it. The fact that it can never be recovered. The period when the airplane seemed most significant, a period that can never be recovered, is the 1920s and 1930s. The airplanes from the true dawn of aviation, the 1910s, are so rickety they just aren't interesting. But the skies of World War I were so cruel and tragic it's just too painful to portray them. When you get to the late '30s you're in the world of the DC-3 and the direction aviation is taking is already carved in stone. And that's why they're boring.

ANIMERICA: What do you think of the animation industry today? Do you think it's heading in a good direction or a bad one?

MIYAZAKI: There's no denying we're in a boring period. There just isn't very much interesting stuff coming out. We're getting too many films whose budget limitations are making their seams show, so to speak, and not enough stimulating works. But the biggest problem is that we're not seeing any new talent emerge.

ANIMERICA: Does that go for television, too?

MIYAZAKI: Yes. But looked at another way, a boring period can be seen as a time for building up the energy needed for the next leap; a time for staffers to build up frustration. It's the compression needed for an explosion. But it's also possible that we could just go on compressing and sputter out.

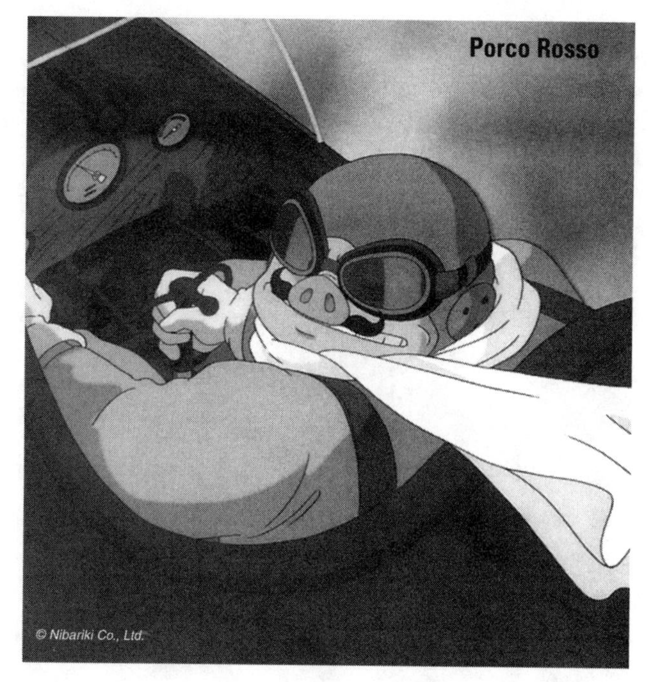
Porco Rosso

ANIMERICA: What do you think about new technologies such as computer graphics?

MIYAZAKI: I don't think it's particularly useful in terms of labor-saving. It's a new form of expression, yes, but my sense is that the introduction of computer graphics has become a sort of competition with video games. If that's the case, well, video games will win. People who want to use computer graphics should use them, but personally I'm not interested.

ANIMERICA: Have you ever considered making a live-action film?

MIYAZAKI: I'm always bemoaning the fact that I haven't got enough energy even for animation. I wonder if I could possibly succeed in another genre.

ANIMERICA: The only work of yours that's appeared in the U.S. (in animated form) at this point is a modified version of *Nausicaä*, and yet your name has become very well established. I believe you once commented that your work wouldn't be understood outside of Japan.

MIYAZAKI: What I meant was that I discovered that my work was a product of a Japanese historical perspective and sense of nature, much more so than I myself had originally thought. I think popular culture tends to be conservative. So I have no plans to start making films

© Nibariki/Tokuma Shoten

with a global market in mind. I want to create enjoyment for Japanese children. If the children of other continents or islands enjoy my work as well, then to me that's just icing on the cake.

ANIMERICA: But the fact is, you already have many fans in other countries.

MIYAZAKI: I'm grateful for that. But Japan will always remain very much the foundation of my work.

ANIMERICA: So far, we've been talking about your work. Let's start focusing on Hayao Miyazaki the man. When you're not busy creating animation or doing manga, what do you do for relaxation?

MIYAZAKI: When I have the time, I like to go up to a cabin I have in the mountains. Sometimes friends will come by to visit me, but I also like to spend time alone. It reinvigorates me, hiking those mountain trails. After working on a film, it usually takes half a year for me to recover my mental and physical balance. I have to set aside time to recuperate. I guess when you add it all up, I'm not really working *that* many hours. [LAUGHS]

ANIMERICA: One thing about the industry which isn't all that well-known abroad is the incredible amount of women working in the actual production of animation. What sort of relationship do you enjoy with the female members of your staff?

MIYAZAKI: One thing I've learned from working with women is that they have the ability to persevere. Men may be faster out of the gate, but I also think men's concentration tends to lag over a period of time. Women, though...they can really dig in there for the long haul, once the goal is set. My experience is that, when working with a big staff, it's always best to have as diverse a group as possible. Group dynamics are always the same, after all; you're just as likely to find the same ratio of "good people" in a group of priests as you are in a motorcycle gang. By "good people," I mean those who can lead and influence the whole group.

ANIMERICA: How about on a personal level? What about women in general?

MIYAZAKI: I don't really have a view toward women in general—like anyone else, there are those whom I like and those whom I don't. But then again, I can usually get along with just about any member of the female sex, so maybe it's correct to say I'm susceptible to feminine charms. [LAUGHS]

ANIMERICA: Even when you're acting only as a producer, I understand that your approach to making films is very hands-on. What do you do when you *can't* get as involved in the actual production? Are there any directors to whom you feel you could entrust one of your films...?

MIYAZAKI: No, but believe me, I'm looking. [LAUGHS] The fact that my name was listed as producer on a recent Takahata film [*the above-mentioned* Omohide Poro Poro, *produced by Studio Ghibli and released in 1991—Ed.*] should be taken as nothing more than an effort on my part to reassure the investors. I didn't do much more producing than that. There are those who define a producer as someone who greenlights a project, secures consent from investors and assembles the staff—especially the director. I define a producer as someone whose fate is intertwined with his film, sharing the joys and heartbreaks of every precious frame. In that sense, as a producer, I was a failure.

ANIMERICA: "A failure"...?

MIYAZAKI: I left everything up to Takahata, you see. We both knew that my involvement as a producer in the film would mean conflict. It was inevitable. Neither of us are the compromising type. The same thing happens when he acts as producer on *my* work. Ghibli desperately needs a new, talented director. We have yet to find one. At this rate, I'll be forced to keep participating in the actual production of films no matter *how* old I get. I wonder how realistic that is....

ANIMERICA: But you're still fairly young—you're still in your fifties, right?

MIYAZAKI: I am a director who actually *draws* animation. Maintaining my current level of involvement can't possibly last much longer. Believe me, I'll be the first to recognize my own limits. And I'd like to retire before someone suggests it to me. [LAUGHS]

ANIMERICA: Is this age speaking, or are we talking about the artistic sensibilities between a director and his audience?

MIYAZAKI: It's not my sensibilities. Up until now, the animation I've been creating has been that which I enjoy myself, and that seems to have worked out okay. No matter how old or young you are, I think it's time to step down when your audience no longer enjoys your work, even though you yourself might. This doesn't apply to me, of course...not yet, anyway. [LAUGHS]

ANIMERICA: So this talk about retiring is basically a matter of stamina, then.

MIYAZAKI: Yes, stamina and concentration. You can bolster your stamina with your concentration, but it doesn't necessarily work the other way around. My particular Achilles heel is my worsening eyesight. It seems to be lowering my concentration. It all comes down to how far you can push yourself. When you're making a film, your life has to revolve around it, both sleeping and awake. You've got to dedicate all your hours to it. Only then can you actually say to yourself, "Hey, I'm making a film!" It's a tough row to hoe, but you can't really break through the "shell" of your "common sense" in any other way. If you can manage it, get really, intensely involved, you don't even catch colds, no matter how fatigued you might become. The last time I was on the verge of coming down with something, I swear I had to fend off the invading cold viruses by chewing them up with my teeth. Isn't that wretched? [LAUGHS]

ANIMERICA: How depressing.... Let's talk about something else.

MIYAZAKI: Okay.

ANIMERICA: Do you feel that your works reflect the spirit of the times?

MIYAZAKI: Of course I do. There has never been a work of art created which didn't somehow reflect its own time.

ANIMERICA: Well then, let's talk about that. What kind of influences do you see in your works of the '70s and '80s?

MIYAZAKI: That's not for me as a filmmaker to explain. The audience should be able to intuit where I'm coming from. I will give a few simple clues, though. *Nausicaä* comes from the new world views regarding nature which came about in the '70s. *Laputa* is my challenge to the children who felt the world and therefore their lives were getting smaller, the possibilities more finite. You could say that among the children of the '70s and '80s, those sensibilities were nothing more than the negative result of that new world view. *My Neighbor Totoro*, now...*Totoro* is where my consciousness begins. It explains how my mind works. That the film was actually made in the first place says something important about what kind of era the '80s was. *Kiki's Delivery Service* shows another side of the '80s, that of Japanese economic prosperity. Even back then, I realized that just like the '80s, *Kiki* was sincere but somewhat lacking in energy. For various reasons, it was a movie I had to make. Commercially, it was a success, but it left me with a personal sense of regret. *Porco Rosso* is a product of the early '90s, of my world views being challenged by real-world events. It's also the product of my resolve to overcome that challenge and build a stronger way of life, a stronger way of looking at things. Right now, I feel as though I understand my own philosophical conundrums a bit better than before, but the answers don't come to me easily, and I'm certain that my next work will reflect that.

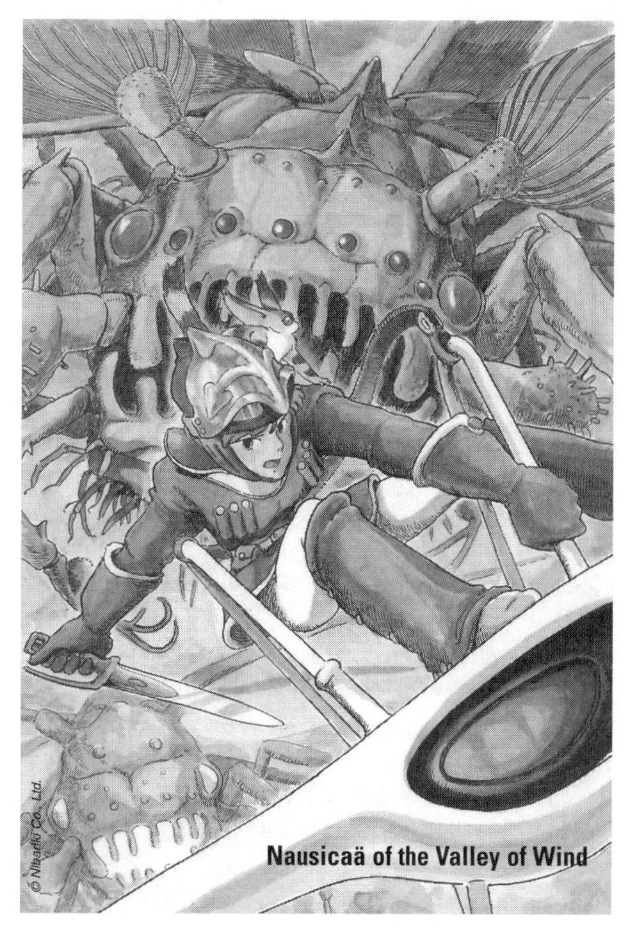

Nausicaä of the Valley of Wind

ANIMERICA: It sounds as though you're moving on to your next creative plateau.

MIYAZAKI: That would be nice, but ultimately it's my own talents which will determine where I end up. Now that the interview is almost at a close...

ANIMERICA: Yes?

MIYAZAKI: ...I want to make sure I'm not creating the wrong impression. While it's true that I do have a cynical side [LAUGHS], I'm usually cheerful and enthusiastic about things. Make no mistake—I'm not staying awake nights worrying about my talent or whether it's time for me to be put to pasture. [LAUGHS] I've always been so busy all my life; there's so many things I've always wanted to do but could never find time for before. If I'm going to be retiring from filmmaking, I'd like to devote my time to more important matters.

ANIMERICA: Such as...?

MIYAZAKI: Making a film means making entertainment for a lot of people. It's not the sort of thing you can quantify. Entertaining a group of people is no better or worse than entertaining just one person and making that one individual happy. For example—this happened the other day—I have this funny-looking little three-wheeled red car which I use for my daily commute. I was parking it downstairs one day when a small child who was passing by just stopped in his tracks, staring open-mouthed. His eyes were just popping out in amazement. His mother, who was with him, nudged him to go but he wouldn't budge. Eventually the boy drew closer little by little and extended his hand as if to touch it. My car is a handmade English model, with this bare Italian motorcycle engine sticking out in front, and I worried that he might burn his hand by touching it so I said something really inane like "Don't touch it—that's hot" or something automatic like that. So the boy gave up and left with his mother. Later on, though, I really started to regret what I'd done. Sure, I was busy and pressed for time, but I really should have invited the little boy and his mother to go for a ride in the car. I could have given that boy a fantastic experience, one which would have lived forever in the fuzzy childhood memories of a five-year-old.

Entertaining a group of people is no better or worse than entertaining just one person and making that one individual happy.

When I talk about devoting my time to more important matters, that's the kind of thing I'm talking about. A personal experience like that is more meaningful than any film. *That* should have been the way of someone who presumes to call himself an entertainer. Someday, maybe for some other small child, next time I'd like to give him a ride.

afterword

The serialization of the *Nausicaä* manga has since ended, but perhaps the largest change in Miyazaki's career came in 1996 when news of a landmark distribution deal between Miyazaki's longtime publisher Tokuma and Disney's Buena Vista distribution house was announced. Reportedly, the bones of the agreement include not only the rights to distribute Miyazaki's films in America, but in Japan, as well. What this means to the mainstream market is that, due to the size and marketing might of Buena Vista, Miyazaki's films would soon be available on a much more widespread basis, and at a much reduced price.

As of this writing, Miyazaki's latest work, a full-length film titled *Mononoke Hime* ("Monster Princess," or, according to Tokuma, "The Princess Mononoke," as the English release title may eventually read), has already debuted in Japanese theaters. With a story set in medieval Japan, it's likely that it'll also be the first of Miyazaki's works to be released directly to a worldwide audience. (It's also interesting to note that, despite a stated aversion to same, *MH* is chock-full with computer graphics- effects.)

For those who've been "into" Miyazaki for a long time now, way back before any rumblings of a possible distribution deal with Disney ever came to light, there seems to exist a certain frustration. It's as though there's a resentment that it's taken an official nod from "the Mouse" to validate or somehow legitimize their interest in an artist many animation fans for years now have felt counts among the greatest filmmakers of our generation... Japanese or otherwise.

Whether (as some fear) Disney's involvement will have a bowdlerizing effect on his films—with a murderous look and her blood-smeared face, *Mononoke Hime*'s eponymous princess is Miyazaki's grimmest heroine yet—remains to be seen. However, despite the fact that Miyazaki has subsequently declared to the Japanese (and, by extension, the world) press that *Mononoke Hime* may be his "last and greatest work," surely the greatest acclaim for this artist is yet to come, as the world outside Japan becomes more aware of his unique filmmaking genius.

Hayao Miyazaki
Select Bibliography & Filmography

MANGA 漫画

Known mainly for his animation work, director Miyazaki has nonetheless managed to create several memorable manga titles, the most well-known of which is no doubt *Nausicaä*. Note that, although he has also been active as an illustrator—he's done cover illustration for Japanese editions of American science fiction novels, for example—the titles listed below are generally those of his more "major" manga works. Note also that manga adaptations of anime features—the closest Japanese equivalent to "Read the Novelization By"—are not included, as it's the anime (and not the manga) artwork which illustrates these individual adaptations.

Sabaku no Tami ("People of the Desert")
砂漠の民

First serialized in SHÔNEN SHÔJO SHIMBUN (1969); published under the pseudonym "Saburo Akitsu." *CURRENTLY IMPORT ONLY*

Kaze no Tani no Nausicaä
("Nausicaä of the Valley of Wind")
風の谷のナウシカ

First serialized in ANIMAGE magazine (1982); also published in a compiled version by Tokuma Shoten. Seven compiled volumes total. *DOMESTIC RELEASE TITLE:* ***Nausicaä of the Valley of Wind*** (Viz Comics)

Shuna no Tabi ("Shuna's Journey")
シュナの旅

First published under ANIMAGE magazine's "AM JuJu" imprint (ANIMAGE is a publication of Tokuma Shoten). Rendered completely in watercolor, the story is notable also for its resemblance to *Nausicaä*, for which some consider *Shuna* to be a predecessor. *CURRENTLY IMPORT ONLY*

Zassô Note: Hikôtei no Jidai
("Notes on This 'n' That: The Age of the Flying Boat")
雑想ノート：飛行艇の時代

First serialized in MODEL GRAPHIX magazine (1989); original source (the story appeared a few color pages at a time, over the course of several issues) for the "*Kurenai no Buta*" or "Crimson Pig" story which would eventually become the animated feature of the same name. *DOMESTIC RELEASE TITLE:* ***Hayao Miyazaki's The Age of the Flying Boat*** (serialized in ANIMERICA, ANIME & MANGA MONTHLY)

ANIME アニメ

Unlike so many other anime videos, most of Miyazaki's works tend not to be animated adaptations of popular manga titles, but original stories or animated adaptations of famous works of literature. In his early projects, especially, his less-elite role as "key animator" no doubt gave him little power to pick and choose the TV series and movies he'd be working on, but, years later, Miyazaki the director/producer still continues his love affair with literature, providing masterpiece after masterpiece using motifs from famous Greek mythology (Nausicaä), 18th century political humor (Jonathan Swift), and even contemporary literature for juveniles in Japan (Eiko Kadono).

Wan-Wan Chûshingura ("'Bow-Wow' Chûshingura")
わんわん忠臣蔵

In-Betweener
81-minute theatrical feature (1963); anime adaptation of the sensational tale (also known as "The 47 Ronin") of murder and revenge which has inspired countless Japanese live-action films and plays. *CURRENTLY IMPORT ONLY*

Ôkami Shônen Ken ("Wolf-Boy Ken")
狼少年ケン

In-Betweener
86-episode TV series (1963~65) featuring occasional direction by Isao Takahata (*Grave of the Fireflies*), Miyazaki's longtime collaborator. *CURRENTLY IMPORT ONLY*

Gulliver no Uchû Ryokô ("Gulliver's Space Travels")
ガリバーの宇宙旅行

In-Betweener
80-minute theatrical feature (1965). Fanciful retake on the Jonathan Swift classic. *DOMESTIC RELEASE TITLE:* ***Gulliver's Travels Beyond the Moon*** (Continental Distributing)

Hustle Punch
ハッスルパンチ

In-Betweener / Key Animation
26-episode TV series (1965~66). Slapstick comedy adventure from Yasuji Mori, the brilliant animator who for many years was as synonymous with an entire era of classic Toei animation. *CURRENTLY IMPORT ONLY*

Rainbow Sentai Robin ("Rainbow-Warrior Robin")
レインボー戦隊ロビン

Key Animation
48-episode TV series (1966~67). Taking their lead from the *Captain Future* series, a talented team animators—including a pre-*Cyborg 009* Shotaro Ishinomori—animate the pulp sci-fi classic. *CURRENTLY IMPORT ONLY*

Taiyô no Ôji: Horus no Dai-Bôken
("The Adventures of Horus, Prince of the Sun")
太陽の王子：ホルスの大冒険

Key Animator / Scene Designer
82-minute theatrical feature (1968). With animation halted again and again due to escalating costs, it's said the film was completed only through the intense devotion of the production staff. Directed by Takahata. *CURRENTLY IMPORT ONLY*

Sora-Tobu Yûrei Sen ("Flying Ghost Ship")
空飛ぶゆうれい船

Key Animator
60-minute theatrical feature (1969); based on a story by Shotaro Ishinomori. One scene in particular animated by Miyazaki—that of a golem—is said to continue in Japan as a fan favorite. *CURRENTLY IMPORT ONLY*

Nagagutsu o Haita Neko ("Puss in Boots")
長靴をはいた猫

Key Animator
80-minute theatrical feature (1969) animating the classic children's story by Charles Perrault. "Pero," the eponymous puss, would eventually go on to become Toei's mascot, appearing in films and promotional materials the same way M. Mouse graces the films of Disney. *CURRENTLY IMPORT ONLY*

Dôbutsu Takarajima ("Animal 'Treasure Island'")
どうぶつ宝島

Key Animator
78-minute theatrical feature (1971) animating the classic adventure story by Robert Louis Stevenson, only (as the title indicates) with animals. *CURRENTLY IMPORT ONLY*

Ali Baba to 40 no Tozoku ("Ali Baba and the Forty Thieves")
アリババと４０匹の盗賊

Key Animator
55-minute theatrical feature (1971) animating the world-famous story...only, in this version, the "thieves" are 40 mangy, manga-looking cats. *CURRENTLY IMPORT ONLY*

Lupin III
ルパン三世

Direction
23-episode TV series (1971-72); based on the long-running manga series of the same name. The directorial touches of both Miyazaki and Takahata (Eps. 6-13 were at least partially directed by either of the two, while Eps. 14-23 were *entirely* directed by them) adds a note of controversy to the series, as some critics have called Miyazaki to task for changing the "nature" of the roguish Lupin III character as created by Monkey Punch (his real name is "Kazuhiko Kato"). *CURRENTLY IMPORT ONLY*

Panda Kopanda ("Panda, Panda Cub")
パンダ・コパンダ

Original Story / Screenplay / Scenic Designer / Key Animator
33-minute theatrical feature (1972) thought by some—and with good reason, once you see the early production designs—as the predecessor to *My Neighbor Totoro*. Directed by Takahata; followed in 1973 by a sequel, "*Panda•Kopanda: Amefuri Circus no Maki* (Panda, Panda Cub and the Rainy-Day Circus)." *CURRENTLY IMPORT ONLY*

Alps no Shôjo Heidi ("Heidi, a Young Girl of the Alps")
アルプスの少女ハイジ

Scenic Design / Scenic Choreography

52-episode TV series (1974) animating the beloved and oft-filmed children's classic by Johanna Spyri. With its loving detail to the ins and outs of daily life, for many, Miyazaki and Takahata's *Heidi* (Takahata is credited as director) showcased anime's ability to focus not only on epic adventures and fantastic premises, but to depict the "little things" in life, as well. *CURRENTLY IMPORT ONLY*

Flanders no Inu ("Dog of Flanders")
フランダースの犬

Key Animator (Assistant)
52-episode TV series (1975) animating the children's story by English novelist Louise de la Ramée, who published under the pen name "Ouida." Featuring storyboards or "picture continuity" (*e-konte*) by Takahata, the series is probably even better known for breaking the hearts of a nation of children when the series' boy-hero, Nero, and his dog, the titular Dog of Flanders, go to their heavenly reward at the series' end. *CURRENTLY IMPORT ONLY*

Haha o Tazunete Sanzen Ri
("Three Thousand Leagues in Search of Mother")
母をたずねて三千里

Scenic Design / Layout / Animator
51-episode TV series (1976); based on the novel "Cuore" by Italian author Edmondo De Amicis. Released theatrically in a compiled version in 1980; directed by Takahata. *CURRENTLY IMPORT ONLY*

Araiguma Rascal ("Rascal the Raccoon")
あらいぐまラスカル

Key Animator
52-episode TV series (1977) animating the autobiographical children's story "Rascal: The True Story of a Pet Raccoon" by Sterling North. *CURRENTLY IMPORT ONLY*

Mirai Shônen Conan ("Future Boy Conan")
未来少年コナン

Direction / Character Design
26-episode TV series (1978); considered by some to be the first "solo" effort from directors Miyazaki and Takahata (Takahata is credited with direction in Episodes 9-10). Based loosely on the story "The Incredible Tide" by Alexander Key (author of the original *Escape to Witch Mountain*); published in Japan under the title "*Nokosareta Hitobito* (The Ones Left Behind)." In 1979, a compilation version was created for theatrical release, but with an ending significantly altered from the original TV series. *CURRENTLY IMPORT ONLY*

Akage no Anne ("Red-Haired Anne")
赤毛のアン

Scenic Design, Scenic Choreography (Eps. 1-15)
50-episode TV series (1979) animating the children's classic *Anne of Green Gables* by Lucy Maude Montgomery. Features direction and scriptwork by Takahata. *CURRENTLY IMPORT ONLY*

Lupin III: Cagliostro no Shiro
("Lupin the Third: Castle of Cagliostro")
ルパン三世：カリオストロの城

Direction / Screenwriting / Continuity
100-minute theatrical feature (1979); second in a series of "Lupin" films, all based on the original manga by creator Monkey Punch. Unlike the first film, *Cagliostro* brought us a Lupin who was more knight errant than hard-boiled thief, and his Clarice—the prototype for a legion of "Miyazaki heroines" to come—found high favor with fans. Ironically, the film is said to have been panned during its original theatrical run, garnering acclaim only after it had been broadcast on national television. *DOMESTIC RELEASE TITLE:* ***Lupin III: The Castle of Cagliostro*** (Streamline Pictures, later Manga Entertainment)

(The New) Lupin III
ルパン三世（新）

Director / Screenplay (Eps. 145, 155; pseudonymously)
155-episode TV series (1977-80) produced in response to high ratings garnered by the first 1971-72 *Lupin* series. Of all 155 episodes, the ones written and directed by Miyazaki—Ep. 145, "Albatross: Wings of Death" and Ep. 155, "Farewell, Lovely Lupin"—shine as the series' most memorable. *DOMESTIC RELEASE TITLE:* ***Lupin III: Tales of the Wolf*** (Streamline Pictures)

Kaze no Tani no Nausicaä ("Nausicaä of the Valley of Wind")
風の谷のナウシカ

Director / Screenplay / Continuity
116-minute theatrical feature (1984); based on Miyazaki's highly acclaimed manga series of the same name. Widely regarded in Japan as one of the finest movies ever filmed—animated or otherwise—English-speaking viewers must (at least, until a new domestic version is released) content themselves with the heavily edited, 90-minute version from New World Video. *DOMESTIC RELEASE TITLE:* ***Warriors of the Wind*** (New World Video)

Meitantei Holmes ("Famous Detective Holmes")
名探偵ホームズ

Screenwriting / Director (Eps. 1-6)
26-episode TV series (1984-85); based on the "Sherlock Holmes" stories by Sir Arthur Conan Doyle. A co-production with Italy's "RAI," the series is also available domestically through Celebrity Home Video, albeit without the little extras such as original song lyrics, the "Image Gallery" segments, etc. *DOMESTIC RELEASE TITLE:* ***Sherlock Hound*** (CHV's "Just For Kids")

Tenkû no Shiro Laputa ("Castle in the Sky Laputa")
天空の城ラピュタ

Original Story / Screenplay / Director
124-minute theatrical feature (1986); based loosely (*very* loosely) on Swift's *Gulliver's Travels.* Miyazaki, whom you'll remember as perfecting his unique brand of "heroines" as far back as 1979, scores big with Sheeta, the little-girl-lost who may hold the key to a fabulous mystery. Produced by Takahata and double-billed in Japan during the time of its initial theatrical release with the "Abduction of Mrs. Hudson" and "White Cliffs of Dover" episodes of *Meitantei Holmes.* Note that, in a dubbed Streamline Pictures version, the film has also received a limited (*very* limited) run in U.S. theaters. *CURRENTLY IMPORT ONLY*

Tonari no Totoro ("Next-Door's 'Totoro'")
となりのトトロ

Original Story / Screenplay / Director
86-minute theatrical feature (1988). Hailed by parents and critics alike as an enchanting piece of family filmmaking, relegating it to the "kiddies only" section of your video library will be doing yourself a disservice, as Miyazaki's message—humanity's need to co-exist with nature—is a prevailing one in his works. As with *Laputa,* Miyazaki also provides the lyrics for the closing song. *DOMESTIC RELEASE TITLE:* ***My Neighbor Totoro*** (Fox Home Video)

Majo no Takkyûbin ("The Witch's Delivery Service")
魔女の宅急便

Director / Screenplay / Producer
105-minute theatrical feature (1989); animates a popular story from the award-winning Japanese children's book of the same name by author Eiko Kadono. The tale of a thirteen-year-old witch and her quest for independence, Jiji, the witch's feline familiar, sparked a brief trademark dispute in Japan owing to his similarity with shipping company Yamato Transport's own logo: a black cat (thus their catchy jingle, "*Kuro-neko* [black cat] *Yamato*"). Also known as "Kiki's Delivery Service." *CURRENTLY IMPORT ONLY*

Omohide Poro-Poro ("Falling Tears of Remembrance")
おもひでぽろぽろ

Producer
119-minute theatrical feature (1991). Miyazaki lends his box-office might to frequent collabor Takahata's film, a poignant look of the "road not traveled" by a twentysomething Japanese woman. Features production by Miyazaki's Studio Ghibli, as ably helmed by character designer/animation director Yoshifumi Kondo. Also known by the studio-supplied English title "Only Yesterday." *CURRENTLY IMPORT ONLY*

Kurenai no Buta ("The Crimson Pig")
紅の豚

Original Story / Screenplay / Director
93-minute theatrical feature (1992) animating the "*Zassô*" or "This 'n' That" notes of Miyazaki's earlier series in MODEL GRAPHIX magazine, the story tells the tale of a heroic aviator (who just happens to look like a pig) who hunts sky-pirates in the skies of 1930s Italy. Like *Majo no Takkyûbin,* which was also the top-grossing film in the year of its release, *Kurenai no Buta* broke box office records of its own. Not only that—due to a deal struck with sponsor Japan Air Lines, lucky international travelers were able to catch the film in-flight, before it screened in theaters. Also known by the Italian-flavored name "Porco Rosso." *CURRENTLY IMPORT ONLY*

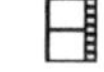

Mononoke Hime ("Princess 'Mononoke'")
もののけ姫

Director / Screenplay
135-minute theatrical feature (1997). Miyazaki's latest and perhaps most "mature" anime film yet, *Mononoke Hime* ("*mononoke*" means literally "the spir-

it of things") is set in Japan's Muromachi era (1333-1568) and movingly details the conflict between a warrior-princess reared to defend a forest and a nature being increasingly impinged upon by upwardly mobile villagers. Said by more than one Japanese critic to borrow heavily from Miyazaki's earlier *Nausicaä*, the film nevertheless packs in more blood, more violence, and an even stronger message than ever before, which forces the question: How is Disney going to explain this one to the PTA...?? *DOMESTIC RELEASE TITLE (tentative):* ***The Princess Mononoke*** (Buena Vista; expected domestic release Summer 1998)

Key

- Japanese comics or "manga" series; may or may not be available in foreign-language (i.e., English) version
- TV series broadcast on-air in Japan. Note that, in the U.S., Japanese TV series are both broadcast on-air (*Ronin Warriors*) and released on home video (*Ranma 1/2*). Others (*Sailor Moon, Dragon Ball*) are available both in broadcast and home video versions
- Direct-to-home-video series; may also include compilations of TV episodes released to home video market
- Theatrical feature; may or may not receive equivalent theatrical release for U.S. version

Masamune Shirow

Interviewed by Trish Ledoux (1993)

Hard-bitten cop Batou from *Ghost in the Shell*

Little more than a decade ago, manga artist Masamune Shirow made his debut with an early version of what would eventually become the popular original animation video *Black Magic M-66* [*"M" for "marionette"—Ed.*] in the Japanese manga fanzine Atlas. Urged by an editor at the small Osaka-based independent publisher Seishinsha to "go pro," Shirow would not publish again until three years later, when his manga opus *Appleseed* was finally completed in 1985. Shirow credits the constant support and encouragement he received from Seishinsha's president Harumichi Aoki for making the series possible in the first place.

"You could say that I was slowly enticed into becoming a manga artist, little by little," Shirow jokes, "but by far the biggest reason has got to be that early meeting with Mr. Aoki." Subsequent manga projects with Seishinsha would include 1988's *Orion*, first published in Seishinsha's manga anthology Comic Gaia and later published in English by Dark Horse Comics, as well as the more widely known *Ghost in the Shell*.

Shirow made a name for himself early in his career with his trademark tremendous attention to detail, extensive technical knowledge, and an unabashed love of the female form. From the cyber-adventures of Captain Motoko Kusanagi in *Ghost in the Shell*, to the trials of the hardcase female police officer Deunan and her cyborg partner Briareos in *Appleseed*, even to Leona and the Tank Police vs. those sexy Puma sisters in *Dominion*, Shirow's works teem with sleek femmes dressed in skintight battlesuits, personal mecha worn like armor, military hardware, cyber-hacker gear, and virtual reality special effects. Although Shirow himself modestly claims that his artwork is "really not that detailed," little things such as the way he carefully distinguishes each gun carried by his characters (right down to the make, model and type of ammunition), to the exquisitely rendered shadings and hatchings on his mecha cockpits that give his stories a sense of detailed reality seldom seen in the manga world.

"From the fan letters I read, I'm guessing that overseas readers like the same scenes as readers in Japan," Shirow says. "It's really a pity that the only way a manga artist can judge how well he's doing with his readers is through the sales of his books." Even so, his books *do* sell—in America, *Ghost in the Shell* has become one of the country's bestselling manga titles ever, breaking into America's "Top 100"-selling comics, a group that's usually the exclusive turf of superhero titles such as *X-Men*. The domestic release of animated versions of his works has pushed his popularity here even higher.

"*Appleseed* and *Ghost in the Shell* are relatively international works," says Shirow. "They transcend national boundaries. Even native speakers may have different reactions to the multiple meanings I've built into the story through the Japanese characters. For example, in Japanese, the nine-headed beast called a 'naga' which appears in *Orion* could be read *kutoryu* in *kanji* (Chinese characters), which could then be corrupted to 'Cthulu,' which is obviously a reference to H.P. Lovecraft's octopus-shaped mythological creature. The 'cubular warheads' are a double pun on the Japanese word *kaku*, meaning both 'cubular' and 'nuclear.' It goes on and on."

Such multilayered meanings are often a feature of Shirow's stories. With the notable exception of *Orion*, which is based on mythological tales of destructive gods, Shirow's manga usually center around fairly pessimistic visions of the future involving mankind having to deal with some variation on a Brave New World—in *Dominion*, it's pollution that's warped society into a form where the crime level is so desperate that the cops need tanks; in *Appleseed*, Shirow posits that utopia is only achievable by making the residents non-human. Man cannot live in the Eden that he has always desired, Shirow claims; only bioengineered perfection is capable of that. For humanity to be perfect, it can no longer be human.

From this viewpoint, *Appleseed* can be seen as setting the groundwork for his later *Ghost in the Shell*, where the great social experiment consists of humans whose bodies are largely machine, and whose minds exist as "ghosts," able to travel through computer "cyberspace" at will. But in *Ghost*, as in *Appleseed*, these kinds of experiments keep running afoul of the fact that humans are...only human.

© Masamune Shirow

As if his work wasn't reason enough to become fascinated with this multi-talented artist, many fans have indulged themselves in speculating why such an otherwise "normal" person (his "day" job is as a teacher in a Japanese high school) would want to lead a double life as a manga artist. About Shirow the person, very little is known. Photos of the reclusive artist are as rare as inexpensive cels at American anime cons, and it's not as though "Masamune Shirow" is his real name, after all.

In this interview, conducted remotely in order to preserve Shirow's carefully guarded privacy, the reclusive artist talks about the proper relationship between manga artist and editor, his early career and influences, his technique, and his assertion that he's unlikely ever to travel to America.

interview

ANIMERICA: Your female characters are usually very good at what they do and very, very dangerous. Many of your male characters, on the other hand, tend to be weak and inefficient. Does this reflect a personal belief, or do you feel that it just makes a better story?

SHIROW: I don't think that *Appleseed*'s Briareos or *Orion*'s Susano or *Ghost in the Shell*'s Chief and Batou are weak or inefficient. I'm not sure I'd say that *Appleseed*'s Deunan or *Orion*'s Seska are particularly smart or dangerous, either. However, considering that my main characters are usually women, there may be some truth in what you say. [LAUGHS]

ANIMERICA: How important to you is scientific and technological accuracy in your work? It seems obvious in works such as *Appleseed* and *Orion*, but what about *Dominion* or *Ghost in the Shell*? Have you spent a lot of time trying to make the science and technology in these works accurate?

SHIROW: For me, manga is entertainment, so scientific accuracy isn't that important. More important than making manga read like some kind of technical manual is making it *interesting*.

ANIMERICA: Let's talk about your background and training as an artist.

SHIROW: I've always enjoyed drawing, but it wasn't until my work was published in a fanzine named ATLAS that I became active as a manga artist. It was published by a group of friends...I was nineteen at the time. Even before then, I was drawing caricatures of my teachers in the margins of my grammar school notebooks and doing illustrations for the school newspaper.

ANIMERICA: What about teaching? When did you begin that career?

SHIROW: I went right into teaching after graduation. The idea of becoming a full-time manga artist had never occurred to me, you see. For various reasons—my frustrations toward the Japanese educational system and how well *Appleseed* was received, to name a few—I ended up becoming the professional manga artist I am today.

We've got a whole generation growing up overseas thinking that anime and manga is just one more form of entertainment and not just some strange, cultish thing from Japan.

ANIMERICA: Have you studied formally? Or do you consider yourself to be self-taught?

SHIROW: No, I've never trained as a manga artist per se, but it's the works I draw every day which are my real training. I did attend an art school in Osaka where I studied oil painting and sketching, but that's so fundamentally different from manga that the only thing I use today from what I learned in those days is maybe some hand control.

ANIMERICA: Would you say that you're influenced by the work of other artists in your field?

SHIROW: It wasn't until recently that I started to read manga or even go to the movies. *Space Cruiser Yamato* was the big thing when I was in junior high, but because I didn't care for its nationalistic or militaristic overtones, I never watched much of it. In high school, *Gundam* was popular, but I was an athlete and so the only time I got to watch it was when I was home with an injury. *Macross* started around the time I was drawing *Black Magic* and it did reach something inside me, but now I feel that if it had satisfied me completely I would probably have stayed in the audience rather than becoming a manga artist.

ANIMERICA: So you *have* been influenced by other artists, even if it's only to go out and create some animation of your own.

SHIROW: Yes. When I was working on the animated version of *Black Magic M-66* I concentrated very intently on the techniques of Hayao Miyazaki, who was then and is now still reigning over the Japanese animation industry. Looking back at *Appleseed* now—not that it's finished yet!—I seem to find nuances strongly reminiscent of Katsuhiro Otomo. In the mainstream film industry there's Terry Gilliam and...oh, there's too many for me to list.

ANIMERICA: Is manga the best forum for your work? If not, what would be?

SHIROW: Well, there's anime of course. But there's also an unfortunate tendency in the anime industry to think of manga artists as outsiders, or as nothing more than the generators of raw material for animation. So there are some things I need to resolve before I go into the animation studio again. Whether manga is the best forum for my work or not...well, since I'm only doing manga right now, I can't say. Becoming a filmmaker holds a certain appeal, but the Japanese film industry has been tired and worn out for a long time now, not like it was during Kurosawa's heyday. I don't think there's much room for the kind of films I'd like to make.

ANIMERICA: Which part of drawing manga do you like the least? Which parts of drawing manga do you like the most?

SHIROW: I'm happiest when I'm thinking up a story, the major props, the stage, and the characters from scratch. I'm most unhappy when being late and missing deadlines forces me to let an unsatisfactory work go out into the world.

ANIMERICA: Speaking of deadlines.... What's your impression of the relationship between a manga artist and his publisher and editor?

SHIROW: The manga artist honors deadlines and doesn't draw lines too fine to print or tones that'll come out black. The editor doesn't interfere with the work unless the artist is going way over the line. I don't know what it's like with other artists and their editors, but for me, I think my editor and I are in an almost ideal relationship of symbiotic trust...except for the universal demand to draw more and more pages, of course. [LAUGHS]

ANIMERICA: I find it interesting that despite cultural differences—or perhaps *because* of them—manga is gaining more acceptance worldwide these days than ever before.

SHIROW: I think the popularity of manga overseas these days owes a lot to anime, even to Nintendo. We've got a whole generation growing up overseas thinking that anime and manga is just one more form of entertainment and not just some strange, cultish thing from Japan.

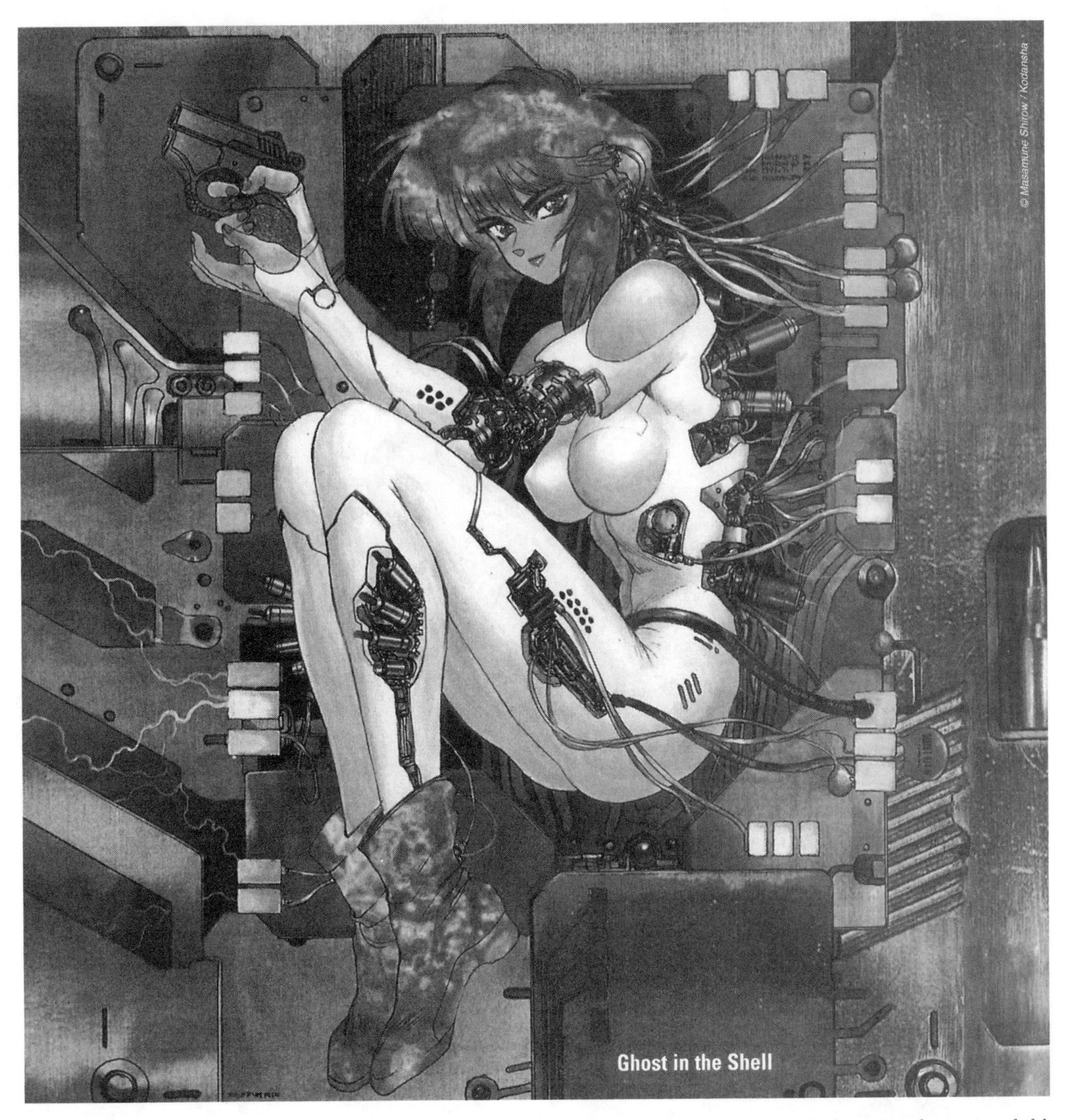

Ghost in the Shell

ANIMERICA: Compared to success in your native Japan, how important is international recognition to you?

SHIROW: Oh, I'm very pleased. It would be foolish of me to delude myself into thinking that international recognition somehow makes me more important, but I do feel proud that my name is known overseas. It also makes me feel that I can't get by with half-hearted art anymore. Not that I can get by with it in Japan, of course—it's just that I now feel an additional obligation to create manga that's truly original and entertaining.

ANIMERICA: Is there a particular manga you feel most proud of? Are there any stories you wish you could go back and re-do before they were published?

SHIROW: Just as parents can't choose to love one child over others, I love all my manga equally. I don't want to go back and re-birth any of them. Unlike childbearing, though, giving birth to manga lets you carry over your frustrations and regrets to the next creation, hopefully making it better. That's one thing you can't do when you're bearing a child. [LAUGHS]

ANIMERICA: One often-used word in describing your manga style is "detailed." How do you feel about this? Is it essential to your work or have you ever thought about using a different art style?

SHIROW: The impression that my manga is "detailed" comes from the details of its content—in reality, the art is not that precise. If you want detail, you should look to the art styles of Katsuhiro Otomo, or to the older stuff by Akira Toriyama (*Dr. Slump, Dragon Ball*). This "detailed content" is important in works like *Appleseed* and *Ghost in the Shell*; it's not so crucial in works like *Dominion* and *Orion*. Detailed art is something beyond the reach of the average manga artist publishing a weekly serial—the artist just can't do it without an army of talented assistants. For an artist like myself, who publishes about as frequently as Halley's Comet, precise detailing is essential to making my works more readable. Also, I simply like to fill in those teeny-tiny little details. [LAUGHS]

ANIMERICA: How did you come up with the idea for the landmate? Some of your fans with backgrounds in engineering wonder if it's based—even a little—on the research now being conducted in the area of human-synthesized movement at the Massachusetts Institute of Technology.

SHIROW: It was quite a while ago, but I do remember seeing a black and white photo of an exoskeleton made by General Electric in a TIME/LIFE book once. That was probably the source of my idea for the landmate. I wasn't aware that it was also being researched at MIT…I wonder what they're going to use it for? The master/slave system is even older. I believe the prototype for the landmate came about when I saw the "magic hands" being used in the medical sector. I'm sure the powered suits in Heinlein's *Starship Troopers* were another inspiration.

ANIMERICA: What sort of books are in the Masamune Shirow reference library? History texts, combat handbooks, firearms guides…? Your references to tactical gear and weapons systems seem so well-researched. Where do you find your reference for combat and SWAT scenes?

SHIROW: Half of it is imported books of military mecha, strange cars, art books, sculpture books, etc. The other half is Japanese books. A quarter of those are biotech books, micro-machine books and non-fiction military robot books, plus a little Greek mythology. Other than that, there are books on insects; I especially have quite a lot of books on bees. And then I of course have a lot of dictionaries and lots of magazines sent directly from the publishers. I average seventeen to eighteen titles a month. Although I'm not sure it counts as reference, I have about the same number of manga as my imported books.

ANIMERICA: So many of your works have been animated. What are your feelings on the animating of your manga stories? Are you involved in the production?

SHIROW: My first involvement was with *Black Magic*. The plan was originally to animate the "Venusian" story directly…the animation company just came knocking on my door one day with the project proposal in hand. I wasn't happy with the idea and didn't want to animate that story, so I drew up storyboards for *Black Magic M-66*. My beginner's curiosity lured me into becoming part of the staff; I even ended up directing it. Although the end result of the animation itself was satisfactory, my relationship with the other staff at the studio ended on a sour note, and I was reluctant to become involved in another project. That's why my only involvement in the *Appleseed* OAV was to give the project my signature and stay otherwise uninvolved. Animation is a group effort. In order to make a good work you pretty much have to put together your own hand-picked team. In preparation for the day when I return to the animation studio, I'm stockpiling storyboards and plots. When I do become involved in animation again—when I have the time—I want to be involved in every possible aspect of production.

ANIMERICA: Do you see the manga and anime worlds of *Appleseed, Dominion, Black Magic* or *Orion* as connected, or do you see them as separate, independent worlds?

SHIROW: Well, ostensibly they're all set in different worlds, but I suppose they could be considered as taking place in one loosely connected universe. There may be a few discrepancies with that, though…. [LAUGHS]

ANIMERICA: As one of the earliest "manga" stories published in English, *Appleseed* has attracted a lot of attention in this country. What was your first reaction when you heard that your manga would be translated into English?

SHIROW: I was about 70% delighted and about 30% stunned that my manga could ever be published abroad. I worried about flopping the art and letting the reader's eye flow vertically rather than horizontally, as the eyes of Japanese readers do. Having my work appear outside of Japan was a real learning experience.

ANIMERICA: How much longer will you continue *Appleseed*? Is the end of the story in sight?

SHIROW: I'd like to take a break after Book Five comes out. There are other stories I'd like to draw. I haven't

Orion

decided on anything specific yet, but I do have several ideas in mind on how to bring the story to a stopping point which can also serve as the conclusion of the entire series, should I make that decision. After all, by the time I get there, I'll probably start thinking about even more stories and then I won't be able to put an end to it. [LAUGHS]

ANIMERICA: Your *Intron Depot* art book is proving to be very popular among your fans in the U.S. Will we see more art collections like this in the future? What about (the long-rumored sequel) *Exon Depot*?

SHIROW: I plan to publish it as *Intron Depot 2*, once I've collected enough color works to fill the pages. It'll definitely be a different sort of book than the first *Intron Depot*. It looks like the publication of *Intron Depot 2* will be about three to four years down the road. *Exon Depot* will be released *long* after *Intron Depot 2* is published.

ANIMERICA: Tell us about Masamune Shirow the man. Do you have any hobbies? What do you do when you're not working on manga?

SHIROW: These days it's nothing more exciting than painting accessories and bottles, I'm afraid. [LAUGHS] Another hobby is making pen shafts and grip handles, although I'm not sure this counts since it relates to my work. I guess I'd have to say that my main hobby is my work...I really don't have many other outside interests. I do enjoy window shopping, or watching TV with friends.

ANIMERICA: Are you interested in traveling to meet your overseas fans someday? In America we hear that you're a very shy person and don't enjoy making public appearances.

SHIROW: I think America is a very attractive country, but I just don't like planes. If I had time, I'd love to come at least once. I'd have to travel by boat or dirigible, though. [LAUGHS] Honestly, though, so long as my manga is published abroad, there's really no need for me to travel in person. My work is a part of me. If that is kept alive overseas, then so am I. After all, I should think my readers would be able to get to know me much better by reading my manga, and in an interview like this, than by talking to me in person. [LAUGHS]

ANIMERICA: Being read is the highest compliment a reader can pay to an author, after all. But what if you *couldn't* be a manga artist? What would you be then?

SHIROW: I taught art at the high school level for five years after I was graduated from college. If for some reason I hadn't become a manga artist, I believe I would still be

Black Magic M-66

teaching...then again, no. Maybe I would have quit anyway. [LAUGHS]

ANIMERICA: What advice would you give to someone just starting out as an animator or comic artist?

SHIROW: My advice is not just for comic artists or animators, but for people in any occupation. Once you make your choice and decide to head in a particular direction, do it with all your might—push yourself to the limit and be as aggressive as possible...without being a nuisance to others, of course. [LAUGHS] If the most passion you can conjure up for something is, "Maybe I could be a manga artist someday," then you're bound to be discouraged at the first sign of trouble, no matter *how* talented you are. After all, they say that the ability to work hard is a big part of what we call "talent."

ANIMERICA: In closing, do have a word for your English-speaking fans?

SHIROW: Enjoy my manga, see you in my next work, and may God bless you.

afterword

Although nearly all of Shirow's main manga series (and the animated versions thereof as well) are available in America and have always been consistently popular, the artist only really reached mainstream attention in the U.S. in 1996, when an animated version of *Ghost in the Shell* was released to worldwide acclaim. Directed by *Patlabor*'s Mamoru Oshii, the film focused less on Shirow's fascination with the *Neuromancer*-like adventures of his human-machine hybrids and zeroed in on the allegorical aspects of the story.

Using stark and moody visuals liberally enhanced with computer graphics, the *Ghost in the Shell* animation was praised as a superlative example not only of state-of-the-art animation, but also of the more "adult" aspects of Japanese animation—in this case, "adult" meaning "mature," as compared to "pornographic."

When released to the American markets barely months after its Japanese theatrical premiere, *Ghost in the Shell* became the first such anime feature to hit the No. 1 spot in *Billboard*'s "Top Ten" of all video sales in the U.S., and has also been one of the first titles to release on Digital Video Disc (DVD), as well as in the by-now obligatory VHS and LD formats. The *Appleseed* manga series, which in Japan is on indefinite hiatus, will most likely be continued in its U.S. edition once the series resumes ("it could be another ten years," as one source put it to us), but until then, Book Four is the most recent volume available.

Masamune Shirow
Select Bibliography & Filmography

MANGA 漫画

One of the world's best-known manga artists, Shirow has, like many other popular creators, published a wide variety of "satellite" books—i.e., research guides, illustration collections, *fumetti*-style anime "film comics," etc. However, because these publications often outnumber the actual manga themselves, we've opted to list them only when there's a possibility they may be confused as sequels to the manga of the same name. Similarly, model kits, CD-ROMs, and novelizations by the author are not included. Shirow, like many other popular creators, has in the past done illustration/conceptual work for video games; note also that he is writer and artist on all titles.

Black Magic M-66
ブラックマジックM66

Early *dôjinshi* or "fanzine" work first published in 1983 with the assistance of Atlas magazine; later republished by Seishinsha (1985) with six additional pages (a *Black Magic M-66* appendix). One compiled volume total. A *Black Magic M-66 Storyboard Collection* ("*e-konte shû*," 1986) is also available from the same publisher. *DOMESTIC RELEASE TITLE:* ***Black Magic M-66*** (Dark Horse Comics)

Appleseed
アップルシード

Published by Seishinsha (1985); four compiled volumes total. Shirow's professional debut. Two "making of" books are also available from the same publisher: *Appleseed Databook* (1990) and *Appleseed Hyper Notes* (1995). *Genga-Ban Appleseed*, a three-volume collector's edition compilation of Shirow's original *Appleseed* artwork in "large-format" size (i.e., before it was reduced for publication), was published from 1988-90, but is available only in specialty shops and the like due to popularity with collectors. Although begun in the pages of Comic Gaia, an anticipated fifth volume in the series has yet at this time to be released. *DOMESTIC RELEASE TITLE:* ***Appleseed*** (Dark Horse Comics)

Dominion
ドミニオン

First serialized in publisher Hakusensha's ComiComi magazine (1986); later republished by Seishinsha (1993). Two compiled volumes total. After the conclusion of the first series, wanting to re-enter the world of *Dominion* once more, Shirow signed on for a sequel, which was to have been serialized in Comic Gaia. When Gaia went on hiatus, however, the series resumed not as a regular serialized title but under the aegis of a Seishinsha compiled volume or *tankôbon*, titled "No More Noise" (1995), thus the "two compiled volumes" listed above. Note that the Seishinsha reprint of the *Dominion* compiled volume includes "Phantom of the Audience," a one-shot stand-alone short story. *DOMESTIC RELEASE TITLE:* ***Dominion*** (Dark Horse Comics)

Kôkaku Kidô-Tai ("Ghost in the Shell")
攻殻機動隊

First serialized in Kodansha's Young Magazine Kaizoku Ban or "Pirate Edition" (1989); a year after the series' 1990 concluded serialization, a compiled volume was released. *Kôkaku Kidô-Tai 2: Man-Machine Interface*, a continuation of the story, began serialization in Japan in the pages of Young Magazine (1991), but as far as can be determined, has yet to be released in compiled form. (An illustration for "Fat Cat," the first story in *Kôkaku Kidô-Tai 2*, can be found on page 86 of *Intron Depot*, however.) Basis for the animated film of the same name. *DOMESTIC RELEASE TITLE:* ***Ghost in the Shell*** (Dark Horse Comics)

Senjutsu Chô Kôkaku Orion ("Super Wizardly Attack Armor Orion")
仙術超攻殻オリオン

Published by Seishinsha (1991); first serialized in Comic Gaia, a Seishinsha manga anthology. Not counting *Intron Depot*, an illustration collection, *Orion* is the only one of Shirow's "major" manga series which has yet to be animated. Interestingly, Shirow says that, before the plans for the manga were finalized, the original idea had been to draw *Orion* in full-color…talk about time-consuming. *DOMESTIC RELEASE TITLE:* ***Orion*** (Dark Horse Comics)

Intron Depot 1
イントロンデポ1

Published by Seishinsha (1992); not technically a "manga" title, per se, but a collection of full-color manga images created by Shirow and compiled from 1981-91. As an added bonus, Shirow's fanatically detailed footnotes and sidebars are provided both in Japanese and in cogent, capably rendered English by the estimable Frederik L. Schodt, author of *Manga! Manga! The World of Japanese Comics* (note to mangaphiles: Schodt also translated the Dark Horse Comics version of *Orion*). Despite being long-anticipated by fans (and perhaps by Shirow himself), a sequel volume, *Intron Depot 2*, has yet to be published. *DOMESTIC RELEASE TITLE:* ***Intron Depot 1*** (Seishinsha)

Exon Depot: Yamazakura ("Wild Mountain Cherry") and Shimban ("Judgment")
イントロンデポ1

First published in Seishinsha's Comic Gaia (No. 8 and No. 12, both in 1992); full-color short stories with pages of no-dialogue manga, one of which—the 11-page "Judgment"—was recently published in the U.S.in the pages of Penthouse magazine's June '97 issue of "Penthouse Comix." As Shirow himself mentions in his foreword to *Intron Depot 1*, "the *Intron Depot* series will not include the *Exon Depot* full-color stories." *DOMESTIC RELEASE TITLE:* ***Exon Depot*** (Penthouse Comix)

ANIME アニメ

As noted above, of all Shirow's "major" manga series, *Orion* remains the only one which has yet to be animated. Although the *amount* of Shirow manga titles to be animated is relatively small, it's important to note that, of all the Japanese animators known to the American public, Shirow's name definitely ranks at the top of the list, not only for the high-profile *Ghost*, but for the ground-breaking *Black Magic* and *Appleseed*, both of which number among the first "anime" videos ever to be released domestically.

Black Magic M-66
Black Magic M (マリオ)-66

Original Story / Screenplay / Director

One-shot OAV (1987) animating Shirow's early work of the same name. As noted, original creator Shirow assumes a rare triple role in taking on not only screenplay duties, but direction, as well. *DOMESTIC RELEASE TITLE:* ***Black Magic M-66*** (U.S. Renditions/Manga Entertainment)

Appleseed
アップルシード

Original Story

One-shot OAV (1988). Exhausted, perhaps, by his heavy involvement in the previous year's *Black Magic*, Shirow is credited for "original story" only in this 70-minute direct-to-home-video tale of life in a perfect—maybe *too* perfect—city of the future called "Olympus." *DOMESTIC RELEASE TITLE:* ***Appleseed*** (U.S. Renditions/Manga Entertainment)

Dominion
ドミニオン

Original Story

Four-volume OAV series (1988-89). Shirow deftly combines cyberpunk sensibilities with over-the-top hijinks (giant, inflatable, phallus-shaped road mines?) in this sometimes serious—but mostly silly—tale of a girl and her tank. Followed a few years later (1993-94) by a sequel OAV series titled "Tokusô Sensha-Tai (Special Assignment Tank Team) Dominion." *DOMESTIC RELEASE TITLE:* ***Dominion Tank Police*** (U.S. Manga Corps) and ***New Dominion Tank Police*** (Manga Entertainment)

Kôkaku Kidô-Tai
攻殻機動隊

Original Story

Full-length theatrical feature (1995); based on the manga of the same name. One of the most "mainstream" anime movies to be released in this country yet, *Ghost* is notable not only in that one-third of its financing came from its U.S. distributor, but that it was the first anime movie ever to place No. 1 on *Billboard* magazine's sales chart for domestic video releases. Directed by Mamoru Oshii. *DOMESTIC RELEASE TITLE:* ***Ghost in the Shell*** (Manga Entertainment)

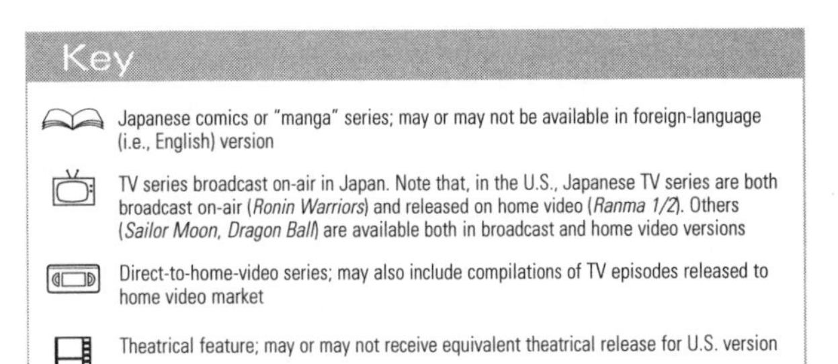

Key

- Japanese comics or "manga" series; may or may not be available in foreign-language (i.e., English) version
- TV series broadcast on-air in Japan. Note that, in the U.S., Japanese TV series are both broadcast on-air (*Ronin Warriors*) and released on home video (*Ranma 1/2*). Others (*Sailor Moon, Dragon Ball*) are available both in broadcast and home video versions
- Direct-to-home-video series; may also include compilations of TV episodes released to home video market
- Theatrical feature; may or may not receive equivalent theatrical release for U.S. version

Ryoichi Ikegami

Interviewed by Satoru Fujii (1993)

In the American comic world, it's nothing new to have an entire team (writer, artist, letterer and inker) working on a single series. In Japan, where manga is thought to be a "one-man universe," an artist such as Ryoichi Ikegami who routinely works with a collaborating writer is unusual, to say the least. More than a mere illustrator, Ikegami has very definite ideas about how his stories should be told, and likes to have a firm story idea in mind before looking for a series' writer.

"The relationship between the writer and myself is similar to that of a screenwriter and a film director," says Ikegami. "Like a director, I decide upon the cast—in manga terms we call that 'character designs'—as well as the cuts or panel layouts in the series.

"Back when my style wasn't really established," Ikegami continues, "there were times when a writer was able to bring out certain talents of mine which I hadn't even known that I'd had. I have learned quite a lot from writers...I think that as a creator of manga, I would have disappeared by now if not for them."

Born in 1944 in Fukui, Japan, Ikegami began drawing his first comic series at the tender age of seventeen. Even then, Ikegami had the magic touch, and two of his first collaborative efforts—*AIUEO Boy* with Kazuo Koike in 1973 and *Otoko Gumi* ("Gallant Gang") in 1974 with Tetsu Kariya—proved so popular they set the pattern for what would turn out to be one of the manga world's biggest success stories. Although many of his earlier works were written and drawn solo, nowadays Ikegami works almost exclusively with collaborators and shows no signs of stopping.

Ikegami is an especially important name for those who've discovered the world of manga through English translations. As one of the first few manga titles to be imported for the mainstream U.S. market, Viz Comics' publication of Ikegami and writer Kazuya Kudo's *Mai the Psychic Girl* in May 1987 helped to establish manga in the American comics scene. Brought onto the marketplace during the late-'80s "black and white boom," *Mai* was an important milestone for American comic readers even though Ikegami says it "wasn't much of a hit" in its native Japan. Two years later, in October 1989, Koike and Ikegami's sophisticated sex-'n'-violence tale *Crying Freeman* was published in English as well, dramatically underscoring the point that not all comics—especially, *Japanese* comics—are for children. In fact, *Freeman*'s frankly adult depiction of erotica and bullet-in-the-head violence shocked many, as much for how well *drawn* it was as for its subject matter.

Not long to follow *Crying Freeman* was one of Ikegami's most critically acclaimed series, *Sanctuary*, written with Sho Fumimura (a.k.a."Buronson," author of the decidedly more fantastic apocalypse-plus-martial-arts drama *Fist of the North Star*). A socio-political thriller which frequently (some say uncannily) mirrored real-world political scandals in the Japanese government, *Sanctuary* fearlessly laid bare (with some discreet sleight of hand on names and physical appearances) the links between the most powerful politicians and the leaders of organized crime that most Japanese have long assumed to exist. The actual governmental scandals contemporary to *Sanctuary's* Japanese publication created such a furor that the final result was a near-total collapse of the most powerful faction of Japan's Liberal Democratic Party (which, in Japan, *Sanctuary* had referred to wryly as the Democratic Liberal Party).

At the time this interview was conducted, *Sanctuary*—which has since ended in both Japan and America—was still a fairly new title on both coasts, and Ikegami was still coming to terms with his own popularity overseas. The surprises in the interview itself mostly have to do with his own artistic influences—for a creator who was responsible for opening the eyes of many American comic artists and readers to the power of Japanese comics, Ikegami professes a love for American comic artists such as Neal Adams, and reveals his role in the creation of the Japanese adaptation of *Spider-Man*.

interview

ANIMERICA: Let's begin with a little bit about your career. I understand you were very young when you made your debut as an artist. Were you doing graphic novels right from the start?

IKEGAMI: I was seventeen or eighteen when I debuted. My start was in the "rental manga" business, drawing a title in an anthology.

ANIMERICA: I remember reading rental manga myself, back in the days when not many people could actually afford to *own* manga. Were you still living in Osaka at the time?

IKEGAMI: Yes, I was.

ANIMERICA: And then you came out to Tokyo.

IKEGAMI: Here's what happened. Shigeru Mizuki [*renowned creator of the spooky comedy* Ge Ge Ge no Kitaro—*Ed.*] saw a short story of mine called "Sense of Guilt," printed in the avant garde manga magazine GARO. Mizuki said to me, "If you really want to become a manga artist, why don't you come to work as my assistant?" I was painting signs in Osaka at the time, and I wasn't particularly thrilled with the business, so I went off to Tokyo with no regrets.

ANIMERICA: When was the first time your own work was published?

IKEGAMI: Let's see. I was twenty-two when I came to Tokyo, and I worked with Mizuki for two and a half years...I must have been twenty-four by the time my own work was printed in a magazine. While I was still working as his assistant I was drawing my own stories, of course. When I finally got my own serial, I asked Mizuki for my freedom. That was late in my twenty-fourth year.

ANIMERICA: What were the names of your early works?

IKEGAMI: The first was titled "Tracker," published in

Crying Freeman

***Spider-Man*, Ikegami-style**

Shônen King magazine. Several of my own original short stories followed in Kodansha's Shônen Magazine. In comparison to other artists working at the time, my style was very realistic. That's probably why I was approached by an editor at Shônen Magazine Extra to do one hundred pages of a Japanese version of the American comic *Spider-Man*. Since I don't read English, a gentleman named Kosei Ono translated it for me. We got all the way up to the fifth volume before the cultural differences sort of did us in.

ANIMERICA: There were a few changes from Ono's literal translation, weren't there? My understanding was that you restructured it for the Japanese version.

IKEGAMI: That's right. I created an original main character named "Yu Komori" and tried to integrate him into the American story, but that didn't go over too well with the Japanese readers. The editors finally decided to ask the Japanese science fiction writer Kazumasa Hirai to write scripts for us, creating a story more tailored to a Japanese audience. The popularity picked up a little after that, but as a series, it never really became a big success.

ANIMERICA: What did you work on after the Japanese *Spider-Man* ended?

IKEGAMI: I did a story called "Rin Alone" for Shônen Magazine based on a script by Tetsu Kariya [*currently writing the gourmet manga series Oishinbo—Ed.*]. His pen name was different back then, but it was Kariya, all right. After that, I started *AIUEO Boy* with Kazuo Koike. *AIUEO Boy* wasn't a manga magazine story; it was published in Weekly Gendai, one of the major general-interest magazines. An editor from Shônen Sunday approached me, saying that he liked my style and wanted to see if that realistic touch could work in a boys' magazine. That's how *Otoko Gumi* ("Gallant Gang") got started. Let me tell you, *Otoko Gumi* really stood out in that magazine...all the other manga were so stylized and cartoony.

ANIMERICA: I remember that I felt the same way when *Otoko Gumi* started. That was around the time *AIUEO Boy* switched publishers, right?

IKEGAMI: Yes. *AIUEO Boy* never was one of Weekly Gendai's more popular titles, and they were kind of giving up on the series anyway, so that's when Koike said to me that he'd like to start over again with Shogakukan. That's why we switched right in the middle of the series to the Shogakukan pictorial magazine, Goro.

ANIMERICA: And then *Otoko Gumi* became a big hit. It ran for about four years, right?

IKEGAMI: Yes. And my name became pretty well-known.

ANIMERICA: After that you started *Otoko Ôzora* [*"Blue Sky Gang," lit. "big sky," implying "lofty goals and endless possibilities"—Ed.*]. That continued for some time too, didn't it?

IKEGAMI: *Otoko Ôzora* was really nothing more than a rehash of *Otoko Gumi*. I'm not quite sure how many stories I did in the boys' magazines after that, but none of them were ever quite as popular as *Otoko Gumi*.

ANIMERICA: And then there was *Mai*. Was *Mai the Psychic Girl* the first story in which your main character was a girl?

IKEGAMI: Yes. But I think Kazuya Kudo, who wrote the script, should share some of the credit for that.

ANIMERICA: Until then it was all a man's world.

IKEGAMI: Yes. I talked with my editor at Shônen Sunday before taking the idea to Kudo. The original idea was to base the character on the Buddhist figure known as "Miroku" or "Maitreya," a Bodhisattva who's supposed to come to Earth as a savior three billion years in the future. By mistake, he comes to present-day Earth. He also comes as a girl.

ANIMERICA: In *Mai*, psychic power is depicted as manifesting in many different ways. Did you come up with those variations while talking with Kudo?

IKEGAMI: Sure. But I also think that Kudo and I must have had the American movie *Firestarter* lurking somewhere in our minds. We didn't want our story to be too close to that, so we came up with a story in which psychically gifted boys and girls could come together to build a new world.

ANIMERICA: There's a character named "Tsukiro," who became a mutant after being experimented on with radiation. Did you have him in mind when you came up with the story for *Mai*?

IKEGAMI: Oh, I think special-effects movies like *Star Wars* are to blame for that one. [LAUGHS]

ANIMERICA: Do you go to the movies often?

IKEGAMI: Sure, all the time. They have a great influence on my work. I probably see all the American films that

I could never entirely swallow the idea of happy endings, you know...probably this penchant for the dark reflects itself in my work.

make their way to theaters in Japan.

ANIMERICA: What did you do after *Mai*?

IKEGAMI: I gave up on trying to top the popularity of *Otoko Gumi* in the boys' magazines. I started a new story called *Kizuyoi Bito* ("Wounded Soul") in SPIRITS magazine. That became a moderate hit.

ANIMERICA: Another story with script by Koike.

IKEGAMI: Yes. When *Kizuyoi Bito* was over, I started wondering if I could re-enter the world of manly romance once more. And that's how *Crying Freeman* started.

ANIMERICA: The graphically depicted sexuality in *Crying Freeman* was a bit of a problem for us in America. We did everything we possibly could to clearly label it as for "mature audiences only," but there are still some states which won't touch it with a ten-foot pole.

IKEGAMI: The sexuality was a problem for us in Japan, as well. Certain members of the Japanese media had tagged it as "poisonous." [LAUGHS] Sure, if you only concentrate on bits and pieces, of course it's going to look lurid. You have to see the work as a whole.

ANIMERICA: The sex and violence is just a part of the whole story.

IKEGAMI: Exactly. We are talking entertainment here, after all. Sure, it's got some sex and violence, but *Crying Freeman* is more than that...if you read it as a whole, you'll realize that it's a story about the dangerous romance of a man's world.

ANIMERICA: It's definitely romantic. The first two volumes of the compilation read more like a love story.

IKEGAMI: I like the first two volumes best myself.

ANIMERICA: What did you do after *Freeman*?

IKEGAMI: There was a story called "Offered." Just like my days in the boys' magazines, it wasn't very popular.

ANIMERICA: Well, as I recall, the story was a bit difficult to grasp.

IKEGAMI: Well, you know Koike...he just loves historicals. He'd wanted to do something dealing with the theory that modern-day Japan and Prussia descend from the same ancestral origins. That's not the kind of story my readers expect from me, though. They expect good-looking, powerful men and beautiful women. When I do something outside of the manly romance genre, for some reason the stories don't do very well.

ANIMERICA: And then...?

IKEGAMI: Next was *Sanctuary* with Sho Fumimura. The idea was to depict something different from *Freeman*, cre-

Sanctuary

Making it seem as though it could happen in "real-life" is probably the most ideal situation a manga artist could hope for.

ate a different kind of man. The series is actually selling pretty well—I think it'll become a big hit.

ANIMERICA: I'm sure the best parts are yet to come. It's a fascinating premise.

IKEGAMI: That's right, and there's more to come! Back when we started *Sanctuary*, the Japanese economy was still booming. The young people of those days—not that they're so different now, mind you—weren't up to putting their lives on the line to accomplish something they believed in. Fumimura and I thought that in order to make a convincing motive for the story, we'd have to make them returnees from the killing fields in Cambodia. It also made them just about the right age.

ANIMERICA: If it weren't for that unusual premise, Asami and Hojo would be nothing more than two megalomaniacs. [LAUGHS] It explains why they've become the way they are, and where they got the drive to make others follow them. The tie-ins with real-world political scandals don't hurt any, either.

Mai the Psychic Girl

IKEGAMI: Yes. It's like I said before, my manga is always expected to be realistic. It's never popular when the story is completely fictional. In *Freeman*, for example, readers expect me to depict the 108 Dragons as though they really exist. In *Sanctuary*, even though the current political structure or the new anti-organized crime law don't come up by name, they're definitely intertwined with the story.

ANIMERICA: In your original version, the ruling political party is known as the "Democratic Liberal Party." In the English version, it's been translated back to the "Liberal Democratic Party," just like in real-life. I think the idea was that a touch of reality would play better in the American market.

IKEGAMI: An American reader once asked me if we'd had any complaints from politicians. What that reader didn't seem to realize was that, in Japan, it's enough just to change the story around a bit and slap a disclaimer on it. You can bet there would've been trouble aplenty if we'd dared to use characters with recognizable faces, though! [LAUGHS]

ANIMERICA: While it's true that *Sanctuary*'s story may only be "inspired" by real-world headlines, it does seem as though events which happen in the manga also happen in the real world.

IKEGAMI: They could very well be true. Making it seem as though it could happen in "real-life" is probably the most ideal situation a manga artist could hope for.

ANIMERICA: What kind of story are you working on these days?

IKEGAMI: Well, aside from *Sanctuary*, I'm working on a new story with a female writer named Soko Ieda scheduled to start very soon in Big Comic Spirits. I've been ill recently and just can't keep up with the weekly schedule anymore, so it'll have to be a monthly serial in a weekly magazine. It's very interesting—we're planning a female main character modeled after the French film *La Femme Nikita*.

ANIMERICA: Here's a question often asked by American fans. In manga, the story and art are usually done by a single person. In the U.S. comics industry, two or more people work together on a single title. Back in your earlier works you wrote your own stories. How is it that you came to work so extensively with collaborators?

IKEGAMI: In the beginning, I did a number of short stories by myself for various magazines. Eventually I noticed that these solo stories were turning out to be

Crying Freeman

very downbeat and not very entertaining. I could never entirely swallow the idea of happy endings, you know...probably this penchant for the dark reflects itself in my work. So that's when I started actively looking for collaborators.

ANIMERICA: Even when you're working with a collaborator, don't you usually come up with the original ideas yourself?

IKEGAMI: That's how it is now, but it wasn't always like that. It wasn't until my own style became more established that I began to search for stories suited to the way I wanted to draw. For example, I think the reason I'm able to portray the manly romance of *Crying Freeman* is the power of Koike's script. Surely, somewhere, I must have had it in me all along, but I don't think I ever would've been able to visualize it without his help. It was Koike who helped me to see *Freeman*.

ANIMERICA: What's it like to work with collaborators? How specific are they in giving details?

IKEGAMI: It all depends on the writer. Someone familiar with manga who only got into writing because he couldn't be an artist is likely to create a script so meticulous, he's probably already got the panel layout in his mind. Some writers create scripts as though they were novels. Either way, it ends up being like a movie script, with details such as actual choreography, panel layout, and the like left up to me.

ANIMERICA: Both *Kizuyoi Bito* and *Crying Freeman* have been animated. What's your impression of these animated versions?

IKEGAMI: I thought *Kizuyoi Bito* might have been a little strained technically, but it got better as the animators got used to the style. By the time the fifth volume of *Crying Freeman* came out, I'm happy to say I was completely satisfied with the work. It can be such a pleasure to see your works animated! Since I draw nothing but static art, it always amazes me to see the characters I created *move*. [LAUGHS]

ANIMERICA: You've got something of a reputation as an American comics fan. Which artists do you like?

IKEGAMI: I've been a fan of American comics since before I worked on *Spider-Man*, but I didn't fall in love until I started studying Neal Adams. I am deeply impressed by his sketches. I've collected all his works, I think, not only *Spider-Man* but *Batman* and *Superman*, too. I'd love to get his autograph.

ANIMERICA: You've got a number of your own fans in the U.S., especially female fans. Your *Mai the Psychic Girl* and *Crying Freeman* seem to be among the most popular. What feelings do you have about your overseas success?

IKEGAMI: One trend which holds true in both *shônen* and *shôjo* or boys' and girls' manga is the increase in stories with female protagonists. No doubt this is one manifestation of today's Japanese women having more social and personal freedom. As you know, *Mai* was one of the first *shônen* manga to feature a girl in the lead role. I'm pleased to hear that *Freeman* is getting read by American women...I think I can understand why they find it appealing, especially that very romantic love story in the first two volumes. I understand that romance novels such as the Harlequin series are very popular in the U.S. They're not so different from *shôjo* manga, you know. I think that if *shôjo* manga were to be introduced on a wider scale to the U.S., English-language publishers of manga could attract an incredible amount of new female readers.

afterword

The story Ikegami refers to in his interview as being based on *La Femme Nikita* became a reality in *Kyoko*, a controversial title which drew much of its inspiration from a much-publicized rape incident on an American army base. Written by Soko Ieda, the story didn't have the usual elements of an Ikegami story—no James Bond-like villains, no superstuds, no globe-trotting romance—and, when asked, he professes to be rather dissatisfied with it. In 1995, though the long-rumored *Mai the Psychic Girl* live-action film still had yet to materialize, *Crying Freeman* was adapted into a stylish live-action film helmed by French director Christophe Gans, with set designs by Alex McDowell (*The Crow*), a soundtrack by Shoji Yamashiro and his Geinoh Yamashiro Group (*Akira*), and starring martial artist Mark Dacascos (*Double Dragon*, *Only the Strong*, *American Samurai*) as the tattooed hero "Freeman" and Julie Condra Douglas (*Gas, Food, Lodging*) as the beautiful Emu, Freeman's victim turned lover. Though the *Crying Freeman* movie has yet, at the time of this writing, to receive wide release in the U.S., Ikegami's *Sanctuary* is another matter. Adapted into both live-action and animated versions in 1995 and 1996, respectively, both versions have subsequently been released for the U.S. market. Currently, Ikegami is at work on a new manga series...and yes, at the San Diego Comic-Con a few years back, he did eventually manage to meet Neal Adams. His new series, *Strain*, will be serialized in English in Viz Comics' new manga anthology, PULP.

Ryoichi Ikegami
Select Bibliography & Filmography

MANGA 漫画

Even as this book goes to press, things are *happening* with Ikegami's career in the U.S. Already well-known for being the creator of *Mai* and *Crying Freeman* (the latter of which, we note, was made into a reasonably-faithful-to-the-manga live-action film), Ikegami's fame in America climbs yet another notch with the announced release of a *domestic* version of his early, until now Japan-only *Spider-Man*. Note that, unless indicated otherwise, Ikegami's involvement is limited to that of "artwork" only.

Spider-Man
スパイダーマン

Published by Asahi Sonorama; five compiled volumes total. Initially written and illustrated by Ikegami; written in later volumes by Kazumasa Hirai (1970). *DOMESTIC RELEASE TITLE:* ***Spider-Man Manga*** (Marvel Comics)

AIUEO Boy
愛飢男BOY

Serialized in Weekly Gendai; written by Kazuo Koike (1973). ("A-I-U-E-O," by the way, are the five vowels of Japanese language; compare with "A-E-I-O-U" in English). *CURRENTLY IMPORT ONLY*

Otoko Gumi ("Gallant Gang")
男組

Serialized in Shogakukan's Shônen Sunday; twenty-five compiled volumes total (1974). Written by Tetsu Kariya. *CURRENTLY IMPORT ONLY*

Otoko Ôzora ("Blue-Sky Gang")
男大空

Serialized in Shogakukan's Shônen Sunday; fifteen compiled volumes total (1980). Written by Tetsu Kariya. *CURRENTLY IMPORT ONLY*

Kizuyoi Bito ("Wounded Soul")
傷追い人

Serialized in Shogakukan's Big Comic Spirits; eleven compiled volumes total (1983). Written by Kazuo Koike. *CURRENTLY IMPORT ONLY*

Mai
舞

Serialized in Shogakukan's Shônen Sunday; six compiled volumes total (1985). Written by Kazuya Kudo. *DOMESTIC RELEASE TITLE:* ***Mai the Psychic Girl*** (Viz Comics)

Crying Freeman
Crying フリーマン

Serialized in Shogakukan's Big Comic Spirits; nine compiled volumes total (1986). *DOMESTIC RELEASE TITLE:* ***Crying Freeman*** (Viz Comics)

Nobunaga
信長

Serialized in Shogakukan's Big Comic Original; eight compiled volumes total (1987). Written by Kazuya Kudo. *CURRENTLY IMPORT ONLY*

Akai Apiru ("Red Duck")
赤い鳩

Serialized in Shogakukan's Big Comic Spirits; six compiled volumes total; written by Kazuo Koike (1988). *CURRENTLY IMPORT ONLY*

Offered
Offered

Serialized in Shogakukan's Big Comic Spirits; four compiled volumes total (1990). Written by Kazuo Koike. *CURRENTLY IMPORT ONLY*

Sanctuary
サンクチュアリ

Serialized in Shogakukan's Big Comic Superior; twelve compiled volumes total (1990). Written by Sho Fumimura. *DOMESTIC RELEASE TITLE:* ***Sanctuary*** (Viz Comics)

Box
Box

Published in Shogakukan's Big Comics (1991); one compiled volume total. Written by Marei Karibu. *CURRENTLY IMPORT ONLY*

Ôritsuin Kumomaru no Shôga
("The Life and Times of Oritsuin Kumomaru")
王立院雲丸の生涯

Serialized in Shogakukan's Shônen Sunday; three compiled volumes total (1992). Written by Oji Hiroi. *DOMESTIC RELEASE TITLE:* ***Samurai Crusader, The Kumomaru Chronicles*** (serialized in Manga Vizion)

Kyoko
今日子

Serialized in Shogakukan's Big Comic Spirits (1995~); ongoing as of press time. Written by Soko Ieda. *CURRENTLY IMPORT ONLY*

Odyssey
オデッセイ

Serialized in Shogakukan's Big Comic Superior; three compiled volumes total (1996). Written by Sho Fumimura. *CURRENTLY IMPORT ONLY*

Kami no Gikyoku ("Drama of the Gods")
神の戯曲

One-shot story serialized in Shogakukan's Big Comic Extra; written by Yuji Nishi (1997). *CURRENTLY IMPORT ONLY*

Strain
ストレイン

Serialized in Shogakukan's Big Comic Superior (1997); ongoing as of press time. Written by Buronson. *DOMESTIC RELEASE TITLE:* ***Strain*** (serialized in Pulp)

ANIME アニメ

For a manga artist who's created as many consistently bestselling manga titles as he, the number of anime adaptations based on Ikegami's work is few. However, there's something to be said in the fact that, of all the artists and creators interviewed in this book, only three—*Guyver*'s Takaya, *Street Fighter II*'s Sugii and, of course, *Freeman*'s Ikegami—can say their works have been made into live-action Hollywood films. Note that Ikegami is credited for "original story" only in each of the following entries.

Crying Freeman
Crying フリーマン

Six-episode OAV Series (1989-93). Also available in a live-action version of the same name, directed by Christophe Gans and starring Mark Dacascos and Julie Condra Douglass. *DOMESTIC RELEASE TITLE:* ***Crying Freeman*** (Streamline Pictures)

Kizuyoi Bito
傷追い人

Five-episode OAV Series (1986-88). *CURRENTLY IMPORT ONLY*

Sanctuary
サンクチュアリ

Single-shot OAV (1995). *DOMESTIC RELEASE TITLE:* ***Sanctuary*** (Viz Video). Also available in a Japan-produced live-action version of same, now available subtitled in the U.S.

Key

- Japanese comics or "manga" series; may or may not be available in foreign-language (i.e., English) version
- TV series broadcast on-air in Japan. Note that, in the U.S., Japanese TV series are both broadcast on-air (*Ronin Warriors*) and released on home video (*Ranma 1/2*). Others (*Sailor Moon, Dragon Ball*) are available both in broadcast and home video versions
- Direct-to-home-video series; may also include compilations of TV episodes released to home video market
- Theatrical feature; may or may not receive equivalent theatrical release for U.S. version

Yukito Kishiro

Interviewed by Seiji Horibuchi (1993)

Yugo, a.k.a."Hugo" from *Gunnm / Battle Angel Alita*

"When I was in high school, my big goal was to win a manga award before graduation," Kishiro says. "It's not as though I felt I was ready to become a real manga artist or anything, but I did think that, after I'd finally mastered the art of inking, I was ready to enter some kind of contest. That's how I came to enter and be nominated for a 'Best New Artist' award from Shogakukan's SHÔNEN SUNDAY magazine in 1984."

Like Rumiko Takahashi, whose *Urusei Yatsura* predecessor *Katte na Yatsura* ("Those Selfish Aliens") won the same award in 1977, Kishiro was soon deluged with offers to "go pro." Unlike Takahashi, however, Kishiro postponed the chance to jump right into the daily grind of a professional manga artist in favor of finishing high school, going on to design school, and then working a newspaper delivery job.

"In the short run, I'd won an award at the age of seventeen," Kishiro says. "In the long run, it was something of a disappointment. I'd reached the point where I was satisfied with my art, but my ideas on how to structure content were still vague. I didn't really know how to shape a story, and there wasn't anything in particular that I'd wanted to say. I was uncomfortable with the level of my work."

In 1988, Kishiro made his second debut as a manga artist with the publication of his story *Kaiyôsei*. Described by Kishiro as a "horror story with somewhat of a profound theme," the story went on to receive an honorable mention in the same contest he'd entered four years earlier.

"At the time, I was flushed with confidence and so full of myself," Kishiro admits with a smile. "I marched right up to the editor and demanded, 'What do you mean, 'honorable mention'!?'" Kishiro laughs. "Fortunately, that particular editor was a very understanding person. When he told me that he thought it was a wonderful story I was somewhat mollified, but then I happened to see some of the notes from the selection process. One of the judges had actually written, 'It's the work of a madman!' That's when I realized I had to try and create a more uplifting story."

In Kishiro's case, it was editorial influence that defined the final shape of what, up until this point, remains his best-known work: *Gunnm* (literally "gun dream"), better known in English as *Battle Angel Alita*. Eluded by an approach for a story he was asked to draw for a Shueisha publication, one of his editors suggested he use a character from a previous, unpublished story. That suggestion—and that sketchily depicted cyborg police officer—eventually became the character of "Gally," or as she's called in English, "Alita" (something Kishiro himself was to humorously reference later in the Japanese version of the series).

A hit in Japan, *Gunnm* was quickly translated into English-, Spanish- and Italian-language editions and greeted overseas with amazing enthusiasm, especially given Kishiro's "unknown" status. A strange but somehow beautiful tale of a gamine cyborg, *Gunnm* inhabits the kind of world which might now be called cyberpunk—a *Max Headroom*-like scrapyard world filled with crumbling mechanized warrens and dubious underworld figures, hulking cyborgs, bounty hunters and misfits of every stripe. Hovering over the entire landscape is a vast technological dream city, which casts its junk down onto the heads of Kishiro's junkyard denizens, who spend their lives searching not only for a way to survive, but for a reason to live. Dark stuff.

With such a success , it should have come as no surprise that *Gunnm* would be chosen for animation. But when KSS approached Kishiro about making his story into an animated feature, he admitted that the idea of his work being animated "took a little getting used to."

"Manga and animation are so different," Kishiro says. "When you're drawing manga, the units you work with to pace your story are the two opposing pages. I just couldn't see how the pacing for the animation could possibly work by looking at the storyboards alone. But then, when I finally saw (the finished animation), I was very impressed with its sense of timing." In the final product (titled *Battle Angel* for its U.S. release), Kishiro's eclectic character designs are interpreted for the animation by Nobuteru Yuki, already well-known for his work on *Record of Lodoss War*, and who would later go on to do the TV series *Escaflowne*, as well as the big-budget, animated *X* movie.

At the time of this interview, Kishiro's *Gunnm* had been running for two and a half years in Japan. The story's publication in English under the "Battle Angel Alita" title was only just reaching the segment of the story with which Kishiro himself seems most taken—the Motorball story, in which armored warriors in cyborg bodies equipped with rollerblades fight a no-holds-barred battle that's somewhere between roller derby, football, and gladitorial combat.

"*Gunnm* is an introspective story," Kishiro continues. "To be honest, when I was first approached about allowing it to be published in foreign-language editions, I wasn't sure it was a good idea. It's kind of an experimental work for me and I didn't think it could be popular, especially not in the United States. To me, it's a never-ending wonder that my work is being translated and read by all sorts of different people."

interview

ANIMERICA: By now you've seen *Battle Angel Alita*, the English version of your manga *Gunnm*. What do you think of it?

KISHIRO: I'm unsure what to make of it, actually...I can't read English. [LAUGHS] I do notice all the mistakes in my art, now that it's been flopped. (Flopping it) really brings out the skew in the line drawings. Looking at it now, I wonder if this particular work isn't a little immature, artistically speaking.

ANIMERICA: In the U.S., flopping pages is simply a fact of

Battle Angel Alita

publishing life. The pages which open to the right in Japan are opened to the left in America. There's no getting around it. There are some artists who hate flopping so much, they refuse to let their work be published abroad.

KISHIRO: Well, imperfections in the artwork *do* become more noticeable when they're printed reversed. But then again, they're usually the kind of mistakes which would be there anyway. They just don't stick out as much in the original.

ANIMERICA: As far as your English-speaking readers are concerned, I don't think anyone regards *Gunnm/Battle Angel Alita* as "artistically immature." The fans seem to love your art....

KISHIRO: Okay, then—it's my perfectionism that's immature. [LAUGHS]

ANIMERICA: Was it always your ambition to be a manga artist?

KISHIRO: I've been drawing manga since before I can remember, but it wasn't until high school that I started to ink my work seriously. I've always liked mecha—*Mobile Suit Gundam*'s had an incredible effect on me—and my art has been affected by it for years. I couldn't draw people, but I could sure draw mecha. [LAUGHS] That's why I used to avoid the problem by drawing monsters, instead of people. My monsters spoke and walked like people...they just happened to be monsters. Eventually it dawned on me that it would be pretty hard to make it as a manga artist if all I ever drew were stories set in reptilian worlds, so in high school I started to concentrate on drawing the human form. The fully realized characters of Yasuhiko [*Yoshikazu Yasuhiko, character designer for the* Mobile Suit Gundam *and* Mobile Suit Zeta Gundam *TV series—Ed.*] were a big influence on me; Rumiko Takahashi's also been a big influence.

I couldn't draw people, but I could sure draw mecha. That's why I used to avoid the problem by drawing monsters, instead of people.

ANIMERICA: So you're saying that your manga has been influenced by animation.

KISHIRO: Oh, yes. Up until high school I watched practically everything. There was a flood of it back then, wasn't there. I guess it reached its high point in the few years immediately after *Gundam*. It's probably fair to say that the golden age of animation ended at 1984.

ANIMERICA: I can't help noticing that you keep referring to *Gundam*.

KISHIRO: Well, I like all the Sunrise shows, really. I loved *Xabungle* and *Votoms*. In fact, I think *Votoms* might have had more of an effect on me than *Gundam* ever did. (*Votoms*) had a four-part composition—the story would conclude at the end of each part, and a new story would start off in a different world for the next. *Gunnm* borrows quite heavily from this style of storytelling.

ANIMERICA: But where did you get your real start? I imagine it must have been sometime around the publication of your story, *Kikai* [*one translation of which is "Machine"—Ed.*], in 1984.

KISHIRO: That's right, and even though I turned down offers to become a professional manga artist after I was nominated for the SHÔNEN SUNDAY "Best New Artist" award, I was always experimenting with ways to shape a story and with techniques of expression. In order to practice my art to the fullest, I started making my own *dôjinshi* (self-published comics). And then, in 1988, I had my second debut.

ANIMERICA: Did it feel different to you, the second time around?

KISHIRO: Well, I felt as though I was through agonizing over my work. I finally had enough confidence to try for recognition again. I drew a story called *Kaiyôsei* and entered it into the Shogakukan contest again.

ANIMERICA: ...Where it won an "honorable mention." What happened then?

KISHIRO: That fall I entered another "New Artist" contest, this time for Kadokawa's COMIC COMP. There wasn't much time before the deadline, so I hurriedly scribbled a story called *Hito* [*"A Man"—Ed.*]. When I was finished, I thought proudly to myself, "Now *this* is my best work!" [LAUGHS] I ended up with another honorable mention.

ANIMERICA: You must have been very disappointed.

KISHIRO: Later, I heard that almost all of the judges had rooted for me, but there was one judge who'd complained that the story was "too didactic." That's how it ended up with an honorable mention. It's still a good story, I think, and it's received well by anyone I show it to now, but then again, at the time, I'd thought *Kaiyôsei* was a masterpiece, too. [LAUGHS]

ANIMERICA: I'm sure it was a valuable learning experience.

KISHIRO: Oh, yes. The best thing to come out of those honorable mentions was that I began working with an editor at Shueisha to improve my only "long" story at the time, *Reimeika*. I really sweated over that one, drawing and redrawing pages. It was never published. Near the end of the summer of 1990, I was asked to draw a story for a special manga compilation Shueisha planned to publish in the fall. The editors at Shueisha had liked the female cyborg police officer in *Reimeika*, and so they suggested I use her. Her name was "Gally" [*"Alita" in the U.S. version—Ed.*]. Of course, the Gally in *Reimeika* was completely different from the Gally in *Gunnm*, but that's how she was born.

ANIMERICA: How did you develop the story from there?

KISHIRO: Usually when I start a story, I tend to work on the plot and theme first—typically, my characters are developed later. This time I was trying to draw something based on one character from a 45-page story. The story itself was pretty run-of-the-mill, actually; in the future, it's the corporations who see to the arrest and detainment of criminals, etc. Like I said, nothing out of the ordinary.

ANIMERICA: And then....

KISHIRO: ...And then, around November, I was contacted by the same editor about making *Gunnm* into a serial. At first, I couldn't believe he was serious, but I went ahead and wrote the script for the first installment. The settings in my short story weren't enough for a potentially long-running serial, so I brainstormed for a while and that's when I came up with the idea of Zalem [*"Tiphares" in the U.S. version—Ed.*]. I had no idea what kind of future—if any—the story had, so I drew *Gunnm* in such a way that it could be more fully developed later.

ANIMERICA: How long was it until you saw your story published?

KISHIRO: Not much more than a month between finishing the script and seeing it begin as a published serial. I don't think I realized it was a reality until I saw the actual magazine itself. [LAUGHS]

ANIMERICA: And how long has it been since *Gunnm* started?

KISHIRO: It's been two and a half years.

ANIMERICA: Tell us more about the world of *Gunnm*. How did you come to create this particular story?

Battle Angel Alita

KISHIRO: I grew up in a place where a forest had been cleared and only a few houses stood. My father was an eccentric who was into dune buggies. He was always digging around at the junkyard looking for parts he could use. He used to take me with him sometimes...I still like spending time at the junkyard. I'm sure most people don't feel that way, but I was always happy to spend time alone there. Sure, I liked being alone anyway, but there was also something comfortable about being alone with the wreckage of things people had abandoned. I guess on the opposite extreme of this feeling is the very real terror I feel when confronted by a brand-new, shiny car. I honestly get the feeling that it's consciously trying to run me down. Old cars, though...they're different. I truly believe there's a kind of nostalgic comfort about being cradled inside the empty shell of an old car.

ANIMERICA: Let's talk about the cyborgs.

KISHIRO: Ah, yes...the cyborgs. [LAUGHS] My relationship with them dates back to the toys of my childhood. I remember this G.I. Joe-type figure manufactured by Takara. It was called "Cyborg One." It was made of clear plastic; the internal mechanisms were easily visible. And its limbs were removable—you could attach different gears and parts in their place. I loved that toy...it's too bad it's been discontinued. That little guy had a profound effect on me. I guess that's why I feel so strongly that cyborgs should always have detachable limbs.

ANIMERICA: And that's why Gally comes from a junkyard.

KISHIRO: I think it's the basis of it, yes. That kind of imagery seems to come to me subconsciously. As for Zalem, I'm not sure what it's supposed to actually signify. In some ways I'm an anarchist—I hate a managed world. There's a certain part of me who thinks that the world of *Mad Max* would be a fun place to live. [LAUGHS]

ANIMERICA: I feel as though I'm really coming to understand your manga.

KISHIRO: Urbanites of the modern world are a lot like cyborgs, you know. They become immediately incapacitated when you cut off their juice. Isn't that what being a cyborg is all about...? From an ideological point of view, I'm against the idea of cyborgs. But I guess the world's come too far for token resistance and half-hearted pleas against technology. In *Gunnm*, what I try to do is focus on the benefits of scientific advance, rather than making some sort of political statement.

Alita in "Motorball" gear

ANIMERICA: Where is *Gunnm* headed? What directions will the story take?

KISHIRO: If the series isn't canceled, I'd like to take my story to Zalem and then do a space story. And even though I don't have the particulars yet, I'd like to reveal Gally's origin in the grand finale.

ANIMERICA: How directly were you involved in the production of the animated *Gunnm*?

KISHIRO: I met with the animation staff right at the very beginning and talked with them about how I'd like to see the story done. Later, at the stage where plot and script decisions were made, I gave them my feedback. When the storyboarding and direction were done, I met with the staff again and talked over a few ideas with them.

ANIMERICA: How do you rate the finished animation?

KISHIRO: Well, back during the storyboards, I'd say things like, "This part is bad" and "Fix this," but it never did get changed. [LAUGHS] Later, after I'd given up all hope, I saw the finished video and thought to myself, "Whoa, it's *moving*!" and "Whoa, it's in *color*!" [LAUGHS] And then I thought they did a pretty good job.

ANIMERICA: But it took you a while to arrive at that conclusion.

KISHIRO: I think part of the problem is that pacing for manga and animation is so different. I just couldn't see how the storyboarding for the anime should work. I had to keep reminding myself that these were professionals working on my story and that I'd have to convince myself that they knew what they were doing.

ANIMERICA: Do you feel it was made well?

KISHIRO: I could go off the deep end on lots of little details, but yes, I think they did a good job. [LAUGHS] You can never be satisfied with *everything*, not unless you're willing to do the whole thing yourself. I did have quite a few of my own ideas...so-and-so's voice shouldn't be like that, that sort of thing. You know what I mean. [LAUGHS]

ANIMERICA: True. For complete satisfaction, an artist has no choice but to draw and produce everything personally. Let's say you've got the opportunity—and the actual time—to do it yourself. Would you...?

KISHIRO: I would like to. My ultimate childhood dream is to a make a live-action movie. Sometimes I think I'm only drawing manga because I can't be making films. In junior high, I really wanted an 8mm camera. There was no way in the world I could have scraped up the $3,000 or so dollars it would have cost back then to have bought it, though. [LAUGHS]

ANIMERICA: What about if someone else wanted to do *Gunnm*? If Hollywood called and said they wanted to make a *Gunnm/Battle Angel Alita* movie, would you give them the go-ahead?

KISHIRO: Of course I would. [LAUGHS] It's my childhood dream, after all. I'd love to see the whole spectacle of Motorball brought to life. I'd love to see those special effects. For the sake of a live-action film, the overall plot could be set aside; the main character wouldn't necessarily have to be Gally. It would be okay with me to make something a little different than the manga version. I think it might be difficult to make the original *Gunnm* the way I envision it in live-action. There are several parts to the story, but I think the Motorball segment by itself could make a great movie.

My ultimate childhood dream is to a make a live-action movie. Sometimes I think I'm only drawing manga because I can't be making films.

ANIMERICA: Okay, let's say the *Battle Angel Alita* movie is being made in the U.S. Who would direct?

KISHIRO: Paul Verhoeven of *Robocop* fame, maybe. Some might say his style is over the top, but I prefer to think of it as "super realism." [LAUGHS] If only for the visuals, *Highlander*'s Russell Mulcahy might be good.

ANIMERICA: I see you're acquainted with American cinema. What about American comics?

KISHIRO: In a small way I'm influenced by them. I was particularly impressed by Frank Miller's *Batman*—now *that* made an impression. [*Frank Miller's famous* Dark Knight Returns *series—Ed.*] That close-up on the Joker's face, with that insane laugh and all those teeth showing.... I guess I'm influenced not by the big picture but by the little details—how an eye or a wrinkle might be drawn, for example.

ANIMERICA: What's your feeling on your comics being read overseas? *Gunnm* is very popular in the U.S., in Italy, even in Spain.

KISHIRO: Up until *Gunnm*, all my works had been hard-boiled; rather than showing what the characters were thinking, I'd just dryly imply it from the action and dialogue. It's possible that the style of *Gunnm* is more like *shôjo* (girls') manga than I'd like to admit. [LAUGHS]

ANIMERICA: Now that *Gunnm/Alita* is such a success, do you feel as though you've finally arrived...?

KISHIRO: Well, my father never was a big believer in manga. He never seemed to think I could go pro. He'd say, "If you're going to draw manga, draw something they'll like all over the world." [LAUGHS] Sure, nowadays manga and animation is getting international recognition, but in the past it was nothing more than a subculture unique to Japan. It was tough enough just trying to make it there...! Now that *Gunnm*'s been translated for foreign editions, I'm not exactly sure how I feel. It *is* my first serial, after all. In many ways, it's still an immature work that I'm making up as I go along. If I had my way, I might have waited until my skill was a bit more polished, until I'd earned the reputation of someone like Frank Miller. That way, people would come to me from overseas with the attitude, "Let's go get that great manga artist Yukito Kishiro!" [LAUGHS]

ANIMERICA: Finally, do you have a word for your American fans?

KISHIRO: I've often wondered what my overseas readers think of *Gunnm*. I'm not all that confident in my communication skills; ever since I was little, I've fretted over whether people were understanding what I was saying or writing. I was a shy child, you know. People are always complimenting me on my penmanship...I think it must be a symptom of my being high-strung. [LAUGHS] I'd like to talk with my fans about how well I've communicated with them, if I ever get the chance to go overseas and visit.

afterword

As it turns out, of course, *Gunnm* was never canceled; in fact, it only recently ended its run in publisher Shueisha's manga mag BUSINESS JUMP. In its U.S. and other "foreign-language" editions, the story lives on although, at least in the case of its English-language publication, the dramatic end—the "grand finale" Kishiro mentions—is definitely in sight.

Ends can also mean new beginnings, and *Gunnm* follow-up *Gunnm Gaiden* (lit., "*Gunnm* Side-Story") has begun appearing in YOUNG JUMP spin-off manga mag ULTRA JUMP, where it replaced the previously published *Gunnm* sorta-sequel *Haisha* (lit., "Ashen One"). Giving readers an extended, Gally-less look at the world of "Motorball" as portrayed in *Gunnm*, *Haisha* is nevertheless drawn in a completely different, even Miller-esque art style. *Haisha* has only just concluded serialization.

The currently running *Gunnm Gaiden*, on the other hand, *does* feature appearances by Gally, although not in the guise you might expect. Because it jumps around so much in the established *Gunnm* universe (some stories take place right after Doc Ido leaves Zalem; others chronicle Gally's adventures during her ten-year span as a "Tuned" agent, adventures not covered in the original *Gunnm* series itself), time is measured one of two ways: BK or AK, as in "Before Koyomi," or "After Koyomi." As readers will no doubt remember, Koyomi is the baby Gally/Alita saved in the first part of the story, who later returns as a teenager. In one story, Doc Ido even has a little black cat named Gally....

As of this writing, neither *Gunnm Gaiden* nor *Haisha* has been licensed for U.S. publication. However, given the tremendous popularity established for his first work as a true manga professional in its diverse foreign editions, the possibility of foreign-language editions of one or possibly both *Gunnm* sequel titles seems inevitable. Also in the "not yet, but probably" category is the long-rumored sequel to the animated *Gunnm/Battle Angel*, which many fans are hoping will focus on Gally's Motorball days.

Just like the scrapyard denizens of his stories, and junkyard days of his own youth, Kishiro has a reputation among his Japanese editors for being something of a packrat. It's never enough for him to jot down just a few notes of info; for even the most minor of gadgets or characters, it's said that he's got to have stacks and stacks of precisely detailed technical info and backstory. If only one could simply organize and collate these notes of his, his editors say, just think of the new stories that could be published. If you consider that both *Haisha* and *Gunnm Gaiden* grew out of the detritus of Kishiro's studio, the saying "one man's junk is another man's treasure" takes on added significance.

Yukito Kishiro
Select Bibliography & Filmography

MANGA 漫画

Comics (manga) series by Yukito Kishiro. In recognition of his growing popularity as a manga artist, it was recently announced in Japan that a collection of his early works would be released—an event the creator himself must surely find encouraging, as those works are next to impossible to find in their non-compiled form. Note that Kishiro is also the artist/writer on all series.

Hito ("A Man")
飛人

First serialized in Kadokawa Shoten's Comic Comp (1988), "Hito" (written with the Japanese characters "jump" + "person") is also the name chosen for an upcoming collection of Kishiro's early works, tentatively scheduled for release in late '97, of which *Hito* itself is only one entry. *CURRENTLY IMPORT ONLY*

Gunnm ("Gun Dream")
銃夢

Serialized in Shueisha's Business Jump (1991); nine compiled volumes total. Concluding its Jump serialization in 1995, *Gunnm* is the series which introduced Kishiro's talent to the wider world. *DOMESTIC RELEASE TITLE:* ***Battle Angel Alita*** (Viz Comics)

Gunnm Gaiden ("'Gunnm' Side-Story")
銃夢外伝

Spin-off manga series currently being serialized in Shueisha's Ultra Jump (1997~), the magazine itself is a spin-off of sister Shueisha manga mag Young Jump. *CURRENTLY IMPORT ONLY*

Haisha ("Ashen One")
灰者

Serialized in Shueisha's Ultra Jump (1995-96); no compiled volumes available as of press time. *CURRENTLY IMPORT ONLY*

ANIME アニメ

Even more so than *Oh My Goddess!*'s Kosuke Fujishima, Kishiro is still at the beginning of his career. Amidst all the rumors which circulate around the creation of a live-action *Gunnm/Battle Angel Alita* movie, a second OAV story—one which would hopefully animate the violent, intense world of Motorball—has been rumored even longer. Although we were unable to officially confirm or deny the rumor with the series' Japanese production staff, inside sources say things look good....

Gunnm
銃夢

Original Story
Two-volume OAV series (1993) which more or less retells an early chunk of the manga story, while also adding some animation-only characters. Note to collectors: The two OAVs are available both in Japan and in the U.S. on a single VHS cassette. *DOMESTIC RELEASE TITLE:* ***Battle Angel*** (A.D. Vision)

Key

- Japanese comics or "manga" series; may or may not be available in foreign-language (i.e., English) version
- TV series broadcast on-air in Japan. Note that, in the U.S., Japanese TV series are both broadcast on-air (*Ronin Warriors*) and released on home video (*Ranma 1/2*). Others (*Sailor Moon, Dragon Ball*) are available both in broadcast and home video versions
- Direct-to-home-video series; may also include compilations of TV episodes released to home video market
- Theatrical feature; may or may not receive equivalent theatrical release for U.S. version

Yoshiki Takaya

Interviewed by Takashi Oshiguchi (1994)

No doubt about it, it was exactly the sort of live-action TV shows which aired in English in syndicated markets across the U.S. in the 1960s and '70s which made *Guyver* creator Yoshiki Takaya the man he is today.

Debuting professionally at the age of twenty-four, Takaya made his mark in 1985 when he published *Guyver* in the premiere issue of Tokuma's monthly manga magazine SHÔNEN CAPTAIN. Despite virtually no professional training (he dropped out of college to work as an assistant for Japanese science fiction/fantasy artist Yuichi Mochizuki at the age of twenty-two), *Guyver* found a ready audience among fans of dark fantasy with its uniquely organic designs and original storyline. The fact that the series was still being published ten years later says a lot about the strength of its popularity.

Takaya says that it was his involvement in a manga *kenkyûkai* or "study group" during college which first started him down the road to his current position in the industry. Soon realizing that the focus of the group was not drawing manga as he had first thought but reading and discussion, it wasn't long before Takaya and several other members of the group left to work on a fanzine called PEN TOUCH. Founded by horror/humor comics creator Ochazuke Nori, Takaya still recalls the fanzine with fondness and speaks of the pseudonymous Nori ("nori" is a type of edible seaweed, and "ochazuke" is rice with tea poured over it, which together makes a popular after-drinking snack) as a man who was "immensely helpful" during the early days of Takaya's career as a manga artist.

When PEN TOUCH eventually folded, almost all of its members went into careers as professional manga artists. "Nori and I still regret the demise of that fanzine," says Takaya with a smile. "The kind of stories that Nori was drawing weren't what you'd call 'popular.' Our fanzine was the only place where he could create his own ideal manga. As for me, I was the group's bad boy—I contributed hardly anything in those days. I think I only did a single eight-page story."

Takaya recalls that over forty live-action TV hero shows crowded the airwaves during the '70s in Japan. Shows by studios such as Tsuburaya and P Production were in their heyday, and Takaya found himself developing an interest which would last well into his adult years. However, the advent of diminishing oil supplies and the specter of a gloomy economy, together with the decline in their popularity among viewers, caused several live-action studios to begin cutting back on the shows Takaya loved. Before he knew it, it was the '80s and the decade had become dark, rather than halcyon, days for live-action as a genre.

"All the live-action shows were disappearing, just like the tides," Takaya says. "To me, it felt as though I was being deprived of something cool just as I was getting into it." Frustrated into action, young Takaya began to create his own adventures on paper. By imitating the formulas of the live-action shows he loved, Takaya's own dynamic, action-oriented manga style was born.

Since the publication of *Guyver* and the start of his professional career, Takaya has never forgotten the influence of those live-action shows, especially those created by P Production. Markedly different from many other live-action production houses of its day, Takaya describes P Production as the first to depict internal strife in the enemy camp, rather than a united front of evildoers. He points to their characterizations—which explored the nature of heroism in a bold and thoughtful way—as one of the studio's most outstanding virtues.

"P Production was always *honest*," Takaya says. "They were never afraid to show the ugliness of people who were weak and selfish." With heroes who displayed such "an amazing voracity" to stay alive, and villains who acted from the strength of their own convictions rather than some hackneyed formula, it's little wonder that a young boy such as Takaya would find himself knee-deep in a life-long love of the genre.

"The masked hero stories actually had a *lot* of deep human drama," Takaya says with conviction, "despite the fact that they were aimed at a younger audience. The masked heroes were really loners, and I liked the fact that P Production heroes weren't invincible. They had human weaknesses, and yet they would somehow manage to overcome them in the end. The requirements of a hero were so clearly spelled out in these shows…they proved that it was okay to have weak points as a human being.

"There was pathos in those shows," Takaya continues. "And you know, that was good stuff."

interview

ANIMERICA: Your love of the live-action/masked hero genre is well known. What is it exactly about these shows that appeals to you?

TAKAYA: Those masked hero stories had some deep human drama—*Lion-Maru the Dark Clouds* and *Tiger Seven*, for example. *The Return of Ultraman* and *Ultra Seven* had those aspects, too. I was drawn to that kind of drama. Those masked-hero shows were really children's shows, but there was really a lot of human drama to be found in them.

ANIMERICA: There was psychological strife behind the mask.

TAKAYA: Yes, exactly.

ANIMERICA: They would fight, and victory would be secured, but there would always be another element, an element of compassion. Like how Tiger Seven is handicapped throughout the story and has to die in the end.

TAKAYA: Right. That script was incredibly well-written, although it doesn't seem to be getting the recognition it deserves. [LAUGHS] Those who really like pathos in their live-action wouldn't have it any other way.

ANIMERICA: Do you think so? P Production's work was different from the other live-action shows….

TAKAYA: Yes, it was. You wouldn't believe how great an influence P Production has had on me. And not only its

Bio-Booster Armor Guyver

heroes—*all* of the P Production characters were just so *real*. Take *Lion-Maru*, for example. Everywhere Lion-Maru goes, the villagers are only thinking about their own safety and refuse to get involved. They betray Lion-Maru without a second thought. They're weak people—that's the only way they can stay alive.

ANIMERICA: What were your favorite shows when you were growing up?

TAKAYA: After the first *Lion-Maru* TV series, I like *Dark Clouds* the best. *Lion-Maru the Dark Clouds* is coming out on laser disc, you know. Ah, I'm just so *glad* to be alive! [LAUGHS]

ANIMERICA: How do you feel about the animated productions of your works? The six-volume *Guyver* video series was recently released in the U.S. and seems to be popular with English-speaking fans.

TAKAYA: Well, the director for the *Guyver* OAV series is also the president of its production company, Visual 80. And Koichi Ishiguro was also the main director of *Lion-Maru the Dark Clouds*. The producers asked me if I had any specific requests for a director when it looked like *Guyver* was going to be animated. I told them that I wanted Ishiguro to direct. At that time, he hadn't directed for a while, but he agreed to come back specifically for this project.

ANIMERICA: That must have been a real thrill for you.

TAKAYA: Oh, yes. Thanks to his direction, even when I watch the English versions of the OAV series, it's very easy for me to follow even though I don't speak the language.

Guyver doesn't fight for some abstract idea like "justice"—Guyver fights because his life is in danger, or because someone close to him is in danger.

Ishiguro's work on this project is just so *solid*—I'm certain that virtually anyone could follow this series through the images alone. Also, his concepts as a director happen to be very close to mine. I guess that's natural, considering how much influence *his* work has had on *my* work. [LAUGHS]

ANIMERICA: How did you get the idea for the Guyver's combat suit? It's not really like a mask....

TAKAYA: ...At first, I was thinking of developing my ideas about heroism with a fairly standard combat-suit story. That was around the time SHÔNEN CAPTAIN monthly manga magazine was starting up. The editor asked if I could come up with something a little more grotesque. I was happy with the initial designs I'd drafted for the combat suit, but even I was wondering if it might not be a little too close to combat suits that readers had seen before, in other series. So I took my editor's suggestions to heart.

ANIMERICA: What sort of ideas or concepts did you use when designing that initial combat suit?

TAKAYA: The theatrical version of *Harmagedon* was popular back then, and the cyborg warrior Vega had left a strong impression on me. So my first idea was based along those lines, together with the idea of a human getting an instant-cyborg operation by putting on the combat suit. There was a bit of a mecha influence there. My editor's suggestion to "make it more grotesque" made me realize that I could make the suit biological. That's how my initial idea of a combat suit was replaced by the idea of a dangerous super-powered being, like something from *Alien*. This is where the idea of "bio-booster armor" came from. Instead of wearing a safe and protective suit, the human is wearing this dangerous alien *thing*, and death is never very far away.

ANIMERICA: Make one mistake, and....

TAKAYA: You got it.

ANIMERICA: It wasn't just the hero of your story that was in danger—I used to read your series back when it was first serialized, and it seemed at the time that the story itself was only one wrong step away from cancellation.

TAKAYA: [LAUGHS] Well, it was initially a one-year deal—they gave me six chapters. They said they'd give me just enough pages for one graphic novel volume and a year to do whatever I wanted, but then I'd have to listen to what they said after that. That's how they lure new writers and artists into the business, after all. [LAUGHS]

ANIMERICA: So when did your editor get the idea to make it grotesque?

TAKAYA: Well, he wasn't all that familiar with the genre at the time. Odds are he just said it on a whim. When I visited his offices with the designs for the Guyver and the storyboards for the first chapter, he said, "This looks fine." It was my current editor who told me this story. He says that after I left the office, my former editor glanced at the material I'd handed him and started worrying if he'd given me the wrong idea, that I'd make it *too* grotesque. My current editor said to him, "It's probably all right." [LAUGHS] That's how these things get started, you know.

ANIMERICA: Considering the times when it came out, the design of the Guyver is very detailed, very complex. There were so many *lines*.

TAKAYA: That's right. I actually wanted to reduce the number of lines, but they just kept on increasing. The biological part is now screentone, but in the beginning, it was all lines. At the time I told myself that I could handle it, keep up with the demands of drawing that complex suit, but I was wrong. I *couldn't* handle it. [LAUGHS] No matter how hard I tried, I never could keep up with my workload. And the editorial department—who knew next to nothing about actual drawing—kept saying, "The Guyver looks too plain. Give him more detail." Where on Earth was I going to add anything to that drawing!? [LAUGHS]

ANIMERICA: Let's talk about the Guyver itself. The control medal at the forehead is the key to the entire suit, isn't it.

TAKAYA: Yes.

ANIMERICA: Even if the main body was destroyed, the control medal could survive.

TAKAYA: You got it. Design-wise, the control medal strongly reminds me of the metallic heroes of old. I still feel it looks really good when the metal parts shine. One thing I was careful about when designing my hero, though—a lot of the old heroes had big mouths and fangs, and I felt that if I went in that direction, I'd be walking into a cliché. Those old heroes—they *bite*. All those power-types end up biting. That's not the case with Guyver, though. His appearance is only for combat, so the Guyver has no need for a mouth. It's not like he has to *eat*, and since he doesn't have a mouth, he doesn't need fangs, either. All those fanged-type heroes have been done to death, anyway. As an organism, the Guyver is a very delicately balanced thing. It's a dangerous alien organism controlled by a single metal control device. I had to consider his reason for fighting. Guyver doesn't fight for some abstract idea like "justice"—Guyver fights because his life is in danger, or because someone close to him is in danger. I wanted him to have a compelling reason to fight, more than other heroes had. Guyver can't just run away from things—he's got (his friends) Tetsuro and Mizuki to worry about. So he has to keep on fighting.

ANIMERICA: What did you think of the first live-action *Guyver* movie?

TAKAYA: We-e-e-l-l-l, I suppose I could say it was an *ambitious* movie. For example, it had its serious parts, like the original manga. In the movie, the FBI agent Max infiltrates the enemy base alone, but then he gets turned into a Zoanoid and dies a tragic death. This is exactly what happened to the father of the main character in the manga. So I could say that the tragic element from the manga was picked up in the movie. But then there are these comedic touches which *aren't* in the original manga, such as the fight with the giant monsters and all that stuff. Everything seemed to be all jumbled together…I think that perhaps the filmmakers were a bit *too* ambitious.

Bio-Booster Armor Guyver

ANIMERICA: The sequel is in production now. I understand that *Guyver: Dark Hero* is going to be much more serious.

TAKAYA: Yes. It's a very serious story, although the flow will still be a little different from the manga.

ANIMERICA: Is this a continuation of the story from the first film?

TAKAYA: Well, we call it a sequel, but the cast is completely different. People watching it will recognize it as a follow-up to the first film, but it's definitely a different sort of experience. It'll probably be easier to understand what the *Guyver* is all about if you see the first film beforehand, but then again, it may not make any difference. This second film is going to be a very serious, rather heavy story.

ANIMERICA: Oh, but they don't forget the action, do they?

How can you have live-action without any catharsis?

TAKAYA: Oh, there's catharsis, all right. It's pretty...well, *good*. [LAUGHS] Obviously I'm very interested myself in seeing how well it will turn out.

ANIMERICA: What do you think of the director, Steve Wang?

TAKAYA: Steve Wang's sensibilities are very close to mine. He grew up watching P Production's *Spectreman*, you know...it got him into this industry. He told me it was broadcast on TV in the U.S. on a show called "Captain Something-or-Other" [Captain Cosmic, *broadcast in the San Francisco Bay Area on KTVU—Ed.*]. He's a creator himself, so he was able to watch a cheap production like that and see beyond to what the producers were trying to say. When I ask him what he likes or knows, he knows he can say the names of shows like *Kikaider* or *Spectreman* to me without embarrassment. He's very fond of transforming heroes. When it comes to the monster-makers in the American special effects industry, all the creative cinematographers and directors tend to lean toward either the occult, or the...well, I guess you could say *freak* stuff. That seems to be the mainstream. Steve Wang is different...he sees the monster as a healthy body, not a freak or mutation, but as a balanced being who just happens to look the way he does. Of course, there are freaky types, too, but they're the exception, not the rule. His feelings on this are one of the reasons I feel artistically close to him as a creator.

Bio-Booster Armor Guyver

ANIMERICA: You're credited with "creative control" on the upcoming film. What did your role really entail?

TAKAYA: Well, Steve Wang came to Japan several times before production began. He showed me the script, and I gave him my opinions on it. If there was something there I didn't understand, I'd ask. I'd tell him to explain to me why a certain sequence was inserted, and if there were things I couldn't agree with, I'd ask for changes. In the end, he left with the script he'd brought mostly intact. This movie is based on his script, so I thought it would be best to leave it all up to him on this one. And considering the cultural differences between Japan and the U.S., I thought that it would perhaps be safer for him to have more control.

ANIMERICA: So you came to an understanding.

TAKAYA: Yes. He loves and respects the *Guyver* manga, and I knew he wouldn't turn the movie into something completely different. From what I've seen, the movie is very strongly permeated with the feel of the original manga. By including more of Steve's ideas on heroism into the film, I decided that it would turn out to be a better movie. It wouldn't be too much fun if all I ever did was intervene from the sidelines and end up turning the movie into something dull. I also realized that the ending of the movie doesn't have to follow the manga exactly. After all, unlike the manga, the movie takes place in the U.S.

ANIMERICA: That's interesting, because the OAV series was produced in Japan, and the live-action films have been produced in the U.S. I wonder if we'll see another live-action *Guyver* movie created in Japan someday...?

TAKAYA: That's something I'd very much like to work on.

ANIMERICA: Would you want to direct this "live-action *Guyver*" yourself?

TAKAYA: Direct it? I don't think I can direct. [LAUGHS] I wouldn't be any good as a director. I'd try too much to keep everyone happy.

ANIMERICA: Do you think it would it be the same with animation? Another *Guyver* OAV series, perhaps?

TAKAYA: I'd say that particular job should be left up to the pros. If a new series were to be made in Japan for a Japanese audience, I'd probably want to have some involvement in it. But it's really the collective efforts of the staff that makes an animated feature, not the original manga. For example, there have been two different animated *Guyver* series produced so far, and I was involved in both of them, completely changing designs and adding finishes to the script. Ultimately, though, it's the director's touches which really shine. And it's no good for the morale of a staff to have the original creator butting in all the time. I would have to think about all these things before I got involved in another animated series.

ANIMERICA: Today's Japanese animation *has* improved in technical quality...except maybe when it comes to the directing.

TAKAYA: Superb direction is very rare, unfortunately.

ANIMERICA: ...Especially when it comes to an OAV series. If it's a six-volume series, there needs to be a coherent story structure for all six volumes—a kind of series composition. The individual episodes need to fit into the larger story structure of the series as a whole. This wasn't always true in the *Guyver* OAV series, from what I understand.

TAKAYA: Well, yes. The manga series had no definite end—it's still going, even now—and it was difficult for the animators to create an ongoing story without some idea of where they were headed. When you consider the additional story elements which inevitably get inserted into an animated version of an original manga story, it was especially hard for the animators to keep the story structure coherent. They also had to worry about staying faithful to the original manga so that they wouldn't alienate the readers of the manga. As for the composition of the animated story...well, I don't think it would be possible to make a good video without frequent and intimate communication between the animators and the original creator. I wouldn't hesitate to get involved in that particular end of the animation.

ANIMERICA: You wouldn't think of writing it yourself...?

TAKAYA: Actually, I *did* write some parts of it. [LAUGHS]

ANIMERICA: How was it?

TAKAYA: It was just like scripting the manga. I tend to write my stories logically, rather than intuitively. At every point along the way I'm stopping and asking myself if the next line is necessary to the story. This process of steps is the same for both manga and screenplays.

ANIMERICA: Would you say the main difference is that, in animation, storyboards come first and only *then* is the script written...?

TAKAYA: Yes. The point between the script and the actual animation production is where the director comes in. I'm a manga artist, and there's no reason I would know much about things such as dialogue length, is there? I wouldn't have a reason to know much about timing, or what sort of things can be expressed through movement. That's why, once the overall shape is formed, the rest has to be left to others. It wouldn't be very interesting if the animation was made with only my input, after all. I'm not a professional animator. A pro's job should be left to the pros.

ANIMERICA: We've talked about how much the live-action shows have influenced your work. Isn't it nice to know that your work is influencing others, too? Steve Wang was influenced by live-action shows, and now he's in the role of director.

TAKAYA: I guess we all influence each other.

ANIMERICA: Do you have any hobbies? Do you build (model) resin kits?

TAKAYA: I'm not good at things that require that much effort. I'm the type who just assembles the parts and plays with the thing. I don't like to paint it. All the *Guyver* kits come pre-colored, right? The people who buy those kits are lucky. [LAUGHS] There was a time when I got into resin kits a little, but they take so much time and I'm just so lazy that not very many of them ever saw completion. I collect videos and laser discs, instead.

ANIMERICA: The stuff from the good ol' days, right?

TAKAYA: Right, right. I think videos are a real treasure. In those days, you watched your favorite shows with all your attention because chances were you'd never again be able to see it. What a *luxury* it is to be able to own those shows on videotape…! I don't think there's *anything* that can beat it.

afterword

As discussed in this interview, Yoshiki Takaya's *Guyver* had already moved from manga to anime to yet another step that most animation and/or manga projects never reach, no matter how popular—live-action. But since *Guyver* had its roots in Takaya's love of costumed live-action, to go the extra step of adapting the story to suited heroes—à la America's popular *Mighty Morphin Power Rangers*—seemed natural, even inevitable.

In the first *Guyver* live-action film, released in 1992, co-directors Screaming Mad George and Steve Wang—Wang already well-known among fans of science fiction, fantasy and horror for his design of the suit from the 1987 film *Predator*—brilliantly realized the physical appearances of the Guyver and his opponents, the monstrous Zoanoids, but in terms of story, they had to deal with more intervention from their own producers than they had expected.

In the end, the result was more comedic than dramatic, and even with the involvement of *Star Wars*' Mark Hamill as a cop looking into the mystery of the Guyver, the film was roundly subject to the slings and arrows of outraged critics. Nonetheless, Wang and George's attempted ode to one of the manga and anime world's most interesting mighty morphin' power heroes set new standards in terms of production design and special effects, and gained enough fans to secure financing for a second movie.

Released direct-to-video in 1995, *Guyver: Dark Hero*, which Wang directed solo, is a much darker and more serious film, which retains Takaya's image of the Guyver as something *dangerous*. Frequently broadcast on cable television, *Guyver: Dark Hero* is one of the more visible offshoots of manga and anime and provides a counterpoint to the brightly colored heroes of the more familiar "rangers."

Yoshiki Takaya
Select Bibliography & Filmography

Key

Japanese comics or "manga" series; may or may not be available in foreign-language (i.e., English) version

TV series broadcast on-air in Japan. Note that, in the U.S., Japanese TV series are both broadcast on-air (*Ronin Warriors*) and released on home video (*Ranma 1/2*). Others (*Sailor Moon, Dragon Ball*) are available both in broadcast and home video versions

Direct-to-home-video series; may also include compilations of TV episodes released to home video market

Theatrical feature; may or may not receive equivalent theatrical release for U.S. version

MANGA 漫画

Not everyone can be a manga wunderkind—unlike the multi-publishing Takahashi's and Ikegami's of the manga world, Yoshiki Takaya has been knee-deep the last eleven years or so in one manga series and one manga series only. That's not necessarily a bad thing, however, as this "one" series of Takaya's has gone on not only to produce fifteen compiled manga volumes to date, but also two separate OAV series, an animated theatrical feature, and two (count 'em, two) live-action Hollywood versions. Plus, let's not forget that the guy's young yet.

Kyôshoku Sôkô Guyver ("Bio-Booster Armor Guyver")
強殖装甲ガイバー

Serialized in publisher Tokuma Shoten's Shônen Captain manga anthology (1986); currently fifteen compiled volumes total. In the summer of '96, an info-packed data book, *Bio-Boosted Armor Guyver Visual Data Files*, was published by Tokuma containing extensive background information on the characters, Zoanoids, villains, and Guyver units found in the series. Note also that three novels based on Takaya's *Guyver* are available: two from Tokuma Shoten's "AM Bunko" series—*Risker no Chôsen* ("Risker's Challenge") and *Dai-San no Kage* ("The Third Shadow")—as well one from the "Animage Bunko" series, *Kyôshoku Sôkô Guyver: Kiei no Kioku* ("The Shadow-Demon's Memory"), as written by Yuji Hayami. *DOMESTIC RELEASE TITLE:* ***Bio-Booster Armor Guyver*** (Viz Comics)

ANIME アニメ

Animated and live-action features based on Takaya's manga series of the same name. Steve Wang, director of *Guyver 2: Dark Hero*, is a long-time fan of both Takaya's work and "monster heroes" in general, and really shows his understanding of the genre in both the live-action *Guyver* films in which he's been involved.

Kyôshoku Sôkô Guyver
強殖装甲ガイバー

Original Story
45-minute theatrical feature (1986); compilation or "digest" version of the first two volumes of Takaya's multi-volume manga series of the same name. A different character designer (among other things) gives this one-shot a completely different feel from either of the two OAV series. Released in its U.S. version on home video, and not theatrically, as it was in Japan. *DOMESTIC RELEASE TITLE:* ***Guyver: Out of Control*** (Dark Image Entertainment)

Kyôshoku Sôkô Guyver
強殖装甲ガイバー

Original Story / Editorial Supervision
Six-volume OAV series (1989-90); based on the Takaya manga of the same name. Japanese high schooler Sho Fukamachi, en route home from school one day, discovers a mysterious unit with which he transforms into the hyper-powered biological combat organism known as "the Guyver." Combined with second OAV series (see below) for purposes of domestic release. *DOMESTIC RELEASE TITLE:* ***The Guyver*** (Manga Entertainment)

Kyôshoku Sôkô Guyver: Act II
強殖装甲ガイバー：ACT II

Original Story
Three-volume OAV series (1991); two OAV episodes included on each 55-60 minute tape. As with the first, 1989 OAV series, episodes from this second OAV series were combined with episodes from the first series for purposes of domestic release. *DOMESTIC RELEASE TITLE:* ***The Guyver*** (Manga Entertainment)

The Guyver

Original Story
92-minute live-action theatrical feature (1992); U.S.-Japan co-production co-directed by Steve Wang and Screaming Mad George and starring Mark Hamill. Wang, of *Predator* fame, gets credit for designing the Guyver itself. Rated PG-13. (New Line Home Video)

Guyver 2: Dark Hero

Original Story
127-minute live-action theatrical feature (1994); directed by Steve Wang. Darker story (written by Wang) comes closer to creator Takaya's original vision. Rated R. (New Line Home Video)

Kosuke Fujishima

Interviewed by Junco Ito (1994)

Keiichi from *Oh My Goddess!*

"Ever get the urge to chop off your drawing fingers?" asks American artist Bruce Lewis when considering the work of Kosuke Fujishima. "I mean it. Ever feel ready to throw in the artistic towel, pick up a meat cleaver, and let fly? 'Won't—' *CHOP!* 'be—' *CHOP!* 'needing—' *CHOP!* 'these—' *CHOP!* 'any—' *CHOP!* '—more!'"

Not to say that other people have this reaction to Kosuke Fujishima's work—on the contrary, Fujishima usually inspires a sense of awe and even adoration for his characters, especially for the (literally) heavenly goddesses of the aptly named *Aa! Megami-Sama*, which, for American audiences, translates to *Oh My Goddess!* (breathless Valley-Girl voice off).

Fujishima's popularity in America owes quite a bit to this charming five-volume OAV series, as adapted from his original manga of the same name. The saga of a young man who becomes the consort of an honest-to-goodness goddess, *Oh My Goddess!* can be seen in some ways as the natural offshoot of one of the most popular of the now well-established "magical girlfriend" genre, Rumiko Takahashi's *Urusei Yatsura*. In the case of *Urusei Yatsura*, the girl in question is a powerful, capricious alien with what might seem like magical powers—Takahashi's original concept for the character having been based on a type of Japanese demon. *Oh My Goddess!* adds the twist of making the "magical girl" sweet and benevolent, as well as all-powerful—a true fantasy goddess. When asked about his influences as a creator, Fujishima lists such diverse stylists as Masamune Shirow (*Appleseed*, *Orion*) and artist Hirohiko Araki (*Baoh*, *Jo Jo's Bizarre Adventures*). He says that he also finds interest in *Batman* and Jean Giraud Moebius, but little of the more hard-edged style of these artists shows in Fujishima's work—even detailed machinery such as cars and motorbikes are rendered in his own distinctive, clean-lined style.

After graduation from high school in Tokyo in the early '80s, Fujishima worked as assistant to manga artist Tatsuya Egawa (*Be Free!*, *Golden Boy*, *Magical Tarurûto-kun*), well-known for his own fluid and lyrical depictions of the female form. Fujishima earned his stripes on the production staff of the film version of Egawa's manga *Be Free!* during its pre-production stage.

In an interview published last July in Italy's MAGAZINE KAPPA, Fujishima told interviewer Rie Zushi, "Over the course of my work (with Egawa's studio), I began taking design seriously for the first time...I also learned a lot about the rudiments of cinematography there." According to Fujishima, it was this real-world experience that enabled him to begin work on his first original stories.

Fujishima did so and in 1986, Kodansha's manga magazine COMIC MORNING PARTY began serializing his debut work *Taiho Shichau zo!* ("You're Under Arrest!"), detailing the offbeat adventures of Natsumi and Miyuki, two mismatched Tokyo female cops with a knack for getting in and out of oddball situations. Natsumi, the wilder of the two, is a strong, hot-tempered girl with a pageboy haircut, while her partner Miyuki is demure and mild-mannered, with longer hair and a more gentle disposition.

Both, however, share in a certain mechanical fetish for cars and motorcycles, and much of the story takes place as they blast around the streets of Shinjuku in their amazing assortment of souped-up vehicles, including a Caterham Super 7, a Nissan Fairlady 240ZG, a Suzuki R2DX, a Toyota S800, a Suzuki GSXR750 touring bike, plus a wide array of scooters, motorbikes, jet skis and motorized skateboards, not to mention their beloved patrol car, a highly modified superstock Honda Today.

Natsumi and Miyuki employ these and many more vehicles in their battle against such enemies of society as lecherous grade-school skirt-chasers (and the grade-school girl-superhero squad that rises to oppose them!), out-of-control paint gun warriors, the menace of the panty-shot breast-cam perverts, and last but not least, their archenemy "Strikeman," a bizarre but good-natured troublemaker clad in punk feathers and a baseball uniform whose fondest wish is to strike out Natsumi with his mean fastball. Of course, Natsumi resignedly blasts his every pitch into orbit...but for Strikeman, there's always next year. Add to this mixture other characters such as the girls' best friend on the force, a stunning brunette with curly hair and dreamy eyes who also happens to be a man, and you've got one very off-the-wall cast.

This combination of cute girls, weird characters and cool gadgetry, all lovingly drawn with Fujishima's sure hand, led to wild success. *You're Under Arrest!* was an immediate hit with readers, attracting a lot of attention to the talented newcomer and eventually running to seven full volumes of collected stories under Kodansha's "Party KC" imprint.

After *You're Under Arrest!*, Fujishima turned his talents to his new manga, *Oh My Goddess!*, which began running in Kodansha's more adult-oriented monthly COMIC AFTERNOON manga magazine in late 1989. A light-hearted fantasy romp drawn from Fujishima's unique personal mythology, *Oh My Goddess!* is the story of young Keiichi: student, motorcycle nut, and freeloader par excellence, who accidentally phones up the spirit world one night from his all-male dorm and ends up summoning an actual goddess instead of the takeout he was trying for.

The goddess, a gorgeous 19-year-old girl (of course), is so grateful for the unintentional diversion Keiichi provides that she grants him one wish...anything he wants! It only takes Keiichi a moment to flip through the options—fame, fortune, and females. But the wish he asks for instead is simply that the goddess stay with him. And so Belldandy, this lovely demure deity from beyond, decides to stay on Earth, right by Keiichi's side. This decision lands the two out the dorm's door after an older student decides to enforce the "males-only" rule, and from that moment on, the two's adventures begin in earnest. Complicating matters are sweet, 13-year-old sister Skuld and white-hot 22-year-old sister Urd (both goddesses in their own right), not to mention Belldandy's archrival, the she-devil "Mara."

You're Under Arrest!

The popularity of *Oh My Goddess!* in manga form made it a natural for animation, and the premiere episode of a five-volume *Oh My Goddess!* OAV series appeared on video shelves in 1993, directed by Hiroaki Goda and featuring character designs by Hidenori Matsubara. The *Oh My Goddess!* animation quickly gained popularity in both Japan and America, and at the time of this interview, the animated series had just been released in America. At the time, a great point of controversy for American fans of the series who'd been following the Japanese work centered around the adjustment of the series name from the Japanese *Aa! Megami-sama* ("Ah! My Goddess") to the more English-colloquial *Oh My Goddess!* Nevertheless, years after the name-change furor has died down, anime fans are left with a series that stays true to its own personal mythology, no matter what it's called.

I think the function of animation is served best when a work with a flavor different from the original comic emerges, even though both the animation and the comic share the same universe.

interview

ANIMERICA: What made you decide to become a manga artist? Did you start as an assistant to anyone?

FUJISHIMA: I started because I love manga—or rather, I liked to draw and create stories. Actually, I think that manga was just the most familiar type of art to me, easily accessible to study and create. That may be closer to the truth. I think I could have gotten into animation just as easily. I was an assistant to Tatsuya Egawa (*Golden Boy, Magical Tarurûto-kun*) for about a year and a half.

ANIMERICA: What was your debut work?

FUJISHIMA: When Mr. Egawa's *Be Free!* manga was going to be made into a live-action movie, I drew the "making of" movie story, called *Making Be Free!!* That was actually my debut work. Essentially, though, *Taiho Shichau zo!* was my first original work.

ANIMERICA: What's the good part of being a manga artist? And what's the not-so-good part?

FUJISHIMA: I can draw what I want to express and have that seen by many people. I've become what I most wanted to be, and there's nothing happier than that. On the other hand, the tough part about being a pro is that I have to go on doing it whether I feel like it or not. You can't always do what you want to do when you want to do it. Also, this might not be as important as other reasons but...well, manga artists don't have to commute to work. [LAUGHS]

ANIMERICA: If you hadn't become a manga artist, what do you think you might have become?

FUJISHIMA: I think I *still* would have become an artist. I don't think I could have gotten away from the fields of design and art. At this point, I can't think of anything else I would have done except become a manga artist.

ANIMERICA: In the case of *Oh My Goddess!*, from where did the inspiration come?

FUJISHIMA: I thought it might be an interesting idea if being a goddess was a job, an occupation. I based it on Norse mythology, which is relatively unknown in Japan.

ANIMERICA: Do you have any spelling preferences for rendering the names of the goddesses in English? I understand that, in the United States, there's been some confusion.... [*This interview took place in Japan.—Ed.*]

FUJISHIMA: Well, Belldandy is spelled with a "B," even though the proper spelling in the actual Norse mythology is "Verdandi." Then there's Urd and Skuld; the spelling of those two names are unchanged [*in Scandinavian mythology, the Norns are the goddesses of fate, with Urd being the goddess of the past, Verdandi the goddess of the present, and Skuld the goddess of the future—Ed.*].

ANIMERICA: Where do you stand on the animated version of *Oh My Goddess!*? What do you think of the quality of the OAV series?

FUJISHIMA: Well, it's based on my drawings, of course, so there are always going to be suggestions I could make as the author to improve it, to create new ideas, and to point out exactly where the animation deviates from my original ideas. But animation is the product of the animators, after all, so I just keep quiet so long as their creative intentions are obvious. Even if it's just a *little* different from the manga...well, let's just say that if the anime is going to end up being exactly the same as the manga, there's no point in animating it. I think the function of animation is best served when a work with a flavor different from the original comic emerges, even though both the animation and the comic share the same universe. Quality-wise, I think *Oh My Goddess!*'s animation is considerably high. I worked on the storyboards for parts of the opening and parts of the ending for the third OAV, so I feel as though the anime is another part of me.

Oh My Goddess!

ANIMERICA: It's looking like the English versions of both the animation and the manga are going to be released soon. Do you have any thoughts on your work being seen in the U.S.?

FUJISHIMA: I don't know how well they'll be received, but I hope that the fans will support them. I never intended to create the story for an international audience, so I'm curious to see how people overseas will perceive it.

ANIMERICA: The number of anime and manga fans overseas is on the rise. Does this come as a surprise to you?

FUJISHIMA: The development of Japanese anime and manga is itself unique, and there are quite a few works of high-quality, so I'd like to see them get greater circulation overseas. It would be nice if my works were included among them.

ANIMERICA: When the U.S. company releasing the animation announced their intention to call it "Oh My Goddess!" rather than "Ah! My Goddess," as had been printed in the manga all these years, a great debate started among fans over what the title should be. Which one best reflects your intentions, "Ah!" or "Oh!"...?

FUJISHIMA: In terms of nuance, I think "Oh!" probably comes closer. However it ends up, I think it should be

You're Under Arrest!

© Kosuke Fujishima/Kodansha, Ltd.

rendered to make better sense in the language of the target country.

ANIMERICA: That's what usually has to happen when titles are brought over to another language. Kishiro's *Gunnm*, for example, became *Battle Angel Alita* in its English version. What about your own works? Do you have a preference one way or the other? How would you feel if the comic and animated versions came out with different titles overseas?

FUJISHIMA: If it's something that fits well in that language, I wouldn't complain. After all, there are movie titles that work much better once they're changed...although there are also those that *don't* work. [LAUGHS] I would like to see that the titles of the comics and the animation stay consistent, however.

ANIMERICA: Since we're already on the general topic...how do you feel about flopped artwork? It seems as though this has become the standard for publication of manga in America.

FUJISHIMA: It's painful. I'm not *that* skilled an artist, and so when the artwork is reversed, all the shortcomings in my drawings become obvious. There's also an artistic consideration. Some panels lose the balance of their composition when they're flopped. If it were possible, I would prefer for everyone to be able to see the original version, the way I intended my artwork to be seen in the first place.

ANIMERICA: Is there anything in particular about the American fans of both your animated and manga work that you would like to know?

FUJISHIMA: Actually, I'd like to know to what aspects of my work American fans are attracted. I'm sure they must have a different perspective than Japanese fans. Cultural differences, most likely.

ANIMERICA: Let's talk a little more about the *Oh My*

Goddess! series. Which goddess is your favorite? Are there any aspects of their character, style or fashion of which you are particularly fond?

FUJISHIMA: I don't really have a favorite, but...well, Urd is always outspoken and has more mature sensibilities, so I like her.

An artist basically draws manga to communicate an idea to others. The idea won't be communicated if the work is understandable only to its creator.... I think the meaning of manga is to have it understood by as many people as possible.

ANIMERICA: Speaking of fashion, your characters are always so beautifully dressed.... Where do you get the ideas for the fashions in your comics?

FUJISHIMA: I study fashion a lot. Often, I find surprises in children's clothes. I'm always ready for a chance to study children's and women's clothes at department stores.

ANIMERICA: As a manga artist, what are your work habits like? Do you work every day of the month? Are you a morning person? A night person...?

FUJISHIMA: I work almost every day, and I'm usually a night person. I don't pull that many all-nighters, however. I find that my drawing skills start going down the drain if I pull too many of those. [LAUGHS] I try to leave a little free time in my schedule when I can help it....

ANIMERICA: How many assistants do you have?

FUJISHIMA: Six.

ANIMERICA: Do you ever have times when being a professional manga artist seems like more trouble than it's worth, times when you feel discouraged?

FUJISHIMA: When I can't think up a story. When I can't draw the way I want to.

ANIMERICA: And what do you do to comfort yourself?

FUJISHIMA: I talk on the phone with friends. Talking to someone in the same business is best. When I see others going through the same thing, I'm comforted that I'm not alone, and I find courage in that.

ANIMERICA: Do you have any advice for fans who want to draw their own manga?

FUJISHIMA: Everyone's goals are different, so I can't make a blanket comment, but an artist basically draws manga to communicate an idea to others. The idea won't be communicated if the work is understandable only to its creator. It just won't work. I think the meaning of manga is to have it understood by as many people as possible.

ANIMERICA: It won't surprise you to hear that there are several publications devoted to comics journalism in America. Do you have your own "theory of manga"?

FUJISHIMA: As far as a theory goes, I guess I've already said it. To be successful, manga needs to be understood by as many people as possible. I have a certain interest in the nature of comics journalism, but I don't have a particular theory other than what I've already expressed.

ANIMERICA: In Japan, manga with highly violent and sexual content is often the target of criticism. Your manga doesn't come under this sort of scrutiny, however, perhaps because the stories are more "pure" and tend to revolve around adolescents. What are your thoughts on sex and violence in manga?

FUJISHIMA: One way of looking at it is that I haven't drawn any explicit sex and violence because it hasn't been necessary. It happens often enough in real life and besides, sex isn't something evil. I think pretending sex and violence doesn't exist only breeds ignorance. There are stories which actually require a certain amount of it to be successfully told. Of course, this is all assuming that the sex and violence isn't done gratuitously.

ANIMERICA: Is there something you keep in mind when you draw manga?

FUJISHIMA: I try to express at least one definite idea clearly. That's my goal.

ANIMERICA: What about the future? What kind of stories would you like to draw?

FUJISHIMA: Right now, for the indefinite future, I'm tied up with the *Oh My Goddess!* series. After that, who knows? I may end up continuing to draw adolescent stories. I'm also interested in stories which explore "male-bonding" friendships and situations.

ANIMERICA: Of all your other works, are there any in particular that you'd like your American fans to read?

FUJISHIMA: I only have two other works, *You're Under Arrest!* and *Striker* [*not the Viz Comics "Striker"—Ed.*], so I guess the choice isn't too difficult. And even though I drew it from a different perspective, *Striker* was created with American comics in mind. Naturally, I'm interested in an American reaction.

ANIMERICA: Let's talk about your hobbies. Do you have

The animated *Oh My Goddess!*

any favorite music or favorite films?

FUJISHIMA: My favorite things are motorcycles, automobiles, airplanes, the sea. Reading. Plastic models. My favorite activities are sleeping, riding motorcycles, drawing pictures and talking on the phone. My favorite music...well, I listen to everything. My favorite movies are *Streets of Fire*, *The Blues Brothers*, *Das Boot*, *The Hidden* and *Terminator 2*. I've also been getting into *Memphis Belle* a lot recently. I bought a sidecar recently—a German sidecar by the name Krauser Domani—and I'm pretty infatuated with that at the moment.

ANIMERICA: Are their any foreign countries you'd like to visit?

FUJISHIMA: Australia. America. Germany. But I'm most comfortable with Japan. I would like to see drag racing and air racing in America someday. The only problem is that I can't speak English. [LAUGHS]

ANIMERICA: Are you interested in mecha and robots? They don't appear much in your work, but....

FUJISHIMA: Sure, I like them very much. Real-life robots are doing wonderful things, and it's fun watching them do their work.

ANIMERICA: Any future plans relating to your leisure time?

FUJISHIMA: I'd like to become a pilot and fly by myself, but that's just not possible with the time I have. The sky is right there, but it's so far away. So I just lie down and watch the sky.

ANIMERICA: As we discussed a little earlier, anime and manga are becoming very popular overseas. There are even anime and manga conventions. Would you be interested in attending one day...?

FUJISHIMA: Hmm, I wonder what sort of things they do there? I only hear rumors....

ANIMERICA: In closing, do you have a message for your English-speaking fans?

FUJISHIMA: If there's anyone out there who reads my manga and is inspired to become a comic artist because of it, then I would really be pleased. I wonder if there is anyone...? [LAUGHS] One of my dreams is to become a world-class manga artist someday. If by some chance I ever achieve that, I would like my fans to be proud and say "I knew him when." You can count on me to try my best, for both our sakes.

afterword

In 1995, with the *Oh My Goddess!* OAV series at an end, and its fans left without any more animated Fujishima magic in their lives, attention turned to *You're Under Arrest!*, the artist's earlier work. Featuring character designs by *Ranma 1/2*'s animation character designer Atsuko Nakajima, *You're Under Arrest!* was adapted for animation in 1995, first as a four-volume OAV series, and then as a Japanese TV series in 1996. Like *Oh My Goddess!*, both the original manga and OAV series have been released for the U.S. market. But as frequent magazine articles in Japanese animation magazines would seem to prove, it's still *Oh My Goddess!* that holds firm sway over the hearts of fans in both Japan and America, who never stop hoping that their goddesses will come back.

Kosuke Fujishima
Select Bibliography & Filmography

MANGA 漫画

Compiled short stories and comics (manga) series by Kosuke Fujishima. Note that Fujishima is both writer and artist for both titles.

Taiho Shichau zo! ("You're Under Arrest!")
逮捕しちゃうぞ
Serialized in Kodansha's monthly Comic Morning (1986); seven compiled volumes total. *DOMESTIC RELEASE TITLE:* ***You're Under Arrest!*** (Dark Horse Comics)

Aa, Megami-sama ("Ah! My Goddess")
ああっ女神さまっ
Serialized in Kodansha's monthly Comic Afternoon (1989); fourteen compiled volumes as of press time. *DOMESTIC RELEASE TITLE:* ***Oh My Goddess!*** (Dark Horse Comics)

ANIME アニメ

Animated adaptations based on Fujishima's comics. Because his career is so relatively recent, only a few titles are listed; however, given his work in related fields such as video game character design ("Tales of Phantasia," "Sakura Taisen"), it's likely we'll be hearing more from him in the future. In fact, an animated version of *Sakura Taisen* is currently in production. Note that Fujishima gets "original story" credit for all entries.

Aa, Megami-sama
ああっ女神さまっ
Five-episode OAV series (1993-94). *DOMESTIC RELEASE TITLE:* ***Oh My Goddess!*** (AnimEigo)

Taiho Shichau zo!
逮捕しちゃうぞ
Four-episode OAV Series (1995-96). *DOMESTIC RELEASE TITLE:* ***You're Under Arrest!*** (AnimEigo)

Taiho Shichau zo!
逮捕しちゃうぞ
Ongoing TV series (1996–). Note that, in a clever reuse of resources, the first four episodes of the OAV series are also the first four episodes of the TV series. *CURRENTLY IMPORT ONLY*

Key

- Japanese comics or "manga" series; may or may not be available in foreign-language (i.e., English) version
- TV series broadcast on-air in Japan. Note that, in the U.S., Japanese TV series are both broadcast on-air (*Ronin Warriors*) and released on home video (*Ranma 1/2*). Others (*Sailor Moon, Dragon Ball*) are available both in broadcast and home video versions
- Direct-to-home-video series; may also include compilations of TV episodes released to home video market
- Theatrical feature; may or may not receive equivalent theatrical release for U.S. version

Yasuhiro Imagawa

Interviewed by Takayuki Karahashi (1994)

In the utopian cities of a past which never happened, forces of domination begin to gather. Giant machines of destruction and sinister villains appear, threatening the delicate balance of a society which runs on a new and perfect power source. When this source is threatened, can the ideal society founded on its energy survive? Will the combined strength of the "Experts of Justice" be able to face down the evil might of "Big Fire," a relentless cabal set on world domination? And how does a young boy in short pants and his glowering giant robot fit into all of this, anyway?

Meet the lifelong fantasy of Yasuhiro Imagawa, director of the hottest OAV series to be animated in years. A retro yet futuristic redux of a classic manga story (and '60s live-action show, known in the U.S. as *Johnny Socko and His Flying Robot*) by the legendary Mitsuteru "*Tetsujin 28*, a.k.a. *Gigantor*" Yokoyama, the seven-volume *Giant Robo* OAV series is directed by a man whose profound respect for the original is obvious in its many walk-on characters and tips of the hat to previous, equally classic Yokoyama series, such as those seen in 1973's *Babel II* TV series (and later OAV remake), as well as in the *Mars* and *Godmars* OAVs.

Attendees at the San Francisco Bay Area anime and manga convention Anime Expo '93 were fortunate to meet the flamboyant director whose mind was instrumental in *Giant Robo*'s OAV launch, although they may not have been able to see that much of him after hours, what with his midnight jaunts to Berkeley's UC Theater to see the cult classic film, *The Rocky Horror Picture Show*. The question is, how did this man—easily one of the most colorful and talkative guests ever to grace these shores, who confessed to Expo attendees that he'd gone to a showing of *Rocky Horror* dressed as the wheelchair-bound Dr. Scott—get into the anime industry?

"In the beginning, I wasn't really thinking of becoming a professional animator as an alternative to going into the family business," Imagawa says. "I thought of it as learning something I enjoyed in place of going to college."

Originally hailing from the southern Japan industrial city of Osaka, Imagawa was graduated from high school at eighteen and enrolled straightaway into Tatsunoko's Animation Technology Research Institute. There, Imagawa studied for about a year and moved on to working with director Hiroshi Sasagawa after he'd left the

Institute and began freelancing. With Sasagawa's encouragement, Imagawa gave directing a try.

"I'm not sure if you would have called me a pro," Imagawa says laughingly. "I got paid for working there…let's just leave it at that. Because of the high standards in-betweeners [*production animators, as compared to higher-status "key" animators—Ed.*] were held to at Tatsunoko, I was able to use what I'd learned at the Institute in my job."

Imagawa gained his first actual directing job in 1981 while working with Sasagawa on an animation special called *The Bremen Four*, which was featured in Japan TV's annual 24-hour summer TV charity telethon. His credit as assistant director on that project led to a job doing storyboards for the TV series *Sentô Mecha Xabungle*, the eclectic sci-fi western created by Yoshiyuki "Father of Gundam" Tomino. Several other Tomino TV projects—*Dunbine*, *L-Gaim*, and the early episodes of *Zeta Gundam*—continued Imagawa's association with Tomino and eventually paid off with a brief involvement with the long-planned *Yamato* OAV series, *Yamato 2520*. Reluctant to discuss the details of his contribution to this new *Yamato* project, Imagawa now professes to be "completely uninvolved" with the project.

That all-important "big break" came for Imagawa with a TV show with which he's still associated to this day, a series known as *Mr. Ajikko*. The story of a young chef and his tongue-in-cheek battles in the realm of food preparation, *Mr. Ajikko* held Imagawa's directorial interest for two years and was the last show he directed prior to beginning his greatest project…his lifelong dream, *Giant Robo*.

"*Giant Robo* is built on the foundations of my feelings for the manga and the live-action television series," Imagawa says. "*Giant Robo* is the animation that I've dreamed of making my entire life.

"It's full of me," he says. "If anything, it's me."

interview

ANIMERICA: What's the best thing about being a director? What's the worst?

IMAGAWA: The best thing is that people enjoy my work. It's best when I come up with a work that everyone—viewers, staff and, of course, myself—agrees is worthwhile. It's best that I get work on reputation alone. [LAUGHS] On the other hand, it isn't too much fun when people have preconceptions about me.

ANIMERICA: Such as being labeled as a director who produces only a certain kind of story, that sort of thing?

IMAGAWA: Exactly. Back in the days when I was working on *Mr. Ajikko*, it would have been wrong to assume that all I could do was cooking shows. By the same token, it would be wrong to assume that all I can do is science fiction now that I'm working on *Giant Robo*. When someone says "Don't pull a *Giant Robo* on us" when I'm working on a totally different kind of story, it bothers me. I correct them by saying, "I never had any *intention* of doing that." Being judged on past works alone is something I definitely like the least. Sure, I may have my own unique artistic signature, but all my works are always different.

ANIMERICA: Let's say there's one thing you keep in mind when you're directing an anime feature. What is that one thing?

IMAGAWA: It would have to be theme, spirit and soul. In my opinion, these are the three things that both crew and audience feel most keenly. I want to make shows that *I* can believe in, too. I want to include "something to believe in" in every show I make.

ANIMERICA: How do you describe the theme, spirit and soul of *Giant Robo*?

IMAGAWA: As you know, one thing I kept repeating when I was in the U.S. last year were those words from *The Rocky Horror Picture Show*, "Don't dream it, be it." Keep in mind that I'm crazy for *Rocky Horror*. [LAUGHS]

Giant Robo

Giant Robo

ANIMERICA: How do you evaluate today's animation industry in Japan?

IMAGAWA: There are two ways to see it: the schedule side and the creative side. Right now, anime production schedules are very tight. It's hard to make the shows you want to make. Then there's budgeting, staff and also time to think about. Animation is basically a system of mass production, and the sometimes-conflicting issues of time and money don't always conveniently resolve themselves.

ANIMERICA: So there are physical limitations. Is there ever a time in anime production when there are artistic limitations, as well?

IMAGAWA: Oh, there are all sorts of artistic limitations. Animation production in Japan these days can currently be described as that of a "copycat industry," beginning at the creator level. Works copied from the past and made to look new, for example.

ANIMERICA: Do you include remakes as being part of this copycat industry?

IMAGAWA: Sure. *Giant Robo* is a perfect example. It's both a remake and a copy. But the thing is, I think that all creative processes begin with imitation. Where creators sometimes err is in copying the wrong things—animation style, design superficialities, etc. What I try to do is grasp the core essence of a show and put my own spirit into it.

ANIMERICA: Continuing this theme, what sort of things do you see in the future for Japan and anime?

IMAGAWA: You're always walking a very fine line in the TV animation industry, always wondering how far you should let creativity run. There are always demands from sponsors and demands from the station, and you have to ask yourself how much priority they should have over creativity. When you think about it this way, you realize that animation is both art and not art, at the same time. I can only wonder how these elements will mesh together in the future, and in what direction they'll take the medium.

ANIMERICA: In the U.S. we're seeing the emergence of a strong English-language anime industry. How will this affect Japan? Will the English market expand business opportunities and profit Japanese creators?

IMAGAWA: No. In the Japanese anime industry, the system demands creative aspects from its creators. But when it comes to financial matters, creators aren't recognized as copyright holders. As for rights, creators have none. There are always a few exceptions, of course.

ANIMERICA: Are you saying that screenplay writers don't get video royalties?

IMAGAWA: Scripts are another matter entirely. Some bring in money; some don't. Some are bought outright. But when it comes to direction and animation, creators don't receive recognition. Therefore, when you ask if the English market will profit Japanese creators, I have to say no. There is no monetary reward in the production of derivative versions.

ANIMERICA: I understand you've worked with *Giant Robo* mecha designer Makoto Kobayashi before. How far back does your business and personal association with him go?

IMAGAWA: It started with my involvement in the *Yamato* project, so I'd have to say it's been about ten years. We saw each other at work, and then the project was shelved, and I didn't see him again for a while. *Giant Robo* gave me the opportunity to associate with him again.

ANIMERICA: Attendees at last year's Anime Expo got to hear all about how much you've been influenced by *The Rocky Horror Picture Show*. Are there any explicit allusions or homages to it in *Giant Robo*?

IMAGAWA: Yes, I think you could say I put something into it...put it in rather blatantly, actually. [LAUGHS] In a way, *Giant Robo* is itself an homage to *Rocky Horror*. I've always wanted to work on something I believe in, and so working on *Giant Robo* was, for me, like the "Don't dream it, be it" line come true.

ANIMERICA: You said that today's animation sometimes tries to find inspiration in the wrong places. Where do you get *your* inspiration...?

IMAGAWA: For me, it's my own daily life, or from the lives around me, or from the news. Events that are happening in real life, and the affairs of the world.

ANIMERICA: Inspiration from everyday life, but to what extent? Let's say you wake up one morning and your toothpaste tube is empty. You've got to throw that one away and open up a new one. Even something inconsequential like that...?

IMAGAWA: It's everything...*including* that. It's everyday life in every sense, not just art imitating art by watching other people's works. So, sure, buying a new tube of toothpaste can be an influence. I might find inspiration by hearing other people's conversations while I'm walking on the street.

ANIMERICA: ...And you'd put all those ingredients into a stewpot called Yasuhiro Imagawa and set that on the stove to boil....

IMAGAWA: Maybe the words uttered by a stranger heard one way by somebody else might be heard by me in an entirely different way. Maybe my imagination would start to run free after hearing those words. That's the fun of it.

ANIMERICA: How does the direction in live-action films appeal to your directorial sensibilities?

IMAGAWA: The impact is...well, *heavy*. In many ways. There are some aspects of live-action which I really envy, but then there are some parts which prompt me to say, "See how much better this can be done in animation? Ha ha." I've always felt that the two are very similar.

ANIMERICA: Does that mean that the same story can be told in both mediums?

IMAGAWA: Well, I suppose the result would be the same. Live-action and animation have the same purpose, after all.

ANIMERICA: So when you say that you've got a lot to learn from live-action, you're talking about a lot of *positive* things to learn.

IMAGAWA: Yes, very much so. There are a great many

There are some aspects of live-action which I really envy, but then there are some parts of it which prompt me to say, "See how much better this can be done in animation?"

directors whom I respect in the live-action field. Recently, I had a bit of a shock when I learned that Federico Fellini had died. I had wanted to see his next work.

ANIMERICA: Despite his age?

IMAGAWA: Whatever might be said about him, I knew that I could always look forward to his next work. Somebody might say, "His latest film is a failure. It just doesn't make sense," but I'd still want to see it.

ANIMERICA: The original idea for *Giant Robo* came from Mitsuteru Yokoyama. There was a TV show—a live-action series also broadcast in the U.S., under the title *Johnny Socko and His Flying Robot*. But your *Giant Robo* is quite different from the live-action series. Is it intentional?

IMAGAWA: Although the *Giant Robo* TV show and manga were developed concurrently, they're both very different. They have their own content, their own shape. The thing about the manga is, it's out of print. Yokoyama's original story isn't around anymore, but the live-action version *is*. My thought was that there was room for another, completely different *Giant Robo*, one which could be animated. Seeing as the manga has become a phantom, I felt that I was free to make a third incarnation.

ANIMERICA: *Giant Robo* has a very epic scale...it sends many messages. What are the themes you particularly value?

IMAGAWA: On an emotional level, there's the theme of destiny between a parent and child.

ANIMERICA: As in a child following in the footsteps of a parent...?

IMAGAWA: Parents and children have an unbreakable bond. There are truths in that bond that no one else—no one who isn't caught up in it—can understand. There's a certain pathos in that. The sorrow of being misunderstood is the theme of *Giant Robo.*

ANIMERICA: On a superficial level, the utopian symbolism of the Shizuma Drive is obvious enough, but is there another level? Is there a message here about nuclear energy?

IMAGAWA: I wanted to examine what happens to mankind when utopian ideals go wrong. Compare that with current world events, if you like...but realize that I have no intention of delivering some sort of lecture on that in the animation.

ANIMERICA: What about in-jokes, references. Anything you'd care to share with us...?

IMAGAWA: Franken Von Vogler's name. Going back to homages, his name—Franken Von Vogler—is an homage to Dr. Frank-N-Furter. In the original manga, his name is Dr. Franken. The "Vogler" part comes from the main character in Ingmar Bergman's film *The Magician*. The full name is Emanuel Von something-something Vogler [*Albert Emanuel Vogler, the 19th-century hypnotist/magician from Bergman's 1958 film—Ed.*]. As mentioned previously, I worked on *Mr. Ajikko*, so I'm often asked if the "Vogler" name came from foie gras [*the Japanese word is "fuowa gura," hence the presumed pun—Ed.*]. Let me say for the record that this is *not* the case. [LAUGHS]

ANIMERICA: In the English version, the pronunciation of Dr. Vogler's name comes out sounding suspiciously close to the brand name of a certain instant coffee, and so there's been some speculation in that direction.

IMAGAWA: Is that so? Well, it's a Swedish film, and Swedish spelling is different from English....

ANIMERICA: I think it may have had more to do with Vogler's "v" being pronounced like an "f," but anyway.... Going back to *Giant Robo*, there's an anime-based manga on which you collaborated with Mari Mizuta that's separate from Yokoyama's original. That manga story's already concluded...will the OAV series end the same way?

IMAGAWA: You could say that, in some ways, the two are similar. This isn't something that will be obvious until you watch the third and fourth OAVs, though. The animation story has gone in a completely different direction. There's a point where it comes close to the manga again, but the conclusion is entirely different.

ANIMERICA: *Giant Robo* has a very retro feel on the screen. It's retro, but it also looks futuristic. Where do the aesthetics for this come from?

IMAGAWA: Back in the earliest OAV planning stages, we decided that Big Fire's goal was eventual world domination. But since World War II, "world domination" has become an obsolete term. There have been wars fought since then which have proved that world domination is an impossibility...it's been shown that it can't happen. But that's Big Fire's goal. So we thought of creating a world where it *would* be possible—a world with today's morality and tomorrow's look—but a world where the term "world domination" would still carry real weight. The sci-fi aspect of the OAV series comes into play with the future technology, but the actual time frame is set a little in the past. That was the premise. The world of *Giant Robo* is a mixture of present, past, and future.

ANIMERICA: So you had this space-time continuum, and you took a knife and made a diagonal cut....

IMAGAWA: Yes. Here I am, sitting in the present. I extend my arms to the past on one side and the future on the other, and then I pull them near.

ANIMERICA: Ah.

IMAGAWA: ...And the filler in between has been taken out. That's how we decided on it. It's like sitting between two girls and pulling them to you with your arms.

ANIMERICA: Patching together all the good parts.

IMAGAWA: Exactly. Just the good parts are pieced together. And the good parts are *really* good. [LAUGHS]

ANIMERICA: Are the retro visuals your concept?

IMAGAWA: Yes. The designs for Giant Robo himself are based on a tractor. In daily life, the most powerful machines would most likely be found on the farm, right? The steam locomotive in the beginning of the first episode is another design which came from daily life.

ANIMERICA: Did Makoto Kobayashi have input on those two?

IMAGAWA: Of course he did. Makoto Kobayashi implemented those ideas, and he also came up with other ideas of his own.

ANIMERICA: Would you say that you share a common vision with him?

IMAGAWA: Sure. When it comes to *Giant Robo*, our visions are very similar.

ANIMERICA: Your direction in *Giant Robo* seems to show a certain fondness for ending episodes with a cliffhanger. Will the OAV series itself end on a cliffhanger, or will there be a proper conclusion?

IMAGAWA: There will be a little left over, but the story itself will conclude at the end of the seven OAV volumes. There may be a few unresolved mysteries. They won't be from the "Day the Earth Stood Still" OAV series so much as unresolved mysteries from the world of *Giant Robo* itself. There'll be a little something to leave you with the impression that the world will continue after the OAV series is over and done.

ANIMERICA: The Warsaw Philharmonic music from the *Giant Robo* OAV series is lavish. Was this also at your request?

IMAGAWA: When it comes to the music, I'd have to give the credit to producer Tokunobu Yamaki. My one request was that they use the aria "Una Furtiva Lagrima" from Gaetano Donizetti's opera, *L'Elisir d'Amore*.

ANIMERICA: "Una Furtiva Lagrima," the famous aria that everyone knows because the great Luciano Pavarotti sings it....

IMAGAWA: Right. I told the producers that this particular aria embodies the theme of *Giant Robo*, the sorrow of others not understanding your true feelings. There's a

Mobile Bushido-Legend G Gundam

Soviet film of which I'm fond, called *An Unfinished Piece for Player Piano* by Nikita Mikhalkov, which uses this aria. [*Released in 1977, director Mikhalkov's* Unfinished Piece *has been described by at least one critic as a "richly ironic and movingly absurd pyramid of love triangles"—Ed.*]

ANIMERICA: It seems the title *L'Elisir d'Amore* also has something to do with the contents of *Giant Robo*.

IMAGAWA: Not intentionally.

ANIMERICA: No?

IMAGAWA: No, but "Una Furtiva Lagrima" does.

ANIMERICA: So you're saying that the Shizuma Drive doesn't really represent an elixir for humanity...?

IMAGAWA: ...Ah! Now I see what you're saying. That wasn't what I intended, though. I guess it all comes down to the interpretation of the world "elixir"—the Shizuma Drive is really more of an idealism issue. It's the gap between reality and dream. That's the reason for the inclusion of the Shizuma Drive here, so I'd have to say it wasn't really intended as some sort of elixir. It really is more like a *furtiva* or "secret" tear.

ANIMERICA: A tear caused by misunderstandings and missed opportunities....

IMAGAWA: ...Yes, and you'll see just how true that is when you watch the fifth and six episodes of the OAV series.

ANIMERICA: As a final question, do you have a message for your fans in the U.S. and in the English-speaking world?

IMAGAWA: First of all, please go see *Giant Robo*. There's just all of me—my drama, my animation, my idea of science fiction—all wrapped up inside of it. I'd like for all of you to watch it until the very end. There are gaps in the production schedule, so there'll be a wait, but please don't become impatient and lose interest. I promise you, it will be worth the wait.

afterword

At the time of this interview, the first volume of *Giant Robo* was just about to debut in the American home video market and the series quickly gained popularity among American fans. But three years later, those fans were still waiting for the final volume to release. Even with the series' popularity, financial concerns had forced Imagawa into working on other projects to support his dream—*Giant Robo* went into one hiatus after another between volumes while its director took the time to direct the TV series *Kidô Butôden G Gundam* ("Mobile Bushido-Legend G Gundam") for Sunrise, and then paused while he worked as a scenarist, writing for the *Hamlin no Violin-Hiki* ("Violinist of Hamlin") TV series in the following year.

G Gundam in particular brought Imagawa a certain notorious acclaim—a self-professed protégé of *Gundam*'s creator Yoshiyuki Tomino, *G Gundam* took the classic space war concept of *Mobile Suit Gundam* and turned it on its head, producing a robot show that seemed to owe more to video games such as *Street Fighter II* than to the sci-fi stylings of *Gundam* animation productions that had gone before it. Though fans who followed the show finally came to realize that what Imagawa had had in mind was a Hong Kong-style over-the-top martial arts drama filled with angst and bravery, Imagawa himself still balefully describes the show as the "black sheep" of the *Gundam* world.

The quirky *Violinist of Hamlin*, about a group of D&D-style adventurers (the leader plays a giant violin), gained Imagawa attention for the surprising drama he'd managed to wring from a nominally comedic manga story. *Hamlin* also gained respect for its animators' creative approach to the show's astoundingly limited low-budget animation, described by some viewers as "inanimation" due to the frequent use of stills. Imagawa then moved on to scripting of the surreal late-night television show *Hareluya* ("Hallelujah") *II Boy*, based on a manga story where the delinquent son of God is sent to Earth as a punishment for his lack of interest in heavenly duties.

However, there's a pot of gold at the end of this particular rainbow. According to comments made by Imagawa during a recent trip to the U.S., the seventh and final volume of *Giant Robo* is, at the time of this writing, just around the corner. As Imagawa himself says, "I promise you, it will be worth the wait."

Yasuhiro Imagawa
Select Filmography

Key

Japanese comics or "manga" series; may or may not be available in foreign-language (i.e., English) version

TV series broadcast on-air in Japan. Note that, in the U.S., Japanese TV series are both broadcast on-air (*Ronin Warriors*) and released on home video (*Ranma 1/2*). Others (*Sailor Moon, Dragon Ball*) are available both in broadcast and home video versions

Direct-to-home-video series; may also include compilations of TV episodes released to home video market

Theatrical feature; may or may not receive equivalent theatrical release for U.S. version

ANIME アニメ

Whether it's combat mecha, combat music, or combat cooking, the work Imagawa has done over the course of his long career has followed a refreshingly consistent path. Most of his work, you'll notice, has been in the service of mecha-heavy anime studio Sunrise, while other works—in particular, goofy *Gundam* franchulate *G Gundam* and the *shôjo*-esque *The Violinist of Hamlin*—are seen by some as distractions which keep him from his "real" work, *Giant Robo*...the seventh and final volume of which is due out in Japan any moment now.

Sentô Mecha Xabungle ("War-Machine Xabungle")
戦闘メカザブングル
Episode Direction / Storyboards
50-episode TV series (1982-83); also known by its production company-supplied English title, "Blue Gale Xabungle." See entry for Tomino. *CURRENTLY IMPORT ONLY*

Sei Senshi Dunbine ("Holy-Warrior Dunbine")
聖戦士ダンバイン
Episode Direction / Storyboards
49-episode TV series (1983-84); followed in later years by a *Dunbine* OAV series (in which Imagawa has no involvement). More commonly known as "Aura Battler Dunbine," the tagline to which even the series' opening theme makes reference. See entry for Tomino. *CURRENTLY IMPORT ONLY*

Jûsenki L-Gaim ("Heavy War-Machine L-Gaim")
重戦機エルガイム
Episode Director / Storyboards
54-episode TV series (1984-85); also known as "Heavy Metal L-Gaim." See entry for Tomino. *CURRENTLY IMPORT ONLY*

Kidô Senshi Z Gundam ("Mobile Suit Z Gundam")
機動戦士Zガンダム
Episode Director / Storyboards
50-episode TV series (1985-86); also known as "Zeta Gundam." See entry for Tomino. *CURRENTLY IMPORT ONLY*

Mr. Ajikko
ミスター味っ子
Director / Episode Direction / Art Continuity
99-episode TV series (1987-89). *CURRENTLY IMPORT ONLY*

Giant Robo
ジャイアント・ロボ：The Animation
Director / Screenplay / Art Continuity / Story Concept
Currently a six-volume OAV series (a seventh has long been announced, yet seems to keep getting pushed back so the director can work on other projects), the *Giant Robo* series has also produced a separate spin-off OAV series focusing on the exploits of curvy agent of justice Ginrei, a series in which Imagawa has no involvement. *DOMESTIC RELEASE TITLE:* ***Giant Robo*** (Manga Entertainment)

Kidô Butôden G Gundam
("Mobile Bushido-Legend G Gundam")
機動武闘伝Gガンダム
Executive Director
49-episode TV series (1995-96); also known as "G Gundam," for short. Known as the "Black Sheep" of the *Gundam* universe, the series plays fast and loose with the established tone of The Franchise, including (among other things) a robot designed to resemble a killer clown...! *CURRENTLY IMPORT ONLY*

Hamlin no Violin-Hiki ("The Violinist of Hamlin")
ハーメルンのバイオリン弾き
Series Coordination
25-episode TV series (1996-97). Lo-budget (the animation budget was so low, it couldn't even afford a "w") series which seems—against all expectation—to have held viewer interest, if only for its story and distinct, Clamp-esque character designs. *CURRENTLY IMPORT ONLY*

Hiroki Hayashi

Interviewed by Takashi Oshiguchi (1994)

"In Japan, the MGM cartoons were on in the afternoons year 'round," says director Hiroki Hayashi, reminiscing about watching the American cartoon *Tom and Jerry* as a child. "I used to watch them every day." As for domestic animation on the airwaves during Hayashi's formative years, it was giant-robot shows such as *Mazinger Z* [Tranzor Z *in the U.S.—Ed.*] which dominated.

"I watched those shows, but I was never fanatical about them," Hayashi recalls. "What really got me interested in animation had to have been *Space Cruiser Yamato*...it was completely different from anything which had come before it. It was like a show from a different dimension."

A member of Japan's *shin-jinrui* or "new generation" of creators who'd grown up watching animation such as *Yamato*, Hayashi also has fond childhood memories of Yoshiyuki Tomino's revamp of the robot show *Mobile Suit Gundam*. "It had good realism, especially for a robot show back then," Hayashi says. "Even when I was a kid I never liked those cartoony, simplified premises, not in robot shows, not in anything."

Unlike many creative types interviewed in these pages—*Battle Angel Alita*'s Yukito Kishiro and *Bio-Booster Armor Guyver* creator Yoshiki Takaya come to mind—Hayashi wasn't driven to find his niche in the anime world because of a passion for anime, but because he wanted a job in the art field.

"I'd wanted to make a living by drawing pictures," Hayashi laughs. Shortly after being graduated from high school, Hayashi enrolled at Japan Design School's two-year graphic design program, but found himself ultimately unsatisfied.

"I think I was misled by the term *design*," Hayashi says. "I thought all I'd have to do was draw. Once I got there, I found out that there were things like typesetting, block copying and other subjects I was supposed to learn. I wasn't good at those tedious tasks."

Fortunately, a friend offered a way out with a job at the animation production house A.I.C. Hayashi gladly accepted and began working as an "in-betweener," one of those people who fill in the frames in between the "key" animation scenes (*Dirty Pair* and *Urusei Yatsura* character designer Tsukasa Dokite and *Fatal Fury* and *Toshinden* character designer/director Masami Obari have both done key animation work for the *Ranma 1/2* TV series, for example).

Hayashi's design training hadn't really prepared him for in-between work, but he tells us that he picked it up quickly enough. Asked if he remembers his first work, Hayashi laughs. "It was in-between animation for some television show...I took on anything and everything."

True to his take-on-everything philosophy, Hayashi's first actual credit on a show was for key animation on the American syndicated program *Thundercats*. Following closely on its heels was *Silverhawks*, and although Hayashi was responsible for key animation on several other similar shows, what he really wanted to do was direct.

The problem was that although Hayashi had years of experience under his belt, he had few on-screen credits. The big break came during an all-night sake-drinking brainstorm with *Gall Force 2* veteran Masaki Kajishima, which resulted in the seeds of what would eventually become *Tenchi Muyô!*, the *No Need For Tenchi!* anime (and, recently, manga) series so popular in the U.S. The two decided to take their idea to Artmic, an industry leader.

"'Let's go with the golden formula' is what I said when we first pitched the project," Hayashi says. "For example, if there was something good about one particular show, we could borrow that. If there was something we liked about another show, we could borrow that, too. Sources could be anywhere—we could extract what we liked from this or that show and put it all together in one OAV series. *Tenchi Muyô!* is that series."

After Artmic declined to pick up the project, Hayashi and Kajishima took it to Pioneer LDC, where a search was currently on for new stories to be featured in their upcoming original animation video line. Pioneer expressed interest in the series and the rest, as they say, is history.

In America, *Tenchi Muyô!* became a cult hit beyond all reckoning—by the time the American arm of the Japanese production company Pioneer LDC began releasing the first six-volume OAV series in a bilingual Japanese/English laser disc format in the U.S., *Tenchi!* fever was in full swing. Names from the series were suddenly in high demand among fans who competed for the privilege to use them as personal nicknames on the Internet. On the real-time chat channel network "IRC," it became fashionable to append "-oh-ki" to one's name in honor of the half-cat, half-rabbit "Ryo-Oh-Ki." Among anime fans, at least, *Tenchi Muyô!* had become nearly as famous, if not more so, than the original works from which it relentlessly borrowed.

Intrigued by the high level of enthusiasm for an OAV series which seemingly came out of nowhere, ANIMERICA got in touch with *Tenchi Muyô!* director Hiroki Hayashi in 1994 to talk about the origins of the series. In this interview, Hayashi not only shares his ideas about the genesis of the series and his hand in selecting its Japanese voice-cast, but also casts ahead to the future, and to what was then his latest project at the time.

interview

ANIMERICA: You began your career in the industry as an animator. And yet here you are, the *Tenchi!* director. Isn't that a little unusual? In my experience, most people who aspire to direct seem more inclined to write than draw.

HAYASHI: I'm sure it's more the exception than the rule. At (production house) A.I.C., for example, it's unusual for someone to go into direction when they started in production.

ANIMERICA: But wasn't it your intention to direct, right from the beginning?

HAYASHI: Yes, that's correct.

ANIMERICA: What was your first directorial credit?

HAYASHI: The first work on which I was given directorial credit was *Gall Force 2: Destruction*.

ANIMERICA: Did you find it difficult to begin directing in the middle of a series? After all, *Gall Force 2* is a sequel, and the characters were already well established by that time.

Tenchi Muyô!

HAYASHI: I didn't really begin to get a feel for what I was doing until *Sol Bianca*. If you notice, I'm credited with storyboards for the first volume. Katsuhito Akiyama is credited with direction. I'm not listed as director until the second volume. It wasn't until then that I began to feel that I was doing what I'd set out to do, concentrating on character and the like. That's not to say what I was doing was any *good*, of course. [LAUGHS]

ANIMERICA: What are some of the other titles on which you've worked?

HAYASHI: I worked on the third and fourth volumes of *Bubblegum Crisis*. I also worked on *Sol Bianca* Volumes 1 and 2. I began working on *Tenchi!* immediately after that. Back in 1990, *Tenchi Muyô!* was nothing more than an ongoing idle discussion between Kajishima and I, and it wasn't until 1991 that it started to look as though the project might become a reality. Actual pre-production didn't start until around 1992.

ANIMERICA: How far back does your association with Kajishima go?

HAYASHI: We've known each other for a long time. We worked together on *Gall Force*. Come to think of it, that's the first series Kajishima ever worked on at A.I.C. He was a fan of (*Gall Force* creator Kenichi) Sonoda's work before he even started. [LAUGHS]

ANIMERICA: How did you and Kajishima go about getting your story produced?

HAYASHI: I was the one responsible for writing down all our ideas. It was Kajishima's job to draw up the storyboards and submit them as a proposal to a production company.

ANIMERICA: How about the plot? What inspired it?

HAYASHI: *Tenchi Muyô!* is inspired by *Gall Force* and *Bubblegum Crisis*. We made up something that resembled a side-story to *Bubblegum* or *Gall Force* and took it straight to Artmic. Unfortunately, they weren't interested. At all. [LAUGHS]

ANIMERICA: *Bubblegum Crisis* is a story of fighting. There's this big corporation controlling everything, and this underground group who fights against the corporation. There's even a heavy subplot with the private police.

HAYASHI: That's *Bubblegum Crisis*, all right. [LAUGHS]

ANIMERICA: But *Tenchi!* isn't heavy at all, although there is some allusion to previous works....

HAYASHI: What I'd had in mind originally was more like a parody of *Bubblegum Crisis* and *Gall Force*. You know, characters going about their daily lives—eating at the dinner table, taking baths—a side-story sort of thing. So many of A.I.C.'s videos were really nothing more than combat stories with characterization tacked on. I wanted to do a show where the characters themselves would be the core of the story. I wanted to do something that had never been seen before.

ANIMERICA: Was the *Tenchi Muyô!* OAV series originally designed to go six volumes?

HAYASHI: No, nothing so organized. The intention was to create a story which could go on indefinitely. It was more like a six-episode block from a thirteen-episode television series. That didn't mesh with what the sponsors had in mind, though, and so it ended up having a conclusion at the sixth volume.

ANIMERICA: From the time the galaxy police show up in the fourth volume and hint at the existence of Kagato, the story just keeps going and going. In fact, the fifth and sixth episodes are just packed with story elements.

HAYASHI: They're dense, all right. [LAUGHS] You wouldn't believe the number of arguments we had while we were making them.

ANIMERICA: Unlike TV, the OAV format doesn't give you too much room for error. When you're dealing with a three- or a six-volume OAV series, even a minor slip-up can have serious ramifications. Is this something you kept in mind while you were plotting the overall story breakdown for the individual episodes?

HAYASHI: No, I didn't have that in mind at all. I was more concerned with trimming down the fat and keeping the pace moving.

ANIMERICA: Let's talk about the *Tenchi Muyô!* characters. They're a fairly familiar comedic trio—a "bad" girl, a "good" girl, and a "straight" girl [*Ryoko, Ayeka and Sasami, respectively—Ed.*]. And then, there's Mihoshi, the type that breaks *all* the rules. [LAUGHS]

HAYASHI: That's right, they're based on a comedy formula. No doubt we had this sort of thing in mind while working on previous video projects, but this time it was *our* story, and we were able to direct the focus as we saw fit.

ANIMERICA: When you look at it one way, *Tenchi!* is like a boarding-house story, where the characters live together in the same house, take baths in the same tub, and eat dinner at the same table.

HAYASHI: I *do* like the dinner scenes. [LAUGHS] But I won't put them in unnecessarily. Tenchi himself is a high-school student. Under ordinary circumstances, he'd be attending classes. But then I'd have to think up reasons for all the characters to follow him there, and one of the things I was careful not to do in this series was create unnecessary characters. It wouldn't surprise me if viewers should happen to find Tenchi's situation a little unusual. I had to content myself with the thought that the *reasons* are all there in the story, even if they're only implied. See, that was one way I could excuse my self-imposed ceiling on the creation of new characters. [LAUGHS]

ANIMERICA: Your voice-actors, especially your female actors, are mostly veterans. You have a couple of veteran male actors as well in Kenichi Ogata and Takeshi Aono, the rather formidable grandfather [*"Sanada" and "Analyzer (I.Q. 9),"* Space Cruiser Yamato; *"Genma,"* Ranma 1/2—*Ed.*]. Was this particular cast something you had decided upon in advance?

Writing a script for something silly has its own dangers. You know very well how silly it is, and yet you still have to spend months producing it. You need a certain kind of enthusiasm to motivate you through something like that.

HAYASHI: In the beginning, I wasn't thinking about the male characters at all. The grandfather you mention is just an ordinary man in the first draft of the story. We didn't realize that he was no longer the same character with whom we'd started out until the actual recording began. We had heated arguments over that, too. [LAUGHS]

ANIMERICA: And what about the character of the older brother? How did you see his character development?

HAYASHI: The older brother was just an older brother. He's as good as dead from the very beginning, so....

ANIMERICA: ...Ah, the tragic, long-lost older sibling. [LAUGHS] Speaking of characters, I have to say that I found Ogata's performance as "Azaka" to be extremely entertaining.

HAYASHI: It wasn't intentional. But during recording he really got into the mood, and we decided to go with it.

ANIMERICA: Both of the two gatekeeper robots, Azaka and Kamidake, they're kind of like sidekicks.

HAYASHI: I wasn't thinking that much about them in the beginning, and after the first two episodes, they didn't show up again for a while. But they proved to be so popular with the fans it was decided that, toward the end of the series, they had to make another appearance.

ANIMERICA: All of *Tenchi!*'s actors certainly do a good job in creating zany characters. Were you there when the decisions were made on the voice-cast?

HAYASHI: I chose them all myself.

ANIMERICA: Really? How about the character of Ryoko? Did she turn out as you'd hoped?

HAYASHI: I'd have to say yes, the voice pretty much fit the image I had of her in my head. And there were no conflicts with the sponsor over casting her, so.... Fortunately, pre-production on this video was long enough that we were able to think about who we wanted for which roles and which recording director we wanted to use. Some of our initial choices may not have been realistic, for whatever reason, but in the end, I think we ended up with most of the cast we wanted. There were several candidates for Kagato's voice, for example, but one important consideration was purely practical—we needed someone who would be easy to work with. And that's how we ended up with Norio Wakamoto.

ANIMERICA: And as the series' sole villain, he doesn't have any gag lines.

HAYASHI: Well, there were plans to make him more humorous, but there was a concern that no one would understand the humor. Actually, I put a lot of humor into the character, but I don't think anyone got it.

ANIMERICA: Going back a little in the series, that first episode really was like a two-person show, wasn't it. It was like a dialogue.

HAYASHI: In retrospect, I think maybe it was a mistake. [LAUGHS]

ANIMERICA: And before the OAV series was even animated, there was a drama CD released. I'm assuming that means the plot was already written up by that point…?

HAYASHI: Yes, that's right. And it's true for all the CDs to come. Personally, I enjoy the drama CDs. For me, the world of *Tenchi!* isn't fixated solely on the animation. I've always wanted the characters to create an interesting world of their own. The thing about drama CDs is, sometimes when you're working on a film, physical limitations pop up and things don't go as you planned. With drama CDs, though, I can capture the atmosphere of a particular moment, and the listener is able to get a feel for the series as a whole within a very short amount of time.

ANIMERICA: Some parts of *Tenchi Muyô!* are very comedic. Are you a big fan of comedy?

HAYASHI: I love comedy movies and slapstick movies. Those really silly American movies, those super-ridiculous ones. I like those.

ANIMERICA: *Bugs Bunny*, that sort of thing?

HAYASHI: Oh, yes. In live-action, I like *Top Secret* and *Hot Shots* and *The Naked Gun*.

ANIMERICA: Comedy's difficult, isn't it. You can't always anticipate how the humor will turn out, and you've said before that the audience didn't always laugh where you'd intended they would.

HAYASHI: That's right. Writing a script for something silly has its own dangers. You know very well how silly it is, and yet you still have to spend months producing it. You need a certain kind of enthusiasm to motivate you through something like that. You start out intending to make a certain part silly, but half a year into production, it's no longer so hilarious. I guess the issue is how to keep up the spontaneity.

ANIMERICA: For example, an idea can be funny when you first think it up, but when it's actually produced, it loses something. Then again, the audience will be seeing it for the first time, and who knows how they'll respond? As director, you've got to make sure that that dramatic tension is maintained. That's tough work.

HAYASHI: No kidding. You start to wonder how something like one of those silly films I mentioned previously can manage to be so funny. *Tenchi!* was the first time I could really explore the comedic potential of animation, and I'm sure there are many places where my lack of experience shows.

ANIMERICA: Is there a *Tenchi Muyô!* manga version?

HAYASHI: Actually, there is. I think it's being published in COMIC DRAGON [*Kadokawa's monthly manga magazine—Ed.*].

ANIMERICA: At Comic Market, I hear they're selling parody fanzines (*dôjinshi*) of *Tenchi Muyô!* rather successfully. Isn't it sort of ironic how the fanzines can be parodying a work which is *itself* supposed to be a parody…?

HAYASHI: It *does* feel strange. As I said before, in creating *Tenchi!*, we felt we had borrowed so much from other works. We thought *we* were doing the parody. [LAUGHS]

ANIMERICA: Once you send an artistic work out into the world, people start to make it their own. They cherish it in its own right.

HAYASHI: Yes. I'm glad to see that our story is taking on a life of its own, so to speak.

ANIMERICA: Did you feel that way during production? For example, did the characters start to take on lives of their own during the dubbing process?

HAYASHI: Sure, but the phenomenon wasn't limited to me. The lyricist understood the characters, and wrote songs appropriate for them without instruction from me.

ANIMERICA: Let's talk about the *Tenchi!* English version. Have you seen it? How do you like it?

HAYASHI: I've only seen the first volume, but the voices are really similar. I don't want this to come off the wrong way, but I used to think that there weren't any foreign voice-actors who could act. I was never impressed by what little I've seen of the European-dubbed Japanese animation. So, relatively speaking, I was pleased to discover, in the English version, that we had people with similar voices who could really act.

ANIMERICA: How about the next series? I understand you're not directly involved in the new *Tenchi!* OAV series.

HAYASHI: That's right.

ANIMERICA: Your involvement is limited to "original concept"…?

HAYASHI: Content-wise, I'm not involved at all. I'm still working on the drama CDs and the songs, but not in the animation.

ANIMERICA: So what's the next project? What will you work on next?

HAYASHI: It's an original story called *El-Hazard*. The story is straight out of those old science-fiction pulp magazines. I've always loved those stories. The "Mars" books by Edgar Rice Burroughs, Edmond Hamilton….

ANIMERICA: Is *El-Hazard* an adventure story?

HAYASHI: Well, I'd like to make it similar to *Tenchi!*, in that the characters will always be the focus. In the case of *Tenchi!*, the aliens came to Earth. In my new story, the people of Earth will travel to alien worlds. It'll be like E.E. Doc Smith's "Skylark" series.

ANIMERICA: The sci-fi stories of a more innocent age.

HAYASHI: Exactly. Those stories have a kind of anything-goes atmosphere that doesn't demand constant rationalization by the reader. It's the kind of place where a character can use an atomic gun without batting an eye, never mind radioactive side-effects. [LAUGHS]

ANIMERICA: Do you intend to have flying machines without a word of technical explanation, then?

HAYASHI: Just block the seventh ray. Fill the tank and you're off…!

Tenchi Muyô!

ANIMERICA: Hey, wait a minute! [LAUGHS]

HAYASHI: There's this experiment which accidentally creates a special solution, see. When you put metal into it, it *floats*…! This is the kind of simple-minded story I'm talking about. A parody of the pulp magazine stories of old. That's the flavor I'm going for.

ANIMERICA: So you're not going to sweat the technical details…? All the mecha has to do is move, that sort of thing?

HAYASHI: Actually, I love mecha. Real mecha, that is. I love to just sit and stare at motorcycle engines. The only problem is, it makes mecha that exists only on paper even less substantial. But these days, I don't really understand these recent engines. I used to like taking them apart, but the modern ones are just too complex…even mechanics have trouble with them nowadays. One thing I do enjoy is games. There's a game section at A.I.C., and I work on projects there from time to time.

ANIMERICA: Game projects? Anything coming up soon you can tell us about?

HAYASHI: I think the first one to come out under our own name will be a *Tenchi!* game. A simple game, really—an adventure game. Like the ones on the NEC PC-98. Sometimes, when I play other games, I think about how I'd do them differently. If I ever get the chance, I'd like to see what I can come up with. Maybe something a little more complicated.

ANIMERICA: It's not shoot-'em-up games for you, though.

HAYASHI: That's right. It's adventure games for me. I have a lot of ambitions in regard to games. There is such a thing as an optimum medium for a story. For example, some stories may not be appropriate for making into films, but they may be enough to make a game. Our company is in the position where it can do things like that now. Not that I'd write the program myself, mind you. [LAUGHS]

ANIMERICA: Finally, do you have a message for your English-speaking fans?

HAYASHI: I'm not very good at this sort of thing...let's just say that I wanted to make something comedic for you, the fans, something you could enjoy even if you don't necessarily understand the language. I hope that I've succeeded.

afterword

After conquering America with the pointy-haired space pirates, galactic manhunters, and cute li'l cabbits in *Tenchi Muyô!*, the work-in-progress that Hayashi refers to in this interview, *El-Hazard*, became a reality in 1995 as an OAV series entitled *Shinpi no Sekai El-Hazard* ("World of Mysteries El-Hazard") released in the U.S. under the title *El-Hazard, the Magnificent World*. Co-written by Hayashi and screenwriter Ryoe Tsukimura, *El-Hazard* retooled the age-old *Prisoner of Zenda* prince-switches-with-pauper plotline by replacing the prince with a princess and making her doppelgänger a Japanese schoolboy who must cross-dress to fulfill his role, with the expected hijinks to ensue.

With its nonstop innuendo and light-hearted pulp sci-fi fantasy setting, *El-Hazard* would eventually go on to achieve almost as much popularity as *Tenchi!* itself, producing a 1995 OAV series, followed by a 1996 TV series and, in 1997, a second OAV series. *Tenchi!* itself continues without Hayashi's involvement, with a second OAV series (already in release in Japan at the time of this interview), two TV series and two theatrical features so far. The Japanese manga adaption of *Tenchi!*—which, in a rare turnaround, wasn't produced until *after* the animation—has since been translated into English and released in the States under a title which is an approximate translation of the Japanese series' title, the *No Need For Tenchi!* by-now so familiar to U.S. fans. An original American comic based on the series has also been produced.

As for what Hayashi might create in the future, who knows what a man with such a knack for balancing grit and slapstick might come up with next?

El-Hazard, The Magnificent World

Hiroki Hayashi
Select Filmography

ANIME アニメ

Spanning two six-episode OAVs series, two OAV specials, three spin-off TV series—a second *Tenchi!* TV series, *The New Tenchi Muyô!*, just started in Japan—as well as a full-length theatrical feature, the anime series known as *Tenchi Muyô!* (a.k.a. "No Need For Tenchi," which is perhaps its closest English translation) has become, since its 1992 Japan debut, a bonafide phenomenon. Credited during the first OAV series for "original story," Hayashi's involvement in the series varies wildly; in some episodes, he's original story/director/screenwriter; in others, he also gets a storyboards or "art continuity (*e-konte*)" credit tagged on. In later series—the second *Tenchi!* OAV series, the *Tenchi!* OAV specials, the *Tenchi!* TV series, the *Tenchi!* movie—Hayashi isn't credited at all; for that reason, those series aren't listed. Note that, although there are currently two separate *Tenchi!* comics being published in the U.S.—an English-translated Japanese adaptation from Viz Comics, as well as a "made in America" version from series distributor Pioneer LDCA—Hayashi the animator is involved creatively with neither.

Black Magic M-66
ブラックマックM66
Key Animator
One-shot OAV (1987) based on the original manga by *Ghost in the Shell*'s Masamune Shirow. *DOMESTIC RELEASE TITLE:* ***Black Magic M-66*** (U.S. Renditions/Manga Entertainment)

Maryû Senki ("Dragon Century")
魔龍戦紀
Key Animator
Three-episode OAV series (1987-89); features animation direction and character designs by *Moldiver*'s Hiroyuki Kitazume, as well as monster designs by *Iczer-One* and *Yotoden*'s Junichi Watanabe. *DOMESTIC RELEASE TITLE:* ***Dragon Century*** (U.S. Renditions)

Bubblegum Crisis 4: Revenge Road
バブルガムクライシス④Revenge Road
Director
Fourth episode in the first *Bubblegum Crisis* OAV series (1988). *DOMESTIC RELEASE TITLE:* ***Bubblegum Crisis 4: Revenge Road*** (AnimEigo)

Explorer Woman Ray
エクスプローラー・ウーマン・レイ
Director
Two-episode OAV series (1989); in the first, Hayashi is assistant director, while in the second, he moves up to director. *DOMESTIC RELEASE TITLE:* ***Explorer Woman Ray*** (U.S. Manga Corps)

Gall Force 2: Destruction
ガルフォース２：ディストラクション
Episode Director
Second episode in the first *Gall Force* OAV series (1990). *DOMESTIC RELEASE TITLE:* ***Gall Force 2: Destruction*** (U.S. Manga Corps)

Bôken! Iczer-3 ("Adventure! Iczer-3")
冒険！イクサー３
Storyboards
Six-episode OAV series (1990) detailing the exploits of android Iczer-1's younger "sister," voiced in the Japanese version by female pro wrestler Cutey Suzuki. *DOMESTIC RELEASE TITLE:* ***Iczer-3*** (U.S. Manga Corps)

Sol Bianca
ソル・ビアンカ
Original Creator / Assistant Director
Two-volume OAV series (1990-91) in which five-woman pirate team named after the months of the year (Janny, Feb, April, etc.) set sail for sci-fi adventure. Hayashi moves up to director as of second volume. *DOMESTIC RELEASE TITLE:* ***Sol Bianca*** (A.D. Vision)

Tenchi Muyô! Ryo-ô-ki
天地無用！（りょうおうき）
Director / Original Concept, also Screenplay / Art Continuity
First, six-episode *Tenchi!* OAV series (1992-93). *DOMESTIC RELEASE TITLE:* ***Tenchi Muyô!*** (Pioneer LDCA)

Shinpi no Sekai El-Hazard ("'Holy World' El-Hazard")
神秘の世界エルハザード
Director / Original Story
Seven-episode OAV series (1995-96). *DOMESTIC RELEASE TITLE:* ***El-Hazard the Magnificent World*** (Pioneer LDCA)

Shinpi no Sekai El-Hazard
神秘の世界エルハザード
Original Concept / Series Coordination
26-episode follow-up TV series (1995-96) to the original OAVs; directed by *Bubblegum Crisis*' Katsuhito Akiyama. *DOMESTIC RELEASE TITLE:* ***The Wanderers: El-Hazard TV Series*** (Pioneer LDCA)

Mahô Shôjo Pretty Sammy ("'Magical Girl' Pretty Sammy")
魔法少女プリティサミー
Original Concept
Ongoing OAV spin-off series (1996-97). As of this writing, the first two volumes have been released domestically. *DOMESTIC RELEASE TITLE:* ***Tenchi Muyô! Pretty Sammy the Magical Girl*** (Pioneer LDCA)

Mahô Shôjo Pretty Sammy
魔法少女プリティサミー
Director
26-episode follow-up TV series (1996-97) to the original OAVs. *TV SERIES CURRENTLY IMPORT ONLY*

Shinpi no Sekai El-Hazard 2
神秘の世界エルハザード２
Original Concept
Follow-up OAV series (1997~); only two volumes available as of press time. *CURRENTLY IMPORT ONLY*

Dai-Undôkai ("Great Sports Meet")
大運動会：Battle Athletess
Director / Original Story
Hayashi parts with the *Tenchi!* franchise at last with this latest OAV (and, in a last-minute update, television) work (1997~). Note that the producer-supplied English subtitle, "Battle Athletess," is not represented in the Japanese, *kanji*-only title. *CURRENTLY IMPORT ONLY*

Key

- Japanese comics or "manga" series; may or may not be available in foreign-language (i.e., English) version
- TV series broadcast on-air in Japan. Note that, in the U.S., Japanese TV series are both broadcast on-air (*Ronin Warriors*) and released on home video (*Ranma 1/2*). Others (*Sailor Moon, Dragon Ball*) are available both in broadcast and home video versions
- Direct-to-home-video series; may also include compilations of TV episodes released to home video market
- Theatrical feature; may or may not receive equivalent theatrical release for U.S. version

Haruka Takachiho

Interviewed by Takayuki Karahashi (1994)

If Haruka Takachiho (autonym: Kimiyoshi Takekawa) isn't the patron saint of Japanese science fiction fanboys, he probably should be. Best-known as the man who created *Crusher Joe* and the *Dirty Pair*, one thing most English-speaking fans probably aren't aware of is, Haruka Takachiho is also an author in his own right.

With his forthright views and championship of the little-appreciated genre of Japanese science fiction, his is a convincing voice for the reexamination of the outdated notion that science fiction is something that only Americans can understand. Just as the ending song from the *Dirty Pair* television series goes ("*dirty stormy destiny*," indeed), Takachiho is a man for whom fate has a lot in store.

The beginning was in 1970, the year Haruka Takachiho went off to college and attended his first science fiction convention. It was at that convention that he met the people who would become the founding members of Studio Nue, among them convention chair Masahiro Noda, now a noted translator of science fiction.

"A bunch of science fiction buddies who met each other at science fiction conventions got together and founded Crystal Art Studio in hopes of doing science fiction work. But once we got started, there was very little related to science fiction. Instead, we got work for animation designs, and staff work for a children's educational show," as Takachiho explains.

Their first animation series was *Zero Tester*, a *Thunderbirds*-inspired tale first broadcast in 1973, the same year that *Casshan*, *Cutey Honey* and *Doraemon* premiered. As the projects which followed *Zero Tester* grew farther and farther away from what Crystal Art was formed to do—work on science fiction—the decision was made to disband the company and start it all over, this time under a new name.

"Our company was like a collective of people doing things that they themselves weren't sure of, never mind explaining to others," remarks Takachiho. "'Nue' refers to the Oriental version of the chimera. So, as an indescribable studio doing indescribable work, we decided to call ourselves Studio Nue."

Until Nue, mecha design was something handled by in-house designers as the need arose. As "outside" specialists hired to design props, the work on *Zero Tester* gained them a reputation for the innovative, and it wasn't long before they were being asked to work on now-legendary, mecha-heavy shows such as *Yûsha Raideen*, *Uchû Senkan Yamato*, *Sei-Senshi Dunbine*, *Combattler V* and *Tôshô Daimos*.

His involvement in Nue aside, however, it wasn't until Takachiho began his next vocation as a writer that his reputation really began to pick up steam. With the publication of two novels—the science fiction action classic *Crusher Joe*, and the by-now infamous *Great Adventures of the Dirty Pair*, which was printed in Japan, in English—Takachiho was setting in action a chain of events which would culminate in a degree of international fame only dreamed of by struggling young animators.

A part of anime apocrypha in its own right, it was the scene-stealing *Dirty Pair* in 1983's *Crusher Joe* theatrical feature which thrust Takachiho into the hearts of anime fans forever. With a continuing video series from Los Angeles-based Streamline Pictures (the *Affair of Nolandia* OAV and, later, the *Project Eden* movie) and a manga-style original comic from Dark Horse (also serialized in the U.K.'s MANGA MANIA magazine), the multinational, multimedia *Dirty Pair* phenomenon proved forever in the minds of anime fans that you never can have too much firepower or too much cleavage.

"I think this story is already well-known in the U.S.," Takachiho says in reference to the start of the series, "but back at the time the *Dirty Pair* was created, there was a very popular women's pro wrestling organization known as the WWWA. And there was this women's tag team by the name of 'Beauty Pair.' I got the inspiration from their name and came up with a completely unrelated story."

But even with the heavy responsibility that comes along with being "Father of the Dirty Pair," Takachiho has never forgotten his roots as a science fiction fan. He still finds time to run a computer bulletin board system (Kadokawa Shoten's Comptique BBS), and he regularly touches base with online fans in the "Miiko's Room" subboard of the FANMIX forum on Nifty Serve, Japan's answer to CompuServe.

Perhaps it is just such a base that keeps him constantly thinking of ways to update his most famous creations, such as in the recent *DP* remake, hot on the Japanese market at the time of this interview—*Dirty Pair Flash*, six-volume OAV series and, basically, a prequel of sorts, which places a brand-new (and, as ever, scantily clad) Pair in a bold, new future.

interview

ANIMERICA: You were a founding member and president of Studio Nue.

Crusher Joe

TAKACHIHO: Yes, I was president from the start.

ANIMERICA: But one day, you decided to become a writer instead.

TAKACHIHO: Nue was a group of creative types, and creative people aren't necessarily good at running a business. We needed someone who could do administrative, accounting, and marketing tasks. I had a knack for them, so I tended toward that position. But it was a company full of creative types, after all, and I had my own creative urges. One day I wrote out an idea I'd been carrying around for a long time and showed it to a publisher. They said, "Let's publish it." After that decision was made, they asked me who I wanted for cover art and illustrations. Since Studio Nue produces illustrations for science fiction, among other things, they thought I'd use one of my own artists. But I happened to know an animator named Yoshikazu Yasuhiko, although no one else seemed to know about him back then except perhaps for fans who were *really* into animation. I'd worked with him on *Yûsha* ("Brave") *Raideen* and I knew how good an artist he was, so I requested him. And that's how the *Crusher Joe* novel came into being.

ANIMERICA: Ah, *Crusher Joe*, the space opera. Were there any space operas in Japanese science fiction literature before *Crusher Joe*...?

TAKACHIHO: There were a few, but Japan also had the wonderful manga artist Osamu Tezuka, and it was he who established the genre as something which had traditionally been depicted through manga. The result was that, although there were many space opera *manga*, there were very few space opera *novels*. Japanese science fiction was heavily influenced by the likes of Arthur C. Clarke, Isaac Asimov and Robert Heinlein's work during the 1950s, so the mainstream literature at that time was heavy science fiction in that vein. Everyone thought space opera was nothing more than a manga genre. So when I incorporated that kind of American style into a space opera novel, it was thought to be refreshing.

ANIMERICA: What was it like, making the transition to writing as a career? You didn't undergo some furtive, ridiculously rigorous training that had you coughing up blood or anything like that...?

I like pro wrestling very much, so there are times when I borrow names from it, but it's not really with the intention of creating homages.

TAKACHIHO: Not at all. [LAUGHS] I actually finished my first novel in two weeks.

ANIMERICA: So it all came to you naturally, then?

TAKACHIHO: Well, I was writing scripts and whatnot before then, and I'd always loved to write, so I had no trouble writing. Except that I hadn't worked on anything of any length, so I was a little nervous, wondering if I could wrap it up well. I think it turned out all right.

ANIMERICA: You've told us the *Dirty Pair* was born from women's pro wrestling. Are there any other homages to wrestling in your work?

TAKACHIHO: No, not too many, although "Crusher Joe" comes from a pro wrestler named Crusher. I like pro wrestling very much, so there are times when I borrow names from it, but it's not really with the intention of creating homages.

ANIMERICA: How about other books? What have you written outside the sci-fi field?

TAKACHIHO: I've been keenly interested in the idea of physical training and fighting for some time now, so in addition to science fiction, I've written quite a few martial arts novels. For that purpose, I've interviewed people doing karate, aikido, *shorinji kenpo*, etc.

ANIMERICA: Do you ever take part in such activities yourself?

TAKACHIHO: Only a little judo in junior high. I haven't done much in the way of martial arts beyond that. I have met a few masters, though, and I think I have a feel for it, and I know enough to discern techniques. The other day, for example, I began sending my son off for kung fu lessons. Kung fu has many top-class techniques that the world should know about, so I'm writing about them in my books. Those who are into martial arts are probably quite aware that the stuff you see in movies is all faked and scripted. Those really high kicks aren't very practical, after all. I wish people could see what sort of moves are *really* used to kill people.

ANIMERICA: Isaac Asimov used to say that science fiction is a literary genre unique to the U.S., and that it doesn't really exist in other countries. In your opinion, are there real science fiction authors who write real science fiction in Japan?

TAKACHIHO: I would say that Sakyo Komatsu has written novels of which the world would be proud. I think he might not be known in the U.S. for anything other than his novel *Japan Sinks*, but his stories have content and scale comparable to Clarke. As for hard science fiction, a writer by the name of Akira Hori writes stories constructed from awe-inspiring details of scientific knowledge. Sure, I think Japanese science fiction has many high-level stories.

ANIMERICA: But will they ever be translated and published outside of Japan?

TAKACHIHO: That doesn't happen often. Stories chosen for publication tend to be short stories with "Japanesque" sentiments. I'm not convinced that the full potential of Japanese science fiction in translation has been explored.

ANIMERICA: Would you say that the stories which are translated are chosen for their Orientalism? The so-called mystique of the Orient?

TAKACHIHO: Yes, I would.

© Haruka Takachiho/Studio Nue • Sunrise, Inc. • NTV

ANIMERICA: But the *Dirty Pair* was translated into English....

TAKACHIHO: That was translated for the Japanese market and published in English for the Japanese market, so I'd say it's a little different from the translations we're talking about. If there were to be opportunities for translation, there are many stories, not necessarily mine, which I would like American people to read. Many of Komatsu's stories, for example.

ANIMERICA: Such as "The Day of Resurrection," perhaps?

TAKACHIHO: Well, that one was made into a movie [*released in 1980 under the title* Virus, *starring Sonny Chiba, Glenn Ford and Olivia Hussey—Ed.*], but there are far better Komatsu stories such as "Who Will Take Over?" or "At the End of the Infinite Flow" or "The Gordian Knot." I think American readers would be shocked silly to read these works in translation. I think they'd be surprised to know these kinds of stories even existed. I'll tell you right now that some stories seem to get translated in Japanese almost automatically, and should you win a Hugo, why, that's even better. I wish books rated as highly in Japan could get the same kind of treatment when they go overseas.

ANIMERICA: It's rare to hear of even Seiun Award winners [*said to be the Japanese equivalent to the Hugo—Ed.*] getting translated into English.

TAKACHIHO: Not just Seiun winners, though, but all the classics we Japanese read and grew up on. Such as Komatsu and Yasutaka Tsutsui. I think it's no good if the classics don't get translated first.

ANIMERICA: On the other hand, a comic version of *Dirty Pair* is published in English from Dark Horse.

TAKACHIHO: I attribute this mostly to the power of animation. Basically, it has pictures despite the language barrier. I think animation fares better if only for the pictures. I think that's how a comic version can spring up or the story itself can become known—animation is a means to overcoming the language barrier. There are a few works made with science fiction in mind, such as *The Wings of Honneamise*, and do I think it's possible to show the caliber of Japanese science fiction through such works.

ANIMERICA: The Dark Horse Comics *Dirty Pair* is an original story. How do you like it?

TAKACHIHO: I tend to think that visual works—including the English comic version, the manga version, the animated version, all versions—are fundamentally different from the novel. For example, I always ask that they come up with an original story when they animate a work of mine. I have a belief that a sufficiently well-written novel cannot be improved by a translation into a visual medium, which is why I make this request. And so, in answer to your question, and without commenting on the story itself, I think original stories must be something suitable for the comic medium.

ANIMERICA: Do you have any ideas for a live-action *Dirty Pair*?

TAKACHIHO: No, I can't say I've been approached with *that* one…at least, not yet. [LAUGHS]

ANIMERICA: What if such a feature were to be made in Japan or Hollywood? Have you given any thoughts to casting?

TAKACHIHO: I love movies very much, but I also love animation very much, too. This time around, *Dirty Pair* underwent a remake, and I've been terribly excited about it. It was fortunate for me that I happened to start a company wanting to go into science fiction and ending up in animation, but I like animation, after all, and I really like to immerse myself in the details of its production. …All of which goes to say, I'd like to continue writing stories with an eye toward having them animated eventually.

ANIMERICA: Do you have any favorite animation titles?

TAKACHIHO: I have to say I mainly watch Hayao Miyazaki's animation. For my viewing material, it's watching stories with a happy ending and without evil people, so that's what I tend to end up watching. As for my own work, *Crusher Joe* was my first, so my feelings for it run deep. And of course, I have other works of which I'm fond for various reasons.

ANIMERICA: But in your own *Dirty Pair* and *Crusher Joe*, evil people are everywhere, and people die right and left.…

TAKACHIHO: It's different when we're talking about *my* stories. [LAUGHS] They tend to go in different directions than the shows I choose to watch.

ANIMERICA: I understand you're involved in running a BBS. Do you value your connections to fandom?

Dirty Pair Flas

TAKACHIHO: I don't really talk with fans. For one thing, there's a big age gap. Even though I like to think I'm still young myself, most of my readers are the same age as my son. When I try to talk to them, it starts to sound more like an old man lecturing a bunch of kids rather than an honest dialogue. [LAUGHS] So I try not to poke my nose into such affairs.

ANIMERICA: Is that so? It was my understanding that you ran some science fiction conventions after you went pro. And before then, you were involved in the science fiction world, were you not?

TAKACHIHO: Yes, but I was still young, then. I started my company when I was 20 or 21 years old. I was still busy doing fan activities until I was 25 or so. —Hey, I *was* young, back then. [LAUGHS] It's a carryover from those days to think of myself as being young…well, you know how it is.

ANIMERICA: Let's talk about your hobbies. Pro wrestling, martial arts, skiing, that type of thing?

TAKACHIHO: Those, and until recently, I was also into motorcycles, at least until I hurt my back. [LAUGHS] These days, I'd say I'm more into skiing.

ANIMERICA: These are all high-adrenaline activities, wouldn't you say?

TAKACHIHO: [LAUGHS] When I was a kid, and until I was in junior high, I was into reading manga and books. I was the type who stayed inside the house all the time. I rarely exercised—I guess you could say I had a little complex going against it. I was suddenly enlightened around the age of thirty or so. I realized that I should be moving my body more often and started to get into many activities. So these sports are things I began to do in the last ten years or so.

ANIMERICA: You like adrenaline, then? *Dirty Pair* and *Crusher Joe* both look like they were written on it, and it's an element in other works of yours yet to be animated, as well.

TAKACHIHO: You could say I have an admiration for all things powerful.

ANIMERICA: What about tractors?

TAKACHIHO: Not tractors. [LAUGHS] More like those powerhouse wrestlers in pro wrestling. Not the Hulk Hogan type; more like the Road Warriors, you know? If you're familiar with pro wrestling, you'll know what I'm talking about. [LAUGHS]

ANIMERICA: You also seem to be into technical things such as networking and computers. Are you also interested in computer games or ham radio?

TAKACHIHO: I'm completely inept at games. I'm just no good at them. I was really into ham radio when I was a kid. The problem was, I was a *kid*—I couldn't obtain the equipment. I've lived thus far without obtaining a license. I have a stronger interest in hardware, gadgets and such. Also, things with motors. Among plastic models, I prefer the ones with motorized parts which move and transform. I've always liked those kinds of models.

ANIMERICA: A battery-operated Valkyrie, for example?

TAKACHIHO: ...That becomes business, so it's not as interesting. It's the same with skiing and martial arts. I got into them as hobbies, but I'd use them for my writing, and they became work. Then I'd start thinking about how I could use them in my work, and I'd lose interest and could no longer enjoy them as hobbies. It's a habit of mine, a...how do you say it? It's like the destiny of a novelist. The pattern is that I think I'm enjoying something purely for pleasure, but eventually it becomes a part of work, and then I can't think of it as anything but source material for writing.

ANIMERICA: Speaking of Valkyries, *Macross* is another Studio Nue show.

TAKACHIHO: Yes. That was from a different department, but we worked on that show, too. *Macross* was of Shoji Kawamori and Kazuki Miyatake lineage. But I wasn't managing it, so I didn't know about the progress of that project.

ANIMERICA: At that time, you were already Haruka Takachiho the writer.

TAKACHIHO: Yes, it was nothing but writing by that time, and I'd already resigned as president.

ANIMERICA: What's your relationship with Studio Nue been like since you became a writer?

TAKACHIHO: Nue handles copyright management, and it's still that way. For example, *Dirty Pair* is copyrighted Haruka Takachiho and Studio Nue.

ANIMERICA: So Nue is your manager.

TAKACHIHO: Yes, and they get a percentage of my income. On the other hand, they also work on animation projects on their own. Right now, Kawamori is working on some *Macross* project with Nue. I'm not really familiar with it; it's called *Macross Plus*. I got a report about it. They seem to be working on it in conjunction with a TV version. Anyway, they let me make a new CD since they made the six-volume *Dirty Pair Flash* OAV series.

ANIMERICA: Will you be singing on this CD?

TAKACHIHO: I won't be singing, but Rika Matsumoto and Mariko Koda, who respectively play Yuri and Kei in the new DP feature, will be. They've released CDs before and can sing, even though they're voice-actors. I submitted a project proposal saying I wanted to make a CD with dramatic dialog and songs in it, and it was accepted. It's been ten years since I last wrote a script, not since *Crusher Joe*.

ANIMERICA: Would you say that this, too, is another version of the *Dirty Pair*?

TAKACHIHO: You could say that. It's scheduled for release on April 25. It's called "Yuri and Kei: The Angels' Holiday." They're on vacation, you see.

ANIMERICA: In closing, do you have a message for your fans in the English-speaking world?

TAKACHIHO: Well, let's see. I've written many space operas, but I've also written many other kinds of novels. I wish you could read all these books from different genres. Of course, if they could be animated...the novels may be in Japanese, but you might have an easier time watching them in animation. I'd like to campaign to get at least some of them animated so that they could be seen not just in Japan, but by people in America, as well. So if you'd like to see that happen too, please root for me. I think that's what I'd like to say.

afterword

Since the time of this interview, *Dirty Pair Flash* has gone on to produce a second OAV series in Japan, *Dirty Pair Flash 2*. In America, the original "Dirty Pair" are enjoying great success, not just for their animated adaptations, but in an original made-in-America comic version, as well.

Conceived of by Toren Smith—head of Studio Proteus, one of the earliest and most influential translation studios in the American anime/manga industry—and artist Adam Warren, who's worked on a *Teen Titans* one-shot and *Gen 13* comic mini-series, the American *Dirty Pair* comic draws its inspiration directly from Takachiho's original "character concepts," which left Smith and Warren (in later installments, Warren produces the series solo) free to come up with their own mythology and adventures for the infamous Pair. Warren is also scheduled to work on another installment in the "made in America" *Bubblegum Crisis* manga series, to be titled "Meat Jacket."

As of 1997, both the animated *Dirty Pair* movies and the *Crusher Joe* films are available in the U.S., with *Dirty Pair Flash* soon to join them. As for future projects—especially science fiction projects—what Takachiho has in mind has yet to be seen.

Haruka Takachiho
Select Bibliography & Filmography

MANGA 漫画

Note that, although they're listed here under "manga," none of the following works are, in fact, Japanese comics, but novels written in Japanese. In the case of the *Dirty Pair* novel, the story was animated, and eventually released here in the U.S. as a "manga-style" American comic written in English by Toren Smith and Adam Warren. Although Toren has since left the series in order to concentrate on comics produced under his own flourishing "Studio Proteus" imprint, Warren keeps the legend alive, gaining notoriety and high acclaim most recently for his work on "*(Bootleg) Gen 13*," a mainstream title loaded to the gills with anime, manga, and Hong Kong action flick in-jokes. For more information on Takachiho's novels, try `www.sfwj.or.jp` on the World-Wide Web.

Crusher Joe: Wakusei Pizan no Kiki
("Crusher Joe: Crisis on Planet Pizan")
クラッシャー・ジョウ：惑星ピザンの危機

Author
Published in 1977; Takachiho's debut as a writer. Followed by several sequels. *CURRENTLY IMPORT ONLY*

Dirty Pair no Dai-Bôken
("The Great Adventures of the Dirty Pair")
ダーティペアの大冒険

Author
Published in 1987. In addition to unleashing upon an unsuspecting public the chaos that is Kei and Yuri, the so-called "Dirty Pa—" ...Uh, make that "Lovely Angels"...*Anyway*, in addition to introducing the characters, the *Dirty Pair no Dai-Bôken* novel went on to win the Seiun Award, the Japanese equivalent to the Hugo. Illustration by Yoshikazu Yasuhiko (*Gundam*), with translation by David Lewis. Followed by a sequel, *Dirty Pair no Dai-Gyakushû* ("The Great Counterattack of the Dirty Pair"). *ENGLISH-LANGUAGE RELEASE TITLE:* ***Great Adventures of the Dirty Pair*** (Kodansha English Library)

ANIME アニメ

Compared to some of the creators in this book, Takachiho's anime contributions may seem a bit slim, but don't let that fool you—active as a writer for more years than some might like to count, Takachiho is a fixture in the science fiction communities of his native Japan, known not only as a novelist and anime screenwriter/producer, but as a Net-happy onliner whose locally operated BBS attracts fans of a similar stripe from all over cyberspace.

Crusher Joe
クラッシャー・ジョウ

Original Story / Screenplay / Editorial Supervision
131-minute theatrical feature (1983). An animated, large-scale sci-fi spectacular that's also not without its humor. Features the first-ever animated appearance of the Dirty Pair, the terrible twosome who would go on to star in one of the most successful series in studio Sunrise's history. Directed, co-scripted, partially animated, character designed, and storyboarded by Yoshikazu Yasuhiko (*Arion, Gundam, Venus Wars*). *DOMESTIC RELEASE TITLE:* ***Crusher Joe: The Movie*** (AnimEigo)

Dirty Pair
ダーティペア

Original Story
24-episode TV series (1985); based on Takachiho's novel of the same name, with character designs by a then-novice Tsukasa Dokite (animation director, *Urusei Yatsura*), as heavily influenced by Yasuhiko's original novel illustrations. A *fumetti*-style "anime film comic" series using actual production cels from the show is also available domestically (with dialogue in English) through Viz Comics. Note that the TV series is also available in Japan in a variety of re-edited and re-released compilation formats. *CURRENTLY IMPORT ONLY*

Dirty Pair no Dai-Shôbu: Nolandia no Nazo
("The Dirty Pair's Great Victory: The Mystery of Nolandia")
ダーティペアの大勝負：ノーランディアの謎

Original Story
55-minute, one-shot OAV (1985); first of non-TV *Dirty Pair* "spin-off" projects. In a break with the established Yasuhiko designs, character designer Dokite takes a chance and goes for a more "realistic" look with Kei and Yuri. (We'll leave it to you to determine whether or not his gamble was successful.) *DOMESTIC RELEASE TITLE:* ***Dirty Pair: The Affair of Nolandia*** (Streamline Pictures)

Dirty Pair: Gekijô Ban ("Dirty Pair: The Movie")
ダーティペア：劇場版

Original Story / Planning Coordinator
80-minute theatrical feature (1987); all-new original story (with a very stylish, "Bond, James Bond"-type opening) in which the Pair square off against a wacky mad scientist, and Kei gets a new boyfriend. *DOMESTIC RELEASE TITLE:* ***Dirty Pair Project Eden*** (Streamline Pictures)

Dirty Pair
ダーティペア

Original Story
Five-volume OAV series (1987); revised Dokite character designs feature a return to a more "anime" style than the "realism" of *Nolandia*. In its original Japanese release, two OAVs were included on each volume, for a total of 10 original anime videos. *CURRENTLY IMPORT ONLY*

Crusher Joe: Hyôketsu Kangoku no Wana and Saishû Heiki Ash
("Crusher Joe: The Ice-Hell Trap" and "Crusher Joe: Final Weapon Ash")
クラッシャー・ジョウ：氷結監獄の罠 & 最終兵器アッシュ

Original Story
Two-volume OAV series (1989). Six years after the original *Crusher Joe* movie, the Crusher Team is back for direct-to-home-video adventures. Character design is by Yasuhiko, while mecha design is by *Macross'* Shoji Kawamori. *DOMESTIC RELEASE TITLE:* ***Crusher Joe: The Ice Prison*** and ***Crusher Joe: Last Weapon Ash*** (AnimEigo)

Dirty Pair: Bôryaku no 005 Ben
("Dirty Pair: The Flight 005 Conspiracy")
ダーティペア：謀略の００５便

Original Story
60-minute, one-shot OAV (1990); Dokite sticks with the safe bet and extends the designs from the '87 OAV series more or less intact to this final—unless, of course, you count *Dirty Pair Flash*—entry into the series (see below). *DOMESTIC RELEASE TITLE:* ***Dirty Pair: Flight 005 Conspiracy*** (Streamline Pictures)

Dirty Pair Flash
ダーティペアフラッシュ

Original Story / Dialogue
Six-volume OAV series (1994). With a new look, new character designs, and even new voice-actors, *Dirty Pair Flash* is more a distant cousin to the original franchise than direct spin-off, despite the fact that Takachiho himself takes credit not only for "original story," but for screenwriting, as well. If nothing else, now we know that the "Dirty Pair" is more than just a pejorative nickname—it's more like an office, in which (presumably) any two buxom, scantily dressed lasses may serve. Nudie transformation sequences á la *Cutey Honey* should prove popular with certain fans (you know who you are). Followed by a second OAV series, *DP Flash 2*. *DOMESTIC RELEASE TITLE:* ***Dirty Pair Flash*** (A.D. Vision)

Key

Japanese comics or "manga" series; may or may not be available in foreign-language (i.e., English) version

TTV series broadcast on-air in Japan. Note that, in the U.S., Japanese TV series are both broadcast on-air (*Ronin Warriors*) and released on home video (*Ranma 1/2*). Others (*Sailor Moon, Dragon Ball*) are available both in broadcast and home video versions

Direct-to-home-video series; may also include compilations of TV episodes released to home video market

Theatrical feature; may or may not receive equivalent theatrical release for U.S. version

Hiroyuki Kitazume

Interviewed by Takashi Oshiguchi (1994)

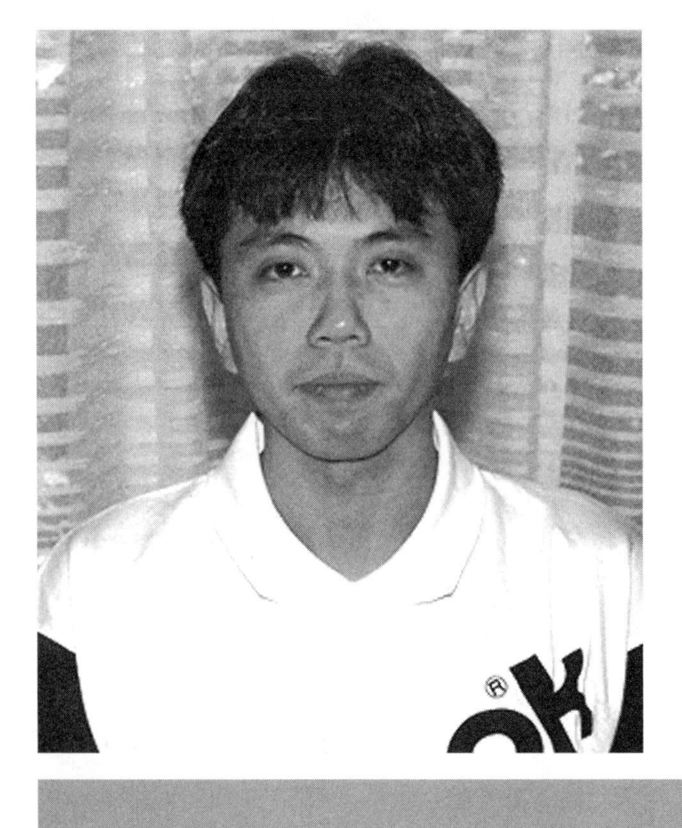

When asked what kind of animation inspired him to become an animator, Kitazume laughs. "Well, it was *Gundam* that made me go into the industry, after all."

He's referring to *that Gundam*, the original 43-episode *Kidô Senshi Gundam* ("Mobile Suit Gundam") television series by Yoshiyuki "Father of Gundam" Tomino, of course. No matter how endearingly camp this 1979 mecha-show-of-all-mecha-shows may seem by today's standards, the series' gritty realism (relative to the time period) and Yoshikazu Yasuhiko's "lifelike" character designs, are mentioned time and time again by anime professionals as one of the first shows to suggest animation's infinite possibilities. Kitazume is perhaps the poster child of the animator who got into animation "because of *Gundam*," especially since he eventually got the chance to make his own mark on the *Gundam* series itself.

"Compared to the animation character designs before him, there was something different about Yasuhiko's style," says Kitazume, who cites the "personality" of Yasuhiko's *Gundam* characters as important influences on his own work. "For ease of animation, designers before Yasuhiko tended toward simplified manga characters. It was unusual for a designer to create animation characters from scratch. But Yasuhiko's drawings have a true design aesthetic. His characters are full-fledged designs that can be viewed as art in their own right."

For a boy who loved animation since elementary school—"around junior high, the (live-action) series *Kamen Rider* really appealed to me for a while, but *Yamato* pulled me back into anime"—Kitazume still thinks of those *Yamato* and *Gundam* days as something special.

"That was an exciting time, with television shows such as *Gatchaman* and so many newly animated theatrical features coming out. I must have been influenced by those. (Those films) were as familiar to me as the television shows I watched during childhood." Inspired by this exciting new age of animation, and Yasuhiko's work—not only on *Gundam*, but on *Combattler-V*, *Raideen*, and other Sunrise and Toei giant robot shows—young Kitazume thought to try his own hand at designing.

"I was doodling since I was little, and I was always very interested in drawing. When the live-action boom shifted back to animation, there was a dramatic improvement in drawing quality. And taken together with my love of drawing. . . ." In his senior year in high school, the time when Japanese students have to make decisions about their future careers, Kitazume told his parents he wanted to become an animator.

"They said 'No,'" Kitazume laughs. "They told me to go to a vocational school instead, to cool my head."

Finally, his parents made a bargain with him. If young Hiroyuki really wanted to become an animator, then nothing else would do but for him to go to animation school. His parents would pay his tuition for the first two years. And so, upon graduation from high school, Kitazume put off job hunting and went merrily on his way to enroll in the animation department of the Tokyo Design Institute. Two years later, he hadn't changed his mind.

"I'd found my vocation," he says.

Kitazume got his official start at Studio Bebow, run by Tomonori Kogawa, while still a student at Tokyo Design Institute. The chance to work with *Gundam*'s creator/director Tomino was an early benchmark in his career.

"At the time, Tomino's latest work was *Ideon*, and Bebow was a studio that worked on that show. So I kind of went there to fulfill my dreams," he laughs.

Kitazume's talent revealed itself early, and he quickly racked up an impressive list of credits on the majority of the shows the prolific animation studio Sunrise was producing at the time—*Xabungle*, *Dunbine*, *L-Gaim* and *Zeta Gundam*, leading finally to his first character design solo on 1986's *Gundam Double Zeta* and his first design work for a theatrical feature, in *Mobile Suit Gundam: Gyakushû no Char* ("Char's Counterattack"). But character design was only the beginning for the multi-talented Kitazume—on his most ambitious original project so far, *Moldiver*, he's credited for original story, as well as director and character designer. As a creator, he cites the omnipresent influence of the great animator Hayao Miyazaki as one of the inspirations that drives his work.

"Back when I saw *Castle of Cagliostro*, I thought it was wonderful, and so much fun to watch...but I thought it was the storyboarding and direction that made it that way, not just the drawing. So I thought animating was fine, but I wanted to direct, too. I wanted to do both. Not just drawing."

interview

ANIMERICA: So, what was your first real job in animation?

KITAZUME: Well, my first job was on the *Ideon* movie. There were two features, *Densetsu Kyoshin Ideon: Sesshoku-Hen* ("Legendary God-Giant Ideon: A Contact") and *Densetsu Kyoshin Ideon: Hatsudô-Hen* ("Be Invoked"). They were going to make new animation for *Contact*, and my first job was making in-betweens for the new animation, which would then be edited into the compilation. As you may know, the *Ideon* movies were based on the TV show. After that, I did in-betweens for TV shows, such as for *Xabungle*.

ANIMERICA: So you were still just an in-betweener back then.

KITAZUME: Yes. I became a key animator in the middle of the next show, *Sei-Senshi Dunbine*.

ANIMERICA: So when were you first on your own?

KITAZUME: When I did *Gundam Double Zeta*.

Moldiver

ANIMERICA: That was your first? I had the impression it was long before that.

KITAZUME: That was the first. I was twenty-four back then.

ANIMERICA: Since then you worked on a few original videos?

KITAZUME: Yes, just one. It was called *Legaciam* (1987). It was around the same time as *Char's Counterattack*.

ANIMERICA: Is it correct that you worked on *Robot Carnival* with your colleague, Hidetoshi Omori, at Studio Bebow?

KITAZUME: Yes, I worked on that with him. I did *Robot Carnival* and *Double Zeta* around the same time. I did *L-Gaim* after *Dunbine*, and after that came *Zeta Gundam*. I left Studio Bebow when *Zeta* was starting up. Right around that time, a producer came to me and said, "I want you to animate the show after *Zeta Gundam*." So that was going to be my first work after going independent. But when I was drawing the characters to audition for that show, it was suddenly decided that *Zeta* would be extended. It was all very last-minute.

I have to fight the urge to use particular styles of my own to establish particular moods. I *could* say it's tough to be the person who has to make those decisions.

ANIMERICA: Not the ideal situation for a first solo work. How much time did you really have?

KITAZUME: Well, *Double Zeta* started in January, but I was drawing the characters for the new show during the summer before. The project went on hiatus in the fall, and I was told to stop my work. It was already October when they told me that *Zeta* was going to be extended. Bright Noah and all the other *Zeta* characters were going to be in it, but (character designer) Yasuhiko wasn't going to be involved anymore. So I was chosen because I was the artist who had worked on the show and could carry on a natural sense of continuity. That's how I ended up working on *Double Zeta*.

ANIMERICA: You've worked on nearly all the Sunrise shows.

KITAZUME: Well, yes. Back then, we were working on about five of the titles being made at Sunrise's Studio No. 2.

ANIMERICA: Were you always freelancing, then?

KITAZUME: Well, after leaving Studio Bebow, I was running a company with a few friends.

ANIMERICA: You've worked on quite a few A.I.C. productions, too.

KITAZUME: I wonder what the first A.I.C. work I did was.... Maybe it was *Iczer-One*. When we were working on *Iczer-One*, (director) Toshihiro Hirano singled out our studio's Hiroaki Oi to do mecha designs for the video. So a colleague from our studio was working on that video...and then I was asked to join. That's how I met Toru Miura—and that's how we started working on A.I.C. titles. Then after *Char's Counterattack*, we disbanded our studio. I'm lazy, and I was getting tired of managing a studio. So I went to A.I.C.'s president and decided to take on any work he brought me. [LAUGHS] I did key animation and everything else under his management.

ANIMERICA: So after *Iczer-One*, you worked mostly on original videos?

KITAZUME: My first work around that time was a video from Kubo Shoten called *Dragon Century*, although that wasn't a big job. Speaking of big jobs, I was involved with the character designs in *Megazone 23, Part Three*. I think that was my first big job since going to A.I.C.

ANIMERICA: Now let's move on to *Moldiver*. *Moldiver* is almost totally your own work, isn't it? You're the creator, character designer and director.

KITAZUME: Yes, I was involved right from the drafting of the proposal.

ANIMERICA: How would you describe *Moldiver* to someone who has never seen it?

KITAZUME: In terms of genre, it's a superhero story. But in most of those kinds of stories, the main character has special abilities to begin with. My premise was: "*What if an ordinary kid suddenly got those abilities?*" And since we're dealing with ordinary kids, the stories wouldn't be that overblown, either. They would have an ordinary beginning, but things might just end up in a big mess. It's an accessible superhero story like that.

ANIMERICA: An ordinary high-school girl tinkers with her brother's mecha and—

KITAZUME: ...And what would happen if that gave her the powers to become a superbeing. That's the theme.

ANIMERICA: Did you prepare the plots for Volumes One through Six before you got the go-ahead?

KITAZUME: No, that wasn't the case. All the volumes were supposed to be self-contained stories. I drafted a couple of story ideas, and some of them got animated as they were. As for the series coordination, about half were Nakamura's ideas [*screenwriter Manabu Nakamura—Ed.*]. The last episode, Episode Six, featured the story of the launch of the spaceship under the "dimensional navigation project." We wanted to make that the backbone of the six episodes, so we started to introduce elements of that from the second episode on.

ANIMERICA: Episode Six looks like a two-parter.

KITAZUME: Yes. In the beginning, we weren't going to make it that big a story. But during the production meetings, we decided there should be an underlying plot. So that's how that came about.

ANIMERICA: Was the character "Moldiver 3" planned from the beginning?

KITAZUME: Well, he was in the plans, but we couldn't come up with the designs until the last minute.

ANIMERICA: What about the idea that the kid would do it? Were the two brothers and sister always going to be involved?

KITAZUME: Yes. That was planned from the beginning. I originally wanted to use this idea for a TV show—like a 50-episode series, including throwaway episodes. But I still wanted it to have a consistent main plot. You know how a TV series has key episodes? We ended up having to condense only those kinds of episodes for the OAV volumes. So we ended up with less time to show the daily lives of the characters. And at the end of those episodes, Nozomu creating Moldiver 3 seemed to happen a little too suddenly—you would have expected something like that if only we'd had more opportunities to show what he was like in daily life. I think it may have been a mistake to have a sudden plot twist like that.

ANIMERICA: How about the female antagonists?

KITAZUME: Those personalities were actually solidified rather late. In the beginning, we wanted to make an "8-Man" [*the hero of the classic 1963 Japanese television series, wherein Higashi Hachiro leads a double life: police officer by day, and crime-fighting android by night—Ed.*]. There'd be eight of them, eight female transforming androids. So when I was drafting the proposal, they all had the same face. I wasn't going to give them individual characters, but that might have been too boring. So instead, we decided to give each of them their own personality.

ANIMERICA: How long did pre-production take?

KITAZUME: I wonder how long that took. Let's see, submitting the proposal and.... It took a while. It was over a one- or two-year span. It took me over a year since the first inspiration.

ANIMERICA: So that means you hadn't decided how the last episode would turn out when you started?

KITAZUME: All the scripts were finished before we started making Episode One. Quite a lot of it was finished before actual production of the film began, but the production was parallel to my work on the *Bastard!!* series. So that's why we had a little delay. It's also why I had a little under

Moldiver

a year to refine my ideas. Afterward, when the writer came in, we came up with all six episodes in a flash. And then, there was a little hiatus before actual production began.

ANIMERICA: Are you going to be working on the new *Yamato*?

KITAZUME: Well, right now, production is pending, but I'm supposed to do it. (Producer) Nishizaki is saying he's making *Yamato*, so I guess it's officially going to be made. [LAUGHS] But in reality, there's no specific talk of when and how. Right now, there are two titles involved. There's the video version, "New Uchû Senkan Yamato," with the Syd Mead-designed ship [*now titled* Yamato 2520—*Ed.*], and then there's "Resurrection of Yamato," using the old designs. "New Yamato" is coming out sooner. It's within the year. I've heard the theatrical version might be on hold until that's taken care of.

ANIMERICA: So you're working on the movie and not the OAV?

KITAZUME: That's right. It's "Resurrection of Yamato." It's the story of resurrecting the *Yamato* that's split in two in *Final Yamato* [*the 1983 theatrical release famous for sacrificing the* Yamato *in one final conflagration, much the same way the* Enterprise NCC-1701 *was destroyed at the end of* Star Trek III: The Search for Spock—*Ed.*]. On the other hand, "New Yamato" has completely new characters. "Resurrection of Yamato" will have Susumu Kodai [*English-speaking fans may recognize this character as "Derek Wildstar"—Ed.*] and a few other characters in their old age, so they're going to appear in a story that takes place some years since the last one.

ANIMERICA: As a *Yamato* fan yourself, what do you think of Syd Mead's designs?

KITAZUME: Well, I have to say it doesn't look like a *Yamato*. [LAUGHS] But I think it can hold its own and there must be ways to make use of it. But I think it'll require a lot of "imprinting" to make it look like it belongs in that universe. I also think it'll be necessary to make it into a series and convince the audience that it is indeed a *Yamato*. Strictly from a design point of view, it doesn't look like a *Yamato*, but....

ANIMERICA: *Yamato* was almost a social movement in Japanese animation, wasn't it? What are your feelings about being involved in a work of which you've been a fan for so long?

KITAZUME: Well, the main reason I joined this project was that it's a theatrical feature. I've been an animator for some ten years now. Granted, I worked on *Char's Counterattack* six or seven years ago, but it may have been a little too big a project for me back then. Since then, I've gotten more experience, and I've gotten a little bit better. So I'd say it was about time for me to work on a theatrical feature...in this case, it just happens to be *Yamato*. It's a film I had great feelings for in my youth, and it's a feature, so I'd like as many people as possible to see it. I hope to show a new generation of people what great animation is. I'm not really too interested in the plot, such as the piecing together of the *Yamato* broken in the previous story. But I think *Yamato*'s impact on the audience will always be big, so that's what I'd like to be involved in.

ANIMERICA: You mentioned that Susumu Kodai will be showing up in his old age. How do you design older versions of characters you love?

KITAZUME: Well, it's similar to what I did in *Char's Counterattack*, after all. —Actually, it was Yasuhiko who had to age Char Aznable after *Gundam* and *Zeta Gundam* so we got to see Char's aging progress. I had a part in *Zeta*'s version of Char, but that was a design with many conditions in mind. As for *Yamato*, the anime scene is different now from how it was back then. At that time, Leiji Matsumoto's popularity was really pulling *Yamato* along. So the issue with me now for this current project is: How much of a Leiji Matsumoto style should be in my characters? It's my feeling that there are more people of a younger generation who are more familiar with the *animated* Kodai than the authentic *Matsumoto* Kodai, so perhaps it's better to update the style. More important than the superficial details of the character design, I want to establish the authentic *feel* of Kodai.

ANIMERICA: They started off with the Matsumoto style, and Kodai's style eventually evolved into what he became over the course of the many sequels. So you'd be adding your style based on that character?

KITAZUME: Yes, back then Leiji Matsumoto's characters were deeply popular in the world, what with *Ginga Tetsudô 999* and such. So the various different styles of Kodai were still regarded as Matsumoto-style characters. But actually, the style has been changing all along. Conversely, the Susumu Kodai that the fans want may not actually be Matsumoto's original Kodai, but the Kodai who's been depicted in the animation.

ANIMERICA: When it comes to character designing, would you say that it's something you make from scratch?

KITAZUME: Well, a lot of my works tend to come with strings attached—I could mention *Gundam*. It may not be a good idea to make the comparison, but you know how (*Macross* character designer) Haruhiko Mikimoto can get away with working on various titles with his own style? I've been forced to change my style depending on the work, so I've been more like a designer than an artist.

ANIMERICA: Designing what fits the world?

KITAZUME: Yes. I'll look for the style that will satisfy what's being sought. I have to fight the urge to use particular styles of my own to establish particular moods. I *could* say it's tough to be the person who has to make those decisions.

ANIMERICA: After all, you have to come up with many, many characters, not just the main ones.

KITAZUME: Yes, but I also think I was extremely lucky to be able to work with Yoshiyuki Tomino. I think that my work with him in the past has become a real asset for me today. *Gundam Double Zeta* had so many subcharacters. For example, even a sideline character like a middle-aged man had to have a profession and social position and personality. I'm sure Tomino must have had his frustrations with me, but still, he trusted me. Ultimately, that forced me into a situation where I had to expand my repertoire, whether I wanted to or not. I think it was good for me. So if I know which direction I need to head in, it's not that hard to come up with the characters and their variations.

***Zeta Gundam*'s "Four Murasame," from this mini-illustration book on Kitazume's character art.**

ANIMERICA: Your previous work, *Sôsei Kishi* ("Genesis Survivor") *Gaiarth*, was another complete original, wasn't it? How do you compare the other aspects of production with character design? Is coming up with everything else actually the hard part?

KITAZUME: Well, a big difference between *Moldiver* and what I did before was that *Moldiver* had comical aspects. Until then, I had worked on science fiction and other serious stories, and the characters had to reflect that setting. But this time, most of the stories were light, so I thought my previous-style characters might be a little too heavy for it. I felt I had to come out with characters that could take on those more light-hearted roles.

ANIMERICA: Like that grandfatherly mad scientist character. He's not really evil, but he's still autocratic.

KITAZUME: Yes. That type of character gets a little hard to handle if you make him too serious. [LAUGHS] I wanted to make him more cartoonish or comic book-like, so in that respect, he's different from what I've designed before.

ANIMERICA: How did your segment in *Robot Carnival* come about? A lot of people in the U.S. know that particular video because it's been released in English.

KITAZUME: I have an acquaintance by the name of Hiroyuki Kitakubo—I helped him out when he was making (an adult anime by the name of) *Pop Chaser*, that's how I got to know him—and he told me, "I'm going to be making this anthology project next. How would you like to work on it?" So I accepted his invitation.

ANIMERICA: So from your short segment in *Robot Carnival* to what you're doing now—what are your aspirations for directing? Do you actually have something in pre-production?

KITAZUME: Well, I got into animation because I liked it. I wanted to transmit the excitement that I got watching animation to today's audience…but it's been far harder than I ever imagined.

ANIMERICA: Have you felt like that on projects besides *Robot Carnival*?

KITAZUME: Yes, I have, especially with *Moldiver*. I had a lot of ideas on how I could entertain the audience, but they didn't always materialize on film.

ANIMERICA: …In other words, the ideas may have been there, but as you coordinated the production and drew the storyboards….

KITAZUME: Yes. You start doubting if what you thought up can actually be expressed on film. It was a monthly release, so there wasn't much time for the amount of work that was needed, and I couldn't spend it all on storyboarding. That's been my big regret. Of course, as the director, I still had to check and coordinate the storyboards even if I wasn't drawing them personally. But I hadn't had experience as a director of a TV show, and I wasn't used to storyboarding myself, so there were many aspects that I had to learn by doing. For example, I wanted to draw the storyboards for all six volumes and compare them to the finished video to see how it compared to my original conception. I couldn't accomplish that.

ANIMERICA: Is storyboarding that difficult?

KITAZUME: Yes. It's especially difficult to control the pacing.

ANIMERICA: There must be many ways to draw storyboards, but to a layman like me, I envision them all the way Hayao Miyazaki does them. In reality, they're usually not like that, are they? Most of them must be more simplified, just showing the movements, or the timing, or the scale. I'm guessing that must be how features are made.

KITAZUME: Actually, the directions are often much more precise and detailed than that.

ANIMERICA: You've mentioned influences from Yoshikazu Yasuhiko to Hayao Miyazaki to Yoshiyuki Tomino. Do you have any other directors who have influenced you? It doesn't have to be someone with whom you've worked. Or is there a director you would like to work with in the future?

KITAZUME: Well, when I was a student, I watched many works by Osamu Dezaki. As for Miyazaki, I used to really look up to him, but his recent works have tended to become rather lopsided. I'd like to make it my agenda to do a different kind of story with a different kind of direction in his kind of style. So in that sense, he's not my goal, but he's always in mind as the figure to surpass.

ANIMERICA: Probably beginning with your work on *Gundam*, your name has become rather well-known in the anime world overseas. What do you think about your works being seen by people who speak another language?

KITAZUME: Well, I could say the same thing for Japan. [LAUGHS] They might still be speaking the same language, but they probably don't know me at all. —Well, it might be different if I drew manga, but I think it's pretty hard to see what I'm thinking aside from the visual messages in the drawing. I think it's the same in Japan or in the U.S.; you won't know me as a person. Actually—although it was quite a while ago—I once received a fan letter from the U.S. But I couldn't read it, so I couldn't reply. [LAUGHS] In that sense, the language barrier is still big, and I'd like to overcome it. But I think that might be pretty hard to do.

ANIMERICA: Do you have any message for your fans overseas?

KITAZUME: As an animator, I hope that you can enjoy the animation I've worked on. I'm happy that you might remember my name, but the best joy comes from you enjoying the production itself.

ANIMERICA: Thank you very much.

afterword

With industry buzz stretching back almost as far as has the next set of *Star Wars* films, the long-delayed *Yamato* project has at last been (partially) realized. *Yamato 2520*, the OAV series which features the Syd Mead-designed *Yamato*, has since begun release in Japan, with future domestic release in English scheduled for the near future by Voyager Entertainment, the New Jersey-based company that also offers the entire run of *Star Blazers* (the U.S. name for the multi-part *Yamato* TV series) on home video.

Moldiver, the six-volume OAV series which Kitazume mentions, has gone on in the U.S. to join the aristocracy in a mini-empire of sorts for Pioneer LDCA, the American distribution arm of Japan's Pioneer LDC, which is also known among fans for its release of the popular *Tenchi Muyô!* series. In the duchy of *Gundam*, we've since seen several entries in the evergreen franchise come and go—Imagawa's "black sheep" *G Gundam*, the uninspired *Gundam X*, as well as the continuingly popular "teen dream" *Gundam Wing*—and, at least as of this writing, mainstream U.S. exposure still eludes "the Big G," as it's been called from time to time.

As for future plans, the big speculation at this point involves Kitazume's rumored involvement in the upcoming *Bubblegum Crisis* TV series (which, in its most recent incarnation, has since morphed into a proposed OAV series). And, of course, there's still the big "Resurrection of Yamato" to which we can look forward.

Hiroyuki Kitazume
Select Filmography

ANIME アニメ

A longtime member of Japan's A.I.C. animation studio—a studio which has, of late, gone on to open a Stateside office, with the expressed intention of developing an overseas market—Kitazume has had his fingers in some of the biggest OAV hits in recent years. The long-delayed "Resurrection of Yamato" project aside, if rumors are to be believed, Kitazume's latest project involves one of the bestselling OAV series ever...do the initials "BGC" ring any bells? Like many others, he has also contributed designs for video games, including the currently Japan-only "Evoluge."

Densetsu Kyoshin Ideon ("Legendary God-Giant Ideon")
伝説巨神イデオン
Animator
39-episode TV series (1980-81). In 1982, the series was re-edited and released theatrically as a two-part movie, *Densetsu Kyoshin Ideon: Sesshoku-Hen* ("Contact") and *Hatsudô-Hen* ("Be Invoked"). Also known as "Space Runaway Ideon." See entry for Tomino. *CURRENTLY IMPORT ONLY*

Sentô Mecha Xabungle ("War-Machine Xabungle")
戦闘メカザブングル
Character Designs
50-episode TV series (1982-83); also known by its production company-supplied English title, "Blue Gale Xabungle." See entry for Tomino. *CURRENTLY IMPORT ONLY*

Sei-Senshi Dunbine ("Holy-Warrior Dunbine")
聖戦士ダンバイン
Animation Direction
49-episode TV series (1983-84); followed in later years by a *Dunbine* OAV series (in which Kitazume, like fellow animator Yasuhiro Imagawa, has no involvement). More commonly known as "Aura Battler Dunbine." See entry for Tomino. *CURRENTLY IMPORT ONLY*

Jûsenki L-Gaim ("Heavy War-Machine L-Gaim")
重戦機エルガイム
Animation Direction
54-episode TV series (1984-85); also known as "Heavy Metal L-Gaim." See entry for Tomino. *CURRENTLY IMPORT ONLY*

Tatakae! Iczer-One ("Fight! Iczer-One")
戦え！イクザー１
Character Designs
Three-volume OAV series (1985-87) on which Kitazume worked with hot and upcoming young animator Toshihiro Hirano (*Dangaio, Vampire Princess Miyu*) at Japanese animation studio A.I.C. *DOMESTIC RELEASE TITLE:* ***Iczer-One*** (U.S. Renditions)

Bôken! Iczer 3 ("Adventure! Iczer 3")
冒険！イクザー３
Animation Direction
Six-episode OAV sequel series (1990) detailing the adventures of Iczer-One's "younger sister," Iczer 3, who happens to be voiced in this anime version by Japanese female pro wrestler, Cutey Suzuki. *DOMESTIC RELEASE TITLE:* ***Iczer 3*** (U.S. Manga Corps)

Kidô Senshi Z Gundam ("Mobile Suit Z Gundam")
機動戦士Zガンダム
Animation Direction
50-episode TV series (1985-86); see entry for Tomino. *CURRENTLY IMPORT ONLY*

Megazone 23, Part III: Eve no Mezame and Kaihô no Hi
("The Awakening of Eve" and "Emancipation Day")
メガゾーン２３ III：
イヴの目覚めand解放の日
Character Designs
Two-volume OAV series (1989) and follow-up to the *Megazone 23* sequels *Part I* and *Part II*. *Megazone 23*, the original 1985 runaway hit which helped to establish the then-nascent OAV industry, is said by some to bear almost no resemblance to its sequels; whether this has anything to do with the (un)involvement of Kitazume is unlikely. *CURRENTLY IMPORT ONLY*

Kidô Senshi Gundam ZZ
機動戦士ガンダムZZ
Character Designer/Assistant Director
47-episode TV series (1986-87); also known as "Gundam Double Zeta." See entry for Tomino. *CURRENTLY IMPORT ONLY*

Relic Armor Legaciam
レリック・アーマーレガシアム
Character Designer
Single-shot OAV (1987) described in Japanese source materials as "sci-fi robot anime from original creator/director Hiroyuki Kitazume, the animation director of (among others) of *Bôken! Iczer 3* and *Gaiarth*." *CURRENTLY IMPORT ONLY*

Robot Carnival
ロボットカーニバル
Director / Screenwriter / Character Designer
90-minute theatrical feature (1987) in which nine of Japan's leading animators tackle the subject of "robots" in an anthology format. Kitazame's contribution is called "Starlight Angel." *DOMESTIC RELEASE TITLE:* ***Robot Carnival*** (Streamline Pictures)

Kidô Senshi Gundam: Gyakushû no Char
("Char's Counterattack")
機動戦士ガンダム：逆襲のシャア
Character Designer
120-minute theatrical feature (1988) which brings closure (?) to the bitter love-hate relationship shared by original *Gundam* TV series hero Amuro Rei and hunky Aryan newtype Char Aznable. See entry for Tomino. *CURRENTLY IMPORT ONLY*

Ryû Seiki: Shinshô A.D. 1990 Riko
Ryû Seiki: Mashô R.C. 297 Rushiria
("Dragon Century: Divine Chapter A.D. 1990" *and* "Mashô R.C. 297 Rushiria")
竜世紀：神章A.D.1990璃子and魔章R.C.297ルシリア
Character Designs / Art Continuity
Two-volume OAV series (1988) in which a dragon suddenly appears in the skies of modern-day Tokyo, carrying over a long-ago war between gods and devils and involving a young girl. *DOMESTIC RELEASE TITLE:* ***Dragon Century*** (U.S. Renditions)

Bastard!! Ankoku no Hakaijin
("The Dark God of Destruction")
Bastard!!暗黒の破壊神
Character Designer
Six-volume OAV series (1992-93), based on the original manga by Kazushi Hagiwara, as serialized in Shueisha's SHÔNEN JUMP. *CURRENTLY IMPORT ONLY*

Sôsei Kishi Gaiarth ("Genesis Survivor Gaiarth")
創世機士ガイアース
Character Designer / Screenwriter / Director
Three-volume OAV series (1992-93); features a far-flung future, a post apocalyptic world, and spell-casting robots. *DOMESTIC RELEASE TITLE:* ***Genesis Surviver Gaiarth*** (AnimEigo)

Moldiver
モルダイバー
Original Concept / Art Direction / Director
Six-episode OAV series (1993). Note that the first letters of each of the six volume titles—*Metamorforce, Overzone, Longing, Destruction, Intruder*, and *Verity*—spell out the name of the supersuit itself. *DOMESTIC RELEASE TITLE:* ***Moldiver*** (Pioneer LDCA)

Key

Japanese comics or "manga" series; may or may not be available in foreign-language (i.e., English) version

TV series broadcast on-air in Japan. Note that, in the U.S., Japanese TV series are both broadcast on-air (*Ronin Warriors*) and released on home video (*Ranma 1/2*). Others (*Sailor Moon, Dragon Ball*) are available both in broadcast and home video versions

Direct-to-home-video series; may also include compilations of TV episodes released to home video market

Theatrical feature; may or may not receive equivalent theatrical release for U.S. version

Shoji Kawamori

Interviewed by Takashi Oshiguchi (1995)

When *Macross Plus* debuted in 1995, it could almost be said that its creator, Shoji Kawamori, was making a comeback. Not that he was ever really *gone* from the animation scene—after a string of successes guaranteed to make most would-be mechaheads green with envy, the fresh-faced thirtysomething animator (34 at the time of this interview), he of the arched brows and the intense eyes, had still barely begun his career, even in an industry known for snatching babes out of design school and impressing them into its service. When you're a mecha designer, you've either got the right stuff, or you don't…and Kawamori certainly did.

1982's breakthrough sci-fi TV series *Chô Jikû Yôsai Macross* ("Superdimensional Fortress Macross") jump-started more than one career with its fresh, new approach to the outer space epic. Like its predecessor, *Uchû Senkan Yamato*, *Macross* had galaxy-spanning combat between alien races, hot-shot pilots and dedicated ship captains. Unlike *Yamato*, *Macross* also had a love triangle and a teen-dream singing star—for anime fans accustomed to the nationalism and high melodrama of *Yamato* and its many imitators, *Macross* certainly was "something different."

Kawamori's main contribution to this new formula was the design of the show's star robot—the transformable, fighter plane-like "Valkyrie." The Valkyrie's success had much to do with the fact that it was one of the first designs whose transforming toy actually transformed as advertised (no pulling off the arms or the head to make the contortions work). When *Macross* was brought to the U.S. as one part of the three-shows-fused-into-one American TV series *Robotech*, the toys made their splash in the West, as well.

A mechanical engineering major and eventual college dropout whose first love was space science, rumor has it that young Kawamori took that first step on the road toward a career as a mecha designer by becoming friendly with staffers at anime design house Studio Nue. A chance to design some gewgaw or other was all it took for the then-sophomore to cast aside a promising academic career at Tokyo's prestigious Keio University and eagerly join their ranks.

Kawamori was born on the twentieth of February, "deep in the mountains of Toyama prefecture." Perhaps it is here, in a region best known for its Gassho-style houses, that his futuristic aesthetic began to develop. Gassho-style houses are 17th century, thatch-roofed buildings with distinctive, very high-peaked roofs, considered by contemporary architects to have an unusually modern design. Environment or education...? In this case, perhaps both.

Either way, Kawamori's design sense gives his works a certain special look that's been sought after by studio after studio ever since the debut of *Macross*' Valkyrie. The innovator's innovator in the world of mecha design, Kawamori has had his finger in more mecha pies than some consider decent—the sleek, jet fighter-influenced Valkyries and the thoroughly alien Zentraedi craft of *Macross*; the heroic Gundam prototype Unit 1 and the hulking nuclear-warhead-equipped Unit 2 of *Kidô Senshi Gundam 0083: Stardust Memory*; the spider-like Roadrunner from the movie *Patlabor 2*; the hyper-realistic F-1 racers of *New Century GPX Cyber Formula 11*; and many more. But Kawamori only really emerged as a director with 1995's *Macross Plus*—the project he once said he would never make.

"I'd once sworn off making sequels," Kawamori muses. "I had my reasons at the time." But once in the '90s, with Japan's so-called bubble economy now burst and the anime industry slumping along into depression like everything else, it was only natural that the innovation of the late '70s and early '80s gave way to more formula product as animators struggled to find new ways to indulge their creativity within the constraints of tight budgets. But with fans clamoring for bigger and better anime, and sponsors demanding a return on their investment, what was an animator to do?

The answer for many companies and creators was then and is now the production of remakes or sequels to once-popular series. Classic TV shows as diverse as *8-Man* (1963), *Kagaku Ninja-Tai Gatchaman* (1972), *Cutey Honey* (1973), *Gundam* (1979), *Chô Jikû Seiki Orguss* (1983) and *The Dirty Pair* (1985) have all been recently reinterpreted as direct-to-video OAV series, theatrical releases, television series, or sometimes, all three. With *Macross Plus*, it was suddenly time for *Macross* once more.

"In the current animation market," as Kawamori says in this interview, conducted when the *Macross Plus* series had only just launched, "it's getting harder and harder for an original project to be approved. A project has to be based on an already-popular story to stand a chance. Of course, if something's got the name *Macross* attached to it, it stands to reason that the chances of approval are very high. Even better, the project can be done the way I want it to be done. In the case of *Macross Plus*, I decided to go with the *Macross* name and make the series I wanted to make."

Kawamori's return with *Macross Plus* expanded the limits of animation technology with exciting new use of state-of-the-art computer graphics and traditional cel techniques. Plus, his work on the simultaneous TV series *Macross 7* fleshed out the *Macross* universe even further with a story that takes place in the future lives of Max and Miria, characters well known to viewers of *Robotech*.

"When I went to the United States, I talked to many people, and they all liked Max," Kawamori comments. "Perhaps Americans like 'genius pilots' better than Japanese do...? I thought to myself at the time that this kind of popularity might prove valuable later down the line, and in a certain sense, it has. You could say that the idea to bring Max and Miria back was an idea that was born during a visit to the U.S."

interview

ANIMERICA: Why did you become an animator? How did you get involved in animation?

KAWAMORI: There was a feature called *Uchû Senkan Yamato*...after I saw the movie, I looked up its design company. They asked me if I'd be interested in drafting some designs. That didn't make me an animator—I was more like production staff. I started out as a designer, after all.

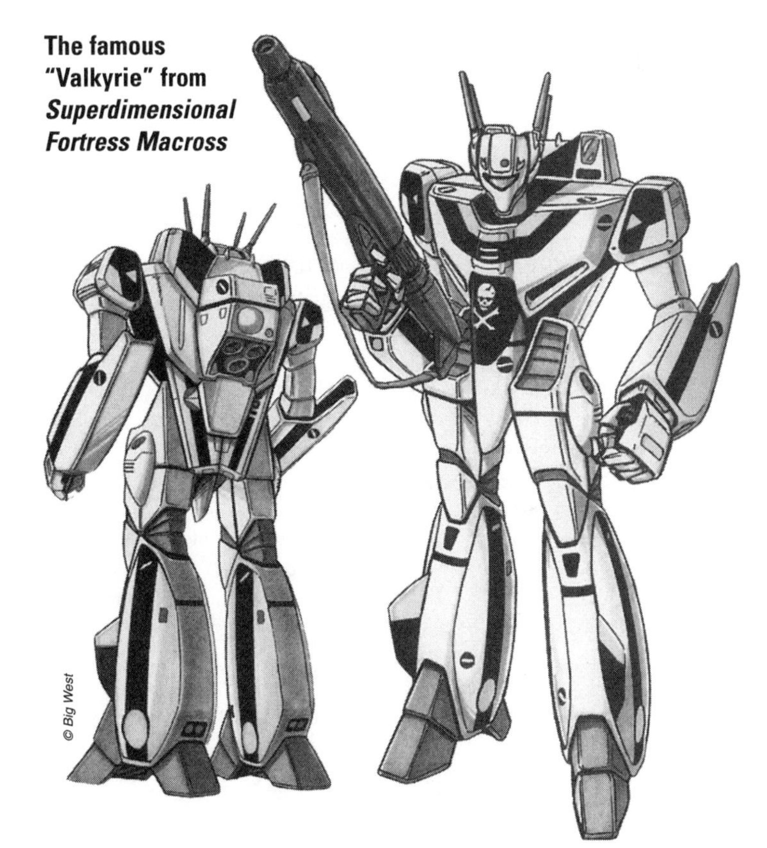

The famous "Valkyrie" from *Superdimensional Fortress Macross*

ANIMERICA: Of mecha?

KAWAMORI: Yes.

ANIMERICA: Planes and other machines, things like that?

KAWAMORI: Yes. [LAUGHS]

ANIMERICA: So did you start with *Yamato*, then?

KAWAMORI: No, I wasn't directly involved in *Yamato*. I *was* offered a design position when I was a freshman in college for the next *Yamato* production, but I didn't want to be distracted during my freshman year. I really got started when I was a sophomore.

ANIMERICA: What was your first work?

In the current animation market, it's getting harder and harder for an original anime project to be approved. A project has to be based on an already-popular series to stand a chance.

KAWAMORI: My first work was as the designer of a "guest" mecha for an episode of the *Uchû Kaizoku Captain Harlock* TV series. [*"Space Pirate Captain Harlock," Leiji Matsumoto's 1978-79 animated TV series.*]

ANIMERICA: So it wasn't a robot?

KAWAMORI: So it wasn't a robot. [LAUGHS] I was designing automobiles in school, since I was an engineering major. If I had stayed on the straight path, I would have wanted to go into space science. [LAUGHS] But, in Japan, there isn't much place for aeronautical engineering on a scale like NASA. So you could say that's one reason I quit.

ANIMERICA: What was your major in engineering?

KAWAMORI: I was a mechanical engineering major. Although, by the time I chose my major, I wasn't attending classes that often.

ANIMERICA: So did you draft blueprints?

KAWAMORI: No, I didn't get that far. *Macross* started when I was a sophomore, and I worked on that....

ANIMERICA: So did you drop out of college because you got too busy with your anime work?

KAWAMORI: Yes. I was working on *Macross* all through my student days.

ANIMERICA: You got into anime mostly by coincidence?

KAWAMORI: Well, yes. It's all a blur how I got thrown into the mine shaft. [LAUGHS]

ANIMERICA: Was that with a certain Mr. Haruhiko Sato [*the "real" name of famed character designer Haruhiko Mikimoto—Ed.*]...?

KAWAMORI: It wasn't with anyone in particular. He and the others were my friends in junior high and high school. Actually, I got to know them in high school and college through a science fiction convention called Kuri-Con.

ANIMERICA: So it all started with science fiction....

KAWAMORI: The people around me were obsessed with science fiction, so I may have been turned off to some aspects of it. Maybe, in one part of my mind, I'd already made the decision not to become an *otaku* ("hardcore fan").

ANIMERICA: Did you jump directly into the *Macross* project after your work on *Captain Harlock?*

KAWAMORI: No. There was a feature called *TechnoPolice 21C* before that. It was a problematic feature; a one-shot.

ANIMERICA: I've always thought of *TechnoPolice 21C* as one of the trailblazers for original animation.

KAWAMORI: It was supposed to be a theatrical release, but production problems wouldn't allow that. There were two other projects before *Macross,* and I was sort of involved with all three projects. And it just happened that the *Macross* idea was approved.

ANIMERICA: What were the other projects?

KAWAMORI: *Macross* was the only project that got approved. I was only involved as a designer or background artist for the others.

ANIMERICA: There's one question my editor insists I ask you: In the U.S., there's a rumor that the fan in the *Macross: Ai•Oboete Imasu ka?* movie who stumbles while trying to get an autograph from Minmei is you. Is this true?

KAWAMORI: Yes, that's me. [LAUGHS]

ANIMERICA: Previously, you've said that you won't make any sequels. So why are you coming back to *Macross* now?

KAWAMORI: In the current animation market, it's getting harder and harder for an original project to be approved. A project has to be based on an already-popular story to stand a chance. Of course, if something's got the name *Macross* attached to it, it stands to reason that the chances of approval are very high. Even better, the project can be done the way I want it to be done. In the case of *Macross Plus*, I decided to go with the *Macross* name and make the series I wanted to make.

ANIMERICA: The *Macross* compilation video *Flashback 2012* gives hints about Minmei and Misa's future. Is there any chance you'll animate a continuation of that story?

KAWAMORI: I don't really want to. I've already used Minmei, Misa and Hikaru in the TV series, and they show up again in the feature version, as well. If they show up for the third time in another movie, you'll be sick of them, too. It won't be a fresh story. I may not do a sequel about the main characters, but a supporting character might get featured, or a side-story-kind-of-sequel might be a possibility.

ANIMERICA: It seems that many American fans tend to think of the *Macross* movie as the "official" *Macross* continuity. What's your opinion?

KAWAMORI: Consider real history. Many different stories have been created based on the same historical facts, haven't they? For example, there are many stories about World War II. It's the same thing with *Macross*. The real *Macross* is out there, somewhere. If I tell the story in the length of a TV series, it looks one way, and if I tell it as a movie-length story, it's organized another way.

ANIMERICA: You have yet to attend an American anime and manga convention as Guest of Honor. Have you ever met any of your American fans?

KAWAMORI: I don't know about fans, but it seems U.S. creators are in my audience. Producers, directors and live-action special-effects people like modelers...I often meet them.

ANIMERICA: How are they different from Japanese fans?

KAWAMORI: They probably aren't fundamentally different, but they seem to be more confident and speak their minds. And also...can I say that their age is different? In Japan, it might be a little strange for a 40- or 50-year-old to be watching animation, but in the United States, you can find a 70-year-old lady watching animation, and there's nothing odd about it.

ANIMERICA: In *Macross* 7, Max and Miria show up. Why?

KAWAMORI: I didn't want to use Minmei and Misa and Hikaru, as I mentioned before, but I did want to portray the supporting characters more. Also, when I went to the United States, I talked to many people and they all liked Max. Perhaps Americans like "genius pilots" better than Japanese do...? I thought that kind of popularity might prove valuable later down the line, and in a certain sense, it has. You could say the idea to bring Max and Miria back

Kenji's Spring

(in *Macross 7*) was an idea that was born during a visit to the U.S.

ANIMERICA: *Macross Plus* the OAV series and *Macross 7* the TV series are being produced by different studios. Why is that?

KAWAMORI: First of all, Bandai's Minoru Takahashi told me it would be impossible to do both at one place. His actual words were, "You know it'll be impossible if you think about the size of Japanese studios." [LAUGHS]

ANIMERICA: So there's a physical constraint.

KAWAMORI: Yes. The other constraints are the respective genres of the two series. There's a world of difference between a TV show and an OAV. It's important to produce a TV show with efficiency, whereas an OAV needs more thoughtful attention.

ANIMERICA: What are the pros and cons of each studio?

KAWAMORI: ...Whoa, that's a hard question. Well, Triangle Staff pays close attention to detail. And Ashi Production is used to making TV shows, so they know how to keep a production schedule. Details might get skipped, but they know how to maintain high-speed intensity.

ANIMERICA: In *Macross II*, the mothership gets destroyed. What happens after that?

KAWAMORI: I haven't watched *Macross II*. [LAUGHS] So, when it comes to *Macross II*, "No comment." If I watch it, I know I'll want to comment on it, y'know...?

ANIMERICA: Why *weren't* you involved in *Macross II*...?

KAWAMORI: Back then, I had sworn off making sequels. I had my reasons at the time. [LAUGHS]

ANIMERICA: Have you seen the English version of *Macross*, the TV series broadcast in English under the name *Robotech*?

KAWAMORI: I haven't given *Robotech* a complete viewing. As for the English version of *Macross: Ai•Oboete Imasu ka?* [*retitled* Superspace Fortress Macross *and released in Japan during 1987 with Japanese subtitles—Ed.*], I've only seen it through the middle of the second reel.

ANIMERICA: Let's put aside *Macross* for a moment. Of all the design work you've done thus far, which has been the most satisfying to you?

KAWAMORI: It would have to be the Valkyrie in *Macross*. I spent the most effort on it, and I have an affinity for it.

ANIMERICA: The toys were great, too, weren't they.

KAWAMORI: Thank you.

ANIMERICA: Japanese animation is well-received in foreign countries these days, especially in the U.S., where they even coined a word for it: "Japanimation." What do you think of this popularity?

KAWAMORI: I'm grateful for it. But on the other hand, I think it's still mostly a popularity that stems from a "it's-pretty-good-for-a-cartoon" mentality. I think anime's popularity has also been boosted by it being a little overrated. I can't help thinking Americans must be comparing anime to the animation they normally see on American TV and saying, "Gee, relatively speaking, anime is much better than this." In my opinion, too, anime can be 100 times more interesting than American animation, but....

ANIMERICA: Tell us about the computer-graphic effects in *Macross Plus*.

KAWAMORI: Because of budgets, the number of shots we can use is limited. But this is an extraordinary budget for a Japanese OAV, and I try my best to use it to best advantage.

ANIMERICA: For example, are computer graphics used for the mecha?

KAWAMORI: That's a possibility. Except that everyone's used to seeing full computer graphics, so it's not too fresh. What I'm doing may not be so expensive, but I'm trying to choreograph something new, such as combining cel animation and computer graphics to show cels moving inside digital space.

ANIMERICA: Is that to take advantage of the different textures?

The Vision of Escaflowne

KAWAMORI: Yes.

ANIMERICA: Do you use computer graphics yourself?

KAWAMORI: I don't have a computer at home, if that's what you mean. [LAUGHS] I think I'd go off the deep end if I ever got my hands on one. Also, it takes a heavy industrial graphics machine to do what I would want to do.

ANIMERICA: At Studio Nue, Naoyuki Kato uses a Macintosh. Don't you ever feel you'd want one yourself?

KAWAMORI: Kato's work is for the medium of print, so all he has to make is one printout. For animation, you'd need ten times more printouts. [LAUGHS] But, if possible, I would like to give computer graphics a try in the future.

ANIMERICA: Is there something new you're working on that you can mention here?

KAWAMORI: Well, something I *can* mention here is a fantasy/science fiction story called *Escaflowne* that I'm working on at Sunrise. Work on it has already started, in fact.

ANIMERICA: Is it an original story?

KAWAMORI: Yes. I can't tell yet if it'll end up as a TV series or video or what. The manga version, which I illlustrate, is already running in Kadokawa's SHÔNEN ACE magazine. The story is by a writer named "Katsu•Aki." Besides *Escaflowne*, I have about ten other game and anime projects.

ANIMERICA: You worked on *Patlabor* too. How was that?

KAWAMORI: For *Patlabor*, my thinking was, you might as well design something that might really exist, right? So, my idea was to work on realistic things like helicopters and cars. For a TV show, it's most important that the mecha are easy to animate, but for a movie, it's possible to be meticulous about details and give as much realism as you want.

ANIMERICA: What might you like to do if you had the time? For example, would you like to direct or supervise the mecha animation?

KAWAMORI: Well, when you're making a film, it's not like you can make a scale model and do wind-tunnel testing, or draft something from the level of the engine structure. It might be fun to try to choreograph my mecha designs and see if I could do it without destroying the sense of realism.

ANIMERICA: What people and designs have influenced you?

KAWAMORI: In terms of design elements, I was influenced by Kazuki Miyatake and Leiji Matsumoto, but I try not to let that show. When I'm doing work under the Studio Nue name, I do use the Nue style. Except for that line of work, I try not to show my influences.

ANIMERICA: Since you like science fiction, you must have a foreign novel you can recommend....

KAWAMORI: My basic influence was NASA. I've had more real-life influences, such as NASA experiments and the Apollo Project. As for design aspects, I'd say all the X-series prototypes. My car influences are real cars. Basically, if I have any animation influences, my policy is to consciously exclude them.

ANIMERICA: Do you and your colleagues influence each other?

KAWAMORI: We try to stimulate each other, but I try not to be influenced.

ANIMERICA: *Patlabor*'s Yutaka Izubuchi, for example?

KAWAMORI: Yes, Yutaka Izubuchi and Mamoru Oshii. Also, Haruhiko Mikimoto, since I collaborate with him a lot.

ANIMERICA: How about directors?

KAWAMORI: I got a non-traditional start in the animation industry, so I can't really say who my role model is. Instead, the little pieces of advice I got from people I collaborated with became my guide. For example, Yoshiyuki Tomino once said to me, "If you want to make something good, you must only watch good works for at least three years. The same goes for being a tailor. You should touch nothing but good clothes for three years." So I thought of not watching any *Macross* TV series for the next three years. [LAUGHS] Also, when I was working on the TV show, famed *Macross* and *Yamato* director Noboru Ishiguro said, "It's always better to break up storyboards according to *sound*, not image." And I had to agree. Besides that, I didn't learn anything formally, and I'm self-taught.

ANIMERICA: How about artwork? For example, do you like American art, or foreign artists like Frazetta, or...?

KAWAMORI: I don't get into things too deeply. When *Gundam* was on the air, I thought I liked Yoshikazu Yasuhiko's art, but that didn't last long...I must be the type who likes the artist's creation more than the artist.

ANIMERICA: What foreign TV shows did you watch when you were little?

KAWAMORI: Definitely *Thunderbirds.* I liked the image of the secret base returning underground. I was so into those ITC shows that I actually *hated Ultraman.* I believed there was no way *modern* weapons could lose against some giant space barbarian. [LAUGHS]

ANIMERICA: Is there anything you'd like to remake if you had the opportunity?

KAWAMORI: That would be everything. [LAUGHS] But I think about the future, for example, with *Macross*, on which I've worked for so long. In that sense, I'm glad I've been able to work on a variety of things, and what's coming may be more interesting than what's transpired.

ANIMERICA: What would you like to work on in the future for TV or film?

KAWAMORI: Whatever I want to do, the cost of labor is rising, and it's becoming more difficult to make an original story. There was a time in the U.S. too when Disney features hit a low, wasn't there? I do have to hope that doesn't happen to anime. Also, in terms of story contents, they're stable now, but there are dangers ahead.

ANIMERICA: How do you spend your free time?

KAWAMORI: I haven't had free time recently. When I do, I try to get work done. [LAUGHS] So recently, I gripe, "I'd like to get some free time so I can get some work done." [LAUGHS]

ANIMERICA: Do you ever take a long vacation and travel abroad?

KAWAMORI: Fortunately, I can go to the U.S. to do research, so I go there often. For the *Macross Plus* research trip, I got to go inside acrobatic planes.

ANIMERICA: There are aspiring animators and mecha designers abroad—do you have any advice for these people?

KAWAMORI: If I have any advice, it's that I think originality is becoming rare worldwide, so you should aspire to be original. I'm happy that you watch "Japanimation" for your inspiration, but I think it's also a good idea to be interested in another field, even if anime is your favorite. Of course, it's easier to get on a creative high when you're focused in a single direction, but it's also important to maintain a balance between such intensity and broader perspectives.

ANIMERICA: I would appreciate it if you could be so generous as to say a few words to your fans in the English-speaking world.

KAWAMORI: There's more *Macross Plus* with even higher energy on the way, so I hope you get a chance to watch it. Also, I'm hoping *Macross 7* can make it on the air in the U.S., so don't forget to write to your TV station! [LAUGHS] I hope you can create a receptive environment so that it will someday be broadcast.

ANIMERICA: Thank you very much for your time.

KAWAMORI: You're welcome.

afterword

In 1996, a manga Shoji Kawamori had been drawing for Kadokawa's SHÔNEN ACE debuted as an animated television show. A twenty-six episode TV series airing from in 1996 and produced by veteran mecha studio Sunrise, *Tenkû no Escaflowne* offered a fantasy-styled world with a knights-in-armor mecha motif that hadn't really been seen in mecha circles since Ryosuke Takahashi's 1984 TV series *Kikô-Kai Galient* was on the air.

As story creator, chief writer and series supervisor, Kawamori took the experience with digital technology he'd gained on *Macross Plus* and pushed the digital envelope even further, bringing the *Escaflowne* series' dragons to life with a blend of traditional cel animation and computerized texture-mapping. Even the robots' high-tech "stealth cloaks" were created with computer graphics. Currently, an *Escaflowne* feature film is in production.

Later, Kawamori would also step in as writer/director of a feature film based on the work of beloved Japanese author Kenji Miyazawa (*Night on the Galactic Railroad*) to create a semi-biographical piece on Miyazawa himself, couched in terms of one of Miyazawa's own stories—*Iihatove Gensô: Kenji no Haru* ("The Illusion of Iihatove: Kenji's Spring"). *Kenji*, in bringing to life the galactic train of the author's imagination, also used extensive computer graphics.

"I think (computer graphics) should be used more," says Kawamori. "But that's only on the premise that an animator will be working on it. Full CG at top budgets may be indistinguishable from live footage, but that type is almost overused in (Japanese) commercials and doesn't have the impact anymore."

As of this writing, Kawamori's *Escaflowne* has yet to be signed for domestic home video release, but those in the know speculate that it won't be long. A feature film version is also in the works. Until then, there's *Macross Plus*, which is now available in its entirety on both VHS and LD, as well as in a compiled "theatrical version."

Shoji Kawamori
Select Bibliography & Filmography

MANGA 漫画

Comics (manga) series by Shoji Kawamori. That Kawamori has done any work in manga at all is surprising, seeing as his background rests chiefly in (anime) mechanical design. Like Kosuke Fujishima, Kawamori is also active in the field of video game design, having contributed designs for the upcoming strategy/simulation "Armored Core," as well as for the bestselling combat simulation "Macross Digital Mission VF-X," both of which are available for the Sony PlayStation.

Tenkû no Escaflowne ("Escaflowne of the Sky")
天空のエスカフローネ

Original Story
Serialized in Kadokawa's Shônen Ace; written by Katsu•Aki (1995); currently six compiled volumes available total. Note that Kawamori is also listed as "original creator" on the "Newtype Novels" series of the same name, as well as in the "Asuka DX" version of the *Escaflowne* comics, *Hitomi: Tenkû no Escaflowne.* *CURRENTLY IMPORT ONLY*

ANIME アニメ

Known for years as the man who put the va-va-voom into the Valkyrie, famed *Macross* mecha designer Kawamori would go on later in his career to tackle the challenge of directing, as well. *Macross Plus,* his luxe, updated entry into the *Macross* universe, expanded the use of computer graphics or "CG" in anime in a way which few fans had seen before; *Escaflowne* and *Kenji no Haru* also pushed the envelope in terms of seamless integration of CG with traditional cel-based techniques.

Chô Jikû Yôsai Macross
("Superdimensional Fortress Macross")
超時空要塞マクロス

Mecha Design
36-episode TV series (1982-83) which, when combined with episodes from two other anime series (*Southern Cross* and *Mospeada*) would go on to become the 65-episode *Robotech.* *DOMESTIC RELEASE TITLE:* ***Robotech*** and ***Robotech Perfect Collection: Macross*** (Streamline Pictures)

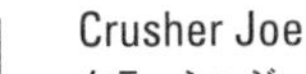

Crusher Joe
クラッシャジョウ

Mecha Design
131-minute theatrical feature (1983) combining the talents of *Gundam*'s Yoshikazu "Yaz" Yasuhiko and *Dirty Pair*'s Haruka Takachiho. See entry for Takachiho. *DOMESTIC RELEASE TITLE:* ***Crusher Joe: The Movie*** (AnimEigo)

Chô Jikû Yôsai Macross: Ai•Oboete Imasu ka?
("Superdimensional Fortress Macross: Do You Remember Love?")
超時空要塞マクロス：愛・おぼえていますか

Direction / Story Continuity / Storyboards
115-minute theatrical feature (1984) which slightly retells events of *Macross* TV series; English-dubbed version also released in Japan under the name "Superspace Fortress Macross" with Japanese subtitles; *Superspace* later released in U.S. by Peregine Film Distributors in 1987 under title "Clash of the Bionoids" with fifteen minutes cut; Bionoids re-released with footage restored by Best Film & Video as "Superdimensional Fortress Macross." *DOMESTIC RELEASE TITLE: See above*

Chô Jikû Yôsai Macross: Flashback 2012
超時空要塞マクロス：Flashback 2012

Direction
30-minute music video (1987) featuring eight of the most popular songs from the animated TV series and theatrical release; includes additional six minutes of footage originally planned to serve as ending to movie; marks Kawamori's directorial debut. *CURRENTLY IMPORT ONLY*

Haja Taisei Dangaiô ("Great Planet Evil-Destroyer Dangaio")
破邪大星ダンガイオー

Mecha Design
Three-volume OAV series (1987-89); Kawamori's design aesthetic really comes to the fore with the giant robot the four must combine to form. *DOMESTIC RELEASE TITLE:* ***Dangaio*** (U.S. Renditions/Manga Entertainment)

Crusher Joe: Hyôketsu Kangoku no Wana and Saishû Heiki Ash
("Crusher Joe: The Ice-Hell Trap" and "Crusher Joe: Final Weapon Ash")
クラシャジョウ：OAV Series
氷結監獄の罠&最終兵器アッシュ

Mecha Design
Two, 60-minute OAV sequels to the TV series (1989); see entry for Takachiho. *DOMESTIC RELEASE TITLE:* ***Crusher Joe: The Ice Prison*** and ***Crusher Joe: Last Weapon Ash*** (AnimEigo)

Kidô Senshi Gundam 0083: Stardust Memory
("Mobile Suit Gundam 0083: Stardust Memory")
機動戦士ガンダム0083:Stardust Memory

Mecha Design
Twelve-volume OAV series (1991-92); see entry for Tomino. *CURRENTLY IMPORT ONLY*

Kidô Keisatsu Patlabor 2: The Movie
("Mobile Police Patlabor 2")
機動警察パトレイバー 2 The Movie

Guest Mecha Designer
115-minute theatrical feature (1993); Kawamori's sole contribution is the long-legged "Roadrunner" police unit. See entry for Oshii. *DOMESTIC RELEASE TITLE:* ***Patlabor 2*** (Manga Entertainment)

Macross Plus
マクロス・プラス

Original Story / Mecha Design / Animation Direction
Four-volume OAV series (1994-95); seen by some as the first "true" sequel to the original *Macross.* Followed in 1995 by a theatrical retelling of the OAV series. *DOMESTIC RELEASE TITLE:* ***Macross Plus*** (Manga Entertainment)

Macross 7
マクロス７

Mecha Design / Series Supervision
49-episode TV series (1994-95) featuring a new generation of Valkyrie pilots as well as character designs by the ever-popular Haruhiko Mikimoto. *CURRENTLY IMPORT ONLY*

Tenkû no Escaflowne
天空のエスカフローネ

Original Concept / Series Supervisor
26-episode TV series (1996); also known as "The Vision of Escaflowne." *CURRENTLY IMPORT ONLY*

Iihatove Gensô: Kenji no Haru
("The Illusion of Iihatove: Kenji's Spring")
イーハトーブ幻想：Kenjiの春

Writer / Director
Single-shot TV special (1996) released on home video the following year in which the life of Japanese author Kenji Miyazawa (*Night on the Galactic Railroad*) is depicted through the anthropomorphic cats Miyazawa himself employed in his own, classic *Galactic Railroad.* *CURRENTLY IMPORT ONLY*

Key

- Japanese comics or "manga" series; may or may not be available in foreign-language (i.e., English) version
- TV series broadcast on-air in Japan. Note that, in the U.S., Japanese TV series are both broadcast on-air (*Ronin Warriors*) and released on home video (*Ranma 1/2*). Others (*Sailor Moon, Dragon Ball*) are available both in broadcast and home video versions
- Direct-to-home-video series; may also include compilations of TV episodes released to home video market
- Theatrical feature; may or may not receive equivalent theatrical release for U.S. version

Kei Kusunoki

Interviewed by Takayuki Karahashi (1995)

The boy is born one day from a human woman, but he is not human. From his dead mother's cooling corpse, he rises. He has no name. An ogre, a monster of legend, he does not bear the traditional horn of the legendary beast, but instead, a legendary sword—*Onikirimaru*, the "Ogre Slayer." The boy who is not really a boy pursues his destiny, to kill his own kind, in the hopes of becoming a true human.

This is the origin of the main character in Kei Kusunoki's *Onikirimaru*, or as it translates to English, *Ogre Slayer*, a macabre, supernatural thriller drawn in the kind of style typically found in *shôjo*, or Japanese girls' comics. Within a genre best known for intense stories detailing relationships and tender love, it's perhaps not what you might *expect*, but....

When you consider that one of the most famous monster stories of all time, *Frankenstein*, was written by a nineteen-year-old girl named Mary Shelley, as well as the evergreen popularity among female readers and filmgoers of the always sexually charged vampire legend, it's worth considering that maybe horror is something female readers and creators are drawn to, for its gothic qualities. The pathos inherent in a horror story hits many of the same notes to which *shôjo* traditionally aspires—the involving soap opera of the characters' lives, loves and deaths, raised to a baroque extreme.

In recent years, some of Japan's highest-profile female creators have been dipping into the horror genre and finding the gold buried there—a kind of renaissance of female-created horror, much of it reaching back to traditional and culturally specific mythology. Rumiko Takahashi with her macabre "Mermaid" series' grisly plot element (in which humans can become immortal by eating a mermaid's flesh) and the *shôjo* supergroup Clamp's moody supernatural thrillers *Tokyo Babylon* and *X/1999* are some of the most prominent examples of horror manga and anime from a uniquely female (and uniquely Japanese) point of view. On this side of the Pacific, American author Anne Rice's bestselling "Vampire" series, beginning with *Interview with the Vampire*, explores the roots of the traditionally European vampire legend, adding a dreamlike, erotic quality and a female-oriented, *shôjo*-esque current. Like Shelley's *Frankenstein*, the driving engines of this new anime gothic are, fairy tale-like, often the human failings that lead to the creation of the monsters, rather than the monsters themselves.

Of her gruesome ogres in *Ogre Slayer*, Kei Kusunoki says, "You can try to run and hide from them, but they're always right next to you. My theme for the story isn't the horror of the ogres themselves, but the vicious human karma that keeps on producing ogres. Ultimately, the most horrible creatures are the humans themselves."

Besides *Ogre Slayer*, another Kusunoki story, *Yôma* ("Bewitching Beast"), has been animated as well, though released in the U.S. under the rather more lurid title *Curse of the Undead: Yoma*. A spooky thriller set in the *Sengoku* or "Warring States" period of Japan, *Yoma* is the story a young ninja searching for a companion, who discovers that his friend is now one of the undead. The atmosphere is dreamlike amid the splatter and gore, providing a feeling of sharp unease as the handsome hero moves through the war-torn landscape in his endless search, monsters slithering out from every dark shadow.

interview

ANIMERICA: Let's start with a simplified profile for your American readers, who may not be as familiar with your work as those in Japan. What was your debut title?

KUSUNOKI: It was a story for Shueisha's RIBON magazine.

ANIMERICA: So it was *shôjo* manga. In the U.S., you would be best known as the author of *Yagami-kun no Katei Jijô* ("Affairs at the House of Yagami") and *Ogre Slayer*. Do you have other titles by which you'd like your American readers to know you…?

KUSUNOKI: Well, that's not something to which I've given much thought. I guess I could say my *shôjo* manga titles.

ANIMERICA: Do you have any specific title in mind? I'm sure you're not going to be happy with just any old title.

KUSUNOKI: Well, if it's something uniquely Japanese that you want, my *Jin-rô Zôshi* is a story about feudal Japan, so it draws from Japanese history. That's a title I'd like to see translated if there's a chance.

ANIMERICA: It's a story with swords?

KUSUNOKI: It doesn't have swords, but it is a feudal-era story. It features monsters and ghosts unique to Japan. They're not ogres, but *Jin-rô Zôshi* ("Man-Wolf Storybook") is a story about the spirits of oppressed women coming back as ghosts. It's a uniquely Japanese horror, a historical horror story. I think *Jin-rô Zôshi* is a uniquely Japanese title.

ANIMERICA: I think you can say *Ogre Slayer* is a horror story, too.

Ogre Slayer

KUSUNOKI: Yes, that's a horror story, too. The main character is in student uniform, and he's got a Japanese sword. From an American perspective, I guess it would be another uniquely Japanese story.

ANIMERICA: The *oni* is a uniquely Japanese monster, after all.

KUSUNOKI: Well, I suppose so. It *is* supposed to be the oldest monster in Japan.

I wanted a character who could slay without hesitation, so he ended up not being human.

ANIMERICA: Well, then, how would you describe *Ogre Slayer* to foreign readers who aren't familiar with this monster?

KUSUNOKI: It's a hideous monster. You can try to run and hide from them, but they're always right next to you. My theme for the story isn't the horror of the ogres themselves, but the vicious human karma that keeps on producing ogres. Ultimately the most horrible creatures are the humans themselves.

ANIMERICA: These ogres eat people.

KUSUNOKI: Yes, but also, the very same people are capable of turning into ogres themselves. The point is in how to avoid becoming one yourself. I think that's what's so fiendish.

ANIMERICA: Is this different from the Occidental (i.e., Western) ogre...?

KUSUNOKI: Actually, I couldn't really figure out what an ogre was, even though the English title says "Ogre Slayer."

ANIMERICA: I believe the ogre is a pagan monster from pre-Christian France that ate people.

KUSUNOKI: Well, my ogres can sometimes be found right around the corner, but usually, they're people who've been drawn into the dark side. Of course, there *are* some puny ones, too.... A uniquely Japanese aspect might be that this monster always has horns on its head. That's something I kept in mind, since it is supposed to be the oldest Japanese monster around.

ANIMERICA: So basically, in other words, what you're saying is, there wouldn't be an *Ogre Slayer* story that takes place outside of Japan.

KUSUNOKI: I think so. ...Yes, that's so.

ANIMERICA: So what we've got is the main character who needs to slay all the ogres in the world. He's a wandering kid, and his desire to become human can only be fulfilled by slaying all the ogres in Japan....

KUSUNOKI: Well...now we're getting into the world-view of the story, and I haven't really thought that much about how I'd explain that to a Western viewer. I guess you could say that the world of *Ogre Slayer* draws from the uniquely Japanese, classical paintings of hell. This would be a different picture of hell than the Occidental idea of it, but since this story takes place within such a uniquely Japanese world-view, I haven't really given much thought to a stage outside of that.

ANIMERICA: The classical Japanese ogre doesn't have much to do with heaven, or nirvana, does it?

KUSUNOKI: You can say that. These ogres are so uniquely Japanese, I haven't really made an effort to figure out how they fit into that kind of framework.

ANIMERICA: Given that *Ogre Slayer* is a horror story, it's not a story with an overwhelming sense of justice.

KUSUNOKI: Well, a blind application of justice—after all, the hero isn't human, and he isn't out there to save other people. If his reason for being was to save people, there would come a time when he would have to make a value judgment and hesitate. I wanted a character who could slay without hesitation, so he ended up not being human.

ANIMERICA: So human justice is completely inapplicable to the main character?

KUSUNOKI: It's not that it's inapplicable, but if that were his only guidance, he'd be lost. That's for the heroine of the episode or the ogre's victim to go through, and his role is pretty much to show up and slay the ogres.

ANIMERICA: So he's more like the chorus from a Shakespearean play.

KUSUNOKI: Yes. [LAUGHS] After all, the story begs the ogre be slain once Ogre Slayer shows up. I wanted the readers to follow the horrors of how one gets taken in by the ogres, how they try to fight them off, and how they end up getting cornered by the ogres. In order to make a story interesting, usually the main character will come out of a disadvantaged position. But that never happens with Ogre Slayer. He just shows up and slays the ogre. The pausing and the hesitating...that I leave up to the other characters.

ANIMERICA: Do you like horror stories, then? Any favorite writers?

KUSUNOKI: Well, I don't have anyone in particular in mind.

ANIMERICA: How about the British horror author Clive Barker?

KUSUNOKI: I know of him. A real "splatter" guy, isn't he?

ANIMERICA: …Well, *yes*, but he's also very psychological and mystical. Then there are other popular horror writers, like Stephen King. But rather than particular authors, you just like the genre as a whole, right?

KUSUNOKI: That's right.

ANIMERICA: Your main character has the desire to become human. Other than being reminiscent of a certain old TV show, was there something you were trying to say with this?

KUSUNOKI: Well, since he's not driven by justice (i.e., a need to avenge), I needed to give him a motive. [LAUGHS] *Ogre Slayer* wasn't originally intended as a serial, but the first short story I drew was popular, and it turned into a serial as I kept on drawing sequels. Initially, I didn't really think deeply about what it meant for him to be immortal and have no name. That's just how he ended up as I kept on drawing him as an ogre who lived many years and wanted to be human. The story just came into being naturally without lending it much deep thought.

ANIMERICA: In terms of dating the material, it's hard with the character wearing a school uniform and showing up the same over two generations.

KUSUNOKI: Yes, although I'm also interested in going back in time to draw a Meiji-era story or a feudal-era story. But right now, he's just in school uniform. The idea of a school uniform wielding a Japanese sword came from the movie *Mishima [1985 film by Paul Schrader detailing the life of controversial 20th-century Japanese writer Yukio Mishima, who advocated militarism and committed ritual suicide in 1970—Ed.]*. And someone looking that age in a school uniform won't look suspicious anywhere he goes. I hear Japanese school uniform looks mysterious to foreigners, as though it were military dress.

ANIMERICA: Especially the boys' uniform.

KUSUNOKI: …And so, I thought he would raise no suspicion in a student uniform if he stayed in Japan.

ANIMERICA: The school uniform would place him around high school-age appearance.

KUSUNOKI: Yes.

ANIMERICA: What would be your favorite books, movies

Affairs at the House of Yagami

or manga—either for your enjoyment or work reference.

KUSUNOKI: Well, the books I purchase tend to be for work reference. I tend to collect them on the criteria of whether or not they inspire me. In that sense, there's Katsuhiro Otomo's *Akira*, with which I'm sure you must be familiar in America.

ANIMERICA: This must be not the animated *Akira*, but the manga?

KUSUNOKI: I like the animation, too. It's great that Otomo himself was involved in the production of the animated version.

ANIMERICA: That's true. Do you have other favorite animated works?

KUSUNOKI: I don't watch a lot of animation, so I can't really say.

ANIMERICA: Your own *Yagami-kun* manga series was once animated….

KUSUNOKI: Yes, but it was told in a voice different from

Affairs at the House of Yagami

my own. When it comes to my own work, I can only come up with suggestions for improvements. But then again, there's an animator by the name of Nobuteru Yuki. I like his works.

ANIMERICA: He has a delicious style.

KUSUNOKI: Very much so.

ANIMERICA: Your characters are all so sexy, too.

KUSUNOKI: Thank you.

ANIMERICA: Your stories are intriguing, but the art is delicious to look at.

KUSUNOKI: Thank you.

ANIMERICA: You must really enjoy drawing those kinds of faces.

KUSUNOKI: Well, I'm also conscious that those faces would sell better. [LAUGHS]

ANIMERICA: ...Back to *Ogre Slayer*, your stories bring up ogre legends from ancient times, but they're usually from the Heian era. Some might be from the feudal era too, but there seem to be none from the later years of the feudal era or the peaceful Edo era.

KUSUNOKI: Well, yes, and if you watch Episode Four of the animation, it tells of temples and shrines that held sealed-in ogres being destroyed during the Meiji Restoration. You can say that the ogres were released during that event.

ANIMERICA: So basically, there was a time when the ogres threatened people, and then there was a peaceful interim. And then, they came back to haunt again.

KUSUNOKI: Yes, and thus, some ogres were slain or sealed. Again, in Episode Four of the animation, you can see slain ogres coming back to life and others being newly born. In my story, the ogres will never go away. It's an ironic theme that as long as there are people, ogres will be born.

ANIMERICA: There is but a fine line between them and humans. It's just like the Bank of Sai [*A Buddhist myth, like that of Sisyphus, wherein children stack stones to build pagodas so that they can ascend to nirvana once the pagodas are complete. But the ogres keep coming back and destroying the pagodas, which serves as a metaphor of unrewarded futility. Unlike Sisyphus, however, the children are innocent—Ed.*]. No matter how many ogres he slays, the humans keep on creating new ones. It's as though man is determined to make sure that he will never be happy.

KUSUNOKI: You can say that.

ANIMERICA: Do you have a new story in the works aside from *Ogre Slayer*?

KUSUNOKI: Well, I'm working on several. There's a comic detective story for Kadokawa's ASUKA magazine called *Daitokai ni Hoero* ("Howl at the Big City"). It's a title that combines the old detective shows *Dai Tokai* ("Big City") and *Taiyô ni Hoero* ("Bark at the Sun"). And there's the *Jinrô Zôshi* I mentioned previously, which is still ongoing. There's also another *shôjo* manga story going on in BOUQUET magazine.

ANIMERICA: Do you have the desire to have your *shôjo* manga titles read in the English-speaking world?

KUSUNOKI: Well, yes, although I don't know if I'll have too many sympathetic readers. And it's a different social structure over there. I don't know. [LAUGHS]

ANIMERICA: Although you may want to keep in mind that some readers may want to read about Japan, too.

KUSUNOKI: That's true. I think my *shôjo* titles have pretty lively characters as compared to some other artists, so I think that what's funny in the story will come across as funny in another language. My stories aren't the popular stream-of-sentiment, cerebral stories, though.

ANIMERICA: I see. Finally, if you have a message for your *Ogre Slayer* readers in the English-speaking world, please go ahead.

KUSUNOKI: I've been pursuing a uniquely Japanese atmosphere in this story, and although it's unlikely any of it could be true, I'd be happy if you can enjoy it.

afterword

Since the U.S. release of her *Yôma* and, as "Ogre Slayer," her *Onikirimaru* anime and manga, the English-speaking world hasn't heard much from Kei Kusunoki.

In Japan, however, it's a whole 'nother story. Commonly described as one of the most beautiful women working in manga today—and, get this, as if *that* wasn't enough, she's also got a twin sister, who's *also* a manga artist—in her native *Nihon*, Kusunoki is active indeed, at one time publishing not only in monthly SHÔNEN SUNDAY (which is where *Onikirimaru* has been serialized from the very beginning), but in a handful of other manga magazines, too: WINGS, ASUKA, MYSTERY DELUXE, BOUQUET, as well as in RIBON, which is where she made her debut at the age of 20.

As of November of last year (1996), Kusunoki began a brand-new series in THE MARGARET, a spin-off 'zine from publisher Shueisha's ever-popular MARGARET, one of the *shôjo* world's most popular monthlies.

Kei Kusunoki
Select Bibliography & Filmography

MANGA 漫画

Compiled short story and comics (manga) series by Kei Kusunoki. Note that Kusunoki is both writer and artist for all titles, the vast majority of which—the exception being *Onikirimaru*, or "Ogre Slayer"—have yet to be published outside of Japan.

Nani ka ga Kanojo ni Toritsuita?
("Has She Been Possessed by Something?")
何かが彼女にとりついた？
First published in Shueisha's "Ribon Original Sôshun (Early Spring)" edition; Kusunoki's debut work (1982). *CURRENTLY IMPORT ONLY*

Boku no Gakkô wa Senjô Datta
("Our School Was a Battlefield")
ぼくの学校は戦場だった
Published in compiled form in Shueisha's "Ribon Mascot Comics" (1984); one volume only. *CURRENTLY IMPORT ONLY*

Gokuendô ("Hall of Hellfire")
獄炎堂
Published in compiled form in Shinshokan's "Paper Moon Comics" (1985); one volume only. *CURRENTLY IMPORT ONLY*

Shûban Kisoku Genshuse Yo!
("Keep to Your Weekly Duties!")
週番規則厳守せよ
Published in compiled form in Shinshokan's "Wings Comics" (1985); one volume only. *CURRENTLY IMPORT ONLY*

Yagami-kun no Katei no Jijô
("Affairs at the House of Yagami")
八神くんの家庭の事情
Serialized in Shûeisha's Zôkan ("Special Edition") Shônen Sunday (1986); seven compiled volumes total. Also published in a Shogakukan "Seven Comics" edition under the same title in four compiled volumes. *CURRENTLY IMPORT ONLY*

Yôma • Zenpen ("Bewitching Beast • Part I")
妖魔・前編
Published in compiled form in "Ribon Mascot Comics" (1986); two volumes total. *CURRENTLY IMPORT ONLY*

Inishie Matsuri ("Ancient Festival")
古祭
Published in compiled form in Shueisha's "Big Comics" (1987); one volume only. *CURRENTLY IMPORT ONLY*

Oni Kogome ("Ogre Monster")
鬼魔
Published in compiled form in Shinshokan's "Paper Moon Comics" (1987); one volume only. *CURRENTLY IMPORT ONLY*

Koishite Furôzun ("Love Me Frozen")
恋してフローズン
Published in compiled form in "Ribon Mascot Comics" (1988); one volume total. *CURRENTLY IMPORT ONLY*

Kusunoki Gekijô ("Kusunoki Theater")
楠劇場
Published in Shinchosha's "Paper Moon Comics" (1988); one-shot short story collection. *CURRENTLY IMPORT ONLY*

Onikirimaru
鬼切丸
Published in compiled form in Shogakukan's "Shônen Sunday Comics" (1988); eleven volumes total. *DOMESTIC RELEASE TITLE:* ***Ogre Slayer*** (Manga Vision)

Tatoeba Konna Yûrei Kaidan
("This Kinda Ghost Story, For Example")
たとえばこんな幽霊奇談
Published in compiled form in "Ribon Mascot Comics" (1988); one volume only. *CURRENTLY IMPORT ONLY*

Momotaro ga Mairu! ("Here Comes Momotaro!")
桃太郎がまいる！
Published in compiled form in "Ribon Mascot Comics" (1989); one volume only. *CURRENTLY IMPORT ONLY*

Kusunoki Kessaku Tampenshû
("Kusunoki Short-Story Masterpiece Collection")
楠傑作短編集
Published in compiled form in "Shônen Sunday Comics" (1990); one volume only. *CURRENTLY IMPORT ONLY*

etc.
エトセトラ
Published in compiled form by Shinshokan (1991); two volumes total. Collection of the artist's illustration work. *CURRENTLY IMPORT ONLY*

"Gomen Nasai" Ko • Power
("The 'Forgive Me!' Kid [Power]")
ごめんなさいこ・ぱわあ
Published in compiled form in "Ribon Mascot Comics" (1991); one volume only. *CURRENTLY IMPORT ONLY*

Jin-rô Zôshi ("Man-Wolf Storybook")
人狼草紙
Published in compiled form in "Wings Comics" (1991); five volumes total. *CURRENTLY IMPORT ONLY*

Circus • Wonder ("Circus Wonder")
サーカス・ワンダー
Published in compiled form in "Ribon Mascot Comics" (1991); one volume only. *CURRENTLY IMPORT ONLY*

Akumade Rabu-Kome ("Bitter End Love-Comedy")
あくまでラブコメ
Published in compiled form in "Ribon Mascot Comics" (1991-94); four volumes total. *CURRENTLY IMPORT ONLY*

Buchikamashi Nemuri-Hime ("Sleeping Headlong Beauty")
ぶちかまし眠り姫
Published in compiled form by Kadokawa's "Asuka Comics" (1992); one volume only. *CURRENTLY IMPORT ONLY*

Daitokai ni Hoero ("Howl at the Big City")
大都会にほえろ
Published in compiled form in "Asuka Comics" (1993); six volumes total. *CURRENTLY IMPORT ONLY*

Ai wa Kakukatariki ("Thus Spake 'Ai'")
愛はかく語りき
Published in compiled form in Shueisha's "Margaret Comics" (1995). *CURRENTLY IMPORT ONLY*

Crime City
Published in compiled form in Kadokawa's "Asuka Comics DX" (1995); one volume only. *CURRENTLY IMPORT ONLY*

Migiko Nihon Ichi!! ("'Japan No. One' Migiko")
みぎこ日本一
Published in compiled form in "Ribon Mascot Comics" (1995); one volume only. *CURRENTLY IMPORT ONLY*

Dokkan Love ("Explosive Love")
どっかんLOVE
Published in compiled form in "Ribon Mascot Comics" (1996); one volume only. *CURRENTLY IMPORT ONLY*

Zoku • Ai wa Kakukatariki ("The Continued 'Thus Spake Ai'")
続愛はかく語りき
Published in compiled form in "Margaret Comics" (1996); continuation of the first series. *CURRENTLY IMPORT ONLY*

Yamada-kun ga Tôru ("Here Comes Yamada")
山田くんが通る
Published in compiled form in Shueisha's "Margaret Comics" (1997); one volume only. *CURRENTLY IMPORT ONLY*

ANIME アニメ

Known in Japan for her trademark historical fantasies (many of which focus on obscure and/or archaic themes), Kusunoki has yet to achieve the same sort of "household name" familiarity enjoyed by other manga artists among American otaku families. Her *Yagami-kun no Katei no Jijô*, the only animated feature of hers which has yet to see domestic release, is a rare comedic departure from her usual, more grim work (see below).

Yôma ("Bewitching Beast")
妖魔
Original Story
One-shot, OAV-length theatrical feature (1989); screened theatrically in two parts (Parts I and II are 38 and 39 minutes each, respectively). The first of Kusunoki's works to be animated, in the U.S., both volumes are available on a single subtitled tape. *DOMESTIC RELEASE TITLE:* ***Curse of the Undead Yoma*** (A.D. Vision)

Onikirimaru
鬼切丸
Original Story
Four-episode OAV series (1994-95); based on the manga of the same name, as serialized domestically in the pages of Manga Vizion. Similar to the domestic release of Kusunoki's *Yôma*, two 30-minute episodes of *Onikirimaru* are each available on one 60-minute volume (two domestic volumes total). *DOMESTIC RELEASE TITLE:* ***Ogre Slayer*** (Viz Video)

Yagami-kun no Katei no Jijô
八神くんの家庭の事情
Original Story / Executive Character Designer
Three-episode OAV series (1990); based on the manga of the same name. In a rare departure from her usual samurai-esque blood and gore, Kusunoki takes a rare comedic detour with this love-comedy tale of a young Japanese boy head-over-heels in love with his own extremely young-looking biological mother. 30 minutes each volume. *CURRENTLY IMPORT ONLY*

Key

Japanese comics or "manga" series; may or may not be available in foreign-language (i.e., English) version

TV series broadcast on-air in Japan. Note that, in the U.S., Japanese TV series are both broadcast on-air (*Ronin Warriors*) and released on home video (*Ranma 1/2*). Others (*Sailor Moon, Dragon Ball*) are available both in broadcast and home video versions

Direct-to-home-video series; may also include compilations of TV episodes released to home video market

Theatrical feature; may or may not receive equivalent theatrical release for U.S. version

Buichi Terasawa

Interviewed by Takayuki Karahashi (1996)

"I was born in the year of the sheep," Terasawa says. "My studio's name, Black Sheep, comes from that." In keeping with his "Black Sheep" sobriquet, Terasawa is forever associated with the color black. Anyone who's ever seen him at a convention (he's attended the San Diego Comic-Con several times) knows that Terasawa can easily be I.D.'d as the man in the black suit and tinted shades, moodily but casually observant, as cool as an agent on a top-secret mission.

"I like black," he smiles. "I also like silver. Gold or silver sprinkled in black is even better." Indeed. Terasawa's Black Sheep Studio business card is matte black, glistening with silver type. Visitors to the office of Terasawa Production are confronted by an all-black interior. The wall is black. The desk is black. All the furniture is black. "I don't use black toothpaste," Terasawa laughs, "but everything inside my dresser is black, so I have a hard time telling my clothes apart. It doesn't help that all my clothes look alike."

So what kind of work can one expect from the Man in Black? A quick look at any of his works provides the answer, and you quickly know at a glance, if not the details of the story, at least what kind of world the story takes place in. Terasawa's manga—whether it's *Space Adventure Cobra*, *Midnight Eye Goku*, *Karasu Tengu Kabuto* or *Red Brand Takeru*—feature a stalwart hero backed up by a woman with an impressive physique and boots that are just made-for-walkin'. It doesn't take a lot to imagine what kind of adventure is in the offering here—fantasy where the men are manly men, and the women are both beautiful and deadly.

Don't let his rep fool you, though. Despite his origins as a *shôjo* (yes, that's right, *shôjo*, as in "girls' comics") manga artist, Buichi Terasawa is as much a fantasy artist in the traditional sci-fi/fantasy mold as Boris, Frazetta, or the Bros. Hildebrandt, whose paintings of bikini-clad lovelies, reptilian alien creatures, and musclemen with chests like tree trunks found so frequently on the covers of sci-fi and fantasy books across America are no different from Terasawa's own sci-fi/fantasy inspired manga work. Terasawa specializes in lovely women dressed in few (and those, skintight) clothes, which are always revealing and usually made of leather and/or festooned with weapons, gun-filled holsters, swords, and whatnot; like Edgar Rice Burroughs' jewel-bedecked Thuvia, Maid of Mars, Terasawa girls adorn their well-endowed, decidedly *female* bodies in G-strings, thigh-high boots, plates of armor, drapes of chain mail, strings of baubles—they're Japanese comic characters, and yet they're a sight no fan of fantasy art or comics would find unfamiliar. Like John Carter, Warlord of Mars, the too-cool hero of your standard Terasawa piece is mostly to be envied not only for his ability to stay alive no matter the gimmick-laden deathtraps set for him by his enemies, but for his knack to stay constantly surrounded by only the most delectable of women.

Asked to name his influences, Terasawa admits a surprising fondness for Disney films, although he's quick to draw a cut-off point between the ones he likes and the ones he doesn't ("the ones made before *The Little Mermaid*, I like," he says. "Not so much the ones after"). Of course, he also names the influences you'd expect the man who created *Cobra* to list, such as Ian Fleming's dashing secret agent. "I've seen quite a few movies, but I'd have to say the James Bond films have probably had the greatest influence," he says. "When it comes to domestic films, I'd have to say the Kurosawa films with heroes, such as *Yojimbo* and *The Seven Samurai*."

In fact, it was Terasawa's fusion of the wandering swordsman stories of Japan with "spaghetti westerns, like the ones starring Clint Eastwood or Franco Nero" which led to the artistic birth of his I'm-too-sexy-for-my-shirt heroes and his I'm-too-sexy-I-don't-even-need-a-shirt heroines. "My manga is a collection of the elements I like," he says reasonably. "I think my idea of a 'hero' probably comes almost entirely from spaghetti westerns; spaghetti westerns with a James Bond-type spin to them. *Cobra* was born when it occurred to me that it would be interesting to have both those different types merged into one."

Terasawa's *Space Adventure Cobra* series is in many ways an archetype of all his other works which followed it, filled with equal parts of manly heroism, gimmicky science, nefarious, comic book-style villains, and plushly proportioned photogenic females. In terms of character, Cobra owes a spiritual debt to Bond less because of a shared appreciation for the fine arts ("although he is more educated than your standard Wild West hero in a spaghetti western," as Terasawa helpfully points out) and more because of an unerring instinct for *survival*.

"Cobra is a survivor not because of his I.Q., but because he's constantly being measured for his ability to make the best of a given situation. In a sense, as a *hero*, Cobra has been genetically selected for his ability to think on his feet." What about Cobra's more...well, how can one put it delicately? how about his more...well...*physical*...aspects?

Terasawa laughs. "Oh, when it comes to the 'physical' attributes, I'd have to say he's definitely in the 'superhero' range."

And what about those sexy Terasawa girls? Here Terasawa is quite forthcoming, speaking fondly of a film probably known more than passingly well by certain cult crowds in this country—1968's *Barbarella*, the campy sci-fi/fantasy flick and *Flash Gordon* redux with an eccentrically costumed Jane Fonda in the title role. In retrospect, the connection makes beautiful, absolutely perfect sense.

"*Barbarella* is a movie I truly love," he enthuses. "I *really* like Jane Fonda. In fact..."—he lowers his voice with a naughty twinkle in his eye—"...Jane in *Cobra* is modeled directly upon Jane Fonda in *Barbarella*." When asked if he was influenced more by the film or by the original *Barbarella* comic by French artist Jean-Claude Forest, Terasawa cheerfully confesses, "For the longest time, I wasn't even aware that there *was* a *Barbarella* comic. Finally, I heard about it and went out and bought a copy. I have to say, though, that the *Barbarella* I know is the one in the movie, which is probably why I didn't enjoy the comic as much. And so, in that sense, I'd have to say that the movie's defnitely had a stronger influence on me."

Terasawa himself is hardly a stranger to the "Based on the comic by..." world. *Midnight Eye Goku*, his "Monkey King"-influenced cyberpunk thriller, was released as a two-volume OAV in 1989; *Karasu Tengu Kabuto*, available on subtitled home video from U.S. Renditions/L.A. Hero, was released in Japan as a one-shot OAV in 1992; while *Space Adventure Cobra* has been produced both as a 1982 TV series, as well

Jane and Cobra

as a 1982 theatrical feature which toured the U.S. to positive critical response. All of which, of course, are based on Terasawa's original manga.

In addition to a CD-ROM game (featuring the actual voices of the characters from the animated series), today the *Cobra* legacy lives on with plans for the brand-new, full-length, CG effects-heavy *Cobra the Psychogun*. Despite numerous production difficulties which have put the film on indefinite hiatus (the bankruptcy of the film's production company, for one), Terasawa is optimistic that the project he thinks of as his life's work will eventually return.

"Sure, I'm tempted to work on other stories when I get bored of *Cobra*," he says, "but somehow, I keep coming back to it." And why wouldn't he? The world of *Cobra* is a great place to be...especially when you're the Man in Black.

interview

ANIMERICA: How did you end up becoming a manga artist?

TERASAWA: The year I failed the college entrance exam, a friend of mine was working on becoming a *shôjo* manga artist. She was submitting works to manga contests sponsored by various magazines, and their prize monies were pretty substantial. Even though it was twenty years ago, we're still talking about something like a million yen! Actually, I wasn't so interested in manga—I *was* intrigued by how big the prizes were, though. Moonlighting drawing manga started to seem like a very good idea. One of my entries just happened to win an honorable mention. I forget exactly how much money I earned, but it enticed me to think it was a great way to moonlight. Eventually, I got the idea that I might actually be able to earn a living doing this. That's how I became a manga artist.

ANIMERICA: Can you tell us more about this first manga?

TERASAWA: Believe it or not, it was *shôjo* manga. I was submitting work for a year or so, and I must have drawn twenty to thirty stories. They were all *shôjo*.

ANIMERICA: And the work which won the honorable mention? What kind of work was that?

TERASAWA: Let's see, I think most of those early stories were science fiction. I don't think I drew that many "ordinary" stories.... Yes, they were all science fiction.

ANIMERICA: So they were science fiction and *shôjo* manga and had roses all over?

TERASAWA: Yes, there were roses. I drew roses, all right. I went out to buy a photo book on roses and used it for reference. [LAUGHS] —Actually, I didn't draw *that* many roses, but I drew some.

ANIMERICA: But you drew enough roses to warrant the purchase of a reference book....

TERASAWA: ...Well, it was *shôjo* manga, after all, but it was still my work, which meant that even back then, I had female characters wearing G-strings. It was pretty bold work. [LAUGHS] It's weird, actually—it may have been *shôjo* manga, but come to think of it, in some ways, I don't think the world view was all that different from that of *Cobra*.

ANIMERICA: Did your *shôjo* manga characters have fluffier hair, though?

TERASAWA: Actually, the hairdo for *Cobra*'s Jane was established during my *shôjo* days. That hairdo comes from Disney's *Cinderella*—actually, no, make that *Sleeping Beauty*. The volume and the spirit for the shape are definitely inspired by *Sleeping Beauty*.

ANIMERICA: And so the Disney connection is revealed. [LAUGHS] You said that you didn't always want to be a manga artist, and chance led you to it....

TERASAWA: Right, I wasn't fully sure what was the right way to draw manga. Fortunately for me, I guess the style I was able to draw from the beginning was also the style I'd become known for.

ANIMERICA: A guiding hand from heaven, would you say?

TERASAWA: ...With impure motives, you might also say. I drew only for the prize money, after all.

ANIMERICA: But money is such an *honest* motive. What would you have become if you hadn't become a manga artist?

TERASAWA: I suppose I'd be a regular office worker, a salaryman. But then again, there are lots of doctors in my family, and there *was* a time I thought about applying to med school.... Hmm. I guess I didn't have a driving desire to become anything else, though, so yeah, I probably *would* have become an office worker or a doctor. In fact, a friend who joined Tezuka Production with me is now a doctor. He attended medical school for a year and decided to try his skills as a manga artist and took a leave of absence. He and I joined Tezuka Production at the same time. He was there for a year, and he probably decided manga wasn't for him. He left Tezuka

Production, went back to school, and today, he's an honest-to-goodness doctor.

ANIMERICA: Are there any manga artists who have influenced you?

TERASAWA: There's Disney, of course, although he's not strictly a "manga artist"; obviously, there's also an influence from my mentor, Osamu Tezuka. While it's true that my art style hardly resembles that of Tezuka, I think that the way I tell a story and layout the panels and pace the story has been influenced by him. Even today, I still remember his best works and learn from them to make my stories more accessible to more readers. If you tell a complicated story in a complicated fashion, you just confuse your readers. What Tezuka taught me was that the way to tell a complicated story is to tell it in a simple fashion, so that everyone—and not just the few—can enjoy it. And then of course, I'd have to count all the older Japanese manga artists as my influence. I've also read American and European works, although perhaps I've seen them more through the movies they're based on than the actual comics themselves. I've also watched many, many an episode of *Tom and Jerry*.

ANIMERICA: Now, about your *Midnight Eye Goku* story. You're obviously familiar with the ancient legend of the *Saiyûki*. He becomes disciple to the priest from China to journey to India to bring home valuable *sutras*, etc. Isn't *Goku* like a modern retelling of the Monkey King legend?

TERASAWA: Well, I wouldn't say *Midnight Eye Goku* has *that* much to do with the Monkey King. When I come up with a main character, for easier visualization on the part of the reader, I just borrow the name or the atmosphere from a legendary figure. I don't necessarily want to retell the legend itself. For example, *Midnight Eye Goku* is obviously based, if only in part, on the Monkey King, while *Red Brand Takeru* comes from the ancient Japanese hero Yamato Takeru. But I'm not really sure what Yamato Takeru did, and it's not like Goku is going off to a modern India to bring home *sutras*. [LAUGHS] I just thought it would be interesting to see a guy with a stick that grows and who's named Goku. In fact, the way it usually works, I come up with the character first and then name him, so it's probably fair to say Goku isn't entirely based on the Monkey King legend.

ANIMERICA: How did you arrive at the idea for the character, then?

TERASAWA: As you know from reading the comics and watching the animation, Goku's basic premise is that he can come into contact with any and every computer through any and every interface. His magic staff is a gimmick too, a way to make the externals flashier, just like Cobra's psychogun. Goku has to have something to pose with, y'know?

ANIMERICA: So your Goku won't be a cloud rider?

TERASAWA: Well, if you go that far, you end up with Son Goku himself. Actually, there already is a Son Goku-type character in *Cobra* who's named, coincidentally enough, Goku. [LAUGHS]

Manga is a visual medium, so people might think the art is the most important aspect. But actually, the story is far more important. A series of pretty pictures does not a manga make.

ANIMERICA: Let's talk about the new *Cobra* movie, *Cobra the Psychogun*.

TERASAWA: Well, there *was* a feature in production with a March '96 release date. It was going to be a pretty good production, too. But the company that was soliciting sponsors to produce the film went bankrupt, so the animation project went back to the starting boards. So, if the current *Cobra the Psychogun* story is to be animated, it will probably be a little further into the future.

ANIMERICA: So the production is on complete hiatus now?

TERASAWA: The animation crew has been disbanded. The work done so far is shelved, and I don't know what will happen to it.

ANIMERICA: How much were you involved in the production?

TERASAWA: I've directed an OAV before [Karasu Tengu Kabuto—*Ed.*], but this was going to be my first theatrical feature. I put a lot of effort into it.

ANIMERICA: Basically, you were the director.

TERASAWA: You could say that, but the most time-consuming task was the storyboard drawing. That took about half a year. And all that effort was suddenly negated, so I'm very annoyed about the whole thing right now.

ANIMERICA: On the other hand, there's the new *Cobra the Psychogun* manga that was serialized in SUPER JUMP magazine that's been made in the style of your *Red Brand Takeru*. How was it, working on the manga?

TERASAWA: The story's finished and it's out in Japan in two compiled volumes. Right now, I'm working on a new story that starts in January called *Galaxian Nights*.

ANIMERICA: What kind of story is it?

TERASAWA: I'm trying to create an atmosphere similar to *The Arabian Nights*, the *Thousand and One Nights*. It's not looking too promising at the moment, but that's the way it's supposed to be.

ANIMERICA: Are you going for the Middle Eastern look and feel now?

TERASAWA: Not at all. [LAUGHS] It just turned out that way. This is one instance where I got started from the name. I hope the one story will have that particular feel, but it's already drifting away from the *Arabian Nights* theme....

ANIMERICA: Is this still a *Cobra* story?

TERASAWA: It's *Cobra*. It's pretty much in the same style as *Cobra the Psychogun*, but it might be a little more evolved. There will be more 3-D renderings in the background. I'll be putting out my manga on CD-ROM.

ANIMERICA: Will it have voice-actors?

TERASAWA: It won't have voice-actors, because this is manga. It might have music and sound effects. The text will be in three languages. Can you guess which ones?

ANIMERICA: Japanese, English, and perhaps...Chinese?

TERASAWA: How did you know? Most people would have said French or Spanish, but yes, the third language is Chinese.

ANIMERICA: I understand Asia has a booming manga market.

TERASAWA: That's for sure. If all 1.2 billion of the Chinese population start reading paper-based manga, the environment is sure to go "Poof."

ANIMERICA: How important is international recognition to you in relation to domestic success?

TERASAWA: I think manga is a form of borderless communication, and those who like my type of work read it regardless of where they live or what language they speak.

ANIMERICA: Does that mean you get fan letters from places such as Liechtenstein or Andorra?

TERASAWA: I'd love to get a fan letter from Liechtenstein—I'd keep the letter just for the stamp! [LAUGHS]

ANIMERICA: Where did you get the idea for *Kabuto*? It feels like such a mismatch to have a feudal wandering swordsman and complex mechanical gadgets....

TERASAWA: Well, it's really supposed to be a ninja story, but it takes place in an alternate world that just happens to resemble feudal Japan with that kind of technological advancement.

ANIMERICA: The same can be said of the *Takeru* world.

TERASAWA: That's my vision of modern Japan. The idea is that it's a world which has made the same kind of technological advances as today's Japan, except it exists in total isolation from the rest of the world.

ANIMERICA: But they use *kanji* (Japanese characters) everywhere.

TERASAWA: Yes, *kanji* is still everywhere.

ANIMERICA: Did you write the lyrics for *Kabuto*'s song yourself?

TERASAWA: I collaborated with the lyricist for the words.

ANIMERICA: How involved were you with the production of the *Kabuto* OAV?

TERASAWA: I drew the storyboards, and I'm credited for direction. I'm supposed to have written it too, but in animation, the screenplay is supposed to get written first, with the storyboards to follow. I was initially unclear on the process, so I ended up doing the storyboards first, which means that the script, which was written later, was based largely on the storyboards. It's a reversal of the traditional order.

ANIMERICA: How do you analyze the secret of your popularity? Is it the good-looking hero? The sexy women? The neat gadgets?

TERASAWA: I think it's different for each reader. Some may like the graffiti on a pillar; others may like the der-

***Cobra*'s "Lady"**

rières of the women characters. The French are big on derrières. I have many derrière photo references of French models in my reference library. [LAUGHS]

ANIMERICA: So the French are big on derrières? Your own manga seem to have a notable lack of cute-girl characters....

TERASAWA: I'm not good at drawing cute things; not children, and especially not "cute" girls. Perhaps that's why I never got far in my *shôjo* manga career.

ANIMERICA: So despite your research in roses, you still needed cute girls. Do you think the French are as big on men's derrières as they are on women's?

TERASAWA: No, I'd say that when it comes to men, they're big on chest shots.

ANIMERICA: Cobra's chest comes from the French model, then?

TERASAWA: You could say that. And his facial features are Italian, especially the nose. Yes, Cobra's nose is definitely an Italian nose.

ANIMERICA: So. Cobra is a combination of James Bond's dandiness, a French buff chest, and an Italian nose. I see. [LAUGHS] Continuing this international theme, do you like American animation and comics?

TERASAWA: I like them, but I probably see them more when they are made into a TV show or a movie.

ANIMERICA: It's no secret that Cobra is a character you keep coming back to, but you do have other characters. Would you say you do these other characters in order not to deplete the creative soil in which the *Cobra* series flourishes, so to speak?

TERASAWA: Maybe. I guess so. Actually, I'm not sure I understand what you're talking about here.... [LAUGHS] Sure, it would be ideal if I could draw everything concurrently. *Midnight Eye Goku* wasn't a story that came out of nowhere—I had lots of story ideas. Some of them had to take place in the modern world to be interesting, which meant they wouldn't be suitable for *Cobra*. I'd accumulate those story ideas, and that resulted in *Goku*. Or when the ideas were historical, they became *Karasu Tengu Kabuto*. So *Goku* wasn't suddenly born out of nothingness; there were many stories waiting just for him when he arrived.

ANIMERICA: *Goku* had its own germination period.

TERASAWA: If I stopped coming up with story ideas now, I'd still have ideas to last me for the next twenty years. Or rather, I have that many stories, but I can't draw fast enough to make them all materialize.

ANIMERICA: There aren't enough media for your ideas?

TERASAWA: No, I'm just slow at what I do. Especially now that I've started using computer colorization, everything's taking even longer. [LAUGHS]

ANIMERICA: What do you do when you're not working?

TERASAWA: Well, the time is spent on my hobbies, like magic. These days, I play games too, such as simulation games. I play fighting games, too.

ANIMERICA: "Magic" as in "*Magic: The Gathering*"?

TERASAWA: What's that?

ANIMERICA: ...Never mind. What about mah-jongg?

TERASAWA: Sure, although I haven't played much recently. But I do like it.

ANIMERICA: Do you win at mah-jongg?

TERASAWA: You bet I do. I'm known to be a good player.

ANIMERICA: Do you have advice for the youths of the world aspiring to become manga artists?

TERASAWA: Well, manga is a visual medium, so people might think the art is the most important aspect. But actually, the story is far more important. A series of pretty pictures does not a manga make. In fact, when you're forced to draw day after day, you can't help but improve technically. But the story—you might want to research topics no one else's pursued. Or think about matters in a way different from other people. I think it's more important to do that, *then* learn how to draw properly.

ANIMERICA: Is there a place that teaches you how to make a story?

TERASAWA: Well, story-making—there's material for that everywhere. You can read a novel. You can pursue your interests. Those kinds of teachers are everywhere.

ANIMERICA: So you can make teachers out of the whole wide world.

TERASAWA: ...But a common trap to aspiring manga artists is making manga your hobby. When it's your hobby, you can just read what you want and enjoy it. Some people pursue that even further and turn into manga critics. But critics aren't creators. Instead, you have to find something that interests you and create with the same passion. If you pursue your interests, you may end up with an interesting topic yourself. So, if you're like me and like mecha as well as female derrières, you could arrange what you like and come up with a story.

ANIMERICA: So you're saying one has to live out one's interests.

TERASAWA: That's right. If you force yourself to draw a story about something you're not interested in, there's no way you can entertain your readers.

ANIMERICA: Finally, do you have a word for the Terasawa fans in the English-speaking world?

TERASAWA: Gee, I'm not really sure what you mean by fans in the English-speaking world. [LAUGHS]

ANIMERICA: Let's say those anime and manga fans who speak English as their native language and read ANIMERICA.

TERASAWA: Well, I'm kind of depressed myself right now that my feature project got shelved. But it's not dead. It'll come back in the future. And I plan to get other stories animated, as well. I'll be working on manga too, but I plan to release the CD-ROM version of the manga by next year. There's also the *Cobra* game, although I don't know if it'll be released for the American market. If it comes out, I hope you get to play it.

ANIMERICA: Thanks for making time for us. Some of our readers may not know that our editor worked for you when she lived in Japan. She especially wanted me to thank you.

TERASAWA: Thank you. And her.

afterword

"Welcome to the zany world of Japanese science-fiction animated features," says reviewer Betsy Sherman in the BOSTON GLOBE REVIEW about a subtitled screening of the *Cobra* movie in Boston, "where triplet princesses with Barbie™-doll figures team with an insouciant hunk whose left hand turns into a 'psychogun' to battle a translucent supervillain who removes his own rib and uses it as a laser sword. It's a superbly animated, moving, comic book that borrows elements from movies such as *Barbarella* and *Star Wars* for its zippy-if-dopey storyline."

As Stan Lee might say, "'Nuff said." Though the hoped-for *Cobra the Psychogun* movie has yet to get off the ground as of this writing, Terasawa has continued to produce manga, much of it computer-colored on the Macintosh—something that hasn't gone without notice in the computer industry.

Terasawa was one of the first to bring his creative endeavors to the public eye with the release of a "Manga Mac Exhibition" CD-ROM, released bilingually through his Tokyo-based management company, A-Girl Co., Ltd. Terasawa can also be described as a pioneer for his work in the field of computer colorization with his manga series *Red Brand Takeru*, which not only utilized a computer for the coloring but also added special effects, such as motion-blurring and multiple images.

It was a vast improvement from an earlier attempt he'd made ten years previously with *Bat*. Like the technology, Terasawa's since moved on to bigger and better tools, including Photoshop, Shade, and Strata 3-D. A self-described "Mac loyalist," he says he's nevertheless toyed with the idea of trying out the Japanese version of Windows 95, despite the fact that it's, as he puts it, "still weak on Japanese peripherals." He's also mulling over the idea of giving a Silicon Graphics computer a try, to improve the speed on his 3-D work.

Terasawa is the first to admit that working on the computer doesn't exactly speed up the drawing process (if anything, he says, it takes longer), but he insists there are compensating merits. In the case of *Cobra the Psychogun*, his techniques allowed him to work on the animation storyboards first, then digitize the line art into the computer, where it could be used as a template for both the concurrently produced *Cobra* manga and CD-ROM. Characters and backgrounds were drawn separately for the CD-ROM, while the manga used another version of them in a new layout. In this sense, perhaps the computerized process can actually be thought of as a time-saver, after all.

With these sorts of advantages, why haven't all manga artists in Japan gone the Photoshop route? As Terasawa explains, "Japanese publishing is basically all typeset, so if someone wants to draw thirty pages of color manga, the magazine's cost would be so expensive that not *all* pages would show up in color. It'll make an expensive *tankôbon* (compilation volume) to produce, and it'll be hard to sell to consumers, too. Manga sort of found its market by making itself cheap and abundant, so if you colorize the art and make it expensive and limited in number like mine, it goes against the establishment. Manga is supposed to be cheap, but my compilations are a case in point. They tend to be three times as expensive as regular manga." But as he's also quick to point out, these manga *don't* sell at a price three times as high.

"Cheaper manga are easier to buy, after all."

Buichi Terasawa
Select Bibliography & Filmography

MANGA 漫画

Once known chiefly as the creator of *Cobra*, these days, Terasawa is known in manga circles for his extensive use of computers—specifically, Macs—in his work, producing as he does volume after volume of painstakingly computer-colored comics. So enthusiastic is he about the potential for computers in the world of manga, Terasawa has even authored a book on the subject, the appropriately titled *Kimi mo Mac de Manga ga Kakeru* ("You, Too, Can Draw Manga on the Mac"), which was recently released through Scholar Publishing.

Space Adventure Cobra
スペースアドベンチャーコブラ

Terasawa's debut title (1977); serialized in Shueisha's weekly SHÔNEN JUMP manga anthology from 1977-84. Like many popular manga series, a variety of editions are available—in this case, not only is there the first 18-volume series, but a ten-volume, larger-format edition, all-color editions, etc. Other variations—including the popular *Cobra Girls* illustration collection—on a *Cobra* theme are available in abundance, such as CD-ROM editions and several computer games. Note that, as of 1995, a completely computer-produced *Cobra* series began serialization as "Cobra the Psychogun" in Shueisha's SUPER JUMP. *DOMESTIC RELEASE TITLE:* ***Cobra*** (Viz Comics)

Black Knight Bat
BLACK KNIGHT バット

Serialized in SHÔNEN JUMP (1985); one compiled volume total. Note that the series is currently being published online, as well, on the web page of Japanese multimedia company "SoftBANK" (`http://www.softbank.co.jp/ilab/bat/m_index.html`), where you can keep up bilingually with the story as it's written. *PRINT VERSION CURRENTLY IMPORT ONLY; ELECTRONICALLY PUBLISHED VERSION AVAILABLE IN EITHER ENGLISH OR JAPANESE.*

Karasu Tengu Kabuto ("Raven 'Tengu' Kabuto")
鴉天狗

Serialized in Shueisha's monthly FRESH JUMP manga anthology (1987); two compiled volumes total in one edition, three in another. (There's also a recent re-release edition available in two volumes.) While you're at it, keep an eye out for a storyboard compilation from the *Kabuto* OAV, as well. *CURRENTLY IMPORT ONLY*

Midnight Eye Gokû
MIDNIGHT EYE ゴクウ

Serialized in Scholar's COMIC BURGER monthly manga anthology (1992); four compiled volumes available total. An illustration collection, *Midnight Scoop*, is available in hardback. *DOMESTIC RELEASE TITLE:* ***Midnight Eye Goku*** (Viz Comics)

Takeru (Red Brand)
タケル

Serialized in Scholar publishing's COMIC BURGER monthly manga anthology (1992); one compiled volume total. Terasawa's most recent series. Note that, unlike the usual black and white of Japanese comics publishing, *Takeru* is published in full color—produced, in fact, on a Macintosh using Adobe Photoshop®. "Takeru: The Letter of the Law," a CD-ROM based on the manga of the same name, is currently in development with Sun Soft and slated for release in late '97. *CURRENTLY IMPORT ONLY*

ANIME アニメ

Animated videos based on Terasawa's works. Because of a certain 1992 MTV music video (see below), name recognition for Terasawa outside his native Japan runs particularly high, despite what might otherwise seem to be a fairly modest roster of anime titles. Frequent appearances at anime, manga, and comic book conventions around the world don't hurt, either.

Space Adventure Cobra: Gekijô Ban
("Space Adventure Cobra: The Movie")
スペースアドベンチャーコブラ：劇場版

Original Story / Screenplay
99-minute theatrical feature (1982); based on the popular manga series of the same name (Terasawa gets partial script credit, as well). This is the movie from which alternative rocker Matthew Sweet gets footage for his MTV music video, "Girlfriend." Athough the film has had a limited U.S. theatrical run, it has yet to be released here on home video. *DOMESTIC RELEASE TITLE:* ***Space Adventure Cobra*** (Streamline Pictures)

Space Adventure Cobra
スペースアドベンチャーコブラ

Original Story
31-episode TV series (1982); follows up the success of the theatrical feature of the same name. Sometimes described in the Japanese press as having an American superhero comic book feel, designs for the character of "Lady" resonate strongly of the "sexy robot" look of Japanese illustrator Hajime Sorayama, whose works have influenced at least one other anime/manga series of which we know. *CURRENTLY IMPORT ONLY*

Midnight Eye Gokû
MIDNIGHT EYE ゴクウ

Original Story / Screenplay
Two-volume OAV series (1989); based on the manga of the same name. A private detective equipped with an eye that can tap into the worldwide computer system as well as a vastly extendable telescoping staff brings the ubiquitous *Saiyûki* "Monkey King" legend to near-future Tokyo in the year 2014. Exceptional mecha design complements a clever story to create one of the OAVs in the '80s worthy of the adjective "original." Long-rumored for domestic release, licensing difficulties seem to be keeping this one in Japan only, at least for now. *CURRENTLY IMPORT ONLY*

Karasu Tengu Kabuto
鴉天狗カブト

Original Story / Series Coordinator / Cel Work
39-episode TV series (1990-91); based on the manga of the same name. Originally broadcast via satellite on NHK, in Japan the series has been released to home video both in a "perfect series" (each half-hour episode, in chronological order), as well as in "digest" form (a condensed version, with only the major storylines retained, and some new footage added). *CURRENTLY IMPORT ONLY*

Karasu Tengu Kabuto: Ôgon no Me no Kemono
("Raven 'Tengu' Kabuto: The Golden-Eyed Beast")
鴉天狗カブト：黄金の目のケモノ

Original Story / Director / Screenplay
One-shot OAV (1992); direct-to-home-video follow-up to the TV series of the same name. A fast-paced and sexy blend of cyberpunk technology and traditional Japanese mythology, Terasawa even helped write the lyrics the rockin' ending theme. *DOMESTIC RELEASE TITLE:* ***Raven Tengu Kabuto*** (U.S. Renditions)

Key

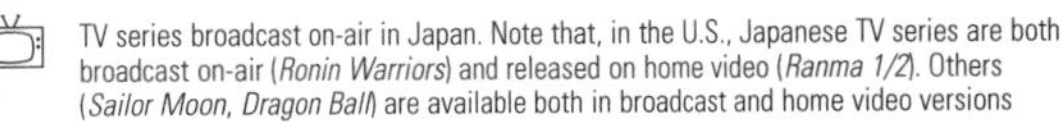

Japanese comics or "manga" series; may or may not be available in foreign-language (i.e., English) version

TV series broadcast on-air in Japan. Note that, in the U.S., Japanese TV series are both broadcast on-air (*Ronin Warriors*) and released on home video (*Ranma 1/2*). Others (*Sailor Moon, Dragon Ball*) are available both in broadcast and home video versions

Direct-to-home-video series; may also include compilations of TV episodes released to home video market

Theatrical feature; may or may not receive equivalent theatrical release for U.S. version

Mamoru Oshii

Interviewed by Carl Gustav Horn (1996)

"When I was twenty-six," Oshii says, when asked how he got into animation at a panel discussion during his tenure as a guest at a U.S. anime convention, "I was out of work, just walking the streets, when I bumped into a telephone pole and saw an ad, 'animators wanted.'" Oddly enough, as an anime director, Oshii made history relatively early in his career, with the first of the OAVs—1983's *Dallos*—and through directing episodes of the *Urusei Yatsura* TV series, but *really* made a name for himself through distinctive motion pictures, such as the *Urusei Yatsura* movie, *Beautiful Dreamer* (1984). Although it strayed rather far from Rumiko Takahashi's own vision of her characters, the vivid, hallucinogenic experience that is the Oshii *UY* nonetheless placed on many "Top Ten" anime film lists in the 1980s.

Angel's Egg (1985) was another early artistic success, about which the 1986 edition of Genkosha's Animation Video Collectors Guide commented, "This is animated art rather than story. It could be brought to a Soho gallery theater." A good example of the level of experimentation in the then-young OAV format, *Angel's Egg* is a cryptic visual feast, featuring delicate and fantastical designs by Yoshitaka Amano (*Vampire Hunter D*, *Final Fantasy* RPG designer). The story follows the meanderings of a fragile waif and her "egg," which she believes contains an angel. She is met during her travels by a soldier carrying a crucifix-like weapon on his back, and the two travel the blasted landscape until the frustrated soldier tires of the mystery and breaks open the girl's egg, which is then shown to contain nothing. Though *Angel's Egg* has almost no dialogue, the film's complex allegorical symbolism—the end of the film featured, among other things, angels rising from the sea into heaven—had nearly everyone who had ever seen it scratching their heads in confusion.

These works already exhibited the elements that would preoccupy Oshii in his career: the symbolic language of dreams, the emergence of reality amidst dreaming, and an epigrammatic use of the Bible.

"I'm not a Christian, but I've been reading the Bible since my student days," Oshii says. "I use it as a prototype for my stories; not for religious reasons, but for ideology and literary inspiration." Oshii's "auteur" reputation no doubt had something to do with mecha and character designer Yutaka Izubuchi (*Patlabor*, *Record of Lodoss War*) being initially reluctant to take on the unusual Oshii as director for his nascent *Patlabor* project in 1988; reluctance was quickly left behind, however, as *Patlabor* became a success as two OAV series, a TV show, and as two theatrical features. In fact, it was Oshii's detailed and intense signature style in 1993's theatrical *Patlabor 2* which led directly to his being tapped to direct the anime adaptation of Masamune Shirow's cyberpunk manga *Ghost in the Shell*.

But shortly before *Patlabor 2* and *Ghost*, Oshii also produced one of his more obscure works—*Talking Head*, a live-action video which also contains brief spurts of anime footage à la anime mockumentary *Otaku no Video*, featuring character designs by none other than *Macross*' Haruhiko Mikimoto. The story of an animation studio torn apart by a murder mystery, the film is a kind of dark art, and confirms that if Mamoru Oshii were not an animation director, he would surely be Japan's analog to David Lynch.

"I really liked the original story of the *Ghost*," Oshii says simply, when asked to explain why he chose to direct the *Ghost* movie, "—but most of all, when I was directing the *Patlabor* films, they possessed a common theme, and I wanted to do more stories of the kind, and when the subject matter of *Ghost* came up, it was perfect."

Reminiscent of the recent slew of futuristic "hacker" movies such as *Johnny Mnemonic* and *Strange Days*, *Ghost in the Shell* depicts a near-future world where computerization has revolutionized society into a cybernetic dreamscape, in which augmented humans live in virtual environments watched over by VR agents; law enforcers are able to download themselves to catch cyber criminals; and the ultimate secret agent of the future is not human, but a virtual reality being, secretly created by the government. Known as "The Puppet Master," it has no physical body, and can freely travel the information highways of the world, hacking and manipulating as required...until the prototype agent decides that it has the right to live a physical life. It appears and makes a demand for asylum—when it is refused, it just as quickly disappears. But how do you capture a being that is nothing more than a ghost...?

Like *Appleseed*, another techno-fetishistic series by Shirow, the *Ghost in the Shell* manga teems with brain-numbing new technology and addresses a similar theme—that the very tools it creates is forcing mankind to evolve into a new kind of being capable of living in the kind of world it has itself produced. The main character, Major Motoko Kusanagi, is a cybernetic being, almost completely artificial, who can "jack" herself into machines and other cyborgs in order to ferret out crimes. This continual out-of-body experience is the theme of the title itself—that the human mind is the "ghost," and that the host body, even that not your own, is but a "shell." Despite critical concern that Oshii's cerebral sensibilities could only serve to further obfuscate Shirow's notorious lack of narrative clarity, others seem to feel that the creative talents of the two made for a perfect match.

Oshii's approach to the *Ghost* material was to gleefully cut whatever did not apply to that desired theme—the pod-like personal robots or "*fuchikoma*" mecha that Shirow so enjoys drawing in the manga (his illustration book *Intron Depot* is chockablock with lithe girls jacked into similarly designed robots), for instance, are not present in the anime—and instead, to develop a strong allegory about man and his spiritual relationship to the viroment in which he's forced to live. The resultant animation, combining state-of-the-art computer animation,

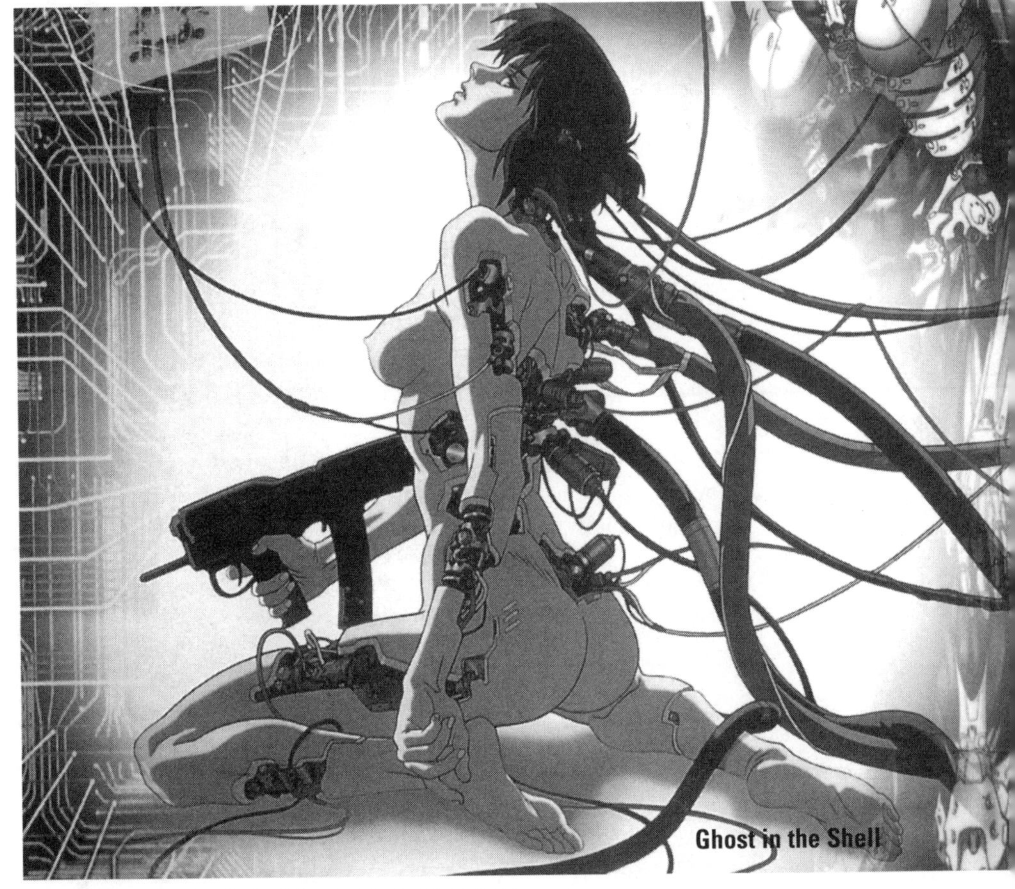
Ghost in the Shell

© Headgear • Emotion • TFC
Patlabor 2

superlative cel work, and Oshii's own blend of reality and dreams, made for one of the most talked-about anime features in recent memory.

Even though the subject matter of his films tends toward the realm of the fantastic, Oshii, as a director, dreams not only in the service of fantasy, but also in the "real world"—witness the overt political themes in the *Patlabor* films. He uses the medium as the Expressionists did painting, not in the photo-realistic copying of reality of the live-action camera eye, but in the tone and line of painting that showed aspects of reality the obviousness of the camera could not, such as the stains of color that reveal hidden details. Oshii loves cities—his camera eye wanders slowly through them in the *Patlabor* films and *Ghost*, moving by day and night, by summer and winter, his eye slowing down their frantic pace, to suggest that what is perceived by their inhabitants as the vital bustle of reality is, in fact, life on the terms of a dream. Oshii himself constructs these scenes before they're ever put on acetate, walking down the rainy streets of Hong Kong and riding flat boats along Tokyo's Sumida River, camera in hand, contemplating. Reality, in his films, is often symbolized by what looms above the track of dreaming: a shattered bridge, a blimp, a tall building which has been planned for a secret purpose. Below, we move through the streets like a slow motorcade. One more turn, and we will be blown into reality; one more turn, and we will realize that if Oshii dreams awake, he dreams wide-awake.

interview

ANIMERICA: First, some of my immediate impressions of *Ghost in the Shell*. One scene that particularly caught my eye was the climactic museum shoot-out, where the machine-gun fire rakes up the medieval "Tree of Life" painting (stopping just before *hominis*, "mankind").

OSHII: The museum was based on the Crystal Palace [*a huge glass hall built for the Victorian Great Exhibition of 1851 in London, and architectural precursor to the modern skyscraper, accidentally destroyed by fire in 1936—Ed.*]. The "Tree" was not from the Palace, but from another European museum which I unfortunately can't recall.

ANIMERICA: I notice such things because they seem to be part of your distinctive art direction—for example, the fish-eye shots used in the *Patlabor* movies. Do they represent a sense of unreality?

OSHII: That is part of it, but I also wished to describe the world from another viewpoint.

ANIMERICA: I had a question about the way the characters appear in *Ghost in the Shell*. It seems to me that they appear more "Western" than is usual in anime. Was this done intentionally?

OSHII: It wasn't intentional. What I wanted to do was to have characters that looked more like a realistic human being, as opposed to your regular anime characters. So, perhaps as a result, they unintentionally came to appear more "Western."

ANIMERICA: How did you first become involved with the film project for *Ghost in the Shell*?

OSHII: About six months after I finished *Patlabor 2*, I got a call from Bandai Visual, and that's when they offered me the director's position.

ANIMERICA: Were you previously familiar with Masamune Shirow's manga of *Ghost*?

OSHII: Yes, and I liked it.

ANIMERICA: What sort of involvement did Shirow have with the film?

OSHII: He had none—it was my project alone.

ANIMERICA: What was it that interested you in directing the film?

OSHII: Well, first of all, I really liked the original story of the comic—but most of all, when I was directing the *Patlabor* films, they possessed a common theme, and I wanted to do more stories of the kind—and when the subject matter of *Ghost* came up, it was perfect.

ANIMERICA: So *Ghost in the Shell* was continuing a theme that was in the *Patlabor* movies? How would you describe this theme?

OSHII: How humanity will change as it deals with new technology.

ANIMERICA: That is perhaps the most basic question of science fiction, isn't it?

OSHII: Well, I'm not so sure.

ANIMERICA: Masamune Shirow is known, even in America, as one of the most distinctive manga artists. But you are also known as one of the most distinctive anime directors. How does Shirow's vision turn into your vision?

OSHII: When I decided to direct the film, I went to see Shirow—and Shirow is very famous for not going out to meet his public [*Just as "Motoko Kusanagi" is a pseudonym for the main character of* Ghost, *"Masamune Shirow" is the enigmatic manga artist's pen name—Ed.*]. I asked him to please, let me direct the film in my own style, with my own ideas—and he agreed, so I was able to proceed. I had the freedom to put *Ghost* into my world, without having to further ask his approval.

ANIMERICA: So Shirow said it was okay for you to take your own approach?

OSHII: Yeah. "Do as you want," as he said.

ANIMERICA: Once you had the okay to take your own approach to filming the manga, what process of adaptation did you follow?

OSHII: First I considered the film's setting, its world.

ANIMERICA: Why should that come first?

OSHII: For me, the actual town, or city environment of the story, is the most important thing—I must set that up before the rest can proceed.

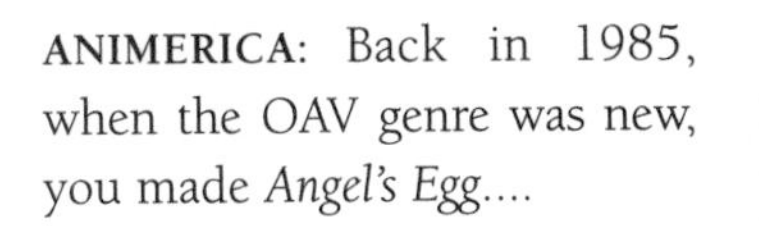

ANIMERICA: Back in 1985, when the OAV genre was new, you made *Angel's Egg*....

OSHII: A decade ago! It had the elements that intrigued me as a film....

ANIMERICA: And they are...?

OSHII: Ruins. I like ruins; I like museums; I like fish; I like birds; I like water...and I like girls. [LAUGHS]

ANIMERICA: Many of your films have quotes from the Bible, and discussions of philosophies from the Bible. Why is that, do you think?

OSHII: I really liked the Bible as a little boy. While a student, I planned to enter a seminary at one point, but didn't. Even now, though, I still read the Bible sometimes.

ANIMERICA: Are you a Christian, or do you just like the Bible for its philosophy?

OSHII: For its philosophy.

ANIMERICA: What was your very first anime movie directing project?

OSHII: It was *Urusei Yatsura: Only You*.

ANIMERICA: ...The first *Urusei Yatsura* movie, yet you also directed the second (*Beautiful Dreamer*), which I think is the one that really made American anime fans begin to notice your distinctive style. Are you interested in dreams?

OSHII: Yes.

ANIMERICA: The elements of your movies—fish, ruins, water—do you dream of these?

OSHII: Ruins arise often in my dreams.

ANIMERICA: Are your films your way of analyzing your dreams?

OSHII: I would say that is about half of it.

ANIMERICA: You've also done live-action films, yet here in the U.S. you're known only for your anime. Can you tell us a little about your live-action work, such as *Talking Head*?

Patlabor 2

OSHII: It's a mystery set in an anime studio. All of a sudden the director disappears in the middle of a film. Another director gets hired, with two missions: complete the anime production and find the missing director.

ANIMERICA: When did it come out?

OSHII: About five years ago? Four years? I can't remember. [LAUGHS]

ANIMERICA: What was your reason for making *Talking Head*?

OSHII: Back then, I was working on a big anime project, and all of a sudden, Bandai canceled it. I was so upset that I asked Bandai if I could direct something else, and they said, "Do whatever you want."

ANIMERICA: What project was that?

OSHII: [LAUGHS] It's a secret.

ANIMERICA: Secret? Does that mean we'll see it someday?

OSHII: I can't really say, you know.

ANIMERICA: Someone who works in the industry, a studio head, once told me that *Talking Head* exposes what it's really like to be an animator.

OSHII: All of the people in the film are modeled after people I actually know, people I've worked with in the industry. I killed them all. [LAUGHS]

ANIMERICA: How is live-action different from animation?

OSHII: Directing anime is much more stressful. With live-action, every (shooting) day is different, and I can work out my stress through the work. And after it's done, the saké tastes better, too. [LAUGHS]

ANIMERICA: What about some of your other live-action films, such as *Akai Megane* [*aka "Red Spectacles," which told the story of combat action in a socially collapsed Tokyo—Ed.*]...?

OSHII: That was made ten years ago, and I made a sequel, *Kerberos*, based on the manga, or as it's called in English, "Panzer Cops," about five years ago. [*The full title is* Hellhounds: Panzer Cops*—Ed.*] However, the story in *Kerberos* actually takes place earlier than that of *Akai Megane*. It's like *Star Wars*—the third film will put everything in order.

ANIMERICA: Getting back to anime, you said that when you make a movie, you consider first the city environment it is set in—and I've noticed that in the *Patlabor* movies, Tokyo is itself an actor—the first one is set in the summer and the second one is set in winter. Each film involves an investigation, but the season lends a real mood, a sensation to it.

OSHII: Yes, of course. It is meant to achieve a psychological effect.

ANIMERICA: Most Americans, I think, will be surprised to see an anime film as political as *Patlabor 2*. The idea that an anime film could be about such real-world, military, and political issues is still a strange one here. Since in

Patlabor 2

Patlabor 2 there is a secret conspiracy between members of the Japanese and American militaries, did you ever wonder how Americans might look at the film when they saw it?

OSHII: I think it may be difficult for Americans to understand. The story is really based on political programs that exist in Japan, so it has quite a few deep meanings within it. In *Patlabor 2*, I wanted to describe the Cold War for Japan. It was a war, but a silent war. When the Cold War existed between the U.S. and Russia, the "stance" of Japan was not to be directly involved. Even though Japan *was* involved, it kept insisting for fifty years that it wasn't. I wanted to describe that fake peace.

ANIMERICA: Do you think another military takeover, as in the 1930s, is possible for Japan today, or was that merely something dramatic for the story?

OSHII: I don't think that it's very possible.

ANIMERICA: When I look at that film, which was made in 1993, nowadays, and I see scenes such as those where the blimp comes down, and gas comes out and starts filling the streets of Tokyo…it's something we're seeing happen now in reality. Did you ever think that kind of thing would happening so soon?

OSHII: I never thought it would happen. When the Tokyo subway was gassed, I immediately thought how glad I was that the film was released *before* the attack happened. [LAUGHS]

ANIMERICA: But in light of such terrorism actually happening in Tokyo, don't you think that people might be more inclined to take *Patlabor 2* more seriously—not just entertainment, but as an actual warning?

OSHII: Not quite. If people were really capable of realizing those dangers, I wouldn't have to make my films.

ANIMERICA: Does that mean you think people still aren't waking up to reality?

OSHII: That's correct.

afterword

Released theatrically in the U.S. to a limited number of theaters, the animated *Ghost in the Shell* brought Oshii international acclaim, and awards from several animation groups who had heretofore barely acknowledged Japanese animators. Oshii's direction aside, *Ghost in the Shell* was an excellent showcase for the cutting edge of Japanese animation at the time—a vision of the future based not on *Akira*'s Neo-Tokyo, but a 21st century Hong Kong: a cyber-cityscape as an overgrown, anachronistic multicultural metropolis, filled with the decaying architecture and relics of past eras packed cheek to jowl with the sleek modern technology, animated with advanced computer graphics combined with traditional cel animation.

As a director of anime for adults (as opposed to "adults-only" anime), Oshii has gone on record criticizing anime's most revered—and financially successful—director, Hayao Miyazaki, for his self-limitation (and perhaps, through Miyazaki's brilliance, implied limitation on the entire medium) as a children's filmmaker, a statement not likely to help his career in animation. During a visit to a U.S. animation convention, 1996's Anime Expo in Anaheim, California, Oshii's answers to questions about his work seemed only to underline his isolation from the "mainstream" of anime, as he claimed that he didn't really watch any anime other than his own, his love for basset hounds (his own dog frequently appears in his animation projects), and that he noticed little difference between fans in Japan and the U.S. "Both groups show a notable lack of females, and both seem to be the 'logic-oriented' type," he commented drily. But when asked to explain his frequent use of "fish-eye" effects in animation, Oshii gave an answer that seemed to sum up his own work, and its dual nature in both the real and surreal, perhaps the best:

"I get asked about that a lot. I'm not really sure about the meaning of that, either. If you pressed me, you could say these are 'eyes' that look at the world of the film from the outside—that these are the eyes, in fact, of the audience."

When the Cold War existed between the U.S. and Russia, the "stance" of Japan was not to be directly involved. Even though Japan *was* involved, it kept insisting for fifty years that it wasn't. I wanted to describe that fake peace.

Mamoru Oshii
Select Bibliography & Filmography

MANGA 漫画

Like many a personality featured in this book, Oshii is known chiefly for his animation work, although—also like others in this book—he's also dabbled in manga from time to time.

Todo no Tsumari ("When All's Said and Done...")
とどのつまり

First serialized in Tokuma Shoten's Animage magazine (1984). *CURRENTLY IMPORT ONLY*

Kenrô Densetsu ("Legend of 'Wolf-Dog'")
犬狼伝説

First serialized in "Amazing Comics" (1988); published in compiled form by Nihon Shuppansha (1990). A "cinematic"-style manga (*gekiga*) story, *Kenrô Densetsu* features an original story by Oshii, art by Kamui Fujiwara, and mechanical designs by Yutaka Izubuchi. The series has been released outside of Japan both in Britain's Manga Mania magazine, as well as in the U.S. In 1991, a live-action version was released theatrically under the title "Stray Dog: Kerberos," featuring direction and screenplay by Oshii. *DOMESTIC RELEASE TITLE:* ***Hellhounds: Panzer Cops*** (Dark Horse Comics)

Seibu Shinjuku Sensen Ijô Nashi
("All's Quiet on the Seibu Shinjuku Front")
西武新宿戦線異状なし

Original Story
Published by Nippon Shuppansha (1994); one compiled volume total. Yasuyuki Ono receives "co-author" credit for a story which posits modern-day Tokyo suddenly thrust into war; a story, by some estimates, not unlike that of *Patlabor 2*. ("Seibu Shinjuku," by the way, is the name of a heavily trafficked transit station in downtown Tokyo.) *CURRENTLY IMPORT ONLY*

Seraphim
セラフィム

Original Story
First serialized in Tokuma Shoten's Animage magazine (1995). Oshii's decision to leave the series prompted a change in his byline, going from "written by" to "original story by" (the series was eventually completed by another writer, Satoshi Kon, who had previously been credited for art only). With its particular motif, *Seraphim*—rendered in Japanese translation as "*tenshi*," or "angel"—is thought by some to have provided inspiration for *Neon Genesis Evangelion*. *CURRENTLY IMPORT ONLY*

ANIME アニメ

Note that for reasons of length, Oshii's non anime- and manga-related work—his live-action films, his computer-game work, his novels and his essay collections—are not included. *Talking Head*, a live-action film with brief anime sequences, is the sole exception, if only because publicity shots of the film showcasing designs by the high-profile Mikimoto have attracted such interest.

Ippatsu Kanta-kun ("One-Hit Kanta")
一発貫太くん

Supervising Episode Director
53-episode TV series (1977-78); heartwarming Tatsunoko ("home of the heroes") comedy about a boy, Kanta, who just can't get enough of baseball. Notable not only for being the series in which Oshii makes his debut, but for the debut of *Kimagure Orange Road*, *Patlabor*, and *Urusei*Yatsura*'s Akemi Takada, who gets credit here for "subcharacter designs." Yoshitaka Amano (*Vampire Hunter D*), a member of Tatsunoko's design staff since the early days of 1973's *Casshan*, is also credited. *CURRENTLY IMPORT ONLY*

Kagaku Ninja-Tai Gatchaman II
("Science Ninja Team Gatchaman II")
科学忍者隊ガッチャマンII

Supervising Episode Director
52-episode TV series (1978-79); sequel to Tatsunoko's wildly popular original *Gatchaman* series first airing in 1972. As with *Ippatsu Kanta-kun*, both Takada and Amano return for design duties, cleaving faithfully to those established in the first show. *DOMESTIC RELEASE TITLE:* ***Eagle Riders*** (Saban)

Zendaman
ゼンダマン

Supervising Episode Director
52-episode TV series (1979-80) continuing Oshii's multi-series association with Tatsunoko. Third entry in the popular "Time Bokan" series, *Zendaman* features, among other things, narration by Japanese voice-actor Kei Tomiyama of *Yamato* and *Galaxy Express 999* fame. *CURRENTLY IMPORT ONLY*

Nils no Fushigi na Tabi
("The Wonderful Adventures of Nils")
ニルスの不思議な旅

Supervising Episode Director
52-episode TV series (1980-81); story of a selfish little boy turned tiny by an elf who has great adventures and learns humility traveling with a flock of geese. Based on the children's book *Nils Holgerssons underbara resa* ("The Wonderful Adventures of Nils") by Nobel-winning Swedish author Selma Lagelöf. Episodes featuring more direct involvement by Oshii—Episodes 36, 49, and 51, to be precise—are said to be held in especially high acclaim by fans. *CURRENTLY IMPORT ONLY*

Ryû no Me no Namida ("Tears of a Dragon's Eye")
竜の目の涙

Director
Educational film (1982); Oshii's first stab at direction for Tatsunoko. *CURRENTLY IMPORT ONLY*

Urusei Yatsura ("Those Obnoxious Aliens")
うる星やつら

Chief Director / Episode Director / Storyboards
197-episode TV series (1981-86); based on the popular manga of the same name by Rumiko Takahashi. In addition to Oshii, the animated *UY* also boasts the character design talents not only of Takada (see above), but direction work by Kazuo Yamazaki (*Maison Ikkoku*) as well as assistant direction by a then-novice Yuji Moriyama (*Project A-Ko*). *DOMESTIC RELEASE TITLE:* ***Those Obnoxious Aliens/Urusei Yatsura*** (AnimEigo)

Urusei Yatsura: Only You
うる星やつら：オンリーユー

Director / Screen Adaptation / Storyboards
90-minute theatrical feature (1983); first in a long and successful series of *UY* films. Takada returns for character design duties. *DOMESTIC RELEASE TITLE:* ***Urusei Yatsura: Only You*** (AnimEigo)

Urusei Yatsura 2: Beautiful Dreamer
うる星やつら２：ビューティフルドリーマー

Director / Screenplay
97-minute theatrical feature (1984); second and definitely the *strangest* of all the *UY* films. In a change of pace, *Please Save My Earth* (*Boku no Chikyû o Mamotte*) and *Maison Ikkoku*'s Kazuo Yamazaki serves as character designer, while Yamazaki and *A-Ko*'s Yuji Moriyama get "animation director" credit. *DOMESTIC RELEASE TITLE:* ***Urusei Yatsura: Beautiful Dreamer*** (U.S. Manga Corps)

Dallos I: Remember Bartholomew
ダロスＩ：リメンバー・バーソロミュー

Co-Director (with mentor Hisayuki Toriumi)
30-minute OAV (1983). A futuristic sci-fi action tale, *Dallos* is also the world's first-ever "OAV," as in animation created expressly for the home video market (as compared to for television broadcast, or theatrical distribution). Note that, of the four-volume OAV series, only the first volume is available here in the U.S. *DOMESTIC RELEASE TITLE:* ***Dallos*** (Best Film and Video)

Tenshi no Tamago ("Angel's Egg")
天使のたまご

Director / Original Story / Script
75-minute original video screened theatrically (1985); Yoshitaka Amano signs on as art director. (Oshii and Amano also collaborate on an illustration book based on the film published the same year.) In the face of routine disbelief, a young girl wanders the wasteland of a post apocalyptic landscape clutching an egg she believes to be divine. Entered at Cannes under the title "*L'Oeuf de l'Ange*." *CURRENTLY IMPORT ONLY*

Twilight Q (2) / Meikyû Bukken File 538
("Twilight Q 2: Labyrinth Objects File 538")
トワイライトＱ（２）／迷宮物件File538

Director / Screenplay
30-minute OAV (1987); second of two volumes in a series envisioned as a

showcase for different directors of differing anime tastes. Note that the first *Twilight Q, Toki no Musubi Hi* ("The Bonds of Time"): *Reflection*—unlike the *Oshii* version of *Twilight Q*—features character direction by frequent collaborator Takada. *CURRENTLY IMPORT ONLY*

Kidô Keisatsu Patlabor ("Mobile Police Patlabor")

機動警察パトレイバー

Director / Storyboards

Seven-volume OAV series (1988-89) for which Oshii provides direction and storyboards for the first five and direction only for the sixth. Based on the popular manga series by Masami Yuki, the *Patlabor* OAV series was the forerunner of what would eventually become a thriving franchise, including two theatrical films (see below), a 1989 TV series and second, 1990-92 OAV series (portions of both these series were also directed by Oshii), and manga. *DOMESTIC RELEASE TITLE:* ***Patlabor: The Mobile Police (The Original Series)*** and ***Patlabor: The Mobile Police (The New Files)*** (U.S. Manga Corps)

Kidô Keisatsu Patlabor: The Movie

("Mobile Police Patlabor: The Movie")

機動警察パトレイバー：THE MOVIE（劇場版）

Director

118-minute theatrical feature (1989) combining political intrigue and a day-after-tomorrow original story with the series' trademark giant police "labors," or patrol robots, thus the title "Patlabor." Character design by Takada; mecha design by Yutaka Izubuchi (*Dunbine*). *DOMESTIC RELEASE TITLE:* ***Patlabor, The Movie 1*** (Manga Entertainment)

Gosenzo-sama Ban-Banzai!

("Let's Really Hear it For the Ancestors!")

御先祖様万々歳！

Director / Screenplay

Six-volume OAV series (1989-90); fanciful story of a girl who, longing to know more about her ancestors, gets into a time machine and ends up doing exactly that. *Maroko,* a 1990 theatrical feature, retells the OAV story and adds new footage. Produced to commemorate the ten-year anniversary of anime's Studio Pierrot, the OAV series also features work by Satoru Utsunomiya, key animator on *Akira. CURRENTLY IMPORT ONLY*

Talking Head

トーキング・ヘッド

Director / Screenplay

105-minute theatrical feature (1992). Troubles at an anime studio motivate this part live-action, part animated murder mystery; surreal sequences á la David Lynch add much fodder for confused head-scratching. Features (sporadic) animated sequences by Haruhiko Mikimoto of *Macross* fame. *CURRENTLY IMPORT ONLY*

Kidô Keisatsu Patlabor: The Movie 2

機動警察パトレイバー：THE MOVIE

Director

114-minute theatrical feature (1993). Top-notch talent including art direction by *The Wings of Honneamise* and *Ninja Scroll*'s Hiromasa Ogura, "guest" mecha design by *Macross*' Shoji Kawamori and *Gundam 0083*'s Hajime Katoki, not to mention the considerable skill of the five-member band known as "Headgear"—Masami Yuki, Akemi Takada, Kazunori Ito, Yutaka Izubuchi, and, of course, Oshii himself—make for one of the best anime movies ever filmed. *DOMESTIC RELEASE TITLE:* ***Patlabor, The Movie 2*** (Manga Entertainment)

Kôkaku Kidô-Tai: Ghost in the Shell

(*lit.,* "attack/assault + husk/cast-off-skin + mobilized force")

攻殻機動隊

Director

85-minute theatrical feature (1995). Obscure, impenetrable manga artist—*Appleseed*'s Masamune Shirow—meets with enigmatic, philosophical filmmaker—Oshii—to create a film hailed by *At the Movies*' own Siskel & Ebert as "unusually intelligent and challenging science fiction, aimed at smart audiences." One of the top films of the year in its native Japan, at one time *Ghost* placed No. 1 on *Billboard*'s video sales chart for the U.S., as well. *DOMESTIC RELEASE TITLE:* ***Ghost in the Shell*** (Manga Entertainment)

Key

Japanese comics or "manga" series; may or may not be available in foreign-language (i.e., English) version

TV series broadcast on-air in Japan. Note that, in the U.S., Japanese TV series are both broadcast on-air (*Ronin Warriors*) and released on home video (*Ranma 1/2*). Others (*Sailor Moon, Dragon Ball*) are available both in broadcast and home video versions

Direct-to-home-video series; may also include compilations of TV episodes released to home video market

Theatrical feature; may or may not receive equivalent theatrical release for U.S. version

Gisaburo Sugii

Interviewed by Toshifumi Yoshida (1996)

Why would an anime director with thirty-plus years in Japan's animation industry under his belt, including Japan's first animated TV series *Tetsuwan Atom* (a.k.a. *Astro Boy*) and "cultured" anime productions such as *Night on the Galactic Railroad* (an adaptation of a story by noted author Kenji Miyazawa) and *The Tale of Genji* (a courtly romance based on the famous 11th century Japanese novel) want to be the one to give animated life to the larger-than-life legends of the video game *Street Fighter II*?

"Actually, until I got involved in the movie, I wasn't interested in the video game," says Sugii. "But when it was decided the movie was going to be made, I got involved with *Street Fighter II* for the first time." In fact, Sugii has tackled the legendary Street Fighters not once, but twice, in both 1994's ultra-serious *Street Fighter II: The Animated Movie* and 1995's more lighthearted weekly Japanese TV series, *Street Fighter II V*.

"There's this *Street Fighter II* poster that's given me a lasting impression," Sugii says, "The impressive thing about the poster, artistically speaking, was that they had all these military planes, but then they just had the fighters from all the various countries standing in front of them, not even facing each other. I thought that was interesting…I can't really express it well in words. I often thought that image might be interesting to produce as an animated movie."

Since the game's debut as a simple one-on-one fighting game featuring only Ryu and Ken and a variety of thugs upon whom you could beat, the *Street Fighter* legacy has expanded to a cast of characters that's attained an immortality of sorts, as the essential archetypes of nearly every fighting game character to come along since. As multinational fighters from different walks of life—Guile, the U.S. Air Force Colonel; Chun Li, the Chinese martial artist in her traditional dress; the Russian Zangief; sumo wrestler E. Honda; the eternal Ryu and Ken; more fanciful characters such as the Indian rubber man Dhalsim and the giant mutant beast Blanka—the cast, in all its incarnations, is unified by nothing more than a desire to be the best at fighting. Each character's individual backstory (usually tacked on after the fact) was always less important than their appearance and fighting style. The idea of fighters with different skills facing and challenging each other, perhaps even learning mutual respect for each other, is a concept similar to so many martial arts sagas where the all-important tournament is the center of the story, everywhere from movies such as *Enter the Dragon* or *Bloodsport* to animation such as *Dragon Ball Z*.

"The audience I had in mind for the film are the gamers who played *Street Fighter II* at the arcades. In the game screen, movements are restricted, and there are game rules, but I thought, those gamers have created their own *Street Fighter II* world in their heads. In the *Street Fighter II* movie, I wanted to present the world that was locked up in their minds, for the battles and the characters. I wanted the movie to be centered on the world imagined by the *Street Fighter II* game lovers."

In a change in tone from the serious, live-action style of the animated movie, Sugii also directed the animated 26-episode *Street Fighter II V* TV series the following year. Based on the adventures of a young Ryu and Ken traveling around the world looking for adventure (much like a martial arts-trained Bill and Ted), *Street Fighter II V* provides the complete backstory for the characters that the movie takes as a given—how they all met each other, how they learned their greatest techniques, their differing philosophies toward their art. The difference in tone between the Japanese TV series and the American-produced, superhero-style *Street Fighter* cartoon series is extreme—in Sugii's version, what's most important to show is what drives the characters to do what they do, and each new introduction gives a human face to the fighting facade.

"Animation is a form of film, so I think the process is pretty much the same. In Japan, especially, the animation industry has more freedom to choose the stories it wants to tell, as compared to other countries where studios like Disney only work on the single subject of fairy tales. I think that, as animators, we're closer to regular live-action filmmakers in that we might be making science fiction or other types of literary works.

"Someone once said that animation is the Japanese Hollywood, and I think that might be true," he continues. "Especially after Osamu Tezuka made *Tetsuwan Atom*, I believe that our thinking process became similar to that of a Hollywood director's movie-making process."

interview

ANIMERICA: How did you get started in animation?

SUGII: I entered Toei Animation just after graduating from high school. Actually, that was really in the early stages, the first few days of Toei Animation when the animation industry was just starting up, and it was rather unlike animation work. Our senior animators taught us in the basics of drawing like upperclassmen teaching their juniors at school. We really learned a lot that way.

ANIMERICA: What was the first work you did? What was your role in it?

SUGII: It was the first major Japanese feature from Toei, *Hakujaden* ("Tale of the White Serpent") [*The same film which Hayao Miyazaki says inspired him to become an animator—Ed.*]. I considered myself very fortunate to have joined the Toei Animation studio at that time. After that, I worked on Japan's first animated TV series, *Tetsuwan Atom*. I've been in animation for over thirty years.

ANIMERICA: Did you always want to become an animator? Or did you originally aspire to another line of work?

SUGII: Well, in my case, when I heard about the first real animation studio opening up in Japan for the first time, I went right away and took the test and got in. I guess my *interest* in animation really started when I was in the fifth grade, when I saw *Bambi*. But, in my junior high school years, there wasn't any information about Japanese ani-

Street Fighter II

mation studios, and I thought I'd have to go to the U.S. to learn animation. So then, when I heard about Toei Animation, I knew I had to do whatever I could to get in. Toei Animation's exam was advertised in the newspaper, and there was competition, where you had about a thirty-in-one chance of getting into the company. That's the way a lot of applicants got in. Back then, there weren't that many jobs for artists, so some of them just wanted a side job at Toei Animation so they could continue with their oil paintings at the studio. But when I joined, what *I* really wanted, was to do animation.

ANIMERICA: What do you think you would be doing now, had you not become an animator?

SUGII: I'd probably be a manga artist.

ANIMERICA: What have been your influences?

SUGII: I liked Max Fleischer. There was one story he did that I really liked, about bugs being chased out of the ground and having to move to a garden on top of a building. I was greatly influenced by this work. You know, I actually like Fleischer's work more than either *Bugs Bunny* or Disney, and, when I was young, my aspiration was to become just like Fleischer.

ANIMERICA: How would you describe the work of the director to someone who doesn't know the animation process?

... the audience I had in mind for the film are the gamers who played the *Street Fighter II* game at the arcades. In the *Street Fighter II* movie, I wanted to present the world that was locked up in their minds...

SUGII: Animation is a form of film, so I think the process is pretty much the same. In Japan, especially, the animation industry has more freedom to choose the stories it wants to tell, as compared to other countries where studios like Disney only work on the single subject of fairy tales. I think that, as animators, we're closer to regular live-action filmmakers in that we might be making science fiction or other types of literary works.

Someone once said that animation is the Japanese Hollywood, and I think that might be true. Especially after Osamu Tezuka made *Tetsuwan Atom*, I believe that our thinking process became similar to that of a Hollywood director's movie-making process. And, aside from a few computerized processes, it's all work done by hand. The most difficult process is giving the animators instructions on minute directions laid out in the storyboards for the hand work.

I'm sure film directors come up with ideas on how the movie should look when they read the script, so that part's the same, but in animation, if one mistaken instruction is given, it takes a huge amount of time and effort to correct it. For example, if you don't already have in your head how fast the scene will be moving if you direct the camera to move so-and-so millimeters at 0.1 millimeter a frame, it may turn out to be too slow or too fast after it's filmed. You have to have those things in mind before the work is even started and instructions are given out. I think that's the real difference between animation and live-action.

ANIMERICA: What does a director do from inception to completion of a project?

SUGII: I often join a project from the planning stages. I tend to join at the planning and scriptwriting stages in order to come up with a world of my own.

ANIMERICA: Are you satisfied with the animation

Street Fighter II

you've made? Were there times when you didn't get what you wanted?

SUGII: My most regrettable work is the animated *Genji*. I couldn't put on film half of what I wanted. It's hard to make the same movie twice, but I'd like to get a second chance at that. Especially the last scene....

ANIMERICA: What was the project with which you're most satisfied so far?

SUGII: That would be *Ginga Tetsudô no Yoru*. This was a work where, through multiple lucky breaks, the intentions of all the staff—from the music writer to the screenwriter and all of the animators—converged. This was the one work I've done where the staff's mind became one for the film.

ANIMERICA: What has changed in you the most since you started directing? Also, how do you get along with your staff on the job? Do you tend to give detailed instructions? Or do you just set the direction and let the staff do the work?

SUGII: My way of thinking has changed 180 degrees between the start of my career up until age thirty-five, and then the ten years since I turned forty-five until now. Until I was thirty-five, I thought that the storyboards *were* the film. As far as I was concerned, the movie was completed in my head when the storyboards were completed. So I thought that the staff's only job was to work according to the storyboards. But since age forty-five, I've come to think of the storyboards as having a temporary existence that is fluid, changing with staff discussion. As long as there's an unchanging central core concept, I've come to think that the details of a production can be free to change. I've come to think that's what it means to make a living, making movies.

Street Fighter V

Until I was thirty-five, my relationship with the staff was to have a reliable crew that would make a movie exactly in the image that I planned it. Now, each movie has its own style and energy, and the staff has to match that. For example, in the *Street Fighter II* movie, the action director was important. If he said certain moves were executed better some other way, it might even affect the plot. So that kind of input could balloon all by itself, as long as the grand concept was still there. Movie making for me now is a collaboration of specialists, such as the technicians, the photographers, and the animators.

ANIMERICA: You were involved both in the *Street Fighter II* movie and the TV series. How did you become interested in them?

SUGII: Actually, until I got involved in the movie, I wasn't interested in the video game. But when it was decided the movie was going to be made, I got involved with *Street Fighter II* for the first time. There was talk of making the game into a movie at my studio, so the project was something I knew about. Then there's this *Street Fighter II* poster that's given me a lasting impression. The impressive thing about the poster, artistically speaking, was that they had all these military planes, but then they just had the fighters from all the various countries standing in front of them, not even facing each other. I thought that was interesting...I can't really express it well in words. I often thought that image might be interesting to produce as an animated movie.

For example, in the movie, Ryu never changes his clothes. During the staff discussion, the producer said, "After a sweaty workout, he probably changes into a T-shirt and jeans." But I refused that. That came from the impression I got from the poster. I wanted to make a weighty, realistic sort of a movie, but *this one thing* had to be my breach of realism. I wanted the characters to be just standing there, unchangeable, including their clothes, just like they seemed in the poster. But they still wanted some change of dress in the movie, so we decided that Ken will get all the fancy changes of dress. [LAUGHS]

ANIMERICA: In a magazine article, you once said that you liked working with game characters because they were so open to your own free interpretation. What *are* your interpretations of the *Street Fighter II* characters? For example, what do you think drives Ryu and Ken?

Street Fighter II

SUGII: Well, the audience I had in mind for the film were the gamers who played the *Street Fighter II* game at the arcades. In the game screen, movements are restricted, and there are game rules, but I thought, those gamers have created their own *Street Fighter II* world in their heads. In the *Street Fighter II* movie, I wanted to present the world that was locked up in their minds, for the battles and the characters. I wanted the movie to be centered on the world imagined by the *Street Fighter II* game lovers.

I think the *Street Fighter II* movie has a different style from regular Japanese movies. I wanted to make it like an American "roller-coaster" movie...you know, where the action is everything. All the drama is removed; it's just up and down like a roller coaster, and it's really the action that propagates the story. It's really game-like. On the other hand, *Street Fighter II V* is a TV series, so instead, it's based around the idea of doing a continuing drama with Ryu and Ken's journey at the center.

ANIMERICA: Are you familiar with American comics and animation? If so, how do you perceive the difference between Japanese and American comics and animation?

SUGII: They have coarse plot development. Very. As for comics, they tend to have a fixed format, and the story develops only within that. It looks like the words in the balloons take precedence over the art.

ANIMERICA: Have you seen the American-produced *Street Fighter* animation? If so, what did you think of it?

SUGII: I've seen the English version. I liked their flashy use of the music. Compared to a Japanese production, it has coarse production values, but that's interesting, too. My productions tend to have more delicate music. The music might start quietly and go on a crescendo, or it might start all of a sudden. I'm really conscious of its use. Perhaps it's the difference between American-style storyboards and Japanese "*e-konte*" picture continuities.

ANIMERICA: What does it mean for you as a director to be recognized overseas?

SUGII: It would make me really happy. It's too bad it's so hard to receive feedback from local fans, but I'm glad that many different people are now seeing my work.

ANIMERICA: Do you have any advice for aspiring animators, or those who are just getting started as artists?

SUGII: Well, I've been doing this for over thirty years, but I still think that this industry will keep on getting more and more interesting. I think that there are many possibilities to explore in mixing computer and hand-drawn animation. In that sense, we're starting to see many kinds of animation that haven't been possible to make before now.

ANIMERICA: What kind of projects do you see in your future, and also, do you have a message for your fans in the English-speaking world?

SUGII: A message? Hmm, I can't come up with one. As for me, right now, I'm working on the *Lupin III* summer special. In Japan, fans have kind of left live-action movies behind, so the opportunity to make a really interesting live-action movie here is rare. But animation—although it's the same with live-action—is a line of work that's interesting because it changes with the spirit of the times. But if the fans leave us, we're out of work. So, I hope both creators and audience can keep on pursuing the kind of works that they want to see.

afterword

The *Lupin III* "summer special" referred to in the interview debuted in 1996 as *Lupin III: The Legend of Twilight Gemini*. Both of Sugii's *Street Fighter* productions have since become available in America; oddly enough, both versions also have sported brand-new soundtracks.

In the case of the bestselling, widely available *Street Fighter II: The Animated Movie*, music by the likes of U2, Alice in Chains and Korn is substituted for the film's original orchestral soundtrack. As for the more character-driven and multi-episodic *Street Fighter II V*, the original TV series opening credits, featuring young Ryu and Ken running toward the screen to the tune of a bouncy pop tune, is replaced by a hard industrial rock theme, as well as by in-your-face fighting scenes to go with the more hardcore music. Fans of the original Japanese opening theme need not despair, however; although the domestic release of the subtitled version contains a newly reedited opening animation sequence, Japanese pop singer Yuki Kuroda's original tune remains intact. For another side of Sugii's work, both *Tale of Genji* and *Night on the Galactic Railroad* are available domestically, as well.

Gisaburo Sugii
Select Filmography

ANIME アニメ

You won't find any manga titles here, and Sugii may be stricly an anime man, but...Oh! What anime! In addition to his well known "literary" films *Night on the Galactic Railroad* and *The Tale of Genji*, Sugii also enjoys a long director-to-creator relationship with best-selling manga author Mitsuru Adachi, whose *Nine* and *Touch* Sugii has helped midwife into animation on many occasions. From Tezuka to video games, comedy to surrealistic tales of medieval witchcraft (!), Sugii is one of the most well-versed directors in the anime industry. It should be interesting to see where he heads next.

Hakujaden ("Tale of the White Serpent")
白蛇伝
Animator
78-minute theatrical feature (1958); Toei's first movie. As an interesting side note, all of the film's roles are filled by two voice-actors only: one a man, and one a woman. Sugii makes his debut as an animator here. *CURRENTLY IMPORT ONLY*

Shônen Sarutobi Sasuke ("Young Sasuke Sarutobi")
少年猿飛佐助
Animator
83-minute theatrical feature (1959). The very first film to use a process known as "Cinemascope" (later renamed "TohoScope"), the historically based *Shônen Sarutobi Sasuke* is remembered today as a "non-anime" anime, incorporating distinctive character designs and a staging that might almost be compared to that of *taiga* or period samurai drama. *CURRENTLY IMPORT ONLY*

Saiyûki ("Journey to the West")
西遊記
Animator
88-minute theatrical feature (1960); an early—but by no means the first!—anime rendition of China's oft-told "Monkey King" legend, a story which appears even today in series as diverse as Buichi Terasawa's *Midnight Eye Gokû* to Akira Toriyama's *Dragon Ball*. Not only is this particular version of *Saiyûki* based on manga by Osamu Tezuka, it's storyboarded by him, as well. *DOMESTIC RELEASE TITLE:* ***Alakazam the Great*** (Orion Home Video)

Aru Machikado no Monogatari
("Tales From a Certain Street Corner")
ある町角の物語
Animator
38-minute theatrical feature (1962); one of manga and anime genius Osamu Tezuka's "experimental" films. According to *Tezuka Osamu Gekijô* ("The Animation Filmography of Osamu Tezuka"), *Aru Machikado* was produced by the animators of Tezuka's own studio "Mushi Pro" with unswerving dedication, the animators even going so far as to identify themselves as "*dôga no mushi*" (animation bugs)—their collective purpose being the transformation of anime as something thought to be "only for children" to something which could be enjoyed by the entire family. *CURRENTLY IMPORT ONLY*

Tetsuwan Atom ("Iron-Arm Atom")
鉄腕アトム
Episode Direction / Animator
193-episode television series (1963-66); generally agreed to be Japan's first anime TV show, although *Otogi Manga Calendar*, a series of five-minute vignettes, beat *Atom* to the airwaves by a good six months. Interestingly, *Atom* is the start of anime on TV in the U.S., as well—broadcast on NBC from 1963-64, it even became a modest syndication hit, going on to inspire the *Dragon Balls* and the *Sailor Moons* and even the Sci-Fi Channel "Festivals of Anime" we see today. *DOMESTIC RELEASE TITLE:* ***Astro Boy*** (The Right Stuf)

Gokû no Dai-Bôken ("Goku's Great Adventure")
悟空の大冒険
Executive Director
39-episode TV series (1967). Returning to the familiar "Monkey King" ground of Tezuka's original manga *Boku no Son Gokû* ("My 'Son Goku'"), Sugii brought a strong Mushi Production flavor to a series in which Tezuka himself had wanted to be involved, but was unable. In an effort to improve ratings, a subtitle, "*Yôkai Rengô* (Monster Federation) Series," was added as of Episode 22. *CURRENTLY IMPORT ONLY*

Dororo
どろろ
Executive Director
26-episode TV series (1969); based on the Tezuka manga of the same name. At the time of its first broadcast in Japan, the use of black and white by Sugii and the other animators of the "realism" school of anime was seen as avant garde, and it's this dramatic mood which so well complements Tezuka's rather bizarre original story, in which a young boy goes a' monster-slaying in feudal Japan in order to recover the 48 parts of his body sacrificed to demon-gods by an overly ambitious samurai father. *CURRENTLY IMPORT ONLY*

Cleopatra
クレオパトラ
Animator
112-minute theatrical feature (1970); fanciful blend of fact and fiction which, in its time, pushed the envelope of what an animated film for adults should and should not be. Directed, choreographed, and screenwriten by Tezuka. *CURRENTLY IMPORT ONLY*

Kanashimi no Belladonna ("Belladonna of Sadness")
哀しみのベラドンナ
Animation Director
89-minute theatrical feature (1973); based on the novel "Witchcraft, Sorcery, and Superstition" by French historian Jules Michelet. An unusual change of pace for Sugii, the "belladonna" of the title is of course a pun, being in Italian both a word for "fair lady" as well as the name of a highly poisonous plant, *Atropa belladonna*, said by historians to have been used by women to dilate the pupils of the eye and create an artificial pallor. *CURRENTLY IMPORT ONLY*

Jack to Mame to Ki ("Jack and the Giant Beanstalk")
ジャックと豆の木
Animation Director
98-minute theatrical feature (1974); based on the familiar fairy tale of the same name. "With its weaving of surreal scenes and nimble action," wrote one critic, "(*Jack to Mame no Ki*) is on a par with Tezuka Production's *Nagagutsu o Haita Neko* (Puss in Boots)." *CURRENTLY IMPORT ONLY*

Manga Nihon Mukashi Banashi
("The 'Manga' Folktales of Japan")
まんが日本昔ばなし
Episode Director
Long-running TV project (1975-91) initially created for the purpose of weaning Japanese children living abroad on the cultural fairytales and folktales of the country they'd left behind. As with 1958's *Hakujaden*, a mere two voice-actors fill each and every role of the 64 episodes the series eventually produced. *CURRENTLY IMPORT ONLY*

Nine
ナイン
Director
84-minute TV special (1983); based on the baseball love-comedy manga series of the same name by Mitsuru Adachi (*Touch*). Re-released shortly thereafter as a theatrical feature. *CURRENTLY IMPORT ONLY*

Nine 2: Koibito Sengen ("Nine 2: Lover's Declaration")
ナイン2：恋人宣言
Director
67-minute TV special (1983). Broadcast approximately eight months after the first *Nine* TV special, *Koibito Sengen* continues the lives and loves of the Adachi story of the same name. *CURRENTLY IMPORT ONLY*

Garasu no Kamen ("Mask of Glass")
ガラスの仮面
Executive Director
23-episode TV series (1984); based on the *shôjo* ("for girls only") manga series of the same name by Suzue Miuchi, as serialized in HANA TO YUME ("Flowers and Dreams") magazine. Sugii, it's said, came aboard the project in response to a request from the series' coordinator, who also happened to be a long-time personal friend. *CURRENTLY IMPORT ONLY*

Nine: Kanketsu-Hen ("Nine: The Final Chapter")
ナイン：完結編
Director
73-minute TV special (1984); continues the animation of original creator Adachi's manga musings on the concept of *seishun* ("youth")—specifically, what it means to be young. *CURRENTLY IMPORT ONLY*

Ginga Tetsudô no Yoru ("Night on the Galactic Railroad")
銀河鉄道の夜

Director / Storyboards

107-minute theatrical feature (1985). Based on the incomplete novel of the same name by Japanese author Kenji Miyazawa, a naturalist, Nichiren Buddhist, and student of Christianity whose own life story was recently animated (using the same anthropomorphic cats) by director Shoji Kawamori of *Macross* fame. One of the most unusual films ever animated, *Ginga Tetsudô no Yoru* is a richly allegorical and symbolic work bearing no relation to the similarly titled *Ginga Tetsudô* (Galaxy Express) *999*...aside, of course, from the fact that both involve galaxy-trotting choo-choo trains. *DOMESTIC RELEASE TITLE:* ***Night on the Galactic Railroad*** (Central Park Media)

Touch: Sebangô no Nai Ace
("Touch: The 'Ace' With the Numberless Back")
タッチ：背番号のないエース

Director / Screenplay

93-minute theatrical feature (1986). "Youth," romance and baseball combine in an original story which capitalizes on the popularlity of the wildly successful *Touch* TV series, which in turn was based on the wildly successful manga series of the same name. *CURRENTLY IMPORT ONLY*

Touch 2: Sayonara no Okurimono
("Touch 2: 'Sayonora' Gift")
タッチ２：さよならの贈り物

Executive Director

80-minute theatrical feature (1986). Of the three *Touch* films released theatrically, this second one of the highest-quality, animation-wise; it's not chopped liver drama-wise, either. *CURRENTLY IMPORT ONLY*

Touch 3: Kimi ga Tôri Sugita Ato Ni
("Touch 3: After You Pass By")
タッチ３：君が通り過ぎたあとに

Executive Director / Screenplay

85-minute theatrical feature (1987). For this third and final film in an unofficial *Touch* "trilogy," a slightly different continuity was created, so as not to conflict with the TV series (a character introduced in the TV series doesn't appear in the movie, for example). Note that, unlike the first two films, Sugii is credited for both "executive direction" *and* "screenplay." *CURRENTLY IMPORT ONLY*

Murasaki Shikibu Genji Monogatari
("Murasaki Shikibu's 'Tale of Genji'")
紫式部源氏物語

Director / Storyboards

105-minute theatrical feature (1987). Adapted from the famed 11th century novel of courtly life and romance in Japan's Heian era by Lady Murasaki Shikibu. *DOMESTIC RELEASE TITLE:* ***The Tale of Genji*** (Central Park Media)

Hiatari Ryoko! Ka•Su•Mi: Yume no Naka ni Kimi ga Ita
("Ryoko Hiatari! Ka•Su•Mi: Inside the Dream, There Was You")
陽あたり良好！KA·SU·MI:夢の中に君がいた

Editorial Supervision

67-minute theatrical feature (1988). Following up on the popularity of the *Hiatari Ryoko!* TV series, the *Hiatari Ryoko!* movie breaks no new ground, but presents its *Kimagure Orange Road*-like love triangle romance in a refreshing and modest way. Based on the manga *Hiatari Ryoko!* by the creator of *Nine* and *Touch*, Mitsuru Adachi, as serialized in publisher Shogakukan's Flower Comics manga anthology. *CURRENTLY IMPORT ONLY*

Sweet Spot
スイートスポット

Director / Screenplay

One-shot OAV (1991) animating the "trendy" manga of the same name by Yutsuko Chusonji, as serialized in monthly Spa! magazine. Comedic, cynical tale of a golf-crazy OL or "office lady" who can't get enough of corny, older Japanese men pasttimes such as heavy after-hours drinking and karaoke. *CURRENTLY IMPORT ONLY*

Nozomi Witches
のぞみ♡ウィッチィズ

Director / Screenplay

Three-volume OAV series (1992); based on the popular manga of the same name by Toshio Nobe, as serialized in weekly Young Jump manga anthology. Light-hearted tale set in the world of high-school boxing, with occasional touches of romance. *CURRENTLY IMPORT ONLY*

Street Fighter II Movie
ストリートファイターⅡムービー

Director / Screenplay

101-minute theatrical feature (1994); based on the Capcom video game of the same name. Kinetic, surprisingly character-rich take on the game's (by now) familiar "eight immortals"—Ken, Ryu, Guile, Chun Li, Dhalsim, E. Honda, Zangief, and Blanka—as they battle the megalomaniacal insanity of Vega ("M. Bison" in the U.S. release). ...Speaking of the domestic version, note that the symphonic soundtrack of the Japanese version has been replaced with a thrash version, featuring the likes of Alice in Chains and Korn. A Sugii-directed TV series—*Street Fighter II V*, as in "victory"—began broadcast on Japanese airwaves starting April '95, and ran 26 episodes. *DOMESTIC RELEASE TITLE(S):* ***Street Fighter II: The Movie*** and ***Street Fighter II V***

Lupin III: Twilight Gemini no Himitsu
("Lupin III: Secret of the Twilight Gemini")
ルパン三世：トワイライト・ジェミニの秘密

Director

90-minute TV special (1996). Despite the loss of beloved title-role voice-actor Yasuo Yamada, "The Franchise" forges bravely on with the cast traveling to adventure-filled Morocco in (mostly) comedic search of a priceless diamond. (*Note to Longtime Series Fans*: After a wait of years and years and years, Lupin and buxom female lead Fujiko finally consummate their relationship...!) *CURRENTLY IMPORT ONLY*

Key

- Japanese comics or "manga" series; may or may not be available in foreign-language (i.e., English) version
- TV series broadcast on-air in Japan. Note that, in the U.S., Japanese TV series are both broadcast on-air (*Ronin Warriors*) and released on home video (*Ranma 1/2*). Others (*Sailor Moon, Dragon Ball*) are available both in broadcast and home video versions
- Direct-to-home-video series; may also include compilations of TV episodes released to home video market
- Theatrical feature; may or may not receive equivalent theatrical release for U.S. version

Leiji Matsumoto

Interviewed by Takayuki Karahashi (1996)

There are many anime legends, but only one Leiji Matsumoto. Against the remakes, parodies and homages that are the trend of much of the anime produced in the '90s, Leiji Matsumoto's signature style stands alone, immediately recognizable, a true original. Like his famous character, the infamous Space Pirate Captain Harlock, Leiji Matsumoto is a man who knows no trend, follows no "fashion," and pledges allegiance to no flag but his own.

A manga artist who began his career as early as 1953, when he won a contest in MANGA SHÔNEN magazine for a 16-page manga titled *Mitsubachi No Bôken* ("The Adventures of a Honeybee") at the age of fifteen, Matsumoto always knew that he wanted to be an artist. He began by drawing for a children's version of a newspaper in high school, and soon after began drawing seriously for magazines. After moving to Tokyo for college, he decided to forgo school to work full-time as a manga artist, but his early career was unsatisfying to him—for fifteen years, he could only find work in *shôjo* manga ("girls' comics"), and the man who later came to be known as the definitive artist of "manly romances" was frustrated.

When he finally managed to break free of *shôjo*, he adopted a new pen name, "Leiji" Matsumoto, in order to distance himself from his *shôjo* work, all of which had been done under his real name, Akira Matsumoto. His breakthrough work, *Otoko Oidon* ("I Am a Man"), the saga of a *ronin* student trying to break into college, was published in 1971 to rave response, and finally set Matsumoto's career on the track. But being a manga artist wasn't all that he wanted to accomplish.

"Since childhood, I've liked Disney and Max Fleischer's American animation," Matsumoto remembers. "The reasons I got into animation were Disney's *Snow White* and Fleischer's *Gulliver's Travels* and *Hoppity Goes to Town*. Also, during the war, when I was still a child yet to go to school, we had black-and-white films of Mickey Mouse and Betty Boop—we called her 'Betty-san'—and we saw them at home. So, even during the war, I was watching *Mickey Mouse* and *Popeye* at home. They stopped showing them in Japan during the war, but we had plenty of them, so we saw them all the time. And since they were on 35mm film, I could see the film and understand how animation works, how each frame is slightly different from the others in sequence. This was before going to kindergarten, so I was perhaps four or five. By the age of five or six, I was already familiar with the mechanism of animation."

Though primarily a manga artist, Leiji Matsumoto's interest in animation led him to work on the show that is often credited with starting the animation "boom" of the '70s, a show which sent out pop culture shock waves that are still washing over us today: *Uchû Senkan Yamato* ("Space Battleship Yamato"), broadcast in the U.S. as *Star Blazers*. Indeed, it was the American broadcast of *Star Blazers* which familiarized a generation of English-speaking viewers with Matsumoto's trademark attenuated style, a distinctive "look" which instantly sets apart his characters, his mechanicals or "mecha," and his futuristic cities. Fans eagerly snapped up Matsumoto's following works: *Uchû Kaizoku* ("Space Pirate") *Captain Harlock*, *Ginga Tetsudô* ("Galaxy Express") *999*, and *Sen-Nen Jo'ô* ("Millennium Queen"), all of which enjoyed healthy popularity.

However, of all his major series, perhaps it is *Space Pirate* which sets the ultimate standard of Matsumoto-style manly romance. His hero, the eponymous Harlock, lives by Matsumoto's ideal of how life should be lived—under debt to no man, to no cause, and with no code to guide him but his own. Such characters are Matsumoto's *oeuvre* to the core; each character's action—such the long-suffering Tochiro's decision to die in order to become the soul of his best friend Harlock's ship, the *Arcadia*—is guided by his own individual conscience, and no other.

"They are all free human beings," Matsumoto says of his characters. "They can do whatever they want and die all of their free will. They have an iron rule of not interfering with each others' paths. But they will go help another in need if they can. They have no bondage to fate. They're all on their own. They are like brothers and sisters who trust each other. In the broad sense, they are family." Matsumoto's own philosophy, too, is in keeping with this sense of following your rugged path to whichever destiny it may lead.

"The way I see it," he says, "I wanted to and chose to become a manga artist. I'm at a point where I can't say, 'I've decided I don't like it.' Your life is a path you chose for yourself, so you have to be responsible for it. Don't whine. If you can't do that, don't choose it in the first place. This is something I make all my main characters say. I think this is true to all occupations. I'm not fond of the idea of switching jobs or the course of one's life work on a regular basis. If it's the way you chose, you should go through with it. I don't think it's sporting to change thinking midway."

At first glance, the usual assumption made by the casual reader or viewer is that each of Matsumoto's works takes place in separate timelines, different worlds. And yet, if you pay enough attention, read/watch enough Matsumoto manga/anime, it becomes apparent that all the stories are linked, twisting and spiraling to form a loosely knit yet infinitely elastic continuity known as the "Leijiverse." In this interview, Matsumoto reminisces about the origins of his legendary characters, such as Harlock and Emeraldas, and about his own philosophies, the ones which drive the "Leijiverse" itself.

Space Pirate Captain Harlock

interview

ANIMERICA: Let's start with your background. You've said that the initial influences that got you into animation were Disney and Fleischer. Do you still like Disney?

MATSUMOTO: Yes, I do. I *think* it's all right to tell you this now.... Around the beginning of the *Showa* 30s (late 1950s) [Showa *years are counted starting with 1926, Year One of Emperor Hirohito's reign, which ended with his death in 1989—Ed.*], a junk merchant came to sell a lot of Disney, Fleischer, and some Soviet animation films. Basically, he was a black marketeer. So the three of us, Osamu Tezuka, Shotaro Ishimori [*creator of* Cyborg 009, *now known under the name "Ishinomori"—Ed.*] bought them. Then we got suspected of buying them for commercial showing and were investigated.

I was most influenced by the movie *Marianne de ma Jeunesse*—in Japan, it was called *Waga Seishun no Marianne.*

ANIMERICA: By the authorities?

MATSUMOTO: Yes. RKO or someone alleged that there were people in Japan using their films for commercial purposes. So a detective in charge of foreign affairs came to us and interrogated us as to what purpose we were going to use those films. The black marketeer was caught—his phone book listed our numbers and addresses—and so we were investigated like falling dominoes. We told them that we'd bought the films for personal research and then were told we could do as we pleased.

ANIMERICA: Since you were innocent to begin with, there was no statute of limitation to worry about either, then.

MATSUMOTO: That's true. But we had no idea what was going on, so we asked if it was all right to do the same thing if another opportunity came up, and that it would be for personal research. They said something like that's no problem. But strictly speaking, considering the relationship between the U.S. and Japan back then, and the issues of film disposal, there might have been some problem. But that was thirty years ago. Or was it forty? Call it something we can now recall and tell as a joke.

ANIMERICA: What do you do when you aren't working? Do you have any hobbies?

MATSUMOTO: Mostly related to anime and manga. Also, this might be rare of a Japanese, but I shoot rifles.

ANIMERICA: Let's talk about *Yamato*. How were you involved in this?

MATSUMOTO: In the beginning, I was asked if I'd do some art designs for them. I took a look, but they had designs that wouldn't fly. And the story wasn't anything becoming of a future space-faring adventure. The art designs weren't usable, nor were the spaceship designs, so I nixed them all and redrew them. And then, I was asked if I'd get involved with everything, including the story. So I got involved with every aspect of the series.

ANIMERICA: So that was for the first one, the TV series, right? How were you involved?

MATSUMOTO: Well, I came up with the designs and story and then made the characters. And then there were the mechanical characters, the mechanisms and spaceships. And then the staging in space. I talked with the art director and discussed how each place should be depicted as realistically as possible. There were twenty-six episodes, and I personally drew about half of the storyboards. The original TV series was the production in which I was most involved.

ANIMERICA: You weren't as involved in the sequels, then?

MATSUMOTO: My involvement started to broaden, and I could no longer do everything myself. I was pretty much fully dedicated with the first feature *Arrivederci Yamato*, but after that, I just worked on the story or the staging or the characters or the designs. The directing tended to be left to others.

ANIMERICA: You previously mentioned you've been influenced by Disney and Fleischer animation. Do you have other influences, such as movies?

MATSUMOTO: As for movies, I am *one* big movie fan. I've seen countless American movies, if they've made it to Japan. Among them, I've loved Errol Flynn's buccaneer swashbucklers and westerns and *The Adventures of Robin Hood*, which is set in England, and others, like knighthood stories. At the same time, I've liked the American science fiction movies *Destination Moon* and *"Kasei Tanken"* [*lit. "Exploration of Mars," probably referring to the 1950 film* Rocketship X-M*—Ed.*] and *Forbidden Planet*. I loved those space stories, so I've been influenced by them. When it comes to female characters, however, I've been influenced more by European movies, especially by French movies. Their actresses' looks and characters were imprinted on me in my childhood, so my characters more or less show their influence. I suppose my women are a fusion of Japanese and European women.

ANIMERICA: Are the European movies you're talking about from the same period as Errol Flynn's?

MATSUMOTO: Most from the period right after his. By *Showa* years, it was *Showa* 29. Basically, French movies from the 1950s. I'm not so interested in older movies, partially because I was still a child when I first saw them. I'm most fond of the French movies from the period when they were switching over from black-and-white to color. Thus, I'm familiar with French actresses from that period. I was most influenced by the movie *Marianne de ma Jeunesse*—in Japan, it was called "*Waga Seishun no Marianne*" ("Marianne of My Youth"). *Marianne de ma Jeunesse* was a French-German co-production, and I was strongly influenced by this movie, so my female characters have hints of Marianne Holt, who played the main character in the movie. I was in my adolescence, so I was strongly influenced.

ANIMERICA: Speaking of Germany, Captain Harlock seems like a Germanic character himself....

MATSUMOTO: Actually, he isn't German. I used to pace my walks saying "*hârokku*" when I was in junior high. I'd be walking home from school marching to the chant "*hârokku, hârokku.*" It wasn't a person's name. So, "Harlock" both does and doesn't have a meaning—it was a marching call. I eventually started using it to draw a buccaneer story.... I drew the character who was to become Harlock for the very first time when I was in my first year of junior high. Back then, his name wasn't Harlock; he called himself "Captain Kingston." He was an English pirate. Strangely enough, he receives secret orders from the Queen of Spain to search for Napoleon's treasure. And he roams the Pacific and not the Atlantic. But he already wears a skull mark on his chest. This was the first pirate story I came up with. His name was Captain Kingston, so however you think about it, he has to be English. It's funny he receives orders from the Queen of Spain in search of Napoleon's treasure in the Pacific. So this pirate did wear a skull mark, but his face was still Errol Flynn's.

ANIMERICA: An English Errol Flynn.

MATSUMOTO: Yes, an Errol Flynn-like pirate. Back then, there were many English buccaneer stories around.

ANIMERICA: I see, so "*hârokku*" was, at first, more like "*here we go, hup, two, three, four*"...?

MATSUMOTO: Yes, I was pacing my walks chanting "*hârokku, hârokku.*" I didn't have in mind what language that was from or anything like that.

ANIMERICA: Do you have other influences, such as comics, manga, paintings...?

MATSUMOTO: As for paintings, I can start with the classics such as Michelangelo and Leonardo da Vinci and go on to American comics such as *Superman* and *Spider-Man* and then Disney. My generation has them all jumbled together. The reason why I've read so many American comics is that, back when I was young, there was a mountain of 10-cent comics left in town by the American soldiers. They were very cheap, so we could buy as many as we wanted. I have almost all comics from the 1940s. As for other influences, there's a Japanese science fiction

Adieu Galaxy Express 999

illustrator named Shigeru Komatsuzaki…I aspired not only toward the creations of Tezuka or Disney or Fleischer, but to those kinds of realistic painting and illustration, as well. When I was a child, I boldly used to think to myself, what wonderful creations could be made if all their good parts were assembled together!

ANIMERICA: How would you say American comics and Japanese manga compare?

MATSUMOTO: The comparison is one I made to myself a long time ago, but it's how I felt at the time. The art, I thought, was wonderfully meticulous and had a polish based on proper drawing skills. As drawings, they were highly complete, and they were in color, so I thought they were wonderful. But when it came to the story, comparing them even to what there was in Japan in the *Showa* 20s, they were still too simple. Each story's exposition-development-twist-conclusions were so short, and lacked complexity. I was more drawn toward the Japanese manga methods that were more like American movies and sophisticated French movies. I'd have to say that, back when I saw the American 10-cent comics, the stories felt really simple to me.

ANIMERICA: To what degree are you usually involved in your animated works?

MATSUMOTO: In important works, such as *Ginga Tetsudô* ("Galaxy Express") *999*, I've been almost fully involved. I'd start with the planning stages, write the story, write the screenplay…the screenplay is usually credited to someone else, but it's basically my writing. Then, there's the character designs, the mecha designs, and the art designs. Basically, I've put my efforts into all of them.

ANIMERICA: Those would include *Galaxy Express*, *Yamato*—and relatively newer but still an oldie, *Waga Seishun no Arcadia*? [*Traditionally referred to in the U.S. as "My Youth in Arcadia"—Ed.*]

MATSUMOTO: Yes. When I wrote the screenplay, I was in the actual location where the story, in the beginning, takes place. I approached the location and wrote it fully in the mood. I drew many design works for that story, too. Think of them as the storyboards prior to the picture continuity. …So, I drew many of those and then handed them to the director. Then we conferred a lot. And then came the dailies and the retakes. Finally, there was the audio, the recording, and the dubbing—and that was the extent of my involvement. It was tiring, but fun.

ANIMERICA: You were almost its director.

MATSUMOTO: You could say that. I was like the director standing *behind* the director.

ANIMERICA: Did you come up with the title, too? From the French movie *Marianne*…?

MATSUMOTO: Yes. Actually, not only that, but there's also an air combat war story that's an element of *Arcadia*. It's one of my manga, titled *Invincible Arcadia*, and it's about a sightscope. *Waga Seishun no Arcadia* is a combination of those two—they're fused together.

ANIMERICA: As for *Galaxy Express*, it's a story about a journey through space, but why is it a train instead of a more traditional spaceship?

MATSUMOTO: I lived by the railroad tracks for the longest time when I was child. It was always my dream to go to places I longed for via train…I was always hearing the rails ringing or imagining the train passing in front of me, flying away into space. And then, when I got to be a creator, I got on that very train and journeyed to Tokyo, back in the days of the steam locomotive. So those two experiences combined together, and when it came time to design a flying train, it couldn't be a modern electric train like the *Shinkansen* (bullet train); it had to be a steam locomotive. That's why it's a train like that. With a train, you can buy a ticket and go anywhere. The story of *Galaxy Express* takes place in a time when there is no need to go through qualifications or paperwork to journey through space. You just need to buy a train ticket, and the train takes you to space. That's what I longed for, so that's what I made. I also thought rockets were a primitive kind of vehicle. Actually, I still think so. So it's partially my memories and also from the thought of that kind of warmth—a feeling of comfort that it's man-run, rather than it being a lump of inorganic computer. It's the idea of bringing an environment just like that on Earth into space.

ANIMERICA: There's a work by Kenji Miyazawa called *Ginga Tetsudô no Yoru* ("Night on the Galactic Railroad").... How does your work relate to that?

MATSUMOTO: I saw it performed in *kami-shibai* [*a traditional Japanese artform, also known as "a shadow play"—Ed.*] when I was a child. Not a movie; *kami-shibai*. In elementary school, we had an assembly in the auditorium and I saw it there. I also read the book when I was in elementary school, so it was in my mind, certainly. But as I've just said, I lived by the railroad tracks for a long time, and what passed in front of me weren't the small local trains but the heavy-class express trains. My fancies came from those. Also, an extreme difference between the two is that my story may have some influence from *Ginga Tetsudô no Yoru* with the train flying off into space, but his story is the experience of dead souls traveling to the next world. Actually, most of Miyazawa's works are like that—he had problems with his health, and died young. So that must be why he wrote like that, but my train was about youth, with infinite possibilities, doing whatever it takes to stay alive. So there was a diverging point somewhere, like trains forking off a junction. In retrospect, I can see that well now.

ANIMERICA: The story of *Galaxy Express* is really harsh, isn't it. For example, Tetsuro's mother is killed by Count Mecha during his human hunts, and then he stuffs her body and hangs it on his wall...but why were Tetsuro and his mother there in the first place, if they knew this sort of thing could happen?

MATSUMOTO: They're in Count Mecha's manor because there is nowhere else left for them to live. That part isn't depicted, but the father disappears and they can't get to Megalopolis without crossing through his manor. And so, there they are. It's very big, including something like a hunting zone just for his recreation. Humans there are like grazing animals.

ANIMERICA: Where does the name "Maetel" come from? And what about "Emeraldas"? Is there a story behind it?

MATSUMOTO: "Maetel" means "mother" in Latin. So it's a corruption of the word *mater*. The name for "Emeraldas" is even simpler. She's a space pirate with a bright, flame-like passion. Usually, an emerald is green, but I heard some of them are red. I heard that, depending on the processing of the mineral, not all of them turn out blue or green. So I thought how wonderful it would be if there were a red emerald. That's how she was named. Her name couldn't be "Ruby," because it wouldn't be interesting. A ruby is gentler; softer. It had to be an emerald, though it's supposed to be red and people may say it's strange. But the luster and the hardness has to be that of an emerald or I can't convince myself. Also, I'll have to tell this as a joke, but I must confess: I thought emeralds were red when I was a child. I didn't think they were green from the name alone. I never saw one. That's another reason. So, I'm left with the idea that it has to be a red emerald or else.

I lived by the railroad tracks for the longest time when I was a child.... I was always hearing the rails ringing or imagining the train passing in front of me, flying away into space.

ANIMERICA: Who is Maetel, really?

MATSUMOTO: She's the woman who travels with an adolescent boy's dreams. She's traveled with millions, tens of millions of boys, so far. In fact, there are as many Maetels are there are boys. That's also how she can show up in any story. All boys have met Maetel in different forms of encounter. That goes for Antares or Emeraldas or Harlock, as well. They are all crossed over, and they can all be separate stories on their own. So if you change perspectives and characters, you can make as many stories as you like. The characters of Shadow and Emeraldas, who were girls in their adolescence, have met someone called Maetel, in the heart, from their childhood, or during a time when they were full of dreams. It's a train ride through one's mind, or the train that travels along with one. And each person has a different journey.... This is starting to sound a little complicated. [LAUGHS]

ANIMERICA: You mentioned previously that you shoot rifles as a hobby. Have you hunted before?

MATSUMOTO: I hunted in Africa. That's when I realized I couldn't be a hunter. It was because of American movies like *Tarzan* and *King Solomon's Mines* that I longed for Africa and exploration. But when I actually shot an animal, a strong sense of shock shot back at *me*. I concluded that I couldn't be a hunter.... The straightforward reason is that I have no need to shoot an animal. Since then, I've been shooting paper targets. I've been poking holes in paper.

ANIMERICA: Where it's more like bowling.

MATSUMOTO: Yes. I wouldn't want to kill another animal. Once was enough. A feeling of regret stayed with me for a long time. It's still with me: "*What cruel deed have I done?*" I went there to realize a childhood dream, and the dream was realized...I went to Africa and hunted. But as I realized my dream, a strong feeling of regret, a shock, came to me. What I was doing was chasing a dream of the past. I was chasing man's dream from a time when humans were less reasoned. I partook in a little of that, and then, it came back to me as a strong shock.

ANIMERICA: Did you keep a material record from that time?

MATSUMOTO: I have it, at home. It was a deed done, so I took responsibility and took it home. I don't usually show it to people, though.

ANIMERICA: We hear it's a gazelle....

MATSUMOTO: Yes. I have a few other things, like bones. And stones from Africa—I have a lot of those. I was still in my thirties when I went there. That I went is something I have no regrets about—it was an invaluable experience. But that I'd be so shocked about the death of an animal...well, I didn't know it'd change me so much. As a memory, it was good that I realized a dream. But the doubts about "Why did I pull the trigger?" remain in me. I reflect about it and feel bad, about that part.

I went to Africa to realize a childhood dream...but as I realized it, a strong feeling of regret, of shock, came to me.

ANIMERICA: You previously mentioned that you like space movies.

MATSUMOTO: There was *Gessekai Seifuku* and *Kasei Tanken*....

ANIMERICA: ...*Gessekai Seifuku*, as in *Conquest of the Moon*, that 19th century—?

MATSUMOTO: ...No, not that Jules Verne one, but a post-war color movie. It's an American color movie I saw in junior high. *Gessekai Seifuku* was the Japanese title [*possibly George Pal's 1955 movie* Conquest of Space—*Ed.*]. *Kasei Tanken* [*"Exploration of Mars," aka* Rocketship X-M—*Ed.*] may have been a movie made before or during the war. Its theme was from atomic to prehistoric. The atomic refers to going to Mars with a civilization dead from nuclear war. So Mars was reduced from an atomic-era civilization to a prehistoric one. In the end, the rocket back to Earth malfunctions and everyone dies. A rare tragic ending for an American movie. Tezuka was certainly influenced by this movie (especially during the part) where the crew falls to Earth and dies. I saw it when I was in high school; junior high or high school. I think it was a revival release, the one I saw. I saw *Lost World* when I was in junior high or high school, too [*the original* Lost World, *that is—Ed.*]. The same with *King Kong*. They were all made before the war, but I saw them after the war was over.

ANIMERICA: Do you see them as science fiction movies?

MATSUMOTO: Yes. Back then, special effects weren't seen for their polish, so it was the story that drew you in. Back then, movies were more entertaining.

ANIMERICA: Times have changed, and today or even ten years ago....

MATSUMOTO: ...Thanks to special effects and computer graphics, there's increased realism, and it's become easier to depict space and the future and dimensional space. So I do wonder if I'll ever get the opportunity to make a non-animation movie with it. I have these ideas for things no one's done before.

ANIMERICA: Should science fiction stories take place in space?

MATSUMOTO: They're not limited to space. They can take place in inner space, in the mind, or across dimensions. It's also possible to make a science fiction story that takes place in the middle of mundane modern society. But I've liked space since I was a child, and that's a fact. In truth, I should have been on Mars by now, according to my childhood plans.

ANIMERICA: I see. You like science fiction movies, but do you read science fiction books?

MATSUMOTO: I used to read them a lot. These days, it's hard to keep track of what's coming out, though. I tend to read a book thoroughly, but afterwards, when I'm quizzed whose book it was, I get confused. But I take a glance at them all.

ANIMERICA: Do you have a favorite author?

MATSUMOTO: When I was a child—I'm sure it's the same everywhere in the world—I liked H.G. Wells and Conan-Doyle's books. There also was a Japanese author by the name of Juzo Unno. I liked his works, too. As for H.G. Wells, he has a book called *The Science of Life*. As it was published in Japan, it's a seventeen-volume series. It had over 10,000 pages of illustrated scholarly discussions of the evolution of life from its origins to the contemporary days of H.G. Wells, according to all known theories of his time. It's a wonderful book. But it's out of print now. It was serialized in a newspaper in England. Its illustrator was very talented, and his illustration of dinosaurs had been the basis for many models, such as those used in movies later on.

Galaxy Express 999

© Leiji Matsumoto

ANIMERICA: ...Speaking of science fiction stories, I think this came from the American pulp era, but there's one of a space pirate climbing up a ladder with a slide rule in his mouth. Without it, he can't calculate his orbits, so it's more important that his life. Do you like that kind of space-adventure story? Exciting, although a little anachronistic?

MATSUMOTO: I haven't seen that one. Hmm...I think space is the last frontier left to mankind. I think it's also a place that can easily accommodate fantasy. It's possible to depict romanticized fantasy there, too. I'm thinking that if I work on it that way, we'll get more children interested in space. And when you have a large group of people, there's bound to be a genius or two in there, so I'm counting on them to get us into space. That's my sense of mission.

ANIMERICA: Woven into *Galaxy Express 999*, too?

MATSUMOTO: Of course. It can be enjoyed for its story alone, but it's also about pursuing the possibilities of youth. My own embarkation is projected there, from the time I came out on that train. Tetsuro's sentiments of leaving Earth are exactly what I was feeling when I was leaving home, onward to Tokyo.

ANIMERICA: What is your own view of humanity's future?

MATSUMOTO: I think humanity will overcome all crises and have a long life in space. I think we're a lifeform capable of that. I think humanity is destined for space and has a duty to go there. That's because if we were to preserve the environment as it is now, humanity must go out to space to prevent overwhelming Earth. I think that's our responsibility for our mother called Earth. So space development is not a fictitious story, but a very important job.

ANIMERICA: Do you think humans will embrace mechanization of their bodies, as in *Galaxy Express*?

MATSUMOTO: Realistically speaking, I think they'll start using machines as medical supplements and eventually end up with something very close to mechanized humans. Ultimately, complete mechanizations may happen. But that's up to the decisions of the people living in that era; it's a decision that can go either way. As a means to achieve eternal life, I think some will either choose biological longevity or become cyborgs. I don't think either is wrong. The next level of decision becomes what will humans *do* with that achieved long life. I think they'll be able to choose the right path.

ANIMERICA: This will be the last question. Do you have a message for your fans in the English-speaking world?

MATSUMOTO: I love animation, and I love drawing manga. I plan on doing this kind of work until I die. I'll be very happy if doing this will help to reduce the distance between you and I, little by little. I'll do my best, so if I ever have the chance to meet you, I'll very much want to talk with you. In the meantime, please take a look at my works and see what I have to say. It was only a dream in the past, that I'd be able to get in touch with people abroad through manga, but I'm very happy that the distance between us is shrinking, little by little. These days, one can make instantaneous communication with the Internet or with faxes. So borders and distance are becoming less of a problem. Conversely, I'm sending out my works as a creator, but I think the time will come when American or Asian or European creators' works will come to Japan as manga and animation. The world is full of talented people—after all, we all have the same number of brain cells—so all these creators can get together and have an exchage, I think nothing could be more fun than that.

afterword

Much as we'd like to think we had something to do with it, the fact is, entirely on its own merits, Leiji Matsumoto's dream project *Galaxy Express 999* began to experience an exciting revival shortly after this interview was published.

In the September 1996 issue of publisher Shogakukan's BIG GOLD monthly manga magazine, the long-promised continuation of his original, roughly 4,000-page *Galaxy Express 999* manga epic took off once more, with writer/illustrator Matsumoto promising to go the distance with *another* 4,000 pages. As of the September '97 issue of ANIMERICA, the new *Three-Nine* saga will be available to English-speaking readers, as well.

Coinciding with the revival of the story in Japan, the first of the classic *Galaxy Express 999* films was released in America uncut and unedited for the first time ever (the 1980 version from Roger Corman's New World Pictures was heavily altered, changing the names of Tetsuro and Captain Harlock, for example, to "Joey" and "Captain Warlock"). *Adieu Galaxy Express*, the 1981 sequel to 1979's *Galaxy Express*, is also available domestically (either subtitled or in English).

There's even more. *Die Walküre*, the long-awaited sequel to Matsumoto's enduringly popular *Uchû Kaizoku Captain Harlock* manga, is in Japan not only being published on paper, it's also being uploaded to the Internet. Electronically published in either Japanese or English, it's one of the first such bold experiments of which we know for a major manga artist to make his work available for no more than the cost of your local dial-up almost the moment it leaves his pen. Set your browser to `http://www1e.meshnet.or.jp/shinchosha/comics_e/index.html` for the English version (it's also available in Japanese, of course), and while you're waiting for your modem to catch up, consider this: According to Matsumoto, brand-new feature film versions of both *Space Pirate* and *Galaxy Express* are currently in production.

As for Matsumoto's personal life, the artist is also active in making his dream of humanity in space a reality, by serving as a chairman of the Y.A.C. or "Young Astronauts Club," a group consisting of about 3,000 members in Japan alone, with more chapters all over the world, and also with a commission from the Japanese version of NASA, the National Space Development Agency (NSDA). At the time of this interview, Matsumoto had been making plans to escort a group of children to an international conference in Washington, D.C. that, unfortunately, had to be canceled due to scheduling conflicts. The closest Matsumoto has been able to get to actual space himself so far has been to send his wristwatch into space with Japanese astronaut Mamoru Mori aboard the Space Shuttle.

"It's a diver's watch, heavy and well-built by Seiko," Matsumoto says. "It's been to many places, from the jungles to the tops of mountains; to Africa and India and the Amazon. Places where the thin air would make you dizzy, cold places, hot places...it's been to many places on Earth. But it's never been to space. I wanted to tag along with it, but the watch, at least, went there and came back. My thinking is, if a watch can get there, so can I."

Leiji Matsumoto
Select Bibliography & Filmography

MANGA 漫画

In the fifty or so years he's been a working manga artist—we've found works of his dating back to *Kasei Akuma* ("Demon of Mars"), in 1947—Leiji "Manly Romance" Matsumoto has yet to slow down. In Japan, it was his award-winning 1954 story *Mitsubachi no Bôken* which launched his career; in the U.S., it was the early '80s, nationally syndicated broadcast of the show we know as "Star Blazers," *Uchû Senkan Yamato*. Although our initial intention was to provide exhaustively complete bibliographies and filmographies for all the interviewees in this book, one fast look at the sheer number of works to Matsumoto's credit (and sheer exhaustion itself) quickly convinced us to scale back a bit. To that end, we've decided to concentrate on his more recent manga titles.

Kôsoku Esupâ ("Speed-of-Light Esper")
光速エスパー
Publisher unknown (1968); two volumes total. *CURRENTLY IMPORT ONLY*

Sensuikan Super 99 ("Submarine Super 99")
潜水艦スーパー９９
Published in Akita Shoten's "Sunday Comics" (1970); two volumes total. *CURRENTLY IMPORT ONLY*

Otoko Oidon ("I Am a Man")
男おいどん
Published in compiled form by Kodansha (1971); nine volumes total. *CURRENTLY IMPORT ONLY*

Sei Bonjin Den ("Exalted Chronicle of an Ordinary Man")
聖凡人伝
Published by Nihon Bungeisha (1973); one volume total. Reprinted in a variety of formats. Part of Matsumoto's popular *yojôhan* ("four-and-a-half-mat room") series. *CURRENTLY IMPORT ONLY*

Ganso Dai-Yojôhan Dai-Monogatari
("The Original Great Story of the 'Great Four-Mat Room'")
元祖大四畳半大物語
Published in compiled form by Asahi Sonorama's "Sun Comics" (1974); six volumes total. *CURRENTLY IMPORT ONLY*

Sexaroid
セクサロイド
Published in Asahi Sonorama's "Sun Comics" (1974); four volumes total. Also reprinted as a new edition in 1992 by the same publisher. *CURRENTLY IMPORT ONLY*

Senjô Manga Series ("'Senjô' [Battlefield] Manga Series")
戦場まんがシリーズ
Published in Shogakukan's "Shônen Sunday Comics" (1974); nine volumes total. Note that each of the nine volumes has a different subtitle, from Vol. 1's *Stanley no Majo* ("The Stanley Witch") in 1974 to Vol. 9's *Eikôdan Kairô* ("Tracer-Bullet Corridor") in 1980. A story from this series, "Ghost Warrior," is also available in English, as published in Frederik L. Schodt's *Manga ! Manga! The World of Japanese Comics* (Kodansha) *CURRENTLY IMPORT ONLY*

Denkô Ozuma ("Lightning 'Ozuma'")
電光オズマ
Published in Wakagi Shobô's "Comic Mate" (1975); three volumes total. *CURRENTLY IMPORT ONLY*

Gun Frontier
ガンフロンティア
Published in compiled form by Akita Shoten (1975); three volumes total. *CURRENTLY IMPORT ONLY*

Panic World
パニック・ワールド
Published in Asahi Sonorama's "Sun Comics" (1975); one volume total. *CURRENTLY IMPORT ONLY*

Uchû Senkan Yamato ("Space Battleship Yamato")
宇宙戦艦ヤマト
Published in compiled form in Akita Shoten's "Sunday Comics" (1975); three volumes total. Reprinted in a variety of editions. *CURRENTLY IMPORT ONLY*

Wadachi
ワダチ
Published in Kodansha's "Kodansha Comics" (1975); two volumes total. Later republished by Shogakukan in a 1993 collector's reprint. *CURRENTLY IMPORT ONLY*

Insect
インセクト
Published in compiled form in Asahi Sonorama's "Sun Comics" (1976); one volume only. *CURRENTLY IMPORT ONLY*

Kikaikajin Toshi: Machiners' City
(Mechanized Human Town: Machiners' City)
機械化人都市マシンナーズ・シティ
Published in Futabasha's "Power Comics" (1976); one volume total. *CURRENTLY IMPORT ONLY*

Ginga Tetsudô 999 ("Galaxy Express 999")
銀河鉄道９９９
Published in compiled form by Shônen Gahôsha (1977); eighteen volumes total. Reprinted over the years in various editions. *CURRENTLY IMPORT ONLY*

Hiruandon ("A Lamp in Broad Daylight")
ひるあんどん
Published by Kiso-Tengaisha's in their "Kiso-Tengaisha Bunko" format (1977); four volumes total. *CURRENTLY IMPORT ONLY*

Hotaru no Naku Jima ("Crying Firefly Isle")
蛍の泣く島
Published by Taitosha (1977); one volume total. Reprinted by the same publisher under their "Hard Comics" imprint in 1994. *CURRENTLY IMPORT ONLY*

Jikan Ryokô Shônen: Milaizer Ban
("Time-Travelling Youth: Milaizer Ban")
時間旅行少年：ミライザーバン
Published in Asahi Sonorama's "Sun Comics" (1977); three volumes total. The "prequel"-like side-story story of Maetel's father, as seen in *Galaxy Express 999*. *CURRENTLY IMPORT ONLY*

Kaerazaru Toki no Monogatari
("The Tale of a Time Which Won't Return")
帰らざる時の物語
Published in compiled form in Akita Shoten's "Akita Manga Bunko" format (1977); two volumes total. *CURRENTLY IMPORT ONLY*

Uchû Kaizoku Captain Harlock ("Space Pirate Captain Harlock")
宇宙海賊キャプテンハーロック
Published in compiled form by Akita Shoten (1977); five volumes total. Reprinted in various editions. *CURRENTLY IMPORT ONLY*

Wakusei Robo•Dangard A ("Planetary Robo•Dangard 'Ace'")
惑星ロボ・ダンガードA
Published in Akita Shoten's "Sunday Comics" (1977); two volumes total. *CURRENTLY IMPORT ONLY*

Yojigen Sekai ("Fourth-Dimensional World")
四次元世界
Published by Shogakukan's in their "Shogakukan Bunko" format (1977); two volumes total. Short story collection. *CURRENTLY IMPORT ONLY*

Dai Junjô-kun ("The Great 'Pure 'n' Simple' Kid")
大純情くん
Published by Kodansha (1978); three volumes total. *CURRENTLY IMPORT ONLY*

Dinosaur Zone
ダイナソア・ゾーン

Published in Nihon Bungeisha's "Goraku Comics" (1978); one volume total. *CURRENTLY IMPORT ONLY*

Dai Sôgen no Chiisana Yojôhan
("Little 'Four-an'-a-Half-Mat Room' on the Big Prairie")
大草原の小さな四畳半

Published in Kiso-Tengaisha's "Kiso-Tengai Comics" (1978); one volume total. *CURRENTLY IMPORT ONLY*

Demodori Shain Den
("The Chronicle of a Divorced Company Woman Gone Home to Mom & Dad")
出戻社員伝

Published in Kiso-Tengaisha's "Kiso-Tengai Bunko" format (1978); one volume total. *CURRENTLY IMPORT ONLY*

Hotaru no Shuku ("Firefly Village")
蛍の宿

Published in Futabasha's "Action Comics" (1978); one volume total. *CURRENTLY IMPORT ONLY*

Kûkan Kikôdan ("Armored Space Corps")
空間機甲団

Published in Kiso-Tengaisha's "Kiso-Tengai Comics" (1978); one volume total. *CURRENTLY IMPORT ONLY*

Kyôryûsô Monogatari ("Dinosaur Village Story")
恐竜荘物語

Published in compiled form in Nihon Bungeisha's "Goraku Comics" (1978); one volume only. *CURRENTLY IMPORT ONLY*

Matsumoto Leiji Roman to Gensô no Sekai
("Leiji Matsumoto's World of Romance and Illusions")
松本零士ロマンと幻想の世

Published by Akita Shoten (1978); one volume total. Illustration collection. *CURRENTLY IMPORT ONLY*

Mystery Eve
ミステリー・イヴ

Published in Asahi Sonorama's "Sun Comics" (1978); two volumes total. *CURRENTLY IMPORT ONLY*

Oyashirazu Sanka
("A Song in Praise of Those Who Know Not Their Parents")
親不知賛歌

Published in compiled form in Seirindô's *Seirindô Kessaku* ("Masterwork") *Series* (1978); one volume only. Fourteenth in a series. *CURRENTLY IMPORT ONLY*

Queen Emeraldas
Queen エメラルダス

Published in Kodansha's "KC Comics" (1978); four-volume series later reprinted by Kodansha in 1990 as a deluxe two-volume reprint. *CURRENTLY IMPORT ONLY*

Sanzen-Nen no Haru ("Three Thousand-Year Spring")
３０００年の春

Published in Nihon Bungeisha's "Goraku Comics" (1978); one volume total. *CURRENTLY IMPORT ONLY*

Torajima no Miime ("Miime the Tiger-Striped Cat")
トラジマのミーめ

Published in Akita Shoten's "Princess Comics" (1978); one volume total. *CURRENTLY IMPORT ONLY*

Gin no Tani no Maria ("Maria of the Silver Valley")
銀の谷のマリア

Published in Suiyôsha's "Grand Comics" (1979); one-volume reprint of the 1958 series. *CURRENTLY IMPORT ONLY*

Majo Tenshi ("Angel Witch")
魔女天使

Published in Kodansha's "KC Comics" (1979); one volume total. *CURRENTLY IMPORT ONLY*

Môsô Oni: Saki Tanpen Kessakushû
("Deluded Ogre: The Collected Short Story Masterworks of 'Saki'")
妄想鬼：サキ短篇傑作集

Published in Kiso-Tengaisha's "Kiso-Tengai Comics" (1979); one volume total. Anthology of illustrated stories by "Saki," the pen name of Scottish novelist and short story writer H.H. Munro; of them all, only the title story is by Matsumoto. *CURRENTLY IMPORT ONLY*

Yamabiko 13-go ("Craft 'Echo' 13")
ヤマビコ１３号

Published by Kiso-Tengaisha (1979); one volume total. *CURRENTLY IMPORT ONLY*

Manga Rekishi Dai Hakubutsukan
("The Great Museum of Manga History")
漫画歴史大博物館

Published by Bronze-sha (1980); one volume total. Scholarly manga reference work co-authored with Satoshi Hidaka. *CURRENTLY IMPORT ONLY*

Dai Furin Den ("'Super Immoral' Chronicle")
大不倫伝

Published in Kiso-Tengaisha's "Kiso-Tengai Comics" (1980); one volume total. *CURRENTLY IMPORT ONLY*

Kareinaru Shôjo Manga ("'Shôjo Manga' at Its Finest")
華麗なる少女マンガ

Published in compiled form by Tokyo Sanzesha (1980); one volume total. Collects earlier *shôjo* manga work published under the name "Akira Matsumoto." (*CURRENTLY IMPORT ONLY*

Matsumoto Leiji Shoki Sakuhinshû
("The Collected Early Works of Leiji Matsumoto")
松本零士初期作品集

Published by Nakano Shoten (1981); four volumes total. Limited-edition reproduction. *CURRENTLY IMPORT ONLY*

Nasuka
ナスカ

Published in Asahi Sonorama's "Sunday Comics" (1981); one volume total. *CURRENTLY IMPORT ONLY*

Shin Taketori Monogatari: Sen-Nen Jo'ô
("The New 'Taketori Monogatari': Thousand-Year [Millenium] Queen")
新竹取物語１０００年女王

Published in Sankei Shuppan's "Waku-Waku Comics" (1981); five volumes total. Reprinted in a variety of editions. *CURRENTLY IMPORT ONLY*

Yamiyo no Karasu no Monogatari
("The Tale of the Crow of Darkness")
闇夜の鴉の物語

Published in Asahi Sonorama's "Sun Comics" (1982); one volume total. *CURRENTLY IMPORT ONLY*

Diver•0 (Diver "Zero")
ダイバー・０

Published in Asahi Sonorama's "Sunday Comics" (1983); one volume total. *CURRENTLY IMPORT ONLY*

Hyôryû Kansen 000 ("Castaway Line 000")
漂流幹線０００

Published by Shônen Gahôsha (1983); four volumes total. Later reprinted in 1994 by Taitosha in a two-volume format. *CURRENTLY IMPORT ONLY*

Shishunki Hyaku Man-Nen ("Million-Year Puberty")
思春期１００万年

Published in Asahi Sonorama's "Sun Comics" (1983); one volume total. *CURRENTLY IMPORT ONLY*

The Sutetekondoru
ザ・ステテコンドル

Published by Asahi Sonorama (1983); one volume total. *CURRENTLY IMPORT ONLY*

Hyôryû 3000-Man Kônen: Shin Machiners (Chikyû Hen)
("Thirty Million Light-Years: The New 'Machiners' [Earth Chapter]")
漂流３０００万光年：新マシンナーズ（地球編）

Published in Asahi Sonorama's "Sun Comics" (1984); one volume total. *CURRENTLY IMPORT ONLY*

Shinkirô Fairy Islander 0 ("Fairy Islander Mirage '0'")
蜃気楼フェリーアイランダー０

Published by Shônen Gahôsha (1984); one volume total. Reprinted in single-volume format in Taitosha's "St. Comics" in 1994. *CURRENTLY IMPORT ONLY*

Arei no Kagami ("Mirror of Arei")
アレイの鏡

Published in compiled form by Sekai Bunkasha (1985); single-volume "film comic" adaptation of the animated series. *CURRENTLY IMPORT ONLY*

Kaitô M ("Mysterious Thief 'M'")
怪盗M

Published in compiled form in Kodansha's "Science Comic" (1985); one volume only. *CURRENTLY IMPORT ONLY*

Hard Metal
ハードメタル

Published by Shogakukan (1986); three volumes total. *CURRENTLY IMPORT ONLY*

Machiners: Kanzen Ban ("Machiners: Final Edition")
マシンナーズ（完全版）

Published in Asahi Sonorama's "Sun Comics" (1986); one volume total. *CURRENTLY IMPORT ONLY*

V2 Panther
Ｖ２パンツァー

Published by Shônen Gahôsha (1988); two volumes total. Reprinted in single-volume format in Taitosha's "Star Comics" in 1994. *CURRENTLY IMPORT ONLY*

Hiraga Gennai
平賀源内

Published by Kôronsha (1989); one volume total. *CURRENTLY IMPORT ONLY*

Mu no Kurobune ("The 'Black Ship' of Nothingness")
無の黒船

Published in Leed-sha's "SP Comics" (1989); two volumes total. *CURRENTLY IMPORT ONLY*

Niebelung no Yubiwa 1: Rhine no Ôgon
("The Ring of the Niebelung 1: Das Rheingold")
ニーベルングの指輪１：ラインの黄金

Published in Shinchosha's "Shinchosha Comics" (1989); one compiled volume published to date. The return of Captain Harlock in an updated, Wagnerian setting. Its sequel, *Die Walküre: Great Harlock*, is currently being serialized on the Internet (see afterword, above). Reprinted in 1992 by Shinchosha. *CURRENTLY IMPORT ONLY*

Yôsei Den ("The Legend of 'Faerie World'")
妖星伝

Published by Nakano Kôronsha (1989); one volume total. *CURRENTLY IMPORT ONLY*

The Cockpit
ザ・コクピット

Published by Shogakukan (1990); five volumes total. Reprints Matsumoto's classic "*Senjô* (Battlefield) Manga" series. *CURRENTLY IMPORT ONLY*

Shinkirô Kidan ("Mirage Stories")
蜃気楼綺譚

Published in Shogakukan's "Big Comics" (1991); one volume total. *CURRENTLY IMPORT ONLY*

Muo no Hosomichi
("The Long and Winding Road Within the Dream")
夢奥の細道

Published in Shogakukan's "Big Comics" (1991); one volume total. *CURRENTLY IMPORT ONLY]*

Kagerô no Monshô ("Crest of the Simmering Heat")
陽炎の紋章

Published in compiled form by Chûô Kôronsha (1994); four volumes to date. *CURRENTLY IMPORT ONLY*

Case Hard
ケースハード

Published in Shogakukan's "Big Gold Comics" (1994); six volumes total. *CURRENTLY IMPORT ONLY*

Tenshi no Jikûbune ("The Angel's Space-Time Craft")
天使の時空船

Published by Ushio Shuppansha (1994); four volumes total. *CURRENTLY IMPORT ONLY*

Kasei Ryodan Danasaito 999.9 ("Mars Brigade 'DNA Sights' 999.9")
火星旅団ダナサイト９９９。９

Published in compiled form by Kôbunsha (1996); two volumes to date. *CURRENTLY IMPORT ONLY*

Matsumoto Leiji no Tobidase! Uchû e
("Leiji Matsumoto's 'Go For It!' Onward to Space")
松本零士の飛び出せ！宇宙へ

Published by Nikkan Kôgyô Shimbunsha (1996); one volume total. 160 pages. *CURRENTLY IMPORT ONLY*

Mugen Kai Hyôryû Ki ("Limitless Sea Castaway Diary")
無限海漂流記

Published in Shogakukan's "Big Gold Comics" (1996); two volumes total. *CURRENTLY IMPORT ONLY*

Miyazawa Kenji Mangakan 4
("Kenji Miyazawa's Manga Museum 4")
宮澤賢治漫画館４

Published by Ushio Shuppansha (1996); one volume total. Anthology work featuring the stories of *Night on the Galactic Railroad*'s Kenji Miyazawa; artists include not only Matsumoto but Osamu Tezuka and others. *CURRENTLY IMPORT ONLY*

ANIME アニメ

If only for his work on the series nationally broadcast on U.S. television as *Star Blazers*, Leiji Matsumoto—note that he spells it with an "L" and not an "R," and that the meaning of the characters in spell out "midnight samurai"—is, with the possible exceptions of *Totoro*'s Hayao Miyazaki and *Akira*'s Katsuhiro Otomo, as close as a manga/anime artist gets to being a household name in America. As of this writing, the latest Matsumoto manga title announced for future animation was *Kasei Ryodan Dana-Saito 999.9* ("Four Nine"); as mentioned in the afterword to this interview, new versions of both *Galaxy Express* and *Captain Harlock* are also said to be in the works.

Uchû Senkan Yamato ("Space Battleship Yamato")
宇宙戦艦ヤマト

Original Story / Series Director / Art Continuity
26-episode TV series (1974-75) abruptly trimmed toward the end of its run due to competition with widely beloved, then on-air *Arupusu no Shôjo Heidi*. Of the ten or so episodes cut from the series, one character—Matsumoto's alter ego, Captain Harlock—would later go on to emerge in a series of his own, *Uchû Kaizoku Captain Harlock* (see below). *DOMESTIC RELEASE TITLE:* ***Star Blazers*** (Voyager Entertainment)

Uchû Senkan Yamato ("Space Battleship Yamato")
宇宙戦艦ヤマト

Art and Line-Art Design
130-minute theatrical feaure (1977) which retells the events of the 1974-75 TV series in abbreviated or "digest" form. Also known as "Arrivederci Yamato," this is the film which ignited the "Yamato" boom in Japan. *DOMESTIC RELEASE TITLE:* ***Space Battleship Yamato*** (Voyager Entertainment)

Wakusei Robo Dangard "A" tai Konchû-Robot Gundan
("Planetary Robo Dangard 'Ace' vs. the Insect-Robot Brigade")
惑星ロボダンガードA対昆虫ロボット軍団

Original Story
25-minute theatrical feature (1977) teaming up the popular cast of the *Dangard A* TV series with a brand-new, made-for-the-movies villain. *CURRENTLY IMPORT ONLY*

Wakusei Robo Dangard A ("Planetary Robo Dangard 'Ace'")
惑星ロボダンガードA

Original Story
56-episode TV series (1977-78); based on the Matsumoto manga series of the same name. Broadcast as part of the "Force Five" series, only 26 of the series' 56 episodes were included in the English-language domestic television adaptation. *DOMESTIC RELEASE TITLE:* ***Force Five*** (Parade Video)

Saraba Uchû Senkan Yamato: Ai no Senshitachi
("Farewell, Space Battleship Yamato: Soldiers of Love")
さらば宇宙戦艦ヤマト：愛の戦士たち

Original Story / Direction / Executive Conceptual Designer
151-minute theatrical feature (1978); paves the way for the later "second season" of the TV series (the only difference is, unlike the movie, the TV series leaves half the cast *alive* at the end, nicely setting the stage for future sequels). *DOMESTIC RELEASE TITLE:* ***Farewell to Space Battleship Yamato: In the Name of Love*** (Voyager Entertainment)

Uchû Kaizoku Captain Harlock: Arcadia-go no Nazo
("Space Pirate Captain Harlock: Secret of the Arcadia")
宇宙海賊キャプテンハーロック：アルカディア号の謎

Original Story
34-minute expanded theatrical retelling (1978) of Episode 13 from the TV series; includes approximately ten minutes of new footage. *CURRENTLY IMPORT ONLY*

Wakusei Robo Dangard A: Uchû Dai-Kaisen
("Planetary Robo Dangard 'Ace': The Great Space Naval Battle")
惑星ロボダンガードA：宇宙大海戦

Original Story
25-minute theatrical feature (1978); based on the 1977-78 TV program. Second in a series. *CURRENTLY IMPORT ONLY*

Uchû Kaizoku Captain Harlock
("Space Pirate Captain Harlock")
宇宙海賊キャプテンハーロック

Original Story
42-episode TV series (1978-79) which, although it takes place in *real-time* chronology several years *before* the theatrical feature *Waga Seishun no Arcadia* and follow-up TV series *Mugen Kidô SSX*, occurs in *storyline* chronology later than either. Based on the Matsumoto manga series of the same name, as first serialized in PLAY COMIC magazine. Broadcast domestically in limited markets as part of *Captain Harlock and the Queen of a Thousand Years* (the other footage came from *Sen-Nen Jo'ô*, another Matsumoto series). *DOMESTIC RELEASE TITLE:* ***Captain Harlock and the Queen of a Thousand Years*** (Harmony Gold); also released on home video (select episodes only)

SF Saiyûki Starzinger ("SF 'Saiyûki' Starzinger")
SF 西遊記スタージンガー

Original Story
64-episode TV series (1978-79) based on the Matsumoto manga of the same name, as loosely adapted from the traditional story *Saiyûki*, or "Journey to the West," which details the exploits of the mischievous Monkey King. A departure from Matsumoto's other, more serious works. *DOMESTIC RELEASE TITLE:* ***Spaceketeers***, one of five series which made up the syndicated strip ***Force Five***.

Ginga Tetsudô 999 ("Galaxy Express 999")
銀河鉄道９９９

Original Story
114-episode TV series (1978-81); based on the manga series of the same name. *Galaxy Express* is Matsumoto's true "manga opus," incorporating as it does characters from other series—*Uchû Kaizoku Captain Harlock, Sen-Nen Jo'ô*—and continuing over the years in a variety of sequels: movies, TV specials, even a recently resumed, all-new manga series. If any one Matsumoto series best represents the "Leijiverse," this is it. *TV SERIES CURRENTLY IMPORT ONLY*

Ginga Tetsudô 999 ("Galaxy Express 999")
銀河鉄道９９９

Original Story / Planning / Animation Choreography
129-minute theatrical feature (1979); based on the TV series of the same name. As much as any two hour-plus film can, *Galaxy Express 999* retells the events of the 114-episode TV series, managing to cover most of the series' major dramatic events, while still providing a fresh look at a story by then very well-known to Japanese viewers. Note that, although Roger Corman's New World Pictures produced an English-language adaptation of their own in 1980, only the Viz Video version is presented uncut and unedited. *DOMESTIC RELEASE TITLE:* ***Galaxy Express 999: The Signature Edition*** (Viz Video)

Ginga Tetsudô 999: Kimi wa Senshi no yô ni Ikirareru ka!?
("Galaxy Express 999: Can You Live as a Soldier!?")
銀河鉄道９９９：君は戦士のように生きられるか！？

Original Story
114-minute one-shot (11 October 1979) expanding with new footage Eps. 12-13 from the TV series, "*Kaseki no Senshi* (Fossil Warrior)," in commemoration of the series' one-year anniversary. *CURRENTLY IMPORT ONLY*

Ginga Tetsudô 999: Eien no Tabibito Emeraldas
("Galaxy Express 999: Eternal Traveler Emeraldas")
銀河鉄道９９９：永遠の旅人エメラルダス

Original Story
60-minute one-shot (3 April 1980) which uses as its base Ep. 22 from the TV series, "*Kaizokusen* (Pirate Vessel) Queen Emeraldas," to explore in more depth the backstory of characters Emeraldas and Maetel. Features an appearance by Reiko Tajima of *Galaxy Express* theatrical fame as the Japanese voice of "Emeraldas." *CURRENTLY IMPORT ONLY*

Ginga Tetsudô 999: Kimi wa Haha no yô ni Aiseru ka!!
("Galaxy Express 999: Can You Love Me as a Mother!!")
銀河鉄道９９９：君は母のように愛せるか！！

Original Story
114-minute, one-shot (2 October 1980) remake of the TV series' Eps. 51-52, "*Tômei Kai no* Artemis (Artemis of the Transparent Sea)." *CURRENTLY IMPORT ONLY*

Ginga Tetsudô 999: Glass no Claire
("Galaxy Express 999: Claire of the Glass")
銀河鉄道９９９：ガラスのクレア

Original Story
17-minute theatrical feature (1980) produced by the animation staff of the TV series, as compared to the staff which worked on the 1979 full-length theatrical film. Basically a remake of Episode 3 from the TV series, a slightly different look at the crystal-clear character Claire is offered; note also that, unlike the actor who appears in the TV series, the movie's Yoko Asagami ("Yuki," *Yamato*) returns to voice the role. *CURRENTLY IMPORT ONLY*

Uchû Senkan Yamato 2 ("Space Battleship Yamato 2")
宇宙戦艦ヤマト２

Original Co-Creator / Series Director
26-episode TV series (1978-79) which expands upon the story first told in the second *Yamato* theatrical feature, *Saraba Uchû Senkan Yamato: Ai no Senshitachi*, only—unlike the movie—leaving half the cast alive at the end, reportedly at Matsumoto's behest. *DOMESTIC RELEASE TITLE:* ***Star Blazers • The Comet Empire*** (Voyager Entertainment)

SF Saiyûki Starzinger II ("SF 'Saiyûki' Starzinger II")
SF 西遊記スタージンガー II

Original Story
Eight-episode follow-up TV series (Eps. 65-73) to 1978-79's *SF Saiyûki*; the heroes get a new transformation, and Princess Aurora gets a new costume. *CURRENTLY IMPORT ONLY*

Uchû Senkan Yamato: Aratanaru Tabidachi
("Space Battleship Yamato: The New Voyage")
宇宙戦艦ヤマト：新たなる旅立ち

Executive Editor / Executive Conceptual Designer
114-minute TV special (31 July 1979) in which the crew of the *Yamato* team up with Desslar while Starsha sends husband Mamoru and infant daughter Sasha to safety in order to sacrifice herself and her home planet. Remade in 1981 for theatrical release via the addition of some never-before-seen footage. Note that, as far as we can determine, the domestic version is the one first broadcast on TV. *DOMESTIC RELEASE TITLE:* ***Space Battleship Yamato: The New Voyage*** (Voyager Entertainment)

Marine Snow no Densetsu ("The Legend of Marine Snow")
マリンスノーの伝説

Original Story / Director / Executive Conceptual Designer
81-minute, one-shot TV special (12 August 1980); fanciful tale of a proposed human city named "Aquapolis," the queen of an underwater race, and their ensuing confrontation over the city's construction. *CURRENTLY IMPORT ONLY*

Yamato yo, Towa ni ("Yamato, Toward Eternity")
ヤマトよ永遠に

Original Story / Direction / Executive Conceptual Designer
145-minute theatrical feature (1980). This time, the *Yamato* must do battle against the evil "Dark Nebula Empire," not only surviving their blitzkrieg-style onslaughts, but deactivate a doomsday bomb, as well. *DOMESTIC RELEASE TITLE:* ***Be Forever Yamato*** (Voyager Entertainment)

Uchû Senkan Yamato III ("Space Battleship Yamato III")
宇宙戦艦ヤマトIII

Director / Executive Conceptual Designer
25-episode TV series (1980-81) featuring a new interstellar crisis (a stray doomsday missile which will cause the Earth to explode in one year's time) and another, hunky new male lead with an attitude problem. *DOMESTIC RELEASE TITLE:* ***Star Blazers • The Bolar Wars*** (Voyager Entertainment)

Sayonara Ginga Tetsudô 999: Andromeda Shûchaku Eki
("Adieu Galaxy Express 999: Final Station Andromeda")
さよなら銀河鉄道９９９：アンドロメダ終着駅

Original Story / Planning / Animation Choreography
130-minute theatrical feature (1981); picks up storywise a few years after the end of the first *Galaxy Express* movie with Tetsuro's continuing adventures against the ever-expanding Machine Empire, Maetel's ever-deepening secrets, and the Conductor's ever-worsening nerves. *DOMESTIC RELEASE TITLE:* ***Adieu Galaxy Express 999*** (Viz Video)

Shin Taketori Monogatari Sen-Nen Jo'ô
("The New 'Taketori Story' Thousand-Year [Millenium] Queen")
新竹取物語１０００年女王

Original Story
42-episode TV series (1981-82) known by English-speaking fans not only for being the precursor to *Galaxy Express,* but as the "other" part of the U.S.-broadcast *Captain Harlock* series. *DOMESTIC RELEASE TITLE:* ***Captain Harlock and the Queen of a Thousand Years*** (Harmony Gold)

Sen-Nen Jo'ô ("Thousand-Year [Millenium] Queen")
１０００年女王

Original Story / Planning / Animation Choreography
121-minute theatrical feature (1982); based on the TV series of the same name. Dara Sedaka—Neil's daughter—provides the movie's main theme. *CURRENTLY IMPORT ONLY*

Waga Seishun no Arcadia ("My Youth in Arcadia")
わが青春のアルカディア

Original Story / Planning / Animation Choreography
130-minute theatrical feature (1982). Although the *Uchû Kaizoku* TV series details Harlock's later adventures, it took this later-day retrofitted "prequel" to give us the full story on what happened *before* Harlock took up heavy drinking. *DOMESTIC RELEASE TITLE:* ***Arcadia of My Youth*** (AnimEigo)

Waga Seishun no Arcadia: Mugen Kidô SSX
("My Youth in Arcadia: Endless Orbit SSX")
わが青春のアルカディア無限軌道SSX

Original Story / Screenwriter
22-episode TV series (1982-83); follow-up to the theatrical *Waga Seishun no Arcadia* animated feature. En route to a mystical place known only as "Arcadia," Harlock rescues orphans, cuddles kittens, and generally hyucks it up, the series turning deadly serious only toward the very end. *CURRENTLY IMPORT ONLY*

Uchû Senkan Yamato: Kanketsu Hen
("Space Battleship Yamato: Final Chapter")
宇宙戦艦ヤマト：完結編

Original Story / Conceptual Design / Direction
158-minute theatrical feature (1983) and, until the recent *Yamato 2520,* presumed series finale. Not only do we get the return of the newly revived Captain Okita, but we get Susumu/Wildstar and Yuki/Nova in a long-anticipated love scene. *DOMESTIC RELEASE TITLE:* ***Final Yamato*** (Voyager Entertainment)

Arei no Kagami ("Mirror of Arei")
アレイの鏡

Original Story / Conceptual Design / Executive Direction
25-minute short theatrical feature (1985); based on an original story by Matsumoto. Two youths search for the fabled planet "Arei," said to be located at the galaxy's end. *CURRENTLY IMPORT ONLY*

The Cockpit
ザ・コクピット

Original Story / Executive Conceptual Designer
Three-volume OAV series (1993) in which original stories by Matsumoto are animated, anthology-style, by three of the hottest directors working at the time: Takashi Imanishi (*Mobile Suit Gundam 0083*), Yoshiaki Kawajiri (*Wicked City*), and Ryosuke Takahashi (*Votoms*). *CURRENTLY IMPORT ONLY*

Yamato 2520
Original Story
Four-volume OAV series (1995-97). A total design overhaul for the *Yamato* (courtesy of *Blade Runner*'s Syd Mead) and a new generation of hot-headed saviors bring the Yamato legend into the '90s. *DOMESTIC RELEASE TITLE:* ***Yamato 2520*** (coming from Voyager Entertainment)

Key

- Japanese comics or "manga" series; may or may not be available in foreign-language (i.e., English) version
- TV series broadcast on-air in Japan. Note that, in the U.S., Japanese TV series are both broadcast on-air (*Ronin Warriors*) and released on home video (*Ranma 1/2*). Others (*Sailor Moon, Dragon Ball*) are available both in broadcast and home video versions
- Direct-to-home-video series; may also include compilations of TV episodes released to home video market
- Theatrical feature; may or may not receive equivalent theatrical release for U.S. version

Ryosuke Takahashi

Interviewed by Takayuki Karahashi (1996)

"I started out at Osamu Tezuka's Mushi Production—that's where I studied directing, although for the first year, I was in production management. That's a position where you can most conveniently learn all the processes involved in animation."

As an animator, the man best known for gritty mecha sagas such as *Sôkô Kihei* ("Armored Trooper") *Votoms*, Ryosuke Takahashi has been in the industry a long time—almost since its very beginning, in fact. "Mushi Production got started just a few years before I joined them," Takahashi remembers. His first project, "in production," was on Mushi Production's first TV show, when Japanese TV animation really began—1963's *Tetsuwan Atom*. Though Takahashi had no special training when he joined the studio, and learned animation on the job, he moved into directing two years later with the TV series, *Wonder 3*, and worked directly with the legendary Osamu Tezuka.

"It was a small company, although it was the largest one outside of Toei back then. Osamu Tezuka himself was the chief director for *Wonder 3*, so I worked directly with him. Among all the people I've worked with directly, he was the most talented, and back then, his works were the ones I liked the most, so I was very excited to start work there." When asked what it was like to work with the legendary Tezuka, Takahashi remarks with a smile, "Aside from his talent, he was a creator after all, so ultimately speaking, he was a man of no small ego. ...His attitude toward his work, that is."

Even with this auspicious beginning, looking back, Takahashi remembers that his childhood dream wasn't to become an animator, but a toy designer. "There was no deep reason behind that. I was a child, after all, and just wanted to make toys and hoped that could be my occupation. These days, I often work with the very people making toys, so I think that's an interesting quirk of fate. Also, I wanted to become a *rakugo* teller. [*A traditional Japanese comedic storyteller—Ed.*] That didn't have a deep reason either—I just liked *rakugo*."

Takahashi really became known among mecha fans as one of the triumvirate of directors—along with *Gundam*'s Yoshiyuki Tomino and *Vifam*'s Takeyuki Kanda—who helmed most of the mecha TV series which dominated the airwaves in the 1980s. But though well-known in mecha circles, Takahashi has always been prolific in other genres, using his hard-earned professional skills directing and scriptwriting for lighthearted *shôjo*-styled shows such as *Akazukin* ("Red Hood") *Cha-Cha, Nurse Angel Lilica S.O.S.*, and *Kodomo no Omocha* ("A Child's Plaything"). "These are all shows made at a company whose president is a friend of mine," Takahashi says. "The studio has the capacity for work that *doesn't* involve too much creative talent, but they're a little weak on positions such as directors that require such creativity. So I got involved by way of helping a friend…and it just so happened that they got to make a lot of *shôjo* shows." Takahashi laughs. "Their staff had many *shôjo* story fans, but I had to teach them how to make stories with the proper exposition-development-twist-conclusion form. Otherwise, when animators work on genres they love, they tend to go out of control, and sometimes end up with an unmarketable film.

"I'm not so sure myself that I'm so slated for mainstream success," he continues. "But I think I know how to be objective about works that aren't my own. When it comes to my own creations or directing, I'm not so good at appealing to the lowest common denominator. But when I'm not directly directing, I think I'm more objective about it."

Always branching out, Takahashi also writes novelizations—at the time of this interview, he was finishing the third novelization for *Kodomo no Omocha*, and making plans to begin a *Votoms* novel at its completion—and dabbling in directing for the live stage, most recently with a stage production based on *Votoms*, and another which was "a present-day story that takes place in a restaurant with a man and a woman."

"Doing live is fun," Takahashi reflects, "but I think I enjoy film more. Since I once wanted to become a *rakugo* teller, I would love live performances if I were performing. As for directing, however, I think film's better."

But even with all his diverse projects, it's still the '80s robot shows and the more recent, gritty battle dramas such as *The Cockpit* and *Chinmoku no Kantai* which most fans associate with Takahashi. Despite his protestations, the label of "mecha director" doesn't really seem like a bad fit. At the time of this interview, his current project, "The Ryosuke Takahashi Project," was at the early planning stage, and Takahashi's sum-up says it all.

"It'll be about robots again," Takahashi said. "But I *always* want to do something new with robots. I don't know yet if they will be something to be piloted or worn, but it'll be anew take on the robot genre."

interview

ANIMERICA: Since you're probably best known as a mecha director…what would you say is the appeal of mecha?

TAKAHASHI: Actually, I'm always frustrated by this question. I don't think I'm particularly strong doing mecha shows. It just happened that the shows I directed at Sunrise were mecha shows. So the audience might take it differently, but I think my distinguishing mark is mecha depicted from the perspective of someone who's not necessarily fluent in mecha.

I don't have a consistent theme, but one thing about myself that always shows is a distrust of authorities.

ANIMERICA: Speaking of perspectives, I think *Votoms* depicts a man's world. It doesn't have many female characters. Is it easier to work from a male perspective?

TAKAHASHI: Well, you can say that I find it easier to portray men than women. Of course, I'm fond of women, but I'm not necessarily drawn toward *drawing* women. So females tend to be few in my works.

ANIMERICA: What would you say is the most important aspect in making a robot show? Would it be the drama, mecha, story, characters?

TAKAHASHI: Well, I can just say they're *all* important for the show's success, but my own standard for a robot show's success is whether its robots have a definitive role in the story. In *Votoms*, that would be the position of the robots as mere weapons in war that gives flavor to the story.

ANIMERICA: So, that's whether you can effectively use the robots as props.

TAKAHASHI: Yes, whether I can keep their position as weapons of warfare in the context of that world.

ANIMERICA: As for *Votoms* itself, where did you get the inspiration for the story?

TAKAHASHI: Well, at the very beginning was an American movie—it was a rodeo story, *Junior Bonner*. They'd travel from town to town in a trailer doing rodeo shows. That was the movie inspiration. So the first idea for *Votoms* was to set it right after the end of some war

Armored Trooper Votoms

or other, with the towns full of surplus robots, like the ones in *Votoms*. There'd be rodeo attractions done with them, and fights against each other offered as a spectator sport. A drifter would be among those competitors.... That was the original idea. Also, from my own experience, right after the end of WW II, there *were* a lot of jeeps in town. Although they were war vehicles, they showed up in town as daily-use vehicles and were used for wilderness driving and for construction. I've always had that picture in mind. I wanted to make a story about robots that were made for war but ended up being used in non-war places. They'd fight against each other and be the object of betting. They're all career soldiers, so they don't know how else to make a living.

ANIMERICA: That's the "battling" they do in *Votoms*. Are you familiar with a video game called *Battletech*?

TAKAHASHI: No. I'm not interested in video games, so I've never played any.

ANIMERICA: It's a multiplayer game where you sit inside robot cockpits and fight against each other. It's "battling" itself. Perhaps the times are finally catching up with *Votoms*. By the way, in the U.S., there's a persistent rumor that Chirico's model is the American actor Steve McQueen. Any truth to this?

TAKAHASHI: No, I just like Steve McQueen. He's not really Chirico's model. Steve McQueen isn't that expressionless. In fact, he looks more like a wrinkled-up monkey. [LAUGHS] I've always liked Steve McQueen from the time he was in the *Wanted: Dead or Alive* TV series.

ANIMERICA: If Chirico's expressionless...well, would he be modeled after other western heroes?

TAKAHASHI: Well...as for westerns, in *Junior Bonner*, the main character [*Steve McQueen—Ed.*] keeps his horse in his trailer, and that's the situational model. But there isn't any direct character model for Chirico. He was created for that show and came to life with Norio Shioyama's character designs. That's because he's a character who was already a young soldier by the time he could remember things and doesn't know any other way of life. Suddenly, the war ends and he's thrown out into town to fend for himself. He has a hard time mixing in. I first thought of making it a story about the social rehabilitation of this misfit who's at the end of his boyhood and at the beginning of his youth. So there is really no specific model for him.

ANIMERICA: Do you ever watch anime on TV and think, "*It's a good story, but it'd be even better with robots*"...?

TAKAHASHI: I don't really watch other anime TV shows. Right now, I *am* working on ideas for a completely new robot show that'll be my original. It'll have robots, and although I don't know yet if they'll be the main feature, there's no way that robots *won't* show up. It isn't so much that it's descended from other mecha shows, but it's been about ten years, and producers are starting to think that they could use an original "Takahashi" show again. But I don't really watch other shows. Just the same, as I turn the fact that I'm not that fluent in mecha to my advantage, I'd like to turn my lack of watching other shows and my vow to not play any video games into a way to preserve my innocence of thought, where I can come up with original perspectives. I'm afraid that if I watch the same shows everyone else is watching, I'll be left with the same perspective as everyone else, and that might deprive my own works of originality. So if I'm to watch anything, I'd like to be watching something different. That's why I do stage. I'm hoping that, for me, doing stage can breathe a new kind of life into my animation.

ANIMERICA: You have been involved in the production of many mecha shows, especially in the 1980s, but did you have any involvement with any of the *Gundam* series?

TAKAHASHI: I wasn't involved in *Gundam*. I was making a show called *Cyborg 009* back then. I was never involved in *Gundam*.

ANIMERICA: Why was that? It seems unusual, seeing that you're a noted director of mecha shows.

TAKAHASHI: The reason? Well, I am of the same generation as *Gundam*'s creator and director Yoshiyuki Tomino—we went through the same periods at the same company, Sunrise, where I made my robot shows. So when Tomino was working on something, that meant that *I* was working on something too. I wouldn't have been able to work on the same thing he was doing.

ANIMERICA: Weren't you involved a little in the original video series, *Gundam 0083: Stardust Memories*, though?

TAKAHASHI: ...Oh, right, *0083*. I wrote the script for that. A junior director of mine when I was at Sunrise was directing it, and I was asked to do the script. That's how I wrote a few episodes for it.

ANIMERICA: So your writing of the series was done to help someone out.

TAKAHASHI: That's right—*0083*'s director changed in mid-production. In fact, the whole staff changed, and there was a staff shortage. That's how my junior friend ended up asking for me.

ANIMERICA: If you look at the new TV shows that are called *Gundam* these days, they're nothing like the original *Gundam* by Tomino.

TAKAHASHI: True.

ANIMERICA: By that token, do you have any urge to get involved now, maybe create your own *Gundam* universe?

TAKAHASHI: No. Unlike the works I've done, *Gundam* is a diverse story. I think it's okay for Tomino to keep on doing *Gundam* sequels himself, but if anyone else were to make a *Gundam* type of story, I think they should be from the generation who grew up on the show. I don't think someone from the same generation as Tomino should work on a *Gundam* show. Realistically speaking, I don't think such a show would be accepted.

ANIMERICA: Your next work is going to be the new *yûsha* [*"Hero" series—Ed.*] series show. What's that work going to be like?

TAKAHASHI: Well, unlike *Gundam*, the *yûsha* series wasn't created by one person like Tomino, so I think anyone is allowed to work on it. I won't be involved in it as a director, though, but as a producer. I'd like to discover new people who can direct robot shows doing this. I think *yûsha* series shows are traditional—not that I'm sure if "traditional" can properly describe *any* robot show—but I think they demand that kind of quality. Shows that have proper exposition-development-twist-conclusions, yet have simple stories—yet those simple stories need to be directed so they are entertaining. That's the kind of talent I'd like to dig up.

ANIMERICA: Can you tell us anything about what kind of show it will be?

TAKAHASHI: Well, the new show still has many things I can't discuss yet, but the basic concept will still be in line with the previous *yûsha* shows, so I don't think it'll have anything really revolutionary.

ANIMERICA: So it'll once again, it'll be hyperactive kids saving the day.

TAKAHASHI: Well, yes, but the *yûsha* robot itself will get more screen time.

ANIMERICA: I'd like to ask you about your non-*Votoms* shows. What were the inspirations for shows like *Kikô-Kai Galient* and *Aoki Ryûsei SPT Layzner*?

TAKAHASHI: I've worked on four robot shows at Sunrise: *Dougram*, *Votoms*, *Galient* and *Layzner*. I don't know what the viewers thought, but I like to think I've made different shows. The same person designed the robots for *Dougram* and *Votoms*, so they might have some visual similarities, but they do have different kinds of robots with different world-views, and different intentions. In *Dougram*, I wanted to depict a society in a world that required robots. In *Votoms*, I wanted to depict the plight of one individual and robots as mere tools. In *Galient*...well, video games may have popularized the notion of robots based on medieval armor now, but back then, the motif was considered a sure flop, so I wanted to challenge that. So the intention behind *Galient* was doing a medieval knights story with robots in place of regular armor. In *Layzner*, I wanted to work on something I had never done before; i.e., robots that are like fighter planes. *Dougram* robots would just run: *thump*, *thump*. Visually, that lacked a sense of speed. *Votoms* robots got smaller and had the "roller dash." *Galient* had the heroic fantasy taste. I wanted to do fighter plane-style robots—something I hadn't done before—in *Layzner*.

ANIMERICA: *Layzner* is a group story, while *Votoms* focuses on an individual. Is this one of your intentional differentiations?

TAKAHASHI: Yes, and also, *Layzner* was made at the same studio that made *Vifam*. It was still within the same Sunrise company, but I was the one who moved to that studio to make *Layzner*, and that studio had a successful precedent in *Vifam*. The producer already had a show like that in mind, so he wanted a fusion of that previous success and my style. That's how *Layzner* came to be.

ANIMERICA: As to your influences, do you watch American TV shows or movies?

TAKAHASHI: Well, when it comes to my generation—you can also say that I don't keep up to date—I like older movies. ...Hmm, yeah, they all tend to be old movies. The movie, "Showdown at O.K. Corral," the one with Henry Fonda [My Darling Clementine—*Ed.*]. My preferences tend to be conditional—for example, it's *Henry Fonda's* "O.K. Corral" movie, although I like John Ford's directing, too. I also like the theme song in

Armored Trooper Votoms

© Kaiji Kawaguchi/Kodansha • Sunrise, Inc.

The Godfather, the one that plays in the opening of the first movie.

ANIMERICA: The "Love Theme from The Godfather"?

TAKAHASHI: Yes. So let's see—I've only seen recent movies sporadically—well, in that sense, it wasn't really American movies that I liked, but American TV shows. I liked *Kojak* and another detective show that was made before that. I watched a lot of westerns from that period. But I think I've been influenced more from Japanese movies. I'm not sure in what form, but I'm sure that *Votoms* has the influences from *Nikkatsu* movies from the late *Showa* 20s to the mid 30s. The series of movies back then that doesn't seem to be taking place in any specific country, such as the *Watari Dori* ("Migrating Birds") series, and *Yujiro* ("Yujiro Ishihara"). I'm not sure myself how these movies have influenced my works, though.

ANIMERICA: Would *Taiyô Zoku* ("Clan of the Sun") be one of them?

TAKAHASHI: *Taiyô Zoku* has a definite location. It takes place at the Shonan beach in Japan. The movies starring Keiichi Akagi and Akira Kobayashi were really obscure about where they were taking place. They'd be toting guns and hauling a guitar on a horse. I'm sure they were made by people who liked American westerns. So I've incorporated a derivative influence from movies already inspired by someone else's works.

ANIMERICA: Do you have a favorite writer?

TAKAHASHI: Well, most of them have nothing to do with animation. I'm not familiar with foreign writers, and I mostly like Japanese drinking novels. For example, Hitomi Yamaguchi and, although he's passed away, Takeshi Kaiko. I like their works.

ANIMERICA: Do you have a consistent theme throughout your works?

TAKAHASHI: I don't have a consistent theme, but one thing about myself that always shows is a distrust of authorities. However much the current situation may put them in good light, I'll always bear a distrust somewhere. I think this consistently shows up not only in my works, but in my private life, too. My generation's political high points would be the student demonstrations against the U.S./Japan Mutual Defense Treaty renewals in 1960 and 1970. In 1960, everyone was left wing, at least in spirit. I didn't trust the left wing, either, though. I always think it's dangerous if everyone blindly follows one single value. I've thought like that since elementary school. So that's something that will always show up in my work. For that reason, I don't think I'll be able to create a big hit. I think this lifelong belief I've had will distract me. I think one needs some kind of respect for authority in order to indulge in the euphoria that's making everyone feel good from a hit film. I lack that, so I don't think I can make a big hit.

ANIMERICA: You've been involved in more light-hearted shows such as *Granzört* and *Wataru*....

TAKAHASHI: Yes, as the scriptwriter. I think the creator aspect in me is just a small portion of myself. Outside that, if anyone has a need for my skills, I'm there. What we do is a group effort, after all, so if you're not the core of a project, I think it's fair to offer your skills in any way that's needed. That'll depend on the demand. I'll do it if there's demand.

ANIMERICA: In that sense, which do you enjoy more, being the leader of your own project, or offering your skills for someone else's project?

TAKAHASHI: First of all, I very much like the simple task of creating a story. I also like creating words. It's not exactly the same as *rakugo* or that I blindly trust the power of words, but I am attracted to words.

ANIMERICA: What is your view on war?

TAKAHASHI: I think it's something that won't go away. As long as humans remain human, it won't go away. That's without making a value judgment on whether that's good or bad. I think it's human nature. Some have described war as "inhuman," but I think that's wrong. It's a *very* human thing.

ANIMERICA: In *Votoms*, after the Uoodo chapter ends and the Kumen chapter begins, Chirico has changed from being a battling gladiator to a mercenary. Does that follow your idea that there's war somewhere all the time, or is there something else involved?

TAKAHASHI: He doesn't want or aspire to become a mercenary but just ends up there. Chirico is already under a sense of emptiness when he first shows up in Uoodo, but his despair is even deeper in the Kumen chapter. There's something that isn't depicted in the TV show, but the OAV series *Last Red Shoulder* fills in the gaps. In the TV show, Chirico is separated from Fyana in Uoodo, and the Kumen chapter starts with his monologue, "I've come to Kumen to forget everything." Well, that doesn't make sense. This is a guy who's never known a woman. He finally finds someone he likes, and it seems she likes him too. How can it be that he wants to forget that all of a sudden? This sudden leap was planned from the beginning and is explained in the OAV series. Chirico bands together with his wartime colleagues to seek vengeance on those who betrayed him. He bumps into Fyana in the process and finds her kissing Ypsilon and is heartbroken. So it's this broken heart that drives him to become a mercenary in Kumen.

ANIMERICA: One thing mecha fans always seem to mention when talking about their favorite shows are the toys and model kits. How are sponsors like toy companies involved in the content of a mecha show?

TAKAHASHI: That's been different over the years, and also different by show. Fifteen years ago, the toy company would base their toys on the mecha that showed up in the show. Ten years ago, the toy company would make requests about using specific mecha in the show, based on past experience of what sold well. Since five years ago or so, the toy companies have been effectively imposing their products into the content of the show. So it's been different throughout the years. I'd like to reset this trend, so in the next *yûsha* show, I'll still have to respect my client, but if there's a confict between the story and the client's merchandising, I'm going to talk it through with them so that the story prevails. I think my biggest job as producer will be to champion the director and his show.

ANIMERICA: Do you ever build your own models based on the robots from your own series?

TAKAHASHI: No, I've never built *any* models. Since I was born, I've never bought one. I've been given a few, but I give those away in return, so I haven't built anything.

ANIMERICA: So what do you do when you're not working? Do you have any hobbies?

TAKAHASHI: Well, I lie around. [LAUGHS] Oh, actually, I like to play, so I'd go play golf or go to the gym and sweat it out. I've also come and gone to the race track for the last thirty years. I'm not a real gambler, but I enjoy horse racing.

ANIMERICA: You sound pretty athletic.

TAKAHASHI: Not really. I think I'm just your average Japanese guy: playing golf, worrying about his health, betting on horses, and drinking.

ANIMERICA: Do you have any advice for aspiring animation directors?

TAKAHASHI: I don't have anything specific, but you have to constantly re-assess your skills and the techniques you've learned as you go through your years in your 20s and 30s and 40s. If you mis-measure yourself, you'll soon be unable to do your work. You have to keep on evaluating what you're good at, what you can do, and how much you're willing to do. You have to evaluate your assets as a creator. If you mis-evaluate, you'll end up spending time on futile efforts, and when you realize it, you'll have disappeared from the production scene.

ANIMERICA: Finally, do you have a message for your fans in the English-speaking world?

TAKAHASHI: Well, I've always been proud of my style. I'll strive to find a new visual style in my next project, so I'd like you to look forward to seeing it. I'm trying to come up with a new style of a robot story, and it's my hope you'll want to see it.

ANIMERICA: Thank you very much.

afterword

The new *yûsha* ("hero") show Takahashi mentioned in his interview made its appearance on Japanese TV for the 1997 spring season—*Yûsha-O Gowgaigâ* ("Hero-King Gaogaigar"), on which Takahashi is working as a producer. As he promised, the *yûsha* gets more screen time, in a high-energy transforming robot romp with *Giant Robo*-like character designs, and a plotline that seems downright nostalgic in its glee for the formulaic fight-of-the-week with big robots as bright and colorful as those of the *Mighty Morphin Power Rangers* wielding nifty weapons. Though Takahashi is working as a producer, not a creator or director on this project, his promise to clear the path for the creator's vision seems to have held true.

Ryosuke Takahashi
Select Filmography

ANIME アニメ

Like Tomino, most of Takahashi's experience falls firmly in the field of TV anime; in fact, as fellow animators who share a frequent affiliation with Sunrise "Home of the Giant Robots" anime studio, they've actually worked on many of the same shows together. When it comes to the field of "hard mecha" shows, few come close to matching Takahashi's accomplishments, as you'll soon see below.

Gokû no Dai-Bôken ("Goku's Great Adventure")
悟空の大冒険

Episode Director
39-episode TV series (1967); see entry under Sugii. *CURRENTLY IMPORT ONLY*

Ribon no Kishi ("Ribbon Knight")
リボンの騎士

Episode Director
52-episode TV series (1967-68); see entry under Tomino. *CURRENTLY IMPORT ONLY*

Sasurai no Taiyô ("Wandering Sun")
さすらいの太陽

Director
26-episode TV series (1971); see entry under Tomino. *CURRENTLY IMPORT ONLY*

Kokumatsu-sama no Otôri Dai
("Kokumatsu's 'Coming Through'")
国松さまのお通りだい

46-episode TV series (1971-72); see entry under Tomino. *CURRENTLY IMPORT ONLY*

Chô Denji Robo Combattler V
("'Super Magnetic Robo' Combattler V")
超電磁ロボコン・バトラーV

Storyboards
54-episode TV series (1976-77); see entry under Tomino. *CURRENTLY IMPORT ONLY*

Manga Ijin Monogatari
("'Manga' Tales of Great Personages")
まんが偉人物語

Episode Director
46-episode TV series (1977-78). Following the enduring popularity of Japan's animated *Manga Mukashi Banashi* and *Manga Sekai Mukashi Banashi* ("'Manga' Folktales of Long Ago" and "'Manga' Folktales of Long Ago From Around the World") comes this anthology-format program, focusing on the lives of diversely famous persons in world history, such as Beethoven, Sir Isaac Newton, and even Babe Ruth. *CURRENTLY IMPORT ONLY*

(Shin) Cyborg 009 ("The New 'Cyborg 009'")
サイボーグ009 （新）

Director
50-episode TV series (1979-80); remake of the classic 1968 program, as based on the manga series of the same name by Shotaro Ishinomori (*Japan, Inc.*) Animated in response to fan demand, character designs retain a traditional feel more in tune with that of Ishinomori's original manga than the animated Toei series from which it sprung some twelve years earlier. *CURRENTLY IMPORT ONLY*

Tetsuwan Atom: Color Ban ("'Iron-Arm Atom' Color Version")
鉄腕アトムカラー版

Screenplay
52-episode TV series (1980-81); brand-new, color version of Tezuka's seminal series. Initially involved almost not at all in the remake—at the time, the new *Atom* was just one more series in a trendy "revival" boom that included remakes of classics such as *Tetsujin 28-go* (*Gigantor*), and others—little by little Tezuka become more involved in production until, by the series' end, his own son was receiving credit as "director of photography." *CURRENTLY IMPORT ONLY*

Sirius no Densetsu ("The Legend of Sirius")
シリウスの伝説

Production Sketch Assistance
108-minute theatrical feature (1981); lush, fable-like "full-animation" fantasy created (or so the anime historians tell us) in response to Disney's *Fantasia*. *CURRENTLY IMPORT ONLY*

Taiyô no Kiba Dougram ("Fang of the Sun Dougram")
太陽の牙ダグラム

Director / Screenwriting / Storyboarding / Original Concept
75-episode TV series (1981-83). After years of working in various genres, Takahashi falls at last into what would eventually become his true metier: the angst-soaked Sunrise mecha drama. Episode direction and storyboarding credits go also to a then-novice Yasuhiro Imagawa (*Giant Robo*). *CURRENTLY IMPORT ONLY*

Sôkô Kihei Votoms ("Armored Trooper Votoms")
装甲騎兵ボトムズ

Original Story / Director / Episode Direction / Screenwriting
52-episode TV series (1983-84); the most nihilistic Sunrise mecha show yet. As Takahashi alludes in his interview, it would seem the inspiration for lead character Chirico Cuvie was a then-young Steve McQueen; once you watch the series—even only a bit of it—you'll understand why. Followed by a three-volume OAV series. *DOMESTIC RELEASE TITLE:* ***Armored Trooper Votoms*** (U.S. Manga Corps)

Kikô-Kai Galient ("Armored World Galient")
機甲界ガリアン

Original Story / Director
25-episode TV series (1984-85); third entry in what had come to be called "Ryosuke Takahashi's 'Real Robot' Series." A tale of gritty mecha combat in a feudal setting (albeit aimed at a younger audience, especially in comparison with *Votoms*), the story was originally planned for a full year's run of 52 episodes, but was abruptly cut short to 26, forcing the story to come to a rushed end. Followed by a three-volume OAV series, the first two of which were compiled from the TV series, while the third, released in 1986, features all-new animation and a slightly skewed retelling of the first series' story. Features mecha design by Yutaka Izubuchi, at that time fresh from a star-making design stint on Tomino's *Aura Battler Dunbine*. Also known as "Panzer World Galient." *CURRENTLY IMPORT ONLY*

Aoki Ryûsei SPT Layzner ("Blue Meteor SPT Layzner")
蒼き流星SPTレイズナー

Original Creator / Director / Screenwriting / Episode Direction / Storyboarding
38-episode TV series (1985-86). Following the success of his previous Sunrise anime mecha show hits—*Dougram*, *Votoms*, and *Galient*—Takahashi gets in up to his elbows with this tale of alien invasion and one lonely warrior's way, featuring mecha design by *Gundam*'s Kunio Okawara. Like *Galient*, an accompanying three-volume OAV series is available which, like and unlike *Galient*, budgets the third volume for an expanded, newly animated retelling of the series' final episode (the plan was to go for a full 52...also like *Galient*). *CURRENTLY IMPORT ONLY*

Yoroiden Samurai Troopers ("Armor-Legend Samurai Troopers")
鎧伝サムライトルーパー

Series Choreography (Eps. 1-19)
39-episode TV series (1988-89); broadcast in the U.S. under the name "Ronin Warriors." Created in response to the wild popularity of Toei's *St. Seiya*, *Samurai Troopers* was the first such "hero-team" show for Sunrise, and it wouldn't be the last—the trend continues today with shows such as the recent *Chôsha Raideen*, in which yet another five-member team of superhunks armor up and wage the war of virtue against evil forces. Followed (so far, in Japan only) by a string of OAV sequels. *DOMESTIC BROADCAST TITLE:* ***Ronin Warriors*** (Graz Entertainment)

Fujiko Fujio "A" no Anime Golf Rulebook
("The 'Anime Golf Rulebook' of Fujiko Fujio 'A'")
藤子不二雄Aのアニメ・ゴルフ・ルールブック

Planning
45-minute one-shot OAV (1988). Thinking of golf, but not sure where to begin? Leave it to Japanese animation—specifically, to Fujiko Fujio "A," one-half of the team which created the lovable, iconographic robot cat from the future, Doraemon—to provide not only tips on play, but four unique characters with whom viewers may identify in their own nine-hole vision quest (what, you think Japan's got the space to waste on eighteen holes?). Directed by Junji Nishimura of *Ranma 1/2* fame. *CURRENTLY IMPORT ONLY*

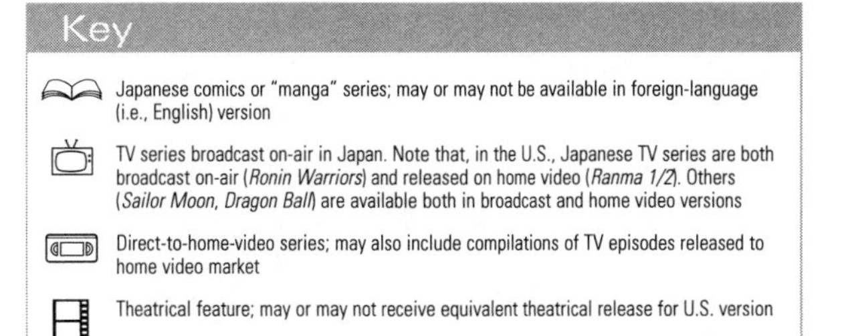

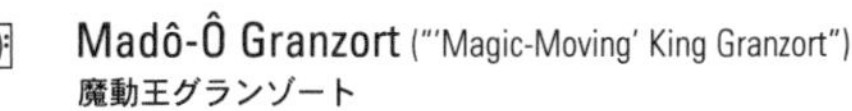

Madô-Ô Granzort ("'Magic-Moving' King Granzort")
魔動王グランゾート

Screenwriting
41-episode TV series (1989-90); wacky mecha comedy that's a far cry from the grit and anguish of Takahashi's earlier efforts. Followed by a string of OAV sequel series (1990-92), the series is also known as "Granzote," a studio-provided alternate rendition of the Japanese "*guranzôto.*" *CURRENTLY IMPORT ONLY*

Mashin Eiyû Den Wataru 2 ("Magic-God' Hero-Legend Wataru 2")
魔神英雄伝ワタル2

Screenwriting
28-episode TV series (1990-91); sequel to the first, 1988-89 *Wataru.* Note the similarity between the sounds produced by the characters "mashin" to the English "machine"—a punning coincidence exploited as a series title by more than one studio. Both the 1988-89 and the 1990-91 series are followed by OAVs; in the first case, by a two-volume series in 1990 and in the second, by a three-volume series released in 1993. *CURRENTLY IMPORT ONLY*

Eiyû Gaiden Mosaica ("Glorious 'Victory-Legend' Mosaica")
英雄凱伝モザイカ

Director
Takahashi reunites with former *Samurai Troopers* collaborator Norio Shioyama (original story, character designs, storyboards) in this science fiction action story released in Japan on home video. *CURRENTLY IMPORT ONLY*

Kidô Senshi Gundam 0083 ("Mobile Suit Gundam 0083")
機動戦士ガンダム0083: STARDUST MEMORY

Screenwriting
Twelve-volume OAV series (1991-92); see entry under Tomino. *CURRENTLY IMPORT ONLY*

Mama wa Shôgaku Yon-Nen-Sei
("Mama's a Fourth-Grader")
ママは小学4年生

Screenwriting
51-episode TV series (1992); see entry under Tomino. Charming tale of a baby from the future who drops into the lap of her schoolgirl mama...hijinks ensue. Like Tomino, an unusually comedic depature for the both of them. *CURRENTLY IMPORT ONLY*

Konpeki no Kantai ("The Deep Blue Fleet")
紺碧の艦隊

Screenwriting
45-minute OAV (1993); based on a bestselling Japanese science fiction novel in which a naval officer dies at the end of World War II and then finds himself reincarnated at the war's *start*...only this time, he's got the benefit of all his past memory and experience. *CURRENTLY IMPORT ONLY*

The Cockpit
ザ・コクピット

Director / Screenplay
Three-volume OAV series (1993); see entry under Matsumoto. Takahashi joins the esteemed company of fellow directors Takashi Imanishi (*Gundam 0083*) and Yoshiaki Kawajiri (*Ninja Scroll*) in his direction and screenwriting of this third OAV based on the manga of the same name by Leiji Matsumoto. The three OAVs are also available as a 78-minute, all-in-one volume. *CURRENTLY IMPORT ONLY*

Chinmoku no Kantai ("The Silent Service")
沈黙の艦隊

Director
100-minute theatrical feature (1995); based on the controversial manga of the same name by creator Kaiji Kawaguchi, in which the Japan Self-Defense Force and the U.S. military collaborate to build a secret, nuclear-powered submarine. *CURRENTLY IMPORT ONLY*

Yûsha-Ô Gowgaigâ ("Hero-King Gaogaigar")
勇者王ガオガイガー

Producer
Recent TV series (1997~); 35 half-hour episodes aired as of press time. *CURRENTLY IMPORT ONLY*

Nanase Okawa

Interviewed by Takashi Oshiguchi (1997)

"Everyone, except for me, went to high school together," says Nanase Okawa, head writer for the all-women manga team known as "Clamp," collectively. "A high school friend of mine got to know these other three—who were all in the same astronomy and meteorology club—first."

Together with Okawa, "everyone," in this sense, means the four women who would gradually come together out of the chaos of the Japanese *dôjinshi* or "self-publishing publications" world to assume their destiny as one of the most reliably bestselling names on the manga scene today: writer and designer Nanase Okawa, artists Mokona Apapa and Mikku Nekoi, and designer and artist Satsuki Igarashi.

"We weren't an artistic collective then, but a group of friends who liked to party together," Okawa remembers. "There'd be twelve or thirteen of us of varying ages, and within that number, there were a certain amount of people who liked to make *dôjinshi*. Even though those people all belonged to different *dôjinshi* circles, we somehow came together, and to commemorate the occasion, we decided to publish a *dôjinshi* under the group name 'Clamp.'"

But what does the word "Clamp" *mean*, we wondered? Is it an homage to the group name which, clamp-like, "holds or presses parts together firmly"? A comment on vise-like deadline pressures on their collective foreheads? A feeble Japanese-language pun on sharp abdominal pains? (We didn't actually *mention* this last speculation, but still, we wondered.)

"No," says Okawa to us with a straight face. "It just means, 'a bunch of potatoes.'"

Ohh-kay.

At first, that early group's activities were far from serious in tone. "A letter would arrive suddenly when a holiday came, telling us when to get together, where to get together, and what we'd be doing once we got there," comments artist/designer Satsuki Igarashi in an interview published in COMICKERS, a specialized Japanese manga magazine. "We'd have sleep-over parties to watch horror movies," adds Nekoi.

"A male friend of ours named Tamayo goes nuts for horror movies," says Okawa. "Whenever there'd be one that he'd particularly want to see, we'd all get together and watch it. There was this one time that we were watching a movie at my place when the lights suddenly went out. We were all sitting there huddled in blankets, watching the movie by candlelight... It was like a scene straight from *Nightmare on Elm Street.*"

"Then there was this other time we all went to Osaka Castle in the middle of the night," chimes in Nekoi. Igarashi adds, "We weren't even of legal drinking age at the time, but for some reason, there'd always be drinks for us left inside the icebox...."

Still, even for a team bound first by a common love of each other's company, the talent and energy expended on their artwork is extraordinary. "People say that an all-female creative group is rare," muses Okawa to us, speaking for the group, "but we don't see it as anything special. We've just found it easier to work together." Collectively, Clamp functions much like American comic artists do, apportioning out each task—writing, drawing, coloring, designing—to the one who does it best. Every aspect of a Clamp manga story is done "in-house," we're told, all handled by one of Clamp's four members. Compare this with many other manga artists in Japan, artists who have assistants to help with screentone, with lettering, with just about *anything*, in fact, short of putting their own names on the page. With Clamp, it's all kept in the four-woman family.

Clamp's works, such as *Tokyo Babylon*, *Magic Knight Rayearth*, *X* (known as *X/1999* in the U.S.) and *RG Veda*, have the fluid, delicate artistic style of much *shôjo* manga or "girls' comics," but the stories—thanks to writer Nanase Okawa—have a distinctly *darker* tone. Many of Clamp's stories, even those aimed at young children, such as *Rayearth*, deal with fate, grim destiny, and sacrifice. In other words, those looking for light-hearted fantasy fare should look elsewhere.

"I think fate is something you choose," muses Okawa. "I think it's a lie that there's a mystical force out there, manipulating your destiny. I think that destiny is something you *choose* to do, even when you're being dictated to by fate."

Considering that most of Clamp's works deal with fate in one form or another, the idea of *choosing* your fate is an important distinction. But if destiny *is* something you can control, then why is it that so many of Clamp's stories seem so *dark*? Does Okawa just not like happy endings? "That's not true," she says. "Basically, all of the characters live the way they want to, so their endings aren't necessarily *all* unhappy. If the characters themselves think they have no regrets, you can't really say that they're unhappy, can you?"

These days, with their grueling schedules, "happiness" to most of the members of Clamp means meeting their deadlines, and putting the finishing touches on the last installment of long serials. But, like the characters in their works, they've each chosen their own paths and are living the way they want to. "I think happiness is different according to each person," says Okawa decidedly. "Everyone is different, so it should be impossible for everyone to think the same. So 'like everyone else' is a phrase I most dislike. I don't know what it's like to be 'just like everyone else,' first of all, and what others consider unhappy might be the happiest situation for someone else. I think you should seek to make *yourself* happy, rather than try to be told by everyone how happy you look."

X/1999

This outlook also applies to how they view their own work. "Basically, what we draw will always just be a drawing, to us. We don't want to get infatuated with the characters and destroy the story," says Okawa. "If you're sensitive about popularity," she says, "you'll start reading fan mail, to find out which of your characters are popular. But that character may be scheduled to die in the next installment. So, although we're really happy to receive mail, and it's encouraging, we just can't stay in this business without doing something that might potentially make our readers hate us."

interview

ANIMERICA: How did you get involved in making manga?

OKAWA: When I was still in Osaka, I had friends with whom we were making *dôjinshi*. We went by the group name Clamp.

ANIMERICA: Were you involved in manga in college?

OKAWA: I didn't really read manga when I was growing up. I did see movies and watch TV and read books, but I only got started in manga when I got to know our current members. They were my friends' friends. In the beginning, we just went to see cherry blossoms and went out at night. [LAUGHS] Eventually, that led into manga.

I think fate is something you choose. I think it's a lie that there's a mystical force out there, manipulating your destiny.

ANIMERICA: So is that when you started scripting, then?

OKAWA: Actually, I was a writer/editor in the beginning. I did the editing, layouts, and the plots. I first went as far as writing the script for *RG Veda*. The editor at Shinshokan said it wouldn't be possible to print the story as it was and asked me for a rewrite.

ANIMERICA: So your *dôjinshi* work just became your job.

OKAWA: Well, a few of us had real jobs while we drew manga, but that wasn't easy. They had to quit in order to concentrate on the manga. Some of us were tormented.

ANIMERICA: Does "Clamp" mean anything?

OKAWA: I wasn't the one who came up with it [LAUGHS], but it refers to a pile of potatoes. Just a bunch of potatoes.

ANIMERICA: I'd like to pry a little more, but what do you find interesting in manga? Are you interested in the writing itself? In your writing becoming illustrated? Or...?

OKAWA: Well, I had a writing job before then. It was for a teen magazine—they often solicit student writers. I was earning pocket money writing for them and other similar magazines. [LAUGHS] So there was that writing work, the fact that I liked movies, and *RG Veda*.

ANIMERICA: So that was your idea.

OKAWA: Well, yes. But I'm not good at fantasy. I've read foreign fantasies, but I didn't own a single Japanese-written fantasy. I was once really into *Dune*, and there was a time I really liked *Dune* and *Captain Future*. I liked that type of science fiction more. I liked them, and I wasn't good at fantasy, but our artist Mokona really liked fantasy. She also really liked Buddhist mythology, so it was me adjusting to her.

ANIMERICA: It's been about seven years since you debuted, and you've put out quite a few titles since then. How has it been?

OKAWA: Well, everyone said a group of girls wouldn't last long. [LAUGHS] One of our merits may be that, with the four of us, we can be objective. What I write is just a story, after all, so I can't always tell if it's interesting. So my first readers would be Mokona and Nekoi, and *they'd* tell me if it's boring. And then, whoever draws the storyboards and draws the panel lines would also be able to tell. In that sense, the group is maybe a good thing.

ANIMERICA: What's it like to be working in a group composed entirely of women?

OKAWA: We can't get work done if we get too emotional. Of course, there are many types of successful women, so I can't generalize. If we tried working together just because we were friends, it'd never work out. Just like marriage, it's a long relationship. Once someone starts getting dependent, it's a bottomless swamp from there. So it might sound cruel, but once your own work is done, you have to get your sleep, even if everyone else has to pull an all-nighter. If you don't, you won't be able to stay up when you have to pull *your* all-nighter. In that sense, working in a group could be tough if you couldn't be cool about it.

ANIMERICA: So you got into writing just because you liked writing. Did you have any special training for that?

OKAWA: Not at all.

ANIMERICA: So you figured things out in your work.

OKAWA: That's true. The few manga I read when I was a child and books and movies must have been my influences.

ANIMERICA: You mentioned that Mokona was drawing fanzine manga since high school. Was she set on becoming a manga artist?

OKAWA: No, a manga artist was the *last* thing she wanted to become. [LAUGHS] She really considers being a manga artist to be tough work. It's difficult to draw manga, so she didn't really think she could endure it. It's a form of integrated art. You draw your own background, act out your own characters. She never thought she could do all that. And then, in manga, you have to draw the same thing three times, in the storyboard, in pencil, and in ink. That used to really pain her. She says she's gotten used to it now, though. These days, she seems to find the most joy in drawing the last installment. It's a long-term engagement, like running a marathon. It's tough, but it's fun.

ANIMERICA: In that sense, there's a catharsis.

OKAWA: Yes.

ANIMERICA: What *did* you want to become?

OKAWA: An officer worker. [LAUGHS] I like menial tasks. But everyone says I can't do that. [LAUGHS] But an office job was waiting for me in Tokyo. In the end, though, I ended up never doing that kind of work.

ANIMERICA: You did get a job?

OKAWA: I got through the interview and had the job. Igarashi and everyone else, too. Our debut just barely prevented us from going off to office work.

ANIMERICA: So you came out to Tokyo to find a job?

OKAWA: Yes, it was to find a job. Graduation was nearing.

ANIMERICA: I'd like to ask about your work. I've heard you have an assistant who keys the text into the word processor for you.

OKAWA: No, I don't. [LAUGHS] It's faster doing it myself.

ANIMERICA: Do the artists have assistants?

OKAWA: No, we do it with the four of us.

ANIMERICA: Isn't that tough?

OKAWA: Yes, but we got used to it. Once we got used it, it's faster to do it yourself than finding the time to tell an assistant what color to use. [LAUGHS]

ANIMERICA: How about the cover art?

OKAWA: We do it ourselves.

ANIMERICA: Do you do *everything* yourselves?

Magic Knight Rayearth

OKAWA: Yes, we do. Kadokawa's NEWTYPE has dedicated designers, so we don't usually have to do work for them, but we did it anyway for *X*.

ANIMERICA: Do you do the calendars, too?

OKAWA: Yes, we do, Igarashi and I.

ANIMERICA: Wow. How do you collect fresh information, inspirations for your work?

OKAWA: We watch TV and hang out with friends. We talk amongst each other. I basically like TV and film. Of course, I like books, too. When I get tired, I see a movie or read a magazine. I like magazines. If you include game magazines and computer magazines, I read a hundred magazines a month.

ANIMERICA: How do you go about creating your characters?

OKAWA: Well, when we create a character, we start with his or her resume. A Japanese resume comes with a photo, doesn't it? The artist fills that in from all three sides, including how the hair is done. We'd forget, otherwise. [LAUGHS] I fill in the history and favorite food and other habits. And then we make four copies.

ANIMERICA: So you have a huge database.

OKAWA: Yes. If you've seen the *Rayearth* character design book, that's the kind of thing we make for *all* our stories. It might be close to the sort of thing that they do at the animation studios.

ANIMERICA: They do something similar in American comics.

OKAWA: Yes. They have specialists for each task in American comics, don't they? Even a dedicated colorist. We might be close to that.

ANIMERICA: In Japan, it's more like animation. There's a manager, a colorist, and all that is done within the four of you.

OKAWA: ...But once you get used to it, it's faster than using an assistant or someone from the outside.

ANIMERICA: That's probably why your readers like you so much. What else is it that you think they like about your work...?

OKAWA: That's a tough one. [LAUGHS] Basically, what we draw will always just be a drawing, to us. We don't want to get infatuated with the characters and destroy the story.

ANIMERICA: I think your *Rayearth* manga in NAKAYOSHI magazine deviated quite a bit from the traditional *shôjo* manga style.

OKAWA: Well, the reason we drew for NAKAYOSHI was that, if we don't re-aim for a lower-age readership from time to time, the age group keeps on going up indefinitely. Of course, our older readers are just as valuable to us. Our NAKAYOSHI editor liked our works and told us we didn't have to change our style. And the editor-in-chief responsible for *Sailor Moon*'s success said his magazine's weakest point was that once girls graduate from elementary school and become junior and senior high school students, they stop reading NAKAYOSHI. They wanted us to draw a story not just for children but a story that they can keep on reading as they grow up. That wasn't so possible from the outset, so in the beginning, *Rayearth* was a little more geared toward younger readers, but we soon reverted to our regular style. [LAUGHS] I'm sure there are grownups who like *Rayearth*, but I personally intended it for elementary and junior high school students. Portions of it may have been a little difficult for them, but we were really lucky. NAKAYOSHI had an editor-in-chief who wanted artists like us. I don't think we would have gotten the serial if they didn't already have *Sailor Moon*. Otherwise, the idea of using robots in a NAKAYOSHI story would have been rejected flat out. [LAUGHS]

ANIMERICA: You said *everything* is your influence. What would be your influences from animation or manga?

OKAWA: For me, it's the manga of *Harmagedon*. That, and *Devilman*. I was really shocked when I read the manga—not the animation—of *Devilman*. When you're young, you think in straight lines. I thought the hero would win. I wonder how old I was then....

ANIMERICA: You must have been in elementary school.

OKAWA: Something like that. It was a real shock. In the end, Devilman loses. That was a *double* shock. I think that shock became the basis for the stories I write. I might have gotten it wrong, but I really found Go Nagai's thesis, that good looks don't necessarily make a good heart, and his ideas on human mass hysteria, scary. And *Harmagedon* as well, even though I didn't like the movie version, actually—I wasn't convinced that what they did was enough to save the Earth. I really liked Rin Taro's direction, though. But my biggest influences are probably Go Nagai and Osamu Tezuka. I really liked *Hi No Tori* ("The Phoenix"), and I cried reading *Black Jack*. *Black Jack* was not what you'd call a conceptual work—it had solid themes like human pathos and greed. That must have been why I liked it.

ANIMERICA: We talked about your movie influences before, but what do you like?

OKAWA: Well, it's not a recent movie, but I like Alan Parker's *Angel Heart*. I like hopeless movies.

ANIMERICA: How did you like *Jacob's Ladder*, then?

OKAWA: Nobody seems to like *Jacob's Ladder*. [LAUGHS] I'm sad. I also like *Silence of the Lambs*, *The Dead Zone*, and Hitchcock.

ANIMERICA: I'm guessing that you must like *Brazil*, then, too.

OKAWA: Yes. [LAUGHS] I really like the director, Terry Gilliam. I'm sad nobody likes *Twelve Monkeys*. [LAUGHS] You could say that *Twelve Monkeys* isn't really his style, but it has wonderful writing. I was moved, but nobody else liked it. [LAUGHS] Also—though he's not as good as he used to be—I like Brian De Palma.

ANIMERICA: How about French movies?

OKAWA: I like them very much. Of course, I like the Hollywood-style contrived happy endings, too. [LAUGHS] But I like the abrupt endings of the French movies. There's always faint music in the background in those movies. You can't tell if it's music or sound effect.

ANIMERICA: Do you keep consistent themes in all your works? Or do you have individual themes for each work?

OKAWA: We don't like to look back and wonder what we wanted to say ourselves, so we come up with a new theme for each story. One thing to say each time.

ANIMERICA: I see. You seem to always depict human fate. Why is that?

OKAWA: I think fate is something you choose. I think it's a lie that there's a mystical force out there, manipulating your destiny. That's the way it was in *RG Veda*'s ending, but it's something you're supposed to be able to change. I think destiny is something you choose to do, even when you're being dictated to by fate. For example, if you're at work and you want to resign, it takes a lot of energy to do so. You'll be losing a stable lifestyle, and if you don't like that, you'll have learn to put up with how things are. But if you want to change things, only you can do that for yourself. If you don't like doing *that*, you let the circumstances dictate your fate. But if you have the determination and resolve, I think you can change your fate.

ANIMERICA: That seems to relate to your view on life.

OKAWA: This is something that gets mentioned in every single interview I do. I *am* an individualist. I hate group responsibility the most of anything in this world.

ANIMERICA: Aren't most creators like that?

OKAWA: Perhaps so. There's one thing about group responsibility that I still can't understand. If someone forgets something, it becomes everyone's fault? For example, in Japan, if one person in your group forgets to bring paint to art class, everyone has to stand in the hall to take responsibility. I never understood that or liked that. I think you need to be responsible for yourself. It probably has to do with the way I was brought up. My parents really scolded me if I pointed fingers. They'd just punish me if I admitted my own responsibility, but they *really* got on my case if I pointed my finger at someone else. My parents didn't like that.

ANIMERICA: I'd like to ask about how *X* came to become a movie. There was X^2 ("Double X") before that, and when that came out, the storyboards for the movie were included....

OKAWA: Yes, a long trailer at the end of the video, you could say. You'd want to see the movie after you saw that.

ANIMERICA: Well, when you're doing manga, you're the writer and Mokona is the artist. But when one of your manga stories is animated, how do you go about getting the visuals you want? How much control do you have?

OKAWA: You have to think for whom the film is being made. Is it for the readers? Is it for ourselves? There are times when we just like the director and leave everything to him. [LAUGHS] It's not just animation, but in all film, the work belongs to the director. If that's not good enough,

Tokyo Babylon

you just don't have it made. But if you can find a good producer, you will be able to talk to the director. Creators will always clash with each other. Can you really say, "Change this, change that" to the guy who thinks he's the best in the world? [LAUGHS] Conversely, once we name a director or designer, we'll leave everything up to him. We'd look at every single work he'd done up to that point and check. Sometimes we strike out.

ANIMERICA: Are you involved with the script of the *X* movie?

OKAWA: I'm among many of the writers.

ANIMERICA: I haven't seen the movie yet myself, but when I hear the story from those who have seen it, they say there are aspects you won't get if you haven't read the manga.

OKAWA: I think it's more upsetting if you *have* read the manga. [LAUGHS] If you're the fan of a certain character, you'll be upset simply by the way he's depicted. You'll complain when he only shows up for a few minutes, or that he's killed off too soon. But if you didn't have those kind of pre-conceived notions, you could take the movie as it's presented. I *do* think there are too many characters for a movie-length story.

ANIMERICA: Where did you get the idea for Kamui?

OKAWA: The basic *X* story is something I thought up in elementary school. Back then, it was the middle of the polluted '70s. There was a time the very existence of humanity was a nuisance to the planet. [LAUGHS] It was the time when the "Gaia" theory was starting to circulate. The idea that Earth itself was one living organism.

ANIMERICA: The question why Kamui has two personalities is something I've always had myself.

OKAWA: I think all persons have dual natures. I'd be afraid of a good man who is only good. Conversely, there are characteristics that are charming in one person, but would be the reason to hate someone else. I think a dual nature is something everyone has.

ANIMERICA: And Kamui is an extreme example of that.

OKAWA: Yes.

ANIMERICA: I think you just gave out a hint, but how did you like the movie?

OKAWA: I'm satisfied. I judge movies by whether they are worth the admission price. What I hate most is walking out without remembering what it was all about. In that sense, there must have been people who really hated it, and others might have gotten sick from all the blood. And some others may not have tolerated all those on-screen deaths. I'm sure those are lasting impressions. Still, I think it was a worthy movie.

ANIMERICA: Rather like *Blade Runner*.

OKAWA: Yes. The first thing we talked over with the director was that the movie had to have a conclusion. I think it's a financial strain for junior and senior high school students to see a movie. They might not have a ¥5000 allowance, but you still have to take admission from them, so the movie should not end without a conclusion. The other agreement was not to make an "anime style" movie. So you would notice when you see it, but it has a faint background music that you can't tell apart from the sound effects. The visuals are also more live action-like. It's more subtle. No one cries when someone dies, and they keep on dying one after another. That's where you get sick seeing the movie. *They* don't cry, and *you* can't cry. At that point, they don't like the movie. I don't think a tearjerker is the solution, either, so perhaps we did manage to hit the target.

I'm not good at love stories. Apparently, my idea of a relationship is different from that of a lot of other people.

ANIMERICA: I see. How were the voice-actors?

OKAWA: I wasn't involved with the voice-actors much, but the director and producer agreed with me to use a young voice for the main character, and give him lots of veteran support in the other roles. In that sense, it's a feature-style casting.

ANIMERICA: I understand the movie was directed by Rin Taro.

OKAWA: Yes. He hadn't directed a movie in nine years. He was saying he wants to do more TV. But he's a "master" now, so no one can casually request him, as he says. [LAUGHS]

ANIMERICA: I'd like to talk about *Rayearth*. The animated series went on for a year and three months. How was it? The manga story was progressing at a monthly pace....

OKAWA: I joined as a writer on the animated *Rayearth* from Part Two. I was requested by director Toshihiro Hirano because he said that it was impossible for someone who doesn't know the manga to animate the story, and when we were discussing Part Two, the manga only had one installment. Hirano had liked Episode Fourteen and the last episode of Part One that I had written, so he wanted me. It wasn't that tough doubling up work on both the TV series and the manga, but I like subplots, and that got me in trouble sometimes with the TV production. I'd take a script to the meeting, and the producer would tell me something was against the TV codes. But then if I changed that, the subplot would fall to pieces. Since I only joined from Part Two, I wasn't fully aware of all the subplots the writers laid in Part One, so that was also troubling.

ANIMERICA: Where did you get the idea that everyone's will is determined by fate?

OKAWA: I consider Earth and Cephiro to be the same. What man does becomes the fate of humanity. The result is the same. It's just more exaggerated in Cephiro.

ANIMERICA: At the end of the *Rayearth* animation, Cephiro is saved. Did you prepare that just for the animation?

OKAWA: No, we always decide on the ending of a story. Part One's ending and Part Two's ending were all decided.

ANIMERICA: Is it true that you named things after the cars you owned?

OKAWA: They are named after cars, as is Cephiro. Children have a hard time learning names in *katakana* [*the Japanese writing system used mainly for foreign words—Ed.*]. But their fathers tend to be driving cars. If characters bear the same names as the cars in people's houses, I thought that would be mnemonic enough.

ANIMERICA: You considered that far.

OKAWA: Of course. [LAUGHS]

ANIMERICA: That's so cute.

OKAWA: I couldn't remember fantasy names if it weren't so, myself. [LAUGHS] I'd be okay if they were Japanese names, but I can't memorize *katakana* names. [LAUGHS]

ANIMERICA: Is Mokona really a god? [LAUGHS]

OKAWA: It's not a god. God isn't the only being capable of creation. We're creators, but we're no gods, are we? This cup might be just a cup from the glass craftsman, but from the glass, the glass craftsman would be its creator.

ANIMERICA: It's a RPG-type world. Do you like RPGs?

OKAWA: I like games, but I don't have the resolve, so I have only finished a few. A reflex-less person like me can take the time to finish RPGs. [LAUGHS] But most shooting games don't have endings, and you need skill. So I tend to play more RPGs. *Rayearth* intentionally traces out an RPG world, but I don't consider it an RPG world, myself. You can tell it's not a simple world, the kind where there's a princess, a villain who kidnaps her, and the main character who saves the day and lives happily ever after. Even if the main characters *thought* that's the world they got into....

ANIMERICA: What do you do in your spare time?

OKAWA: Spare time? [LAUGHS] I don't have much of that, but I nap, play with the cat, or play video games. Or I might go see a movie. Recently, I get too analytical seeing a movie, professionally. I can't fully become part of the audience.

ANIMERICA: Do you follow any TV shows?

OKAWA: I like *The X-Files*, especially the second season.

ANIMERICA: How about *Star Trek*?

OKAWA: I like it, but Mokona is the one who really likes *Star Trek*. I've liked hardcore stories that boys usually tend to like more than girls, ever since I was little. That's my preference in mysteries and horror, too.

ANIMERICA: How about *Hill Street Blues*, then?

OKAWA: *Hill Street Blues* was aired by an Osaka station, so they kept on showing it late at night. I've watched the entire series. Osaka keeps on endlessly re-running imported shows late night, so in that sense, I was blessed. American TV shows are completely different from Japanese. In an American story, they don't dedicate one case to a whole episode. They have two or three cases going on at the same time. And at the end, everything concludes happily.

ANIMERICA: What kind of music do you like?

OKAWA: I've always liked Sting.

ANIMERICA: That's pretty old, for your generation.

OKAWA: Perhaps so. But I come from an age when MTV was on when you turned on the TV. Prince was just barely there. I still like progressive rock over computer sounds.

ANIMERICA: How about film music?

OKAWA: I like that too. *Blade Runner*. Eric Serra. I like John Williams too. I like those difficult-to-distinguish pieces like *Superman* and *Raiders of the Lost Ark*. I was also impressed by the Argentine tango in *Twelve Monkeys*. I liked the director's sense.

ANIMERICA: Aside from Clamp's manga *X*, which is currently running in ANIMERICA, there isn't that much *shôjo* manga being published in the U.S. Do you think it has something to do with the size of the eyes? I think Mokona's philosophy is reflected there, but are Clamp's "big eyes" a conscious effort?

OKAWA: Mokona's taste is big, there. The charm of her characters is in the expressions in their eyes. We do change styles a little, depending. We'll probably change styles according to the story.

ANIMERICA: ...I don't mean the drawing style per se, but are you conscious of the size of their eyes? The current trend in Japanese *shôjo* manga is to use small eyes. How is it to intentionally have big eyes amid that?

OKAWA: Well, that must be Mokona's sense of balance. She uses their eyes for expression, after all. I don't know. It's not like we can change the style for current stories. It's just that we might have smaller eyes in future stories. As I just mentioned, we try to vary our style as much as possible. The new *Card Captor Sakura* story that's after *Rayearth* is of a different style, with finer lines.

ANIMERICA: Is that something you can really control?

OKAWA: Yes, we can. First of all, you start with a thorough understanding of the work. You consider the characters to be actors. We're the directors and the stylists and the camera operators. And, for us, the ending of a story is pre-determined, so it's easier to act it out. That's one of our conditions when serializing a story. We won't extend a story just because it gets popular. Of course, lack of popularity could give it a premature axing. [LAUGHS] So far, we haven't experienced that yet.

ANIMERICA: So as the creator, you have to really understand your characters.

OKAWA: Yes. If you think of your characters as actors, you get requests. Like "she should cry cuter." But if the "director" doesn't have that kind of grasp and just films with the flow, you just end up with a dull movie. [LAUGHS]

ANIMERICA: Many manga artists just make a cold start with the dialogue.

OKAWA: There are many artists who are successful that way. But I can't do it. —Oh, yes, I've heard about the way Shotaro Ikehata, when he was running a newspaper serial, wrote: "And then, someone came out from the shadow...." It was a great cliffhanger, but then his editor asked who it was, and he replied, "Actually, I haven't thought that far ahead yet." [LAUGHS] I was surprised to learn that those types of artists really exist.

ANIMERICA: Do you ever need to wait for an inspiration?

OKAWA: Not me. I basically don't need time to come up with a story. I could come up with one in ten minutes. Of course, I'd need more time for the details.

ANIMERICA: But you could come up with the basic guideline.

OKAWA: Yes. But I can't write unless I know what I'm writing for.

ANIMERICA: I see. Does that mean listening to your editors?

OKAWA: Well, if the editors want us, there must be a reason for it. Conversely, we'd be most vexed to be asked to write "a story like *X*." [LAUGHS] We can't draw the same story twice. We'd know that this was one of those editors who has no ideas of their own. It's easier on us if they're frank and tell us why they want us.

ANIMERICA: I see. That's interesting.

OKAWA: ...But there *are* stories that we want to do. We take those to the publisher ourselves. *X* was such a title.

ANIMERICA: You've collaborated with Takeshi "*Elemental Masters*" Okazaki before. How is it different to collaborate with a male artist?

OKAWA: As long as we have the same sensibilities, it's fine. The most troublesome situation happens if we don't have a common topic. If the other person doesn't get it when I mention a scene from a certain movie or a passage from a novel, that's a problem. That's when our conversation ends. For example, there might be this great actress, and I want her to be the model for our character, and he says, "I've never seen her." That closes all channels. So as long as that's cleared, it doesn't really matter if a collaborator is really older or much younger.

ANIMERICA: So you collaborate well with Okazaki because he has that sensibility?

OKAWA: Well, Mr. Okazaki first said he wanted to draw someone else's story. He wanted to do a love story.

ANIMERICA: How do you like doing love stories? You don't usually have a love story as the central plot.

OKAWA: I'm not good at love stories. Apparently, my idea of a relationship is different from that of a lot of other people. I really got a lot of complaints when I once wrote that people love themselves the most, and that they only do something for others because it makes *them* feel good to see others made happier. —Hey, I'm okay if the person I'm seeing has an external affair. Nobody ever believes me when I say that.

ANIMERICA: I don't know what to say. One could almost say that's quite masculine. —No, actually, that's not masculine. Men aren't like that either.

OKAWA: It's not that I lack the desire to be exclusive, but I'll be most troubled, for example, if the person I'm seeing right now has another affair, and that inconveniences me. But if that doesn't happen, I don't want to be scolded for thinking someone else is good-looking. Perhaps I like to go out of my way to avoid trouble. [LAUGHS] I hate fighting.

ANIMERICA: I'm sure there are aspiring manga artists in the U.S., especially ones that are reading *X* in ANIMERICA. Do you have any advice for them?

OKAWA: Perhaps it's most important to have a firm grasp of what you're drawing *for*. Is it for money? Is there something you really want to draw for which you'll endure any hardship to make it happen? If you know what your goal is, you probably won't get discouraged when you're only halfway there.

afterword

Since this interview, Clamp has finished their serialization of *Rayearth* in NAKAYOSHI, and has since moved on to a number of brand-new manga serials: *Wish*, *Card Captor Sakura* and *Shin Shunkôden* ("New Legend of the Spring Scent"). The animated *Rayearth* ran two seasons on Japanese TV and is currently in the process of being *re*-adapted for an OAV series, which retells the story in a different sequence of events. For instance, instead of the three girls magically traveling to the world of Cephiro, in essence, the magic comes instead to Earth with a series of terrible earthquakes, and then an amazing storm and light show over Tokyo Tower appears....

The feature-film version of Clamp's manga, *X*, was a great success during its Japanese theatrical run in the summer of 1996, especially when you consider that it's based on a *shôjo* or "young girls'" comic, which traditionally falls into a subgenre of the manga publishing world. The *X/1999* manga itself—the title was revised slightly to avoid conflict with another comic of the same name—first released in English in a monthly stand-alone format and later moved to the pages of ANIMERICA,where it enjoyed a two-year run before going on hiatus, presumably to resume at a later date. In the meantime, not only are there several *X/1999* graphic novels to read, but an English adaptation of the *X* movie is scheduled for upcoming domestic release, as well.

Clamp's *Magic Knight Rayearth*, long considered by fans as the logical follow-up to *Sailor Moon* on American television, has yet to air in the States (though an English "pilot" was once produced at Vancouver's Ocean Studios), but the manga has been made available in a new English-language manga-anthology magazine titled MIXX ZINE, which also serializes Takeuchi's *Sailor Moon*.

Currently, the group's work seems to be more and more in demand for TV, as 1997 brought the debut of a new series so much in the "Clamp style" that it even carried the name—***Clamp Gakuen Tanteidan*** ("Clamp Campus Detectives"), based on an original manga by the team.

Clamp
Select Bibliography & Filmography

MANGA 漫画

As mentioned in Nanase Okawa's interview, the four-woman supergroup "Clamp" got its start in the underground fanzine or "dôjinshi" scene, meaning (among other things) that their works display an unusual intensity uniquely appealing to hardcore fan or "otaku" sensibilities. Like most successful manga creators, many of their works have been animated with even more, no doubt, to come.

Gakuen Tokkei Deukarion ("Campus 'Special Police' Deucalion")
学園特警デュカリオン
First serialized in Kadokawa Shoten's Newtype magazine "100% Comics" (1990); two compiled volumes total. *CURRENTLY IMPORT ONLY*

Clamp Gakuen Tantei-Dan ("Clamp 'Campus Detectives'")
CLAMP学園探偵団
First serialized in Kadokawa Shoten's "Asuka Comics DX" (1990); three compiled volumes total. *CURRENTLY IMPORT ONLY*

Shira-Hime Shô ("All About 'Shira-Hime'")
白姫抄
Published in Kobunsha's "VAL Pretty Comics" (1990); one volume total. *CURRENTLY IMPORT ONLY*

Tokyo Babylon
東京BABYLON
Published by Shinshokan (1990); seven compiled volumes total. *CURRENTLY IMPORT ONLY*

RG Veda
聖伝
First serialized in Shinshokan's "Wings Comics" (1989); ten compiled volumes total. *CURRENTLY IMPORT ONLY*

20 Mensô ni Onegai! ("Ask it of '20 Masks'!")
20面相におねがい!
First serialized in Kadokawa Shoten's Newtype magazine "100% Comics" (1990); two compiled volumes total. *CURRENTLY IMPORT ONLY*

Fushigi no Kuni no Miyuki-chan ("Miyuki-chan in Wonderland")
不思議の国の美幸ちゃん
First serialized in Kadokawa Shoten's Newtype magazine "100% Comics EX" (1994); one compiled volume total. *CURRENTLY IMPORT ONLY*

Magic Knight Rayearth
魔法騎士レイアース
First serialized in Kodansha's Nakayoshi magazine (1993); three compiled volumes available total. *DOMESTIC RELEASE TITLE:* ***Magic Knight Rayearth*** (serialized in MixxZine)

Magic Knight Rayearth 2
魔法騎士レイアース2
Published in Kodansha's "KC Deluxe Comics" (1995); three compiled volumes total. Picks up where the first *Rayearth* series left off. *CURRENTLY IMPORT ONLY*

Rex: Kyôryû Monogatari ("Rex: A Dinosaur Story")
REX:恐竜物語
First serialized in Kadokawa Shoten's "Asuka Comics DX" (1993); one compiled volume total. Manga adaptation of the summer live-action film of the same name, as written by Masanori Hata and illustrated by Clamp. *CURRENTLY IMPORT ONLY*

Watashi no Suki na Hito ("The One I Love")
わたしのすきなひと
First serialized in Kadokawa Shoten's "Young Rosé Comics DX" (1993); one compiled volume total. *CURRENTLY IMPORT ONLY*

X
X
Published by Kadokawa Shoten's "Asuka Comics" (1992); ten compiled volumes to date. *DOMESTIC RELEASE TITLE:* ***X/1999*** (serialized in Animerica, Anime & Manga Monthly)

Card Captor Sakura
カードキャプターさくら
Serialized in Kodansha's Nakayoshi magazine (1996); three compiled volumes to date. *CURRENTLY IMPORT ONLY*

Shin Shunkôden ("The New 'Legend of Spring-Scent'")
新・春香伝
Published by Hakusensha (1992); one volume to date. *CURRENTLY IMPORT ONLY*

Wish
WISH
First serialized in Kadokawa Shoten's "Asuka Comics DX" (1995); two compiled volumes available to date. *CURRENTLY IMPORT ONLY*

Clover
Serialized in Kodansha's monthly Amie manga magazine (1997); one compiled volume to date. *CURRENTLY IMPORT ONLY*

ANIME アニメ

Anime adaptations based on original manga works by Clamp. Note that, with the exception of Okawa's involvement as a writer in both the second season of *Rayearth* and in the feature-length *X* movie, group involvement is limited to that of "original story" only.

RG Veda
聖伝
Original Story
Two-volume OAV series (1991-92) animating in epic romantic style the Vedic scriptures, or "Rig vedas" (*seiden*, the characters chosen to spell out the series' title, literally translate to "holy legend"). *DOMESTIC RELEASE TITLE:* ***RG Veda*** (U.S. Manga Corps)

Tokyo Babylon
東京BABYLON
Original Story
Two-volume OAV series (1992-94) in which a fashionable spiritualist—dressed in inimitable Clamp style—investigates strange goings on in modern-day Tokyo. *DOMESTIC RELEASE TITLE:* ***Tokyo Babylon*** (U.S. Manga Corps)

X2 ("Double X")
X2(ダブル・エックス)
Original Story
One-shot OAV music video (1993) setting various imagery from the *X* manga series to music by a group named, appropriate enough, "X"; thought of by Okawa, apparently, as "one long trailer" for the full-length (and big budget!) *X* movie. Directed by Rin Taro (*Galaxy Express 999, Dagger of Kamui*). *CURRENTLY IMPORT ONLY*

Magic Knight Rayearth
魔法騎士レイアース
Original Story
49-episode TV series (1994-95) based on the manga series of the same name; followed by a separate, second TV season (for which Okawa joined the writing team), as well as by an OAV series, which was ongoing as of press time. *CURRENTLY IMPORT ONLY*

Fushigi no Kuni no Miyuki-chan ("Miyuki-chan in Wonderland")
不思議の国の美幸ちゃん
Original Story
One-shot OAV (1995) detailing sweet young thang Miyuki's fantastic—mostly adults-only—adventures in a Wonderland only loosely based on that created by Lewis Carroll. *DOMESTIC RELEASE TITLE:* ***Miyuki-chan in Wonderland*** (A.D. Vision)

X
X
Original Story / Screenwriting
98-minute theatrical feature (1996) based on the manga series of the same

name; features direction by Rin Taro and character designs by Nobuteru Yuki (*Record of Lodoss War*). *CURRENTLY IMPORT ONLY, BUT SCHEDULED FOR FUTURE DOMESTIC RELEASE VIA MANGA ENTERTAINMENT*

Clamp Gakuen Tantei-Dan

学園探偵団

Original Story

TV series based on the manga series of the same name (1997); ongoing as of press time. *CURRENTLY IMPORT ONLY*

Key

Japanese comics or "manga" series; may or may not be available in foreign-language (i.e., English) version

TV series broadcast on-air in Japan. Note that, in the U.S., Japanese TV series are both broadcast on-air (*Ronin Warriors*) and released on home video (*Ranma 1/2*). Others (*Sailor Moon, Dragon Ball*) are available both in broadcast and home video versions

Direct-to-home-video series; may also include compilations of TV episodes released to home video market

Theatrical feature; may or may not receive equivalent theatrical release for U.S. version

index

This index contains references to films, TV series, OAV releases, places, people, businesses, and organizations found throughout this book. Style guidelines are established as follows:

- short stories, novels, TV series, films, operas, arias, foreign words, etc. are set in *italics* (i.e., *The Great Adventures of the Dirty Pair*);
- character names are set in "quotes" (i.e., "Derek Wildstar");
- personal names are given last name first, first name last (i.e., Takahashi, Rumiko);
- when two or more versions exist of a given work, information is listed under the original, Japanese title (i.e., Astro Boy [see *Tetsuwan Atom*]);
- translations of composition titles are set roman;
- titles of magazines and similar publications are set in SMALL CAPS.

Please note that neither filmography nor bibliography references are included in this chapter.

character index

general index

U

W

Julie Davis

A graduate of the University of Michigan, Julie Davis first became interested in Japanese animation in high school with the TV show *Star Blazers*. Years later, a chance meeting at San Diego Comic-Con led to work on ANIMAG, THE MAGAZINE OF JAPANESE ANIMATION, and finally, to an editorial position at ANIMERICA, ANIME & MANGA MONTHLY. She has also contributed work to *The Complete Anime Guide*. Her favorite anime titles always seem to include a healthy dose of angst.

Satoru Fujii

Viz Comics Managing Editor Satoru Fujii is (together with Executive Editor Seiji Horibuchi) not only a co-founder of San Francisco-based Viz Communications, but also a former member of the counterculture who used to hang out in Haight-Ashbury and play in a band.

Seiji Horibuchi

After being graduated with a degree in law from Tokyo's prestigious Waseda University in 1974, Viz Comics Executive Editor Seiji Horibuchi moved to the United States, where he has lived ever since. His wide-ranging interests include art and architecture; he spends his free time with his wife and two children, and playing golf.

Carl Gustav Horn

A world traveler at an early age, Carl Gustav Horn was first exposed to anime in the form of *Speed Racer* on AFRTS while living in Iran in 1973. Though he spent many of his formative years in Texas, he has lived in the San Francisco Bay Area since 1982, and has contributed to the anime magazines ANIMAG, ANIME U.K. (and its later incarnation ANIME FX), as well as to the webzine EX. An assistant editor on ANIMERICA, Horn's life ambition is to write the ultimate history of eclectic anime studio Gainax.

Junco Ito

Founder and chief director of A-Girl Co., Ltd., globetrotting journalist Junco Ito manages the career of international anime and manga superstar Buichi "Cobra" Terasawa and is said to be best pals with Naoko Takeuchi, the creator of *Sailor Moon*.

Takayuki Karahashi

A graduate in mathematics from the University of California at Berkeley, Takayuki Karahashi traces his roots as an anime fan back to his childhood, when he watched *Daitarn 3* on the air in Japan. A veteran of ANIMAG, Taka has worked as a translator on numerous anime and manga titles; he also regularly serves as staff translator not only for ANIMERICA, but also for Anime Expo, America's largest and best-known anime convention. He remains spiritual advisor to the staff of the magazine, thanks to his otherworldly sense of calm.

Trish Ledoux

An anime fan with deep roots, Trish Ledoux has been editor of not one, but two influential American magazines on anime: ANIMAG, and ANIMERICA. Currently pursuing a second major (this time, in English literature—the first was in Japanese) at San Francisco State University, she has worked as translator and scriptwriter on more video and comic titles than she can easily count. Author of *The Complete Anime Guide*, an exhaustive review of all titles available in domestic translation, Ledoux has been or will be extensively interviewed and/or quoted on the subject of Japanese animation in both the television and print media by CNN International, *The Washington Post*, *Wired*, The Sci-Fi Channel, *Newsweek Japan*, ABC's *World News Tonight with Peter Jennings*, and more.

Bruce Lewis

An infamous Net gadfly and editor of the quarterly rantzine, "Bruce the Psychic Guy," Bruce Lewis is perhaps best known as a writer for the *Robotech* comics *Invid War* and *Aftermath*. In 1995, Lewis—together with John Ott and Tim Eldred—formed Studio Go!, a small group dedicated to writing and drawing manga adaptations of popular anime titles for CPM Comics such as *Gall Force: Eternal Story*, *Project A-Ko* and *M.D. Geist*. Studio Go! also collaborated on the comic magazine *Star Blazers: The Magazine of Space Battleship Yamato*.

James Matsuzaki

A fan of anime and manga since 1988, James Matsuzaki has served as president of his local anime club, as well as having also held the position of editor at the small press anime magazine V-MAX. Besides anime, his other interests include American history and the Italian Renaissance.

Takashi Oshiguchi

As manager of Japan's *Manga no Mori* ("Comics Forest"), the largest anime/manga merchandise specialty chain in that country, Takashi Oshiguchi has been involved in the industry not only as a retailer but also as a journalist for many years. He writes occasionally for Japan's ANIMAGE magazine and has had his own column in the comic trade journal COMIC BOX. Currently, Oshiguchi writes a monthly column for ANIMERICA on the Japanese anime scene, something which he has done since the magazine's inception.

Toshifumi Yoshida

Once told by his mother, "You'll never make a living reading comics and watching videos all day," Toshifumi Yoshida delights in proving her wrong on the first of each and every month, which is when he gets his paycheck. A veteran of ANIMAG, Yoshida began working as a freelance translator on some of the first Japanese animation titles to be released in the U.S., which led eventually to a full-time position as video producer for Viz Video. He traces his days as a consultant on U.S. translations of manga back to his comic book store employee days of the late '80s, which was when Viz Comics' Seiji Horibuchi asked his opinion about a translated version of the comic *Area 88*.

Frederik L. Schodt

A writer, translator and interpreter who lives in San Francisco, the Japanese-fluent Frederik L. Schodt is one of the most respected names in the American anime and manga community, and is the author of several books on manga and Japanese culture, such as *Manga! Manga! The World of Japanese Comics*, *Inside the Robot Kingdom*, *America and the Four Japans*, and most recently, *Dreamland Japan*.

rights and clearances

Kumi Kobayashi

A native of Kyoto, Japan, Kumi Kobayashi came to the U.S. in 1990, and graduated with a B.A. in English Communications from Notre Dame Women's College. She remembers watching *Cutey Honey* and *Alps no Shôjo Heidi* on television with her sisters when she was growing up in Japan and, with enough convincing, can still sing the theme songs to both. Her favorite manga titles include the breathless *shôjo* titles *Rose of Versailles* and *Banana Fish*.

Hyoe Narita

"Mr. Mysterious and Exciting" Hyoe Narita hails from Japan, where he gave up an influential job as an editor at one of Japan's largest publishers, Shogakukan, to move to America and take on a managing editor position at the markedly more laid-back offices of Viz Comics/Viz Video. His interests include music and manga.

layout and design

Ted Szeto

Born in the bayous of Mississippi, Ted Szeto is a graduate of California College of Arts and Crafts. He loves hot chocolate and spends his free time wandering the streets of San Francisco and collecting weird magazines to inspire his layouts.

image index and copyright credits

Yoshiyuki Tomino
page 9: image from *Mobile Suit Gundam: Gyakushû no Char* © Sunrise • Sotsu Agency
page 10: image from *Mobile Suit Gundam* © Sunrise • Sotsu Agency
page 11: image from *Byston Well Monogatari: Garzey no Tsubasa* © Yoshiyuki Tomino • Garzey's Wing Production Committee

Rumiko Takahashi
page 17: image from *Ranma 1/2* © Rumiko Takahashi/Shogakukan, Inc.
page 19: image from *Maison Ikkoku* © Rumiko Takahashi/Shogakukan, Inc.
page 21: image from *Urusei Yatsura* © Rumiko Takahashi/Shogakukan, Inc.
page 22: image from *Ichi-Pound no Fukuin* © Rumiko Takahashi/Shogakukan, Inc.
page 23: image from *Inu-Yasha* © Rumiko Takahashi/Shogakukan, Inc.
page 23: image from *Ningyo ("Mermaid") Saga* © Rumiko Takahashi/Shogakukan, Inc.

Hayao Miyazaki
page 27: image from *Tenkû no Shiro Laputa* © Nibariki/Tokuma Shoten
page 28: image from *Mononoke Hime* © Studio Ghibli Co., Ltd. • Nibariki • TNDG
page 30: image from *Tonari no Totoro* © Nibariki/Tokuma Shoten
page 31: image from *Kurenai no Buta* © Nibariki Co., Ltd.
page 32: image from *Majo no Takkyûbin* © Nibariki/Tokuma Shoten
page 33: image from *Kaze no Tani no Nausicaä* © Nibariki Co., Ltd.

Masamune Shirow
page 38: image from *Ghost in the Shell* (Dark Horse Comics) © 1991 Masamune Shirow/Kodansha • Studio Proteus • Dark Horse Comics
page 39: illustration from *Intron Depot* (illustration collection) © Masamune Shirow/Seishinsha
page 41: image from *Kôkaku Kidô-Tai* (manga) © Masamune Shirow/Kodansha
page 42: image from *Senjutsu Chô Kôkaku Orion* © Masamune Shirow/Seishinsha
page 43: image from *Black Magic M-66* © Masamune Shirow

Ryoichi Ikegami
pages 47, 51: images from *Crying Freeman* © Ryoichi Ikegami/Shogakukan, Inc.
page 48: cover image from *Spider-Man* © Marvel Comics
page 49: image from *Sanctuary* © Ryoichi Ikegami/Shogakukan, Inc.
page 50: image from *Mai the Psychic Girl* © Ryoichi Ikegami/Shogakukan, Inc.

Yukito Kishiro
pages 54, 55, 57, 58: images from *Gunnm* © Yukito Kishiro/Shueisha, Inc.

Yoshiki Takaya
pages 63, 65, 66: images from *Kyôshoku Sôkô Guyver* © Yoshiki Takaya/Tokuma Shoten

Kosuke Fujishima
pages 70, 73: images from *Aa, Megami-sama* (manga) © Kosuke Fujishima/Kodansha Intl., Ltd.
pages 71, 74: images from *Taiho Shichao zo!* © Kosuke Fujishima/Kodansha, Ltd.
page 76: image from *Aa, Megami-sama* (anime) © Kosuke Fujishima/Kodansha • TBS • KSS

Yasuhiro Imagawa
pages 79, 80, 81: images from *Giant Robo* © Hikari Productions • Amuse Video • Plex • Atlantis
page 83: image from *Kidô Butôden G Gundam* © Sunrise • Sotsu Agency • TV Asahi

Hiroki Hayashi
pages 87, 88, 91: images from *Tenchi Muyô!* © A.I.C./Pioneer LDC, Inc.
page 92: image from *Shinpi no Sekai El-Hazard* © A.I.C./Pioneer LDC, Inc.

Haruka Takachiho
page 95: image from *Crusher Joe* © Haruka Takachiho/Studio Nue • Sunrise, Inc.
page 97: image from *Dirty Pair* © Haruka Takachiho/Studio Nue • Sunrise, Inc. • NTV
page 98: image from *Dirty Pair Flash* © Haruka Takachiho/Studio Nue • Sunrise, Inc.

Hiroyuki Kitazume
pages 103, 105: images from *Moldiver* © A.I.C./Pioneer LDC, Inc.
page 107: illustration from *Kidô Senshi Zeta Gundam* © Sunrise • Sotsu Agency (published in *Light Pink* by Am JuJu)

Shoji Kawamori
page 111: image from *Chô Jikû Yôsai Macross* © Big West
page 113: image from *Iihatove Gensô: Kenji no Haru* © Kenji Miyazawa • TV Iwate • Group TAC
page 114: image from *Tenkû no Escaflowne* © Shoji Kawamori • Kadokawa Shoten • Sunrise • TV Tokyo

Kei Kusunoki
pages 119, 120, 123: images from *Onikirimaru* © Kei Kusunoki/Shogakukan, Inc.
pages121, 122: images from *Yagami-kun no Katei Jijô* © Kei Kusunoki/Shogakukan, Inc.

Buichi Terasawa
pages 127, 130: images from *Space Adventure Cobra* © Buichi Terasawa

Mamoru Oshii
page135: image from *Kôkaku Kidô-Tai* (anime) © Masamune Shirow/Kodansha • Bandai Visual • Manga Entertainment
pages 136, 137, 138: images from *Kidô Keisatsu Patlabor 2* © Headgear • Emotion • TFC

Gisaburo Sugii
pages 143, 144, 146: images from *Street Fighter II* (movie) © Capcom Co., Ltd. • Sony Music Entertainment
page 145: image from *Street Fighter II V* (TV series) © Capcom • Group TAC • Amuse • Yomiuri Telecasting Co., Ltd.

Leiji Matsumoto
page 151: illustration from *Uchû Kaizoku Captain Harlock* © Leiji Matsumoto
page 153: image from *Sayonara Ginga Tetsudô 999: Andromeda Shûchaku Eki* © 1981 Toei Animation Co., Ltd.
page 154, 157: illustrations from *Ginga Tetsudô 999* © Leiji Matsumoto

Ryosuke Takahashi
pages 165, 167: images from *Sôkô Kihei Votoms* © Sunrise, Inc.
page 168: image from *Chinmoku no Kantai* © Kaiji Kawaguchi/Kodansha • Sunrise, Inc.

Nanase Okawa
page 173: image from *X* (manga) © Clamp/Kadokawa Shoten
page 175: image from *Magic Knight Rayearth* © Clamp/Kodansha • TMS
page 177: image from *Tokyo Babylon* © Clamp/Shinshokan